Renewing Biblical Interpretation

The Scripture and Hermeneutics Series

Craig Bartholomew, Series Editor
Colin Greene, Consultant Editor

Forthcoming volume, November 2001:

After Pentecost: Language and Biblical Interpretation

Renewing Biblical Interpretation

Edited by
Craig Bartholomew
Colin Greene
Karl Möller

paternoster press

Zondervan

CHELTENHAM & GLOUCESTER
College of Higher Education

BRITISH & FOREIGN BIBLE SOCIETY

First published 2000 jointly
in the UK by Paternoster Press, an imprint of Paternoster Publishing,
P.O. Box 300, Carlisle, Cumbria, CA3 0QS
Website: www.paternoster-publishing.com
and in the United States of America by
Zondervan Publishing House
5300 Patterson Ave SE, Grand Rapids, Michigan 49530

06 05 04 03 02 01 00   DC   7 6 5 4 3 2 1

British Library Cataloguing in Publication Data
A catalogue record for this book is available from the British Library
ISBN 0-85364-034-3

Library of Congress Cataloguing in Publication Data
Renewing biblical interpretation / Craig Bartholomew, series editor; Colin
J.D. Greene, consultatnt editor; Karl Möller, editor.
p.cm. — (Opening the book for a new millennium)
Includes bibliographical references
ISBN 0-310-23411-5
1. Bible—Hermeneutics—Congresses. 2. Bible—Criticism, interpretation,
etc.—Congresses. I. Bartholomew, Craig G., 1961- II. Greene, Colin J. D.
III. Möller, Karl. IV. Series.
BS476.R45 2000   00-043726

Cover Design by Gert Swart and Zak Benjamin, South Africa
Typeset by WestKey Ltd, Falmouth, Cornwall
Printed in the United States of America
Printed on acid free paper

Contents

Contributors

Craig G. Bartholomew is Research Fellow at Cheltenham & Gloucester College of Higher Education. He is the author of *Reading Ecclesiastes: Old Testament Exegesis and Hermeneutical Theory*. He has also edited *In the Fields of the Lord: A Calvin Seerveld Reader* and co-edited *Christ and Consumerism: A Critical Analysis of the Spirit of the Age*.

H. Dan Beeby was Professor of Old Testament at Tainan Theological College, Taiwan. He also taught at Selly Oak Colleges, Birmingham, and was involved, with Lesslie Newbigin, in 'The Gospel and Our Culture' movement. He is now a consultant to The British & Foreign Bible Society. His publications include *Grace Abounding: A Commentary on the Book of Hosea* and *Canon and Mission*.

Walter Brueggemann is William Marcellus McPheeters Professor of Old Testament at Columbia Theological Seminary, Decatur, Georgia. He has authored numerous books, including *Theology of the Old Testament: Testimony, Dispute, Advocacy; A Commentary on Jeremiah: Exile and Homecoming* and *Cadences of Home: Preaching among Exiles*.

Brevard S. Childs was, until his recent retirement, Sterling Professor of Divinity at Yale University. He has authored numerous books, including *Biblical Theology of the Old and New Testaments; Old Testament Theology in a Canonical Context* and *Introduction to the Old Testament as Scripture*. His commentary on the book of Isaiah is forthcoming in the Old Testament Library series.

Colin Greene is Head of Theology and Public Policy at The British & Foreign Bible Society. He is the author of *Christology and Atonement in Historical Perspective* and *Christ in Cultural Perspective* (forthcoming).

Trevor A. Hart is Professor of Divinity at the University of St. Andrews. His books include *Regarding Karl Barth: Essays toward a Reading of His Theology; Faith Thinking: The Dynamics of Christian Theology* and (with Richard Bauckham) *Hope Against Hope: Christian Eschatology at the Turn of the Millennium.* He is also the editor of *Justice the True and Only Mercy: Essays on the Life and Theology of Peter Taylor Forsyth.*

Mary B. Hesse FBA is a historian and philosopher of science, and Emeritus Professor in Philosophy of Science in the University of Cambridge. She has authored numerous books, including *Revolutions and Reconstructions in the Philosophy of Science; The Structure of Scientific Inference and Models* and *Analogies in Science.*

Brian Ingraffia is Associate Professor in English at Biola University, La Mirada, California. He is the author of *Postmodern Theory and Biblical Theology: Vanquishing God's Shadow.*

Neil MacDonald is Meldrum Lecturer in Systematic Theology at the University of Edinburgh. He is the author of *Karl Barth and the Strange New World Within the Bible: Barth, Wittgenstein and the Metadilemmas of the Enlightenment.*

Rex Mason was, prior to his retirement, Lecturer in Old Testament Studies at the University of Oxford. His books include *Propaganda and Subversion in the Old Testament* and *Preaching the Tradition: Homily and Hermeneutics after the Exile.* He has also written commentaries and study guides on some of the Minor Prophets.

Karl Möller is Project Administrator for the Scripture & Hermeneutics Project, Cheltenham & Gloucester College of Higher Education, and Course Coordinator at The Open Theological College. His book, *A Prophet in Debate: The Rhetoric of Persuasion in the Book of Amos*, is due to be published in the coming year.

Thorsten Moritz is Senior Lecturer in New Testament at Cheltenham & Gloucester College of Higher Education. He is the author of *A Profound Mystery: The Use of the Old Testament in Ephesians.* He has also co-edited *Christ and Consumerism: A Critical Analysis of the Spirit of the Age.*

John Riches is Professor of Divinity and Biblical Criticism at the University of Glasgow. He is the author of *A Century of New Testament Study; The World of Jesus: First-Century Judaism in Crisis; Jesus and Transformation of Judaism* and *Conflicting Mythologies: Identity Formation in the Gospels of Mark and Matthew.* He has also written a study guide on the Gospel of Matthew.

Christopher R. Seitz is Professor of Old Testament and Theological Studies, University of St. Andrews. His books include *Word without End: The Old Testament as Abiding Theological Witness; Zion's Final Destiny: The Development of the Book of Isaiah* and *Theology in Conflict: Reactions to the Exile in the Book of Jeremiah.*

Walter Sundberg is Professor of Church History at Luther Seminary, St. Paul, Minnesota. He has co-authored *The Bible in Modern Culture: Theology and Historical-Critical Method from Spinoza to Käsemann.*

Al Wolters is Professor of Religion and Theology/Classical Languages at Redeemer College, Ancaster, Ontario. He is the author of *Plotinus, 'On Eros': A Detailed Exegetical Study of Enneads III, 5; Creation Regained: Biblical Basics for a Reformational Worldview* and *The Copper Scroll: Overview, Text and Translation.*

Nicholas Wolterstorff is Noah Porter Professor of Philosophical Theology at Yale University. He has authored numerous books, including *John Locke and the Ethics of Belief; Divine Discourse: Philosophical Reflections on the Claim that God Speaks* and *Reason within the Bounds of Religion.*

Stephen I. Wright is Director of the College of Preachers and Associate Lecturer at Spurgeon's College, London. He is the author of *The Voice of Jesus: Studies in the Interpretation of Six Gospel Parables.*

Abbreviations

AB	Anchor Bible
AnBib	Analecta biblica
ATD	Das Alte Testament Deutsch
BBB	Bonner biblische Beiträge
BibInt	*Biblical Interpretation: A Journal of Contemporary Approaches*
BIS	Biblical Interpretation Series
BKAT	Biblischer Kommentar: Altes Testament
BZAW	Beihefte zur *ZAW*
CBQ	*Catholic Biblical Quarterly*
CTJ	*Calvin Theological Journal*
EKKNT	*Evangelisch-Katholischer Kommentar zum Neuen Testament*
EuroJT	*European Journal of Theology*
EVB	*Exegetische Versuche und Besinnungen*
HALAT	Ludwig Köhler et al. (eds.), *Hebräisches und aramäisches Lexikon zum Alten Testament* (5 vols.; Leiden: E.J. Brill, 1967–1995)
HAR	*Hebrew Annual Review*
HUCA	*Hebrew Union College Annual*
Int	*Interpretation*
JAOS	*Journal of the American Oriental Society*
JETS	*Journal of the Evangelical Theological Society*
JR	*Journal of Religion*
JSNTSup	*Journal for the Study of the New Testament*, Supplement Series
JSOT	*Journal for the Study of the Old Testament*
JSOTSup	*Journal for the Study of the Old Testament*, Supplement Series
JTS	*Journal of Theological Studies*
KAT	Kommentar zum Alten Testament
NCB	New Century Bible
NEB	New English Bible

NRSV	New Revised Standard Version
OBS	The Oxford Bible Series
OBT	Overtures to Biblical Theology
OTL	Old Testament Library
SBT	Studies in Biblical Theology
SJOT	*Scandinavian Journal of the Old Testament*
SJT	*Scottish Journal of Theology*
TLZ	*Theologische Literaturzeitung*
TOTC	Tyndale Old Testament Commentaries
TS	*Theological Studies*
TynBul	*Tyndale Bulletin*
VT	*Vetus Testamentum*
WMANT	Wissenschaftliche Monographien zum Alten und Neuen Testament
ZAW	*Zeitschrift für die alttestamentliche Wissenschaft*
ZDPV	*Zeitschrift des deutschen Palästina-Vereins*

Foreword

For at least a decade it has become commonplace to speak of a crisis in biblical interpretation. Most everyone engaged in the study of the Bible is fully aware that the enterprise has run into real difficulty. The present crisis has been described in different ways: methodological impasse, conflicting private agenda, loss of clear direction, extreme fragmentation, unbridgeable diversity, and even a deep sense of resignation. Fortunately, the editors of this volume have not sought to focus too long on our present malaise, but have sought boldly to break away from this litany of despair in search of a new beginning.

At the outset there are important reasons for attempting to revive biblical interpretation. The very intensity of the conflicting voices serves to confirm the impression that the problem of biblical interpretation does not arise from apathy. Indeed, just the opposite. When a strong, new feminist voice first arose to protest a cultural injustice, its proponents sought almost immediately to establish a fresh relationship with the Bible. Likewise, practitioners of postmodern hermeneutics applied their new tools to the task of rethinking the nature and function of western literature by using biblical examples. Or again, many of the most probing, recent discussions of the philosophy of language used biblical models, almost by reflex, by which to mount a case for a new approach. Cannot one draw the implication that in spite of confusion and conflict in respect to biblical interpretation, there is an unexpressed consensus that the Bible still possesses a seriousness of content and an evocative power for raising basic questions which offers hope in a search for its renewed understanding in the twenty-first century?

It would, of course, be folly for any one group to project a rigid agenda for finding the way out of the impasse. The new search must begin from a variety of vantage points even when the connections linking them are at present tenuous. The editors of this volume have been wise in throwing the net wide. What can be learned from reviewing the history of interpretation in both a positive and a negative sense? How might the new interest in the philosophy of language contribute to rethinking the function of every interpretation including those of the Bible? It was not by chance that several essays included in this volume stressed the importance of the social dimension involved, both in the authoring and construing of a text for a particular group at some specific point in time, and for a concrete goal.

A more difficult question lies in determining how one moves from simply celebrating diversity or embracing pluralism as the ultimate end. Lying at the heart of a genuine renewal of biblical interpretation must be the will and the openness to learn from debate and from the competing experiences of others. Yet more is involved than merely changing one's opinion or conforming to a majority vote. Rather, one can only hope that the impact of the subject matter itself when viewed from different perspectives creates a coercion which overcomes traditional party lines.

To use an illustration. I think that it is a correct historical observation to say that the shift of biblical interpretation within the English-speaking world happening in the late nineteenth and early twentieth centuries did not occur primarily because of a breakdown in the traditional conservative apologetic for biblical inerrancy, but rather from a widespread sense of fresh religious illumination associated with the application of the historical-critical method by liberal scholars such as S.R. Driver, G.A. Smith, W. Sanday and F.C. Burkitt. Conversely, two generations later the cultural optimism of leading scholars such as Ritschl and Harnack very quickly lost credibility when their biblical interpretation failed to address the demonic depths of human folly revealed to all in the catastrophe of World War I. This historical analogy is also a reminder that the search for renewal is not for a timeless ideal, divorced from human struggle, but for interpretation which is both responsible and faithful to the challenge of today's world.

While respect for diversity and openness to disagreement are always a requirement for serious reflection, it is equally important that both individuals and groups of colleagues do not seek to reach a consensus all too quickly, especially through easy compromises. What is needed is the courage to probe deeply into the material and to anticipate growth, change, and transformation in the very struggle for divine truth. One lesson to be learned from the past is that the Bible has a quality of calling forth an active response from its readers before revealing its profoundest secrets. To repeat an often forgotten maxim: the more profound the interpreter, the deeper the interpretation.

One final word seems in order. How does one test whether one is moving toward genuine renewal? One practical indication will be the extent to which our hermeneutical experiments lead us closer to the biblical text rather than increasing our distance from it through endless abstraction. Simply more talking about the Bible will hardly guarantee renewal. Again, does the audience that profits from our interpretation seem to grow in size, strength, and diversity, or is the interpretation received by a decreasing number of the already convinced? Lastly, is our approach to the Bible a means of providing a safe defence within a circle of wagons from all attacks, or does it aid in receiving a gracious gift, inviting its readers to a shared encounter with God who offers a way of human life commensurate with the will of a gracious Creator? Could it be that the persistent, existential claims of the Bible are what drive a new generation forward in anticipation of genuine discovery?

Brevard S. Childs

ACADEMIC *WITH AN OPEN BOOK*:
an interpretation

Our cover illustration – 'Academic *with an Open Book*' – was commissioned for this volume. The ideas, design, sketch and final painting were developed by sculptor Gert Swart and artist Zak Benjamin in consultation with Craig Bartholomew. The cover design is intended to interact with and explore the ideas discussed in the volume.

'Academic *with an Open Book*' is a contemporary reworking of Rembrandt's *Philosophe en Meditation*. 'Academic *with an Open Book*' speaks powerfully alone, but it is also fascinating to compare it with the Rembrandt (*see page xx*). Gert Swart notes that in the Rembrandt there is a distinct feeling of Yin and Yang – the tail of the one half starting from the top of the stairs to the pool of light incorporating the window and philosopher's head. The tail of the other half starts from the light at the feet of the philosopher, and goes up the stairs to a 'pool of darkness', completing the Yin-Yang motif. In Chinese philosophy Yin and Yang are opposing principles complementing each other, but in the Rembrandt the tension between them is focused in the person of the philosopher with his 'light' head and dark lower body.

The Rembrandt is full of contrasts that express the tension in the painting:

* light vs. dark
* the seen stairs vs. the mysterious, forbidding unseen stairs
* ascent vs. descent
* the open book vs. the closed meditative philosopher.

Gert Swart notes that the Yin-Yang motif also forms a circular feeling – mandala – a striving for wholeness. It is significant in this respect, that the female figure stoking the fire in the bottom right-hand corner is excluded from the circle. The philosopher's book is open but the philosopher seems closed and disconnected from the book, the world outside and whatever lies at the top of the staircase! The philosopher is at the centre of unresolved tensions in the context of a light-darkness struggle for wholeness.

'Philosopher *with an Open Book*' Rembrandt

'Academic *with an Open Book*' Gert Swart and Zak Benjamin

In the Swart-Benjamin reworking, the content has been compressed into a square which creates a feeling of stability. Within the square there is an obvious circular feeling which speaks of resolution and completeness. Both the square and the circularity speak of wholeness. The figure of the academic has been flattened and opened up to create a sense of urgency and of hope. The ethos of 'Academic *with an Open Book*' is thus radically different from the Rembrandt.

The search for wholeness must surely include the encompassing of the feminine. The right hand of the flattened figure is at the book, but the left hand extends to the excluded female. The window is compressed to form four quarters and a cross. The light (the Word) travels across and is focused in the book, bathes the figure and leads up the spiral stairs to the beginning of the dark side.

At this point, one's eye moves across to the face of the figure that is compelling the viewer to re-examine. The spiral staircase seems to have a whiplash effect in the square. We have split the atom and explored outer space; but, where do we stand? It is as if the staircase posits all of our lofty thoughts back at our feet for reappraisal.

The 'cut-out' flat person is filled with Greek script from a section in the Gospels referring to Pontius Pilate sentencing Christ. The questioning face and this ambivalent text raise in an acute fashion the role of the interpreter in his or her role in relation to the open book and the world. Indeed, the literal heart of the academic is in the dead centre of the composition. Carl Jung observed that the Greek cross (with all sides of equal length) was used extensively prior to the Renaissance; after the Renaissance the Latin cross was used – the horizontal beam was elevated as man moved more into the intellectual side of his nature, spelling imbalance.

Thus, in a variety of ways 'Academic *with an Open Book*' explores the possibilities and challenges of academics working with the Bible as Scripture. The reworking alerts us to the potential and significance of an open Book – the open Book mediates resolution and potential wholeness into our brokenness. But that very possibility calls for urgent re-examination of a host of issues. That re-examination is what The Scripture and Hermeneutics Seminar is all about.

Craig Bartholomew

Introduction

When it comes to the Bible, there is a lot at stake for the church and for the world. The God and Father of Jesus Christ who speaks and addresses us through the canon of Scripture by the Holy Spirit is utterly central to Christianity. Without the voice of the Living God addressing us through Scripture, Christianity collapses into so much empty rhetoric, and the world is left without the redemptive, recreative Word of God.

In the great judgement passage in Amos 8, the prophet speaks of a terrible time of famine, 'not a famine of bread, or a thirst of water, but of hearing the words of the LORD' (Amos 8:11, NRSV). A case could be made (although opinions will vary considerably here) that we are approaching such a famine in the west. The sojourn of the Bible *as Scripture* in the modern world has been a chequered one, to say the least. The Bible continues to be a best-seller in western culture, but increasingly it is a closed book, a resident alien, for much of our culture. It is either marginalized by the academy and privatized by our culture, or embraced at a popular level but increasingly only as another consumer product. Under the aegis of historical criticism the Bible has been scrutinized 'scientifically' in the academy in an unprecedented way over the last 150 years, and yet, at the outset of a new millennium with so many challenges facing humanity, biblical studies is in a state of flux with no clarity about how best to proceed in reading the Bible.

It would be wrong to suggest that the opening of the Bible as Scripture to our culture depends on the academy, as if the Bible was not first of all God's word for God's people. However, the academy has been and is hugely influential in the modern world in which rationality is so highly prized, and one cannot reflect on the journey of Scripture in our world without thinking long and hard about its story in the academy.

In the academy it is widely recognized that the *historical-critical paradigm* no longer dominates biblical interpretation the way it did even fifteen years ago. The historical-critical paradigm of interpretation has its immediate roots in nineteenth-century Germany, with folk like de Wette and Wellhausen as its (immediate) fathers, and by the start of the twentieth century English and North American scholarship too was in its grip. For most of the twentieth century biblical interpretation in one way or another has been shaped by this paradigm. This is not to say that *now*, at the start of the new millennium, biblical interpretation has undergone a paradigm shift. Many – perhaps most – scholars still work within the old paradigm, but there is a pervasive sense that the historical-critical paradigm can no longer be taken for granted, and if it is to be adopted than it will have to be argued for in competition with alternative hermeneutics. A number of developments in the latter half of this century have resulted in this changed situation.

In the 1970s biblical scholarship experienced a *literary turn*, with serious implications for a predominantly historical method of interpretation. While biblical studies could still operate within a framework of 'critical' analysis, if not quite of 'historical' critical analysis, the openness to literary theory was to have huge implications once the postmodern debate – with its roots in literary studies – exploded.[1] As the postmodern debate shifted from the arts and literature to a reassessment of the foundations of western culture as a whole, this too would impact biblical scholarship, but at the foundational, rather than just the literary, level. In the 1990s the postmodern turn impacted biblical interpretation. Post-structuralism provided a variety of indeterminate ways of reading Scripture, and, philosophically, the critique of the assumptions of modernity inexorably turned towards historical criticism with its deep indebtedness to post-Enlightenment historiography. Increasingly the pluralism and fragmentation of postmodernism have become evident in biblical studies. The result is that a plurality of ways 'forward' are being proposed.

Some suggest that historical criticism remains the right direction for biblical interpretation. Recent criticisms may have a point, but, from this perspective, our response should not be to forsake historical criticism; we should reform it and get it back on track. John Barton's inaugural is redolent of this approach in his argument that we should be wary of the calls for a religious hermeneutic in biblical studies.[2] Rather, we should recentre biblical studies in critical, Enlightenment values. John Collins argues even more strongly for maintaining the dominance of historical criticism.[3] Others, in postmodern fashion, espouse a methodological pluralism in which all methods are equal

---

[1] H. Bertens, *The Idea of the Postmodern*, 17, notes that 'The debate on postmodernism as it has been variously defined since the 1960s has its origins in American literary and cultural criticism and it is from there that it moves into all the other fields and disciplines where it has in the last twenty-five years manifested itself.'

[2] *The Future of Old Testament Study*.

[3] 'Is a Critical Biblical Theology Possible?'

on the hermeneutic smorgasbord, even if some are more equal than others![4] Mark Brett, for example, acknowledges the validity of Childs's canonical approach, provided it is made one of numerous possible methods.[5] David Clines argues for a market philosophy of interpretation which celebrates a diversity in which interpreters of the Bible do what sells and what we enjoy.[6] Another important recent development is the effort to revive a *theological* hermeneutic in biblical studies. For Vanhoozer we should develop a trinitarian, general hermeneutic, whereas Childs, Watson and Seitz argue for a theological hermeneutic in biblical studies.[7]

As a result of this pluralism there is a pervasive sense in the academy that biblical interpretation is subjective and inescapably so. We appear to have gone from an era in which Scripture had a clear meaning which could be discovered by historical criticism apart from faith, to an era of uncertainty and wild pluralism[8] in which one meaning is as good as the hundreds of others, so that faith may be welcome but relativized. In different ways both these contexts – which coexist uneasily in the academy – close, rather than open, the Book. Both problematize an approach to the Bible as Scripture. If the danger of historical criticism was to confine the Bible to the past, the danger of postmodernism is to make it so contemporary that all we hear are the echoes of our own voices. Either way we are in danger of a famine of the Word, or as Luther might have put it, we are in danger of being burdened with a closed book and so remaining unfed.[9]

In my opinion, the postmodern turn is not only a time of danger, but also of *immense* opportunity. It has loosened up the regnant paradigms and provides an opportunity to reassess the foundations of biblical interpretation in the academy. And, it is in this context that The Scripture and Hermeneutics Seminar has developed. I had the idea of a consultation of scholars to assess the crisis – as I see it – in biblical interpretation, and when I took this idea to Martin Robinson and Colin Greene at the British and Foreign Bible Society seeking funding, I discovered that they were looking for someone to develop and partner such a project.

---

[4] It is important to note that what appears to be a very open espousal of all methods and approaches excludes methods like Childs's canonical approach, which argues that this is the right way for Scripture to be read.

[5] *Biblical Criticism in Crisis?*

[6] 'Possibilities and Priorities'; *The Bible and the Modern World.*

[7] Vanhoozer, *Is There a Meaning in This Text?*; Watson, *Text, Church and World*; Seitz, *Word Without End*; Childs, *Introduction to the Old Testament as Scripture.*

[8] See Bernstein, 'The Varieties of Pluralism'.

[9] Luther, *D. Martin Luthers Werk*, 55/1.10.14–15, in a preface to his early lectures on the Psalms: 'lest we should be burdened with a closed book and so remain unfed'.

The first of The Scripture and Hermeneutics Seminar consultations took place in Cheltenham in April 1998. The theme for this meeting was the crisis in biblical interpretation and the sort of answers being proposed by advocates of speech-act theory such as Anthony Thiselton, Nicholas Wolterstorff and Kevin Vanhoozer, all of whom were present. We were not agreed at this consultation whether speech-act theory has the resources to take biblical interpretation forward, but it became clear that any attempt to renew biblical interpretation in the academy would require a process with multiple consultations to address the key areas we thought required attention.

Thus was born The Scripture and Hermeneutics Seminar, a ten-year project headed by Craig Bartholomew and based in the School of Theology and Religious Studies at Cheltenham and Gloucester College of Higher Education (CGCHE). The Seminar is a partnership project between the British and Foreign Bible Society and CGCHE. Its ambitious aim is to facilitate a renewal of biblical interpretation in the academy that will help reopen the Book for our cultures.

The Seminar is thus *academic*. It recognizes the fundamental importance of opening the Book at all levels in our cultures, but the Seminar itself is an academic initiative, aimed first at biblical interpretation in the academy.

The Seminar is *interdisciplinary*. Meir Sternberg rightly notes that biblical studies is at the intersection of the humanities,[10] and the Seminar is based on the understanding that at this intersection interdisciplinary insight is required if biblical studies is to be saved from some of its isolation and fragmentation, and for new ways forward to be forged. It has been a delight at our consultations to find philosophers rubbing shoulders with educationalists and theologians, and missiologists working with literary scholars to renew biblical interpretation.

The Seminar is *Christian*. Modernity has marginalized faith in the great public areas of culture but this is a travesty of a Christian perspective in which faith relates to the whole of life. The Seminar is ecumenical and has a wide range of Christian perspectives represented within it. However, it is a rule of the Seminar that faith is not to be excluded from the consultative process that forms the heart of the Seminar. We have been asked about Jewish and other faiths being involved, and we are keen that such dialogue should emerge. However, we have judged it important to keep the Seminar's Christian character intact at this stage so that the interdisciplinary and faith dynamics have time to be nurtured.

The Seminar is *communal*. The modern academy is deeply individualistic. But we recognize that a renewal of biblical interpretation will require communal work. And a great aspect of the Seminar is the emerging sense of community among Christian scholars of diverse disciplines.

---

[10] *The Poetics of Biblical Narrative*, 21, 22.

The Seminar has identified a series of issues that require attention if we are to work towards a renewal of biblical interpretation in our day. However, it was felt that before attending to specific issues we should hold a consultation to assess the current state of biblical interpretation in the academy. This was the focus of our September 1999 consultation at Selwyn College, Cambridge, at which we were particularly privileged to have Professors Brevard Childs and Walter Brueggemann present. The consultation was called The Crisis in Biblical Interpretation, and the papers from that consultation form the basis of this book. At this stimulating event, it became clear that not all of us thought that biblical interpretation was in a crisis. Some did, others were reluctant to emphasize this. We were all agreed though, that biblical interpretation needs renewal, hence the title of this volume: *Renewing Biblical Interpretation*.

It is our view that biblical interpretation is a complex area whose renewal requires attention to many different aspects. The aim of this volume is to try to get these areas clearly on the table, so that in future volumes we can take up individual areas and explore them in considerably more depth. In what follows I will give some sense of the emerging geography of the key elements that we think need to be addressed if biblical interpretation is to be renewed. I am acutely aware from our consultations, that how one describes this geography will not be unprejudiced (in Gadamer's sense of pre-judgement). No doubt, others in the Seminar would describe the geography differently, and if you read the chapters of this book carefully you will pick up on the nuanced differences amid a significant consensus.

The more sophisticated and theologically aware models for biblical hermeneutics recognize nowadays the need to integrate *three key elements or strands* in their approach to the Bible, namely the historical, the literary and the theological.[11] In this volume all three of these elements are discussed. Table 1 overleaf shows how some chapters fit into this perspective.

Other chapters overlap these categories. In Chapter 1, for example, I discuss the rise of historical criticism, and examine some of the theological hermeneutics being proposed today. Neil Beaton MacDonald's chapter on philosophy of language connects with theological and literary issues. And, there are numerous other connections that can and should be made.

A further major aspect of this volume is the concern with *foundational* issues. There is a recognition by many of the contributors that underlying the three strands of history, literature and theology, are deeper epistemological and ontological issues, that shape the way we think about literature and history. I argue that modern biblical interpretation has been shaped *philosophically* from the start and that deep analysis and renewal must take account of the role of philosophy if we are to move forward. I suggest that some of the contemporary

---

[11] Sternberg, *Poetics*, is a great example of this.

Table 1.

Key Strands	Chapters	
History		
	Greene:	philosophy of history and interpretation
	Sundberg:	the social effect of historical criticism[12]
	Riches:	response to Sundberg
	Möller:	renewing historical criticism[13]
Literature		
	Wright:	aesthetics and biblical interpretation
	Ingraffia:	deconstructing the tower of Babel[14]
	Hart:	imagination and biblical interpretation
	Wolterstorff:	response to Hart
Theology		
	Seitz:	a case for serious *theological* interpretation
	Beeby:	a missional hermeneutic

proposals about a theological hermeneutic for biblical interpretation have not yet addressed this issue sufficiently. I am concerned to open up the question of the relationship between theology and philosophy in biblical interpretation. Seitz, by comparison, argues that concern with general hermeneutics may miss the really central theological issues.

Issues of language are central to postmodernism and especially postmodern notions of the literary. Neil Beaton MacDonald looks at how philosophy of language might help biblical interpretation, especially in terms of scriptural typology. And Colin Greene argues that the philosophy of history has been deeply influential in historical criticism and that a renewal of biblical interpretation must involve developing an adequate theology of history.

This interplay between philosophy and the three main strands, history, literature and theology, can be illustrated as follows in Table 2.

If these three strands of history, literature and theology, *and* the underlying philosophical and theological issues are taken seriously, what sort of biblical hermeneutic might result? Al Wolters' chapter on confessional criticism is a major attempt at mapping out a unified and yet nuanced biblical hermeneutic

---

[12] The difficulty with any model is that none of the chapters fits exactly in any of these categories. Sundberg's text is about far more than the historical dimension of the Bible. It focuses upon the social effects of biblical criticism which has been mainly historical. Likewise Möller's chapter deals with dimensions of the text other than the historical and with the relationship between faith and historical criticism.

[13] See n. 12.

[14] Ingraffia's chapter ranges across philosophy, hermeneutics and literary theory, and again is hard to position exactly.

Table 2.

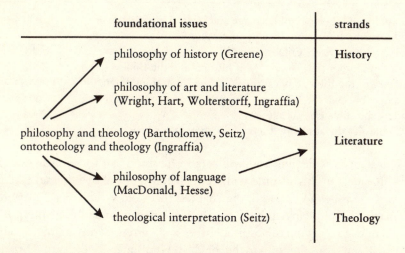

foundational issues	strands
philosophy of history (Greene)	History
philosophy of art and literature (Wright, Hart, Wolterstorff, Ingraffia)	
philosophy and theology (Bartholomew, Seitz) ontotheology and theology (Ingraffia)	Literature
philosophy of language (MacDonald, Hesse)	
theological interpretation (Seitz)	Theology

which integrates the above strands. Thorsten Moritz critically analyses Tom Wright's critical-realist hermeneutic which is another recent attempt at a unified hermeneutic. Karl Möller argues for a renewed historical criticism. And Dan Beeby pleads for a place in the sun for a missional hermeneutic alongside other approaches. Beeby's paper, of course, with its missional concern, takes us back again to the foundational issues that shape hermeneutics at the deepest levels.

Overall these resulting proposals can, I suggest, be visualized as in Table 3.

None of these areas is uncontested. One of the joys of the Cambridge consultation was the high level of expertise involved, and the responses to papers that are included in this volume give the reader a good sense of how the debate might proceed with respect to these issues.

The series of themes that the Seminar plans to address in forthcoming consultations are shown in Table 4.

Table 3.

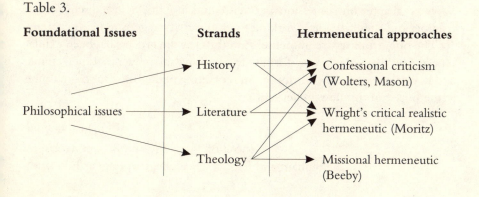

Foundational Issues	**Strands**	**Hermeneutical approaches**
	History	Confessional criticism (Wolters, Mason)
Philosophical issues	Literature	Wright's critical realistic hermeneutic (Moritz)
	Theology	Missional hermeneutic (Beeby)

Table 4.

Philosophy and theology of language and biblical interpretation	2000
The use of the Bible ethically and politically:	
a dialogue with Oliver O'Donovan	2001
History, philosophy and theology of history, and the Bible	2002
The story of the Bible: biblical theology and biblical interpretation	2003
Reading a book of the Bible in relation to key hermeneutical issues	2004
Reading the Bible canonically	2005
The Bible and the academy: the view both ways	2006

This agenda is flexible and will require revision as the Seminar does its work. Readers of this volume will recognize how the above themes take up many of the issues addressed in the chapters that follow. This year (2000) the Seminar will explore in depth the question of language and biblical interpretation. Language is central to postmodernism and current hermeneutics, and the results of our consultation, to be held at Redeemer College in Ontario, Canada, will be published as Volume 2 of The Scripture and Hermeneutics Series. Walter Brueggemann's retrospect alerts us to the importance of ideological readings, and these will feature in our 2001 consultation on the ethical use of the Bible. Several of our papers raise the historical issue and this will be our focus in 2002. And so on.

Issues are already surfacing that we will also need to address, issues that do not fit easily into the above agenda. In my opinion, a central issue is that of the relationship between a strictly theological hermeneutic for biblical interpretation, and issues of general hermeneutics and philosophy. Then, we have received a proposal that we should include a consultation devoted entirely to the question of a *missional hermeneutic*. This picks up on Dan Beeby's chapter. Contemporary missiology is a fascinating area and one can easily see the value of an interface between biblical hermeneutics and missiology.

We desire, wherever possible, to make the connections between hermeneutics and exegesis. In this volume that connection is most apparent in Al Wolters' chapter on confessional criticism and in Chris Seitz's discussions of readings of Daniel. We are working to ensure that exegesis remains central.

The opportunities are immense! And thus far, the process has been exhilarating. This first volume goes forth with our hope and prayer that the Seminar and its publications will contribute to a reopening of the Book for our cultures at the outset of this new millennium.

Craig Bartholomew (Rev Dr)

February 2000

School of Theology and Religious Studies

Cheltenham and Gloucester College of Higher Education

Bibliography

Barton, J., *The Future of Old Testament Study* (Oxford: Clarendon Press, 1993)

Bernstein, R.J., 'The Varieties of Pluralism', *American Journal of Education* 95.4 (1987), 509–525

Bertens, H., *The Idea of the Postmodern* (London: Routledge, 1995)

Brett, M., *Biblical Criticism in Crisis? The Impact of the Canonical Approach on Old Testament Studies* (Cambridge: Cambridge University Press, 1991)

Childs, B.S., *Introduction to the Old Testament as Scripture* (Philadelphia: Fortress Press, 1979)

Clines, D.J.A., 'Possibilities and Priorities of Biblical Interpretation in an International Perspective', *BibInt* 1.1 (1993), 67–87

—, *The Bible and the Modern World* (Sheffield: Sheffield Academic Press, 1997)

Collins, J.J., 'Is a Critical Biblical Theology Possible?' in W.H. Propp, B. Halpern and D.N. Freedman (eds.), *The Hebrew Bible and Its Interpreters* (Indiana: Eisenbrauns, 1990), 1–17

Luther, D.M., *D. Martin Luthers Werke: Kritische Gesamtausgabe*, vol. 55 (Weimar: Bohlaus, 1993)

Seitz, C.R., *Word Without End: The Old Testament as Abiding Theological Witness* (Grand Rapids: Eerdmans, 1998)

Sternberg, M., *The Poetics of Biblical Narrative. Ideological Literature and the Drama of Reading* (Bloomington, Indiana: Indiana University Press, 1985)

Vanhoozer, K., *Is There a Meaning in this Text?* (Grand Rapids: Zondervan, 1998)

Watson, F., *Text, Church and World: Biblical Interpretation in Theological Perspective* (Edinburgh: T. & T. Clark, 1994)

1

Uncharted Waters: Philosophy, Theology and the Crisis in Biblical Interpretation

Craig G. Bartholomew

'One can say with some justification that the beginnings of biblical criticism are initially far more a philosophical than a theological problem . . . in dealing with these questions . . . The church historian finds himself or herself transported into the largely uncharted area which lies between philosophy and theology'.[1]

Those who devote themselves to the study of Sacred Scripture should always remember that the various hermeneutical approaches have their own philosophical underpinnings, which need to be carefully evaluated before they are applied to the sacred texts.[2]

Introduction

If we are to discern the cancer and the many opportunities of the current state of biblical interpretation we must work at a depth diagnosis so that the solutions we propose contribute towards a genuine renewal of biblical interpretation. In this chapter I argue that unless we have the *question of philosophy* firmly in sight we will always be in danger of missing the depth of the problems, and the opportunities confronting us.

My argument develops as follows: First, I will argue that the crises of both modernity and biblical interpretation are at least philosophical, if not more than philosophical, and that these crises are connected. Secondly, I will look at some

---

[1] Scholder, *Birth*, 5,6.
[2] John Paul II, *Faith*, 85.

key examples in biblical studies to indicate how philosophy inevitably shapes biblical interpretation, whether acknowledged or not. Thirdly, I will look at the response to the crisis in biblical interpretation of 'theological interpretation', and show that this still leaves open the question of how philosophy relates to theology. Fourthly, I will explore several models of the theology-philosophy relationship and argue that an integrative model is required for biblical interpretation.

The Crises of Modernity and Biblical Interpretation as Philosophical

Postmodernity has become the catchphrase for our time. In an era of fragmentation and pluralism, and incredulity towards metanarratives, it is astonishing – and instructive! – that such broad-brush analysis is so pervasive. I am reluctant to concede that we have moved from modernity to postmodernity – if one must use modernity as the centre from which one analyses western culture then I would prefer to speak of *late* modernity or *high* modernity.[3] Apart from the problem of trying to do cultural analysis with a club rather than a scalpel when one works with these wide-ranging categories, from a Christian perspective I think it is a mistake to think that so-called postmodernism has moved *radically*[4] beyond modernity. The human autonomy that is fundamental to modernity, for example, remains as entrenched in postmodernism as in modernity. We may no longer be sure that human autonomy is the basis from which we can find truth, but then *we* will manifest our courage by bravely learning to live without that hope.

What the 'post' in postmodern does get at is the fundamental *philosophical* challenge that aspects of the modern worldview have recently been subjected to. In terms of epistemology the very possibility of *representing the world truthfully* has been radically challenged – witness the variety of positions taken in this regard by Habermas, Norris, Lyotard, Foucault, Rorty and Derrida. With this has come an awareness of the extent to which the post-Enlightenment, modern worldview is itself a tradition among traditions. Not all would agree with this of course, but it is precisely here that the battle rages. Gadamer, for example, argues that the Enlightenment perspective has its own prejudices and that these are specifically directed against the Bible as Scripture.[5] All this raises

---

[3] See Bartholomew, 'Modernity'. 'High modernity' is Anthony Giddens's phrase. See his *Modernity*, 4, 7–22.

[4] i.e. at root.

[5] Consider the following two quotes from Gadamer in his *Truth and Method*: 'The historical critique of Scripture that emerges fully in the eighteenth century has its dogmatic base, as our brief look at Spinoza has shown, in the Enlightenment's faith in

in an acute fashion the challenge of (genuine) pluralism and questions at root the post-Enlightenment belief in progress.

Lest you think I am imagining the extent to which postmodernism involves a philosophical crisis, let me refer to a few recent authors in this respect. David Lyon says that 'The postmodern, then, refers above all else to the exhaustion of modernity.'[6] In his book on humanism, Carroll concludes:

> Our story is told. Its purpose has been simple, to shout that humanism is dead, has been so since the late nineteenth century, and it is about time to quit. Let us bury it with appropriate rites, which means honouring the little that was good, and understanding what went wrong and why.[7]

Similarly in his *Cosmopolis*, Stephen Toulmin says of modernity that

> What looked in the nineteenth century like an irresistible river has disappeared in the sand, and we seem to have run aground . . . we are now stranded and uncertain of our location. The very project of Modernity thus seems to have lost momentum, and we need to fashion a successor programme.[8]

This crisis is certainly more than just philosophical, but it is certainly not less than a philosophical crisis. There are historical, social, cultural, technological and economic dimensions to the present ferment in western culture. But, if as Derrida insists, every academic discipline has a philosophical subtext, then the philosophical aspect of the crisis is perhaps most significant for academic work, not least biblical interpretation. In an interview with Kearney, Derrida, rightly in my opinion, argues that

> In all the other disciplines you mention, there is philosophy. To say to oneself that one is going to study something that is not philosophy is to deceive oneself. It is not difficult to show that in political economy, for example, there is a philosophical discourse in operation. And the same applies to mathematics and the other sciences. Philosophy, as logocentrism, is present in every scientific discipline and the only justification for transforming philosophy into a specialized discipline is the necessity to render explicit and thematic the philosophical subtext in every discourse. The principal function which the teaching of philosophy serves is to enable people to become 'conscious', to become aware of what exactly they are saying, what kind of

---

reason' (182). 'Enlightenment critique is primarily directed against the religious tradition of Christianity – i.e., the Bible . . . This is the real radicality of the modern Enlightenment compared to all other movements of enlightenment: it must assert itself against the Bible and dogmatic interpretations of it' (272).

6 Lyon, *Postmodernity*, 6.
7 Carroll, *Humanism*, 228–232.
8 Toulmin, *Cosmopolis*, 3.

discourse they are engaged in when they do mathematics, physics, political economy, and so on. There is no system of teaching or transmitting knowledge which can retain its coherence without, at one moment or another, interrogating itself philosophically, that is, without acknowledging its subtextual premises; and this may even include an interrogation of unspoken political interests or traditional values.[9]

Derrida is, I think, right about philosophy being foundational to all scientific disciplines[10]. And it is as one interrogates the philosophical subtext of modern biblical interpretation that the extent to which it is indebted to modernity becomes apparent. However, philosophically modernity is now in crisis, and through its rootage in modernity, biblical interpretation is unavoidably affected by this crisis. Indeed, we will not understand the crisis in biblical interpretation unless we discern its connection with the broader philosophical crisis of modernity that, *inter alia*, postmodernism signifies. The logic of my argument is as follows:

(1) It is legitimate to describe the dominant method of interpreting the Bible in the last 150 years or so as *historical criticism*. There is a variety of historical criticisms and all sorts of developments within this period,[11] but there is a commonality within that variety under the umbrella of what might be called the modern worldview, and it is important for post-Enlightenment biblical scholars to represent the situation this way! Part of the mythology of modernity is what Toulmin pejoratively calls the standard account of modernity.[12] This is the view that modernity began in the seventeenth century and represents the progressive triumph of reason. In this context historical criticism is thought of as the standard way of studying the Bible objectively.

(2) The philosophical subtext of the historical-critical method is post-Enlightenment philosophies of history, and nineteenth-century historicism in particular, as Ernest Nicholson acknowledges in his 1986 inaugural. Nicholson points out that the name historical criticism indicates its source. It emerged from the historical thinking that emerged out of the Enlightenment, received further impulses from Romanticism, and burgeoned in the German historical school of the nineteenth century.

To a remarkable extent, indeed to a greater extent than has often been realized or acknowledged, it was this historical thinking that provided the basis of biblical

---

[9] Kearney, 'Jacques Derrida', 114, 115.
[10] See, e.g., Clouser, *Myth*, 59–68.
[11] A point made strongly by Anthony Thiselton at our 1998 consultation.
[12] Toulmin, *Cosmopolis*, 13–17. See Bartholomew, *Reading Ecclesiastes*, 54–57 for a summary of Toulmin.

hermeneutics in the nineteenth century, and more than the theologians and biblical scholars themselves it was the leading figures of the German historical school – Barthold Gustav Niebuhr, Wilhelm von Humboldt, Leopold von Ranke, Johan Gustav Droysen, Theodor Mommsen, and others – who created the interpretive framework and provided the method.[13]

The scientific revolution of the sixteenth and seventeenth centuries is followed by a historiographic revolution in the nineteenth century, and historical criticism embodies the application of post-Enlightenment historical philosophy and methodology to the Bible.

(3) The philosophical subtext of historical criticism, namely modernity and historicism, has now been radically questioned by postmodernism, and can no longer so easily be taken for granted. Here again I find Derrida helpful. He points out that deconstruction makes us aware of the philosophical and theoretical presuppositions at work in every critical methodology and makes us 'aware of what we are in fact doing when we subscribe to this or that *institutional way of reading literature*'.[14]

(4) The 'postmodern' interrogation of modernity and thus, albeit indirectly, of the philosophical subtext of historical criticism, and the resulting ferment in philosophy of science, literary studies, etc. meant that sooner or later biblical studies would experience the crisis of modernity signified by postmodernism. Indeed, the literary turn in the 1970s in biblical studies meant that biblical interpretation was particularly open to moves in the literary field, and it was from literary studies that the immediate postmodern impetus came.[15] One only has to glance at the postmodern smorgasbord in literary studies to see a reflection of what is going on in biblical studies today.

Indeed, the implication of postmodern notions of *the literary* for biblical interpretation is a good example of the importance of philosophy for biblical studies. It is common knowledge that much postmodernism is post-phenomenological. Ricoeur, Derrida, Levinas and Marion, for example, have their theoretical roots in Husserl's phenomenology. And phenomenology is quintessentially modern in its attempt to intuit knowledge of an object truthfully.[16] Under the influence of phenomenology Derrida started a doctorate on the ideality of the literary object – a project he never completed.[17] Derrida

---

[13] Nicholson, *Interpreting the Old Testament*, 16.
[14] Kearney, 'Jacques Derrida', 125.
[15] See Bartholomew, 'Modernity'.
[16] See Fuchs, *Phenomenology*.
[17] See Derrida, 'Time', for a discussion of his development since he registered this thesis title in 1957.

came to see that phenomenology is wedded to a 'metaphysics of presence' and part of his deconstruction of phenomenology involved coming to see all texts as literary in a strange Derridean sense that is bound up with Derrida's critique of the metaphysics of presence and logocentric understandings of 'the book'.[18]

Derrida and deconstruction are surprisingly influential in literary and biblical studies nowadays. Biblical scholars generally encounter deconstruction at the level of application to a biblical text, and often have no idea where these bizarre readings come from. One may, for example, be at a conference and experience a most unusual deconstructive reading of say, Esther, in which an aporia in the text is identified so that the book's message is shown to be subverted by elements in its own story. In order to begin to evaluate such readings it is vital to understand what one is not generally told at such sessions, namely that the subtext of such a deconstructive methodology is Derrida's *philosophy* of language and literature, and it is this which drives deconstructive methodology.

No doubt the precise influences of philosophy on exegesis are complex and often hard to trace, and certainly the influence is not just one way. Theory construction is a complex process with all sorts of things going on in its ecosystem. However, what I have argued here is that philosophy is at the heart of modernity and is central to the crisis signified by postmodernism and experienced by biblical interpretation. It is the link between modernity and historical criticism via post-Enlightenment philosophies of history that convinces me that biblical interpretation today is in crisis. The roots of this crisis reach back into the origins of modernity and historical criticism, but insofar as postmodernism challenges the foundations of modernity, so too are the foundations of historical criticism challenged. Thus, any attempt to address the crisis in biblical interpretation must take account of philosophy as the subtext of all academic disciplines and not least of biblical studies.

Some Examples of How Philosophy Impacts Biblical Interpretation

Derrida, as we have seen, insists that every discipline has a philosophical subtext. However, reading most historical-critical biblical study since Wellhausen one would not think so! A crucial aspect, therefore, of assessing the present crisis of biblical interpretation, is to examine the route we have taken to arrive at where we are today. Indispensable to understanding the present will be (re)telling the story of our journey thus far. Of course, one is intensely aware that where we see ourselves today will affect how we tell that story. And how we tell the story will tell a lot about where we position ourselves today.

---

[18] For Derrida on literature see, in particular, his *Acts of Literature*.

Nevertheless there is a historical constraint to the story of biblical studies and it is an important element in assessing our situation today.

There are not many books which examine in depth the development of biblical studies. New Testament studies are in general better served here, I suspect, than Old Testament studies.[19] Re-examination of this history, I suggest, is an important part of understanding the crisis in biblical interpretation. For the purposes of this chapter I will focus on a key figure at the 'origins' of modern biblical criticism, look at a crucial shift in biblical interpretation that takes place in Wellhausen's work, take note of philosophical influence on the development of biblical theology, and then bring the discussion into our present situation.

W.M.L. de Wette

Rogerson describes de Wette as the 'founder of modern biblical criticism'.[20] Rogerson recognizes de Wette's indebtedness to his predecessors but maintains that de Wette's work inaugurated a new era in critical Old Testament scholarship. De Wette was the first to use a critical methodology to articulate a view of Israel's history quite different to that implied in the Old Testament.[21] Especially because of his doctorate on Deuteronomy and his seventh-century dating of it, and his association of the promulgation of Deuteronomy with the reign of King Josiah, de Wette is most well known as an Old Testament critic. However, de Wette wrote substantially on the Old Testament, the New Testament and on Christian theology. He stands therefore at the origin of biblical criticism as a whole.

De Wette grew up in a Protestant family and studied at the University of Jena where his illustrious teachers included Fichte, Schelling, Hegel and Griesbach. For de Wette the major challenge to his faith came, however, from Kant. In 1798, the year before de Wette came to Jena, Kant published his *Der Streit der Fakultäten* in which he outlines an understanding of religion within the bounds of reason alone.[22] As Rogerson says:

---

[19] For the history of Old Testament interpretation see Kraus, *Geschichte*, and Rogerson's works. For New Testament see Neill and Wright, *Interpretation*.

[20] Rogerson, *de Wette*. Where to locate the origins of modern biblical criticism is controversial. I think that de Wette is *a* key figure in terms of the radical application of Enlightenment philosophy to the Bible but the impetus in this direction lies earlier with Spinoza. Resolution of this issue is not crucial for my argument. De Wette is, on all accounts, *a* hugely influential father of modern criticism, and bears scrutiny as such.

[21] Rogerson, *Criticism*, 28,29. On de Wette and biblical criticism see also Howard, *Religion*.

[22] *Religion within the Limits of Reason Alone* is the title of an earlier book (1793) by Kant, in which he develops the view of religion also expressed in *Der Streit* (1798).

However illustrious his Jena teachers were, the greatest initial impact that was made upon de Wette came from the philosophy of Kant. Indeed, for the remainder of his life, de Wette remained, intellectually, a sort of Kantian; and he spent many years of his life trying to reconcile his intellectual acceptance of Kant with his aesthetic and almost mystical instinct for religion.[23]

Kant's view had radical implications for religion and biblical interpretation. There is no agreed interpretation of the Bible, but a religion of reason, because it gets at universal truths of reason, can yield this. Religion is reduced to morality and Christian theology is adjusted accordingly. The contingent truths of history cannot be revelatory since revelation is disclosed through reason.

De Wette found Kant's approach very illuminating but it left him feeling alone and bereft of God in the world. Schelling helped de Wette to develop a critique of Kant's overprivileging of philosophy as final arbiter in all disciplines. For Schelling God as the Absolute was primary and reason a part of the Absolute by which the individual could perceive the Absolute in the particular. Religion is the contemplation of the Absolute as it is manifested in nature, history and art. Mythology, in this context, is to be regarded positively, because it is an attempt to grasp the Absolute. Schelling's understanding of mythology profoundly influenced de Wette's approach to the Bible, especially to the Old Testament.

De Wette sought for a philosophy that combined the best insights of Kant and Schelling. It is probably from Tieck and Wackenroeder's *Phantasien über die Kunst* that de Wette made the discovery that he felt replaced his lost faith with a better and higher faith. *Phantasien* argues that art and religion are two mirrors which allow the true spirit of things to be known. In his *Eine Idee über das Studium der Theologie* de Wette argues that theology must begin with the contemplation of art. It is art which brings down from heaven 'the divine in earthly form, and bringing it into our view you move the cold and narrow heart to accept feelings that are divine and mediate harmony'.[24] From art one can move to nature, history and finally theology.

In his dissertation (submitted 1804) and in his *Aufforderung zum Studium der hebräischen Sprache und Literatur* (1805) de Wette developed a portrait of the history of Israelite religion which differed radically from that of the Old Testament itself and which formed the basis for the development of critical scholarship in the nineteenth and twentieth centuries. According to Rogerson, it is here that de Wette's major contribution lies. But where, asks Rogerson, did de Wette get this portrait from? From reading the text, from reading it in a way not constricted by theories of unity of authorship, but also, says Rogerson, by

---

[23] Rogerson, *de Wette*, 27.

[24] Ibid., 15.

reading the Old Testament through the grid of a certain view of religion. In his dissertation this is, according to Rogerson, a view of religion as developing from a simple to a complex phenomenon which de Wette probably got from Schelling's *Philosophie der Kunst*. The *Aufforderung* contains a devastating attack on the historicity of the Old Testament, motivated by de Wette's view of religion and mythology. From Kant de Wette had learnt, and learnt well, that the contingent truths of history cannot be revelatory. Probably from Karl Philipp Moritz's *Die Götterlehre* (1791) de Wette learnt that myths were never history but poetry, and although myths were fantasy they could contain sublime ideas.

Rogerson perceptively comments that

> Looked at, then, from the perspective of the literary and philosophical world of his day, de Wette was not a rationalizing critic who summarily dismissed the historical value of the Old Testament. It was widely accepted among biblical scholars that the Bible contained myths. De Wette simply applied to their interpretation *a view derived from literary and philosophical interpretation*: that they were to be seen as instances of fantasy-inspired poetry, expressing the ideas of the people.[25]

Like Vater, but unlike Eichhorn with his documentary hypothesis of the Pentateuch, de Wette in his *Beiträge* argues for a fragmentary hypothesis of the Pentateuch. De Wette's great concern is to show that everything in the Pentateuch is mythical. Thus, stories with miracles, or ones in which God speaks are mythical because such events contradict general experience and the laws of nature. Thus the Pentateuchal stories are generally of no value for the historian but of great value for the theologian because of their witness to religion. The Pentateuch 'is a product of the religious poetry of the Israelite people, which reflects their spirit [*Geist*], way of thought, love of the nation, philosophy of religion'.[26] Similarly, in his 1811 commentary on the Psalms de Wette argues that in many cases it is impossible to determine the historical contexts of many psalms but this does not matter because what is important is religion expressed in poetic form.[27]

De Wette's Heidelberg colleague, the philosopher Fries, was very influential in bringing de Wette's philosophy of religion to maturity. In the context of the early influence of Kant, de Wette continued to struggle with the relationship between reason and revelation. De Wette accepted that the final arbiter of whether something was revelation must be reason but worried that this put reason in God's place. Fries helped de Wette to distinguish between reason (*Vernunft*) and understanding (*Verstand*). 'Verstand' is the means whereby a

---

[25] Ibid., 49. Italics mine.

[26] Quoted ibid., 55.

[27] See Parker's comment that de Wette is a rationalist and mystic at the same time. Rogerson, *de Wette*, 66.

person arranges sense perceptions into an ordered whole. 'Vernunft' is connected with moral and aesthetic experience:

> One outcome of this view of things was that de Wette obtained a new way of con-
> sidering the relation between revelation in historical terms and reason. Revelation
> in historical terms was no longer to be judged by its correspondence with the empir-
> ical understanding of reality; rather, it was to be judged by its correspondence with
> the understanding of eternal values mediated by reason (*Vernunft*) reflecting upon
> moral and aesthetic experience.[28]

As regards Christ, through Fries's influence de Wette came to see Christ as 'the
aesthetic expression of the ideal within the contingency of history'.[29]

This gives us some idea of the development of de Wette's biblical hermeneutic. One is struck by the profound influence of philosophical and theological issues on de Wette's thought. But, how are *we* to evaluate this narrative of de
Wette's hermeneutic? Rogerson makes several points at the end of his biography of de Wette. He argues that de Wette's most obvious weakness is his
weddedness to the philosophy of Fries. If he had only been more eclectic or obscure
he may have achieved a greater reputation! According to Rogerson:

> De Wette was convinced that biblical interpretation and theology were concerned
> with reality, and that reality could only be understood with the help of philosophy.
> In this he was surely right. Implicit in Christian belief are claims about the nature of
> reality, about the sort of world in which we live and about the sort of things human
> beings are. Although philosophy in a broad sense does not seek to provide answers
> to these questions, it does offer critiques of attempted answers, it exposes contradic-
> tions and tautologies and offers conceptual frameworks for deeper reflection. Those
> who claim to have no philosophy are simply unaware of their philosophical presup-
> positions.
>
> In using philosophy so unashamedly in his biblical interpretation, theology and eth-
> ics, de Wette was standing in an honourable tradition reaching back through
> Protestant scholasticism to Aquinas and the church of those centuries that produced
> the classical creeds of Christian orthodoxy. This was one reason why de Wette re-
> jected such orthodoxy, believing that it was based upon inadequate philosophy . . .
> we cannot fault de Wette's sincerity in making his views about the nature of reality
> affect his biblical interpretation and his theology . . .[30]

Rogerson also reflects on de Wette's continual focus on the relationship of biblical criticism to Christian belief:

---

[28] Ibid., 78.
[29] Ibid., 88.
[30] Ibid., 267, 268.

Was this any worse than privileging a particular view of the life and significance of Christ because it is held by a believing community? It is probably better, in that de Wette could give reasons for his position, whereas one wants to ask why a believing community thinks about Christ in the way it does.[31]

Furthermore, Rogerson notes that de Wette's aesthetics were tied to an ontology:

> It is here, it seems to me, that de Wette demands that we add to our agenda an item long since neglected. What is the status of aesthetic experience in theology and biblical studies? . . . There must be a place for an attempt to integrate biblical studies more closely with an aesthetic-literary exploration of reality.[32]

Rogerson has made a major contribution to biblical studies with his historical work on its development. However, in his evaluation of de Wette, his own views come more clearly into sight. We need to reflect on de Wette *and* Rogerson's evaluation of de Wette.

First, de Wette. Rogerson himself acknowledges that one of the great virtues of de Wette is his honesty and his quest for integrity in the sense of integration. Three ways in which de Wette is of major significance for our discussions are as follows:

(1) De Wette recognized that human perspectives or worldviews are unified and he saw the unavoidable connections between one's view of reason and history and religion, that is, one's philosophy, and how one reads the Bible. He has much to teach us in this respect. Modernity has been characterized by an explosion in knowledge and a strong differentiation into disciplinary and subdisciplinary areas. An effect of this is that scholars take longer and longer to specialize in less and less. There is little time and often no encouragement for scholars to descend into the subtexts of their disciplines and so connect up with the larger issues that impact their scholarship. This also means that biblical students and scholars are ill equipped for the foundational challenge of postmodernism.

De Wette's work is a reminder that, like it or not, our view of the world and our understanding of reason, religion and language, etc., will shape the way we work with the Bible. The great merit of de Wette is his consciousness of these influences.

(2) De Wette recognized the *fundamental role of philosophy* in academic analysis. He saw, as it were, that philosophical scaffolding is always in place when academic construction is being done, even if scholars are not aware of it. Always

---

[31] Ibid., 268.
[32] Ibid., 270.

an epistemology is assumed, always some ontology is taken for granted, always some view of the human person is in mind. De Wette is remarkably contemporary in this respect, for he was alert to the philosophical subtext that Derrida insists upon, but of which many contemporary scholars seem blissfully unaware .

In recent decades scholars of hermeneutics like Thiselton have reminded biblical scholars of the fundamental importance of philosophy and philosophical hermeneutics for biblical interpretation.[33] However, as Thiselton notes, biblical scholars tend to remain philosophically illiterate and thus destined to work within outworn paradigms.[34] De Wette's work is a salutary reminder of *all* the ingredients involved in biblical interpretation.

(3) De Wette believed that the true philosophy was that done in the Kantian/ Schelling/Friesian tradition, and his life's work is devoted to rethinking religion the Bible and theology within that framework. Especially in our 'postmodern' times this commitment to Kantian philosophy is controversial. But, whatever one thinks of de Wette's Kantianism, his candour is refreshing as is his quest for integration of his worldview with his scholarship and his theology.

Scholars continue to work with philosophical paradigms shaping their work, of course, but generally they ignore these paradigms with the result that they are hidden from view and their scholarship has the appearance of neutral, objective analysis. De Wette's openness about his paradigm enables one to get a look at the total picture that makes up his ideas, and this puts the reader in a position to examine and evaluate his work in its totality.

Secondly, Rogerson. Rogerson agrees with de Wette that philosophy is unavoidable in theoretical analysis. To claim to be free of philosophical presuppositions is simply to be unaware of them! So de Wette is to be commended because of his consciousness of his philosophy. But then Rogerson makes some extraordinary moves. He asserts that Christian belief implies certain philosophical positions: 'Implicit in Christian belief are claims about the nature of reality, about the sort of world in which we live and about the sort of things human beings are.'[35] And then, on *this* basis, de Wette is commended for adopting a

---

[33] See, e.g., Thiselton's *Two Horizons* and *New Horizons*, and Bartholomew, 'Three Horizons'.

[34] In 'Communicative Action', 137, Thiselton notes that 'Curiously, the limits of scientific method to explain all of reality seem to be appreciated more readily in the philosophy of religion than in biblical studies. Views and methods that students in philosophy of religion recognize as "positivist", "reductionist", or even "materialist" are often embraced quite uncritically in issues of judgement about, for example, acts of God in biblical narrative. In place of the more rigorous and judicious exploration of these issues in philosophical theology, biblical studies seems too readily to become polarized.'

[35] Rogerson, *de Wette*, 267.

Kantian framework and fitting religion within it. Rogerson does note that it would have been better if de Wette had been a bit more eclectic and obscure about his philosophical indebtedness. But, what has happened to the philosophical positions that Christian belief implies? Unless Christian belief implies that we adopt the framework of Kant's secular city and then search for a place for religion within the limits of reason?

In this way, de Wette *and* Rogerson focus in an acute way the legacy of Kant in biblical interpretation and theology. The contradictions I discern above in Rogerson's evaluation of de Wette probably stem from an assumption on Rogerson's part that Kant's philosophy is compatible with Christian belief. This is not an unusual view as the image of Kant as the 'philosopher of Protestantism' reminds us.[36] There is a strong tradition in liberal Protestant theology of Kant's philosophy as a mediator between faith and modern culture. However this assumption on Rogerson's part unhelpfully obscures just what is at stake in de Wette's and Rogerson's embrace of Kant in this way. As Beiser shows,[37] even in Kant's day his views were very controversial and the issues of theology and God in relation to Kant's philosophy were fiercely debated. In recent decades Kant's anthropology has come in for strong criticism from liberation and feminist theologians and from postliberals,[38] reminding us at the very least that 'the Cartesian-Kantian model of the self is historically contingent, rather than the indispensable conceptual device for properly framing the issue of faith and transcendence'.[39] It is true that evaluation of Kant as a 'Christian thinker' remains controversial today.[40] Personally, I think Michalson is right to argue that Kant's immanentism and view of human autonomy subvert theism so that Kant, as much as Hegel, should be understood as facilitating the transformations in European culture that we associate with the rise of atheism rather than being foundational for a mediating theology.[41] From this perspective Kant is a key figure on the Luther-Kant-Feuerbach-Marx trajectory, and one of whom, as Buckley notes in his explorations of the origins of atheism, Christian thinkers should be cautious.[42] The implications for theology and biblical interpretation are clear:

---

[36] Michalson, *Kant*, 1.

[37] *Fate.*

[38] Michalson, *Kant*, 128ff.

[39] Ibid., 136.

[40] For different perspectives on Kant and Christianity see Westphal, Wolterstorff, Wood, Michalson, Plantinga, 'Christian Philosophy', etc.

[41] Michalson, *Kant*, 127.

[42] Buckley, *Origins*, especially 322–333. Buckley, 332, 333, rightly notes that 'The atheism evolved in the eighteenth century was thus not to be denied by the strategies elaborated in the revolutions of Kant and Schleiermacher: it was only to be transposed

The consistent subordination of divine transcendence to the demands of autonomous rationality strongly suggests that Kant's own thought . . . is moving in a non-theistic direction rather than in a direction with obviously constructive possibilities for theology . . . the religious feature may remain present, but that is not where the real life is, any more than the twitching body of a beheaded reptile indicates real life. As a result, Kant's own example is hardly a comforting model for those committed to holding divine transcendence and a modern sensibility in proper balance. In his case, the balancing act cannot be sustained; his particular way of endorsing modernity is finally too self-aggrandizing.[43]

Whether or not de Wette is the father of modern biblical criticism in any final sense, his work is highly significant for the discipline in its embrace of a Kantian philosophical framework. This has all sorts of theological and exegetical implications, and Rogerson's assumption of the compatibility of Kant with a Christian perspective indicates just how powerfully and often unconsciously this father figure continues to influence biblical interpretation. One may – which I do not! – wish to argue that Kant is a helpful mediating figure for biblical interpretation between faith and modern culture, but then the case has to be argued, and not assumed. Rogerson rightly notes that de Wette's lasting achievement was to apply historical criticism to the Bible so as to produce a history radically different to that of the Bible itself. Nicholson notes the indebtedness of Reuss, George, Vatke and crucially Wellhausen to de Wette.[44] What tends to be forgotten is de Wette's indebtedness to Kant in moving Old Testament scholarship in this direction in the first place.

Wellhausen

De Wette's concern with and openness about his philosophical pedigree is illuminating. It is also unusual in modern Old Testament study. In the second half of the nineteenth century a style of Old Testament study developed which played down or even denied the philosophical element in historical criticism and got on with literary and historical study. Wellhausen's work marks this transition,[45] and has set the paradigm within which Old Testament scholars have worked ever since.

The enormous influence of Wellhausen on modern Old Testament study is well known. His philosophical indebtedness remains, however, a matter of

---

into a different key. Argue god as the presupposition or as the corollary of nature; eventually natural philosophy would dispose of god.'

[43] Michalson, *Kant*, 137.

[44] *The Pentateuch*, 4.

[45] And Kuenen's. On Kuenen's work see Dirksen and van der Kooij, *Abraham Kuenen*.

controversy. In his day Wellhausen was accused of bringing Hegelian and evolutionistic principles to bear on the Bible.[46] The accusations continue today. And they are not without foundation. Vatke, who influenced Wellhausen, was quite open about his indebtedness to Hegel and devotes the opening 170 and closing 120 pages or so of his *Biblical Theology* (1835) to a Hegelian understanding of the nature of religion in general and Old Testament religion in particular.[47]

However, it is too easy simply to damn Wellhausen as Hegelian and Darwinistic. Historical influence is complex, and furthermore, detailed studies done of Wellhausen's work and methodology show that he cannot be classified as Hegelian and Darwinistic in any straightforward sense. The most thorough of these is Perlitt's (1965) *Vatke und Wellhausen*. The subtitle explains what Perlitt is after: 'Presuppositions from the philosophy of history and historiographical motives for the representation of the religion and history of Israel by Wilhelm Vatke and Julius Wellhausen' (my translation). Perlitt notes the similarities of Wellhausen to Vatke but also their differences. For example, Wellhausen, unlike Vatke, does not see post-exilic Judaism as a positive development,[48] whereas a Hegelian view of history would push one in this direction as it does with Vatke. And, in his finding of a secure starting point for the history of Israel in the formation of Israel as a people, Wellhausen follows the organological method of the historical school *and* Hegel and Vatke.[49] Likewise with his view of progress, Perlitt points out that Wellhausen does not need Hegel or Evolutionism: 'The concept of development stretching from Lessing via Herder, Goethe, Schleiermacher and idealistic philosophy to De Wette, Ranke and Wellhausen has, of course, a specific, common foundation and colouring in its application to history'[50] (my translation). Perlitt argues later that Wellhausen's view of Israel's development is akin to 'historicism's

---

[46] Perlitt, *Vatke*, 154ff.

[47] See Rogerson, *Criticism*, 69ff., and Kraus, *Geschichte*, 194–199. Rogerson, *Criticism*, 70, nevertheless says that 'the main part of the book . . . is a critical account of the history of Old Testament religion; although organized around certain key Hegelian ideas, they constitute a profound and detailed analysis of many problems undoubtedly raised by the content of the Old Testament, and it is quite possible to read this section independently of the long opening and closing theoretical sections. Indeed, although it may be permissible to disregard the parts of the *Biblical Theology* that are blatantly statements about religion in Hegelian terms, the same cannot be done to Vatke's detailed treatment of the Old Testament text. Furthermore, it appears that later scholarship took seriously the historical-critical parts of the Biblical Theology while ignoring the theoretical parts.'

[48] Perlitt, *Vatke*, 177.

[49] Ibid., 172.

[50] Ibid., 178, 179.

individualizing concept of development' (my translation) of which Herder is a prime example.[51] The relationship of Wellhausen to the philosophies of his day is complex and such areas of overlap with Vatke and Hegel do not demonstrate strong dependence.

Perlitt notes, furthermore, that Wellhausen, like the Dutch critic Kuenen, firmly rejected the imposition of alien philosophies upon the Bible: Wellhausen and Kuenen 'agree completely at least in the rejection of pre- and alien philosophical determination'[52] (my translation). In contrast to Vatke, Wellhausen began his work with philological and text-critical analysis of the biblical text. 'Thus Wellhausen proceeded in a methodologically secure way from literary analysis to historical criticism'[53] (my translation). Perlitt finds Wellhausen to be in total agreement with Kuenen at this point. Kuenen asserts that 'Criticism gives us or must give us history, true history. The critic is the assistant of the history writer; he assembles the building blocks which the other needs/uses for his work'[54] (my translation). For Kuenen, historical criticism of the Old Testament thereby follows the recognized method of historical science. Perlitt discusses Wellhausen's literary and historical analysis of the Pentateuch and concludes:

> Thus comparisons of sources and reflections about the historically possible lead from insight to insight. 'To think that the cultus goes back to pre-Mosaic use is, without question, more natural than to think that God or Moses should suddenly have invented or introduced the right ritual for sacrifice.' (P 56) The evidence for a general and multifaceted growth imposes itself everywhere. Thus, one is able to penetrate such religious traditions, which reflect the thinking of a specific epoch, and rediscover 'that which is simply historical, that which is, so to say, world historical'.[55] (My translation.)

Although the goal of all history writing is to be presuppositionless, Wellhausen was well aware, as is Perlitt, that this cannot be achieved.[56] The historian and what he or she brings to the task always influences history writing. Thus Wellhausen's project is to be carefully distinguished from empiricism and from positivism. Wellhausen has his own passions that motivate his history writing. In his work on the prophets Wellhausen's concern with the individual

---

[51] Ibid., 185. On the key role of 'development' in nineteenth century historiography see Mandelbaum, *History*.

[52] Perlitt, *Vatke*, 160.

[53] Ibid., 168.

[54] Ibid., 169.

[55] Ibid., 175.

[56] Ibid., 206, 207.

personality of the prophet exposes, according to Perlitt, the inner passion of Wellhausen's history writing:

> It is not the perspective from a longitudinal slice based on the philosophy of history that elevates the prophets above that which precedes and follows them, but the . . . love for the personal, the individual, which Wellhausen actually does not share with Vatke, but with the historical Romanticism influenced by the spirit of the time of Goethe (which from this perspective extends to Nietzsche), and also with Schleiermacher and de Wette.[57] (My translation.)

This anticipates Perlitt's discussion of the three main motives that shape Wellhausen's writing of the history of Israel. We will return to this later. Suffice it here to note that Wellhausen was aware that history writing is never a neutral, totally objective enterprise.

However, despite this awareness, Wellhausen's response to Strauss's *Leben Jesu* manifests where his real sympathies lie with respect to philosophical influence on biblical study. Wellhausen wrote:

> Because Strauss showed and acknowledged himself to be a child of Hegel in his concept of myth, his book was judged simply as an extension of so-called Hegelianism. Biblical criticism, however, did not in general develop under the influence of philosophical ideas . . . Philosophy does not precede, but follows [biblical criticism], in that it seeks to evaluate and to systematize that which it has not itself produced. The authors – who were friends – of the two great theological works of 1835 [Strauss's *Life of Jesus* and Vatke's *Biblical Theology*] were certainly Hegelian. But, that which is of scholarly significance in them, does not come from Hegel. As Vatke is the disciple of, and the one who brings to completion the work of, de Wette, so Strauss completes the work of the old rationalists. The true value of the *Life of Jesus* lies not in the philosophical introduction and concluding section, but in the main part which in terms of its extent exceeds the others by far.[58] (My translation.)

Perlitt and Rogerson note how this statement exemplifies Wellhausen's view of philosophy and biblical study:

> Where Wellhausen positions his own work in this clear distinction between biblical criticism (as science) and philosophy (as an interpretation which follows criticism and merely systematizes it), can after all not be doubted . . .[59] One must rather proceed from particular impulses which arise from the exegesis. . .[60] (My translation.)

---

[57] Ibid., 200.
[58] Quoted ibid., 204.
[59] Ibid., 204.
[60] Ibid., 205.

With those statements we see the extent to which Wellhausen differed from de Wette and Vatke. Their extensive treatments of the nature of religion indicate a strong awareness of the influence of philosophical questions upon the process of discovery in their work. Wellhausen has a different view of the relationship between the process of discovery and philosophy. It is a view in which discovery is relatively uncontaminated by philosophy – Old Testament research uncovers the facts, and systematic philosophy can follow the facts but should not precede them.

Rogerson is alert to philosophical influence on biblical studies, and acknowledges that biblical criticism has been more influenced by philosophy than Wellhausen allows. However, he quotes from Wellhausen's discussion of Strauss's *Leben Jesu* and then in agreement with Wellhausen argues that

> If biblical criticism is defined as the investigation of the literary processes which brought the books of the Bible to their extant form, together with a critical evaluation of the history and culture of ancient Israel and Judea so as to interpret biblical material in its original historical and cultural setting, it is difficult to see how philosophy, even defined very broadly, can affect such investigations. Surely, the reconstruction of the history of Israel, or of the apostolic period, involves the use of an historical method unaffected by philosophy. Further, the conclusion, based upon the alteration of the divine names and other criteria in the 'Flood' narrative of Genesis 6–9, that this narrative is a combination of two originally separate written accounts, is something else that in no way depends upon philosophy . . . I am happy to agree that in many of its technical procedures, biblical criticism is not affected by philosophy.[61]

What appears to have happened here is that Wellhausen – and Rogerson, and so many others! – have adopted a radically different understanding to de Wette and Vatke of how philosophy relates to biblical criticism. For de Wette, biblical interpretation is shaped by one's view of religion and one's philosophy. For Wellhausen and for Rogerson, philosophy follows on from biblical interpretation and scholarship. The effect is dramatic! In one fell swoop, as it were, what Toulmin calls the standard account of modernity is entrenched in biblical criticism, thereby obscuring the tradition in which this style of biblical interpretation is embedded. That Wellhausen's (and Rogerson's) comments occur in relation to Strauss's *Leben Jesu*, indicates just how much may be obscured by this perspective.[62] The observation of the text by Wellhausen and his followers now becomes objective and scientific, (relatively) unadulterated by philosophical perspectives. Wellhausen's consequent decontextualization of Old Testament research is a good example of Toulmin's characterization of modernity,

---

[61] Rogerson, 'Philosophy', 63.
[62] On Strauss, see *inter alia* Harrisville and Sundberg, *Bible*, 89–110.

and indicates a direction which became ever stronger in Old Testament studies.

Although Perlitt is right to distinguish Wellhausen from positivism,[63] the effect of Wellhausen's approach to biblical study is in a positivist direction in the sense that historical criticism is now understood to uncover the facts of Israel's history, and to be scientific and objective in this regard. Perlitt acknowledges that Wellhausen has his own passions that shape his history writing,[64] but these do not seem to worry Perlitt too much in terms of the scientific nature of Wellhausen's project.

Perlitt identifies three main motives in Wellhausen's history writing: Wellhausen privileges (1) the original over the artificial or unnatural, (2) the individual over the collective, and (3) the profane over the holy.[65] Perlitt looks at Wellhausen's negative view of the effect of the exile, the priestly code and centralization and concludes that

> A preliminary summary of the evidence which has been presented leads to the conclusion: Wellhausen had an almost constitutional aversion to everything artificial, schematic, constructed, secondary, derived; consequently he was attracted to the original, the organic, the natural, the simple. The course of the investigation so far does not make the origin of these inclinations appear doubtful. In the background stands first of all Herder's preference for the time of the patriarchs, for the youth of the people, for its natural growth.[66] (My translation.)

As regards Wellhausen's motive of individuality, we have already referred above to the effect of this upon his study of the prophets. Similarly Wellhausen criticizes the priestly code because it, by its stress on the connection of the whole, destroys the individuality of the particular story.[67] 'All these references indicate only that Wellhausen's occasional very high evaluation of historical individuality is situated rather in the line from Herder to Carlyle than in that from Hegel to Comte'[68] (my translation). Wellhausen, thirdly, prefers the profane to the holy. The former is original and national, whereas the latter marks later stages in Israel's development and relates to the international.

Perlitt, writing in 1965, may have been able to overlook the influence of these motives as seriously prejudicing the objectivity of Wellhausen's work. It is much harder to do that nowadays. For example, we are aware in Old Testament study that the romantic historicism that underlies Wellhausen's and

---

[63] See, e.g., Perlitt, *Vatke*, 183.
[64] Ibid., 207.
[65] Ibid., 206ff.
[66] Ibid., 211.
[67] Ibid., 213.
[68] Ibid., 215.

Gunkel's quest for the individual prophet detracts from the prophetic books in the shape we have received them.[69] One may still wish to pursue Wellhausen's approach and continue the endless search for, say, Ur-Amos,[70] but nowadays it is harder to do this without being aware of the prejudices it embodies. And the profane-holy distinction is intensely troubling, as is Wellhausen's negative view of the Judaism that follows the exile. Wellhausen's view of development may indeed not be that of Hegel and Darwin but it is historicist,[71] and it does shape his reading of the Old Testament in a major way. Wellhausen's discussion of *Volk* and *Blut* is hard to read in a post-Holocaust context without some sense of incipient anti-Semitism.[72]

So, the motives that fire Wellhausen's work are far from presuppositionless. It is easy to understand how the historicism that Wellhausen depended upon in the late nineteenth century might appear to be presuppositionless. Iggers points out that German historicism in the nineteenth and twentieth centuries has two principal meanings. The representatives of the first are those very figures Nicholson refers to as underlying historical criticism,[73] namely Niebuhr, Wolf, von Ranke, Böckh, Mommsen and Droysen. The roots of this classical historicism are located in von Ranke's rejection of Hegelian *a priori* conceptualizations of history and attempt to ground history in *a posteriori* concern with particulars.[74] This emphasis, in the late-nineteenth-century context of 'Wissenschaft for the sake of Wissenschaft',[75] easily gave the aura of pure science to historicism and historical criticism. However, historicism's concern with facts 'as they actually are' should not detract from the very real philosophy of history embodied in historicism and evident in Wellhausen's work.

The same is true of Wellhausen's literary work. I am not suggesting that Wellhausen and his followers imagined what they saw when they read the Pentateuch, for example. Their scholarship is based on hard work on the basis of what they *saw* when they studied the Old Testament. But it remains what *they* saw.[76] Assessment of their legacy and re-evaluation of it at this time must

---

[69] See Brett, *Criticism*, 89–93.

[70] See Karl Möller's chapter.

[71] See Mandelbaum, *History*, for the centrality of 'development' in nineteenth-century historicism.

[72] Perlitt, *Vatke*, 219.

[73] See above.

[74] Iggers, 'Historicism'.

[75] This is Max Weber's description. See Howard, *Religion*, 103, 104, for this reference and a useful description of the priority of 'Wissenschaft' in the second half of the nineteenth century in Germany.

[76] As Greenstein, 'Theory', 90, points out, 'Whether we see a whole text or a defective one involves a range of beliefs. To engage in our work as Biblicists means we must exercise our beliefs.'

take account of *both* these poles of their knowledge. As regards the Pentateuch, it is significant that since the 1970s the documentary theory has been in sharp decline.[77] Norman Whybray even came to argue that the Tetrateuch could have been written by one person, albeit in the exile or later.[78] In his recent book, subtitled *The Legacy of Julius Wellhausen*, Nicholson continues to argue that 'The work of Wellhausen, for all that it needs revision and development in detail, remains the securest basis for understanding the Pentateuch.'[79] Nicholson's is a most useful overview of current and earlier views of the Pentateuch. What is however, remarkable, is that his assessment of Wellhausen's legacy takes place without any consideration of Wellhausen's philosophical framework or hermeneutic or of the significance of frameworks and hermeneutics in general!

There are copious other ways in which to expose the close links between philosophy and biblical interpretation. I mention briefly two: the development of modern biblical theology, and postmodern readings which aim to set texts in play.

Biblical theology

Biblical theology has been in a crisis for decades now, certainly since Gilkey and Barr 'sounded the death knell' of the Biblical Theology Movement in 1961.[80] Reading the history of biblical and Old Testament and New Testament theology is an illuminating and surprising experience. Even with introductory texts like Reventlow's two volumes and Hayes and Prussner's *Old Testament Theology*, one immediately finds oneself immersed in *philosophy*. We cannot explore this in detail here. Suffice it to highlight representative elements in this respect:

(1) Gabler's 1787 Altdorf inaugural is widely regarded as the inaugural too of biblical theology as a modern, independent discipline. However, his approach is deeply rationalistic, as is apparent, for example, in his distinction between the historically situated ideas of the Bible and universal ideas, and his privileging of the latter. Biblical theology in Gabler's scheme thus becomes a preparatory step for the rational 'philosophy' of systematic theology. And this rationalistic distinction has shaped biblical theology ever since. As Reventlow notes, 'The subsequent history of the discipline was to be governed essentially by the

---

[77] See, e.g., Nicholson, *Pentateuch*.

[78] Whybray, *Making*.

[79] Nicholson, *Pentateuch*, vi.

[80] See Hayes and Prussner, *Old Testament*, 241–243. In the literature on biblical theology there are regular references to the flux and crisis in the discipline.

juxtaposition of a historical and a systematic discipline; this already presents us with the one great axis around which the whole complex of problems resolves.'[81]

(2) Gabler was important in his understanding of biblical theology as an historical discipline, and this emphasis soon led to the separation of biblical theology into Old Testament theology and New Testament theology. Initially, as with de Wette, for example, this separation was under the rubric of biblical theology, but soon separate works started to appear. Even more significant a sign was the influence of the nineteenth-century idea of 'development' upon biblical theology. This influence facilitated a monumental shift from biblical theology to the history of Israelite religion, evident for example, in Vatke and Bauer.[82]

(3) Vatke and Bauer are conscious of the philosophy of history they bring to bear on the Old Testament. Crucially, however, 'Future developments were characterized rather by *a move from any conscious philosophy of history* in the name of historical positivism and evolutionism.'[83] We have already tracked this development in Wellhausen's work and noted its importance and how it continues to shadow Old Testament studies.

(4) After World War I Gunkel's history of religions school emerged. The chief influence on this school was Herder! Schleiermacher too influenced Gunkel in the latter's view that the aim of exegesis is neither the thoughts nor feelings of the author, but their personality.

And so we could continue, looking at the further development of Old Testament theology, the development of New Testament theology[84] and the vicissitudes of biblical theology. The massive and inextricable influence of philosophy on biblical theology is clear. It is encouraging that we are again seeing a renewal of biblical theology, but I suggest that projects of Old Testament, New Testament and biblical theology require philosophical scrutiny and input if these disciplines are to be constructively renewed.

---

[81] Reventlow, *Problems*, 4.

[82] See ibid., 4, 5.

[83] Ibid., 6.

[84] As an Old Testament scholar most of my examples are drawn from the Old Testament. However, they could as easily be drawn from New Testament studies. The quest for the historical Jesus is deeply philosophical. And one of the great strengths of Tom Wright's work on New Testament theology is its attention to the philosophical and theological foundations of the discipline. See Thorsten Moritz's chapter in this volume.

Setting texts in play

Finally, on to postmodern readings that aim to set texts in play. But let us take a slightly circuitous route to this discussion. Biblical scholars are well aware of James Barr's influence on word studies – there are a variety of moves in this respect that are strictly forbidden to any self-respecting scholar since Barr's criticism of the approach to language of the Biblical Theology Movement in his *Semantics* and *Biblical Words for Time*. Barr acknowledges his indebtedness to modern semantics and stresses that biblical scholars need the insights of modern semantics in their exegetical work. What Barr does not say but what Anthony Thiselton argues, is that what Barr essentially did, was to mediate Ferdinand de Saussure's influence into biblical studies.[85] Saussure is rightly acknowledged as the father of modern linguistics and Thiselton shows how the main planks of his thought are at the heart of the changes Barr initiated in biblical scholarship.

What neither Thiselton nor Barr does, but what Derrida insists upon, is to examine the philosophical subtext of de Saussure's semantics.[86] Not surprisingly Derrida concludes that the subtext of Saussure's semantics is the *metaphysics of presence* and that Saussure's view of language contain aporia waiting to be deconstructed. Particularly vulnerable, according to Derrida is Saussure's notion of the arbitrariness of the sign. When pushed to its logical implications, Saussure's concept of the sign shows that language and meaning cannot be contained by distinctions between diachrony and synchrony and context. The latter, so regularly appealed to by biblical exegetes, cannot for Derrida ever be sufficiently saturated so as finally to contain meaning. The resulting *dissemination* of meaning cannot be contained, and thus a push here, a nudge there and a text is set in play with meaning darting all over the place.

As I have argued elsewhere, Derrida's reading of the Tower of Babel narrative is a classic example of setting a text in play.[87] So too are Kermode's reading of Mark[88] and Stephen Moore's readings of the gospels.[89] Derrida's notion of locating an aporia in a text – all texts are assumed to have them – and then deconstructing a text by pushing at this point underlies David Clines's deconstructive readings of biblical texts.[90]

Biblical scholars normally encounter these playful readings of the Bible in unusual papers at Old and New Testament Studies conferences. And naturally, for traditional historical-critical scholars or orthodox scholars, they are a shock.

---

[85] Thiselton, 'Semantics', 75.
[86] See Derrida, *Of Grammatology*, Part 1.
[87] Bartholomew, 'Babel and Derrida'.
[88] Kermode, *Genesis*.
[89] See bibliography.
[90] See bibliography.

What is not normally declared or spotted is that such readings are, as Derrida insists – at least of other readings – earthed in a philosophical subtext. James Barr's biblical exegesis and Stephen Moore's readings of Luke are *both* rooted in particular philosophies of language. Barr leans on Saussure, and Moore is indebted to postmoderns like Derrida and Foucault. And Derrida is indebted to Heidegger, Nietzsche and twentieth-century Jewish thinkers like Levinas, Benjamin and Scholem in his view of language. *An* important element in finding a route through our present crisis must therefore be of asking which of these *philosophies* of language are right?

Before we proceed, let us list the questions that focus where we have come to in our analysis:

(1) If in response to de Wette we ask whether philosophy is indispensable in theoretical analysis, it would appear that the answer is Yes! There is always a philosophical subtext to biblical exegesis. Notions of ontology, epistemology and anthropology inevitably shape biblical interpretation. The only question is *how* they shape interpretation.

(2) It is the *how* of the relationship between philosophy and biblical interpretation that has increasingly moved to the foreground in our analysis. How does Christian belief relate to, say, philosophy of language? Does Christian belief, as John Rogerson says, imply philosophical positions? And can these be articulated? Can reason in this way operate within the limits of religion, thereby turning Kant on his head? And where does Christian theology fit in to all of this?

A Theological Response?

In true post-Enlightenment tradition much biblical criticism has stressed the need for theology to be kept out of its practice. Theology, from this perspective, would contaminate biblical criticism's search for the truth about the Bible. One should let truth fall where it may and then, but only then, can one assess the theological value of the Bible with integrity. Rogerson says, for example:

> De Wette insisted, rightly we must say, that questions about the authorship and accurate history of the Bible were matters for historical investigation, and that the Bible's historical content could only be defended by historical criticism.
>
> The second line of attack was to insist that, since faith was not a matter of knowledge (*Wissen*) or understanding (*Verstand*), the religious truth of the Bible had nothing to do with its historicity, and was perceived by faith and intuition.[91]

---

[91] Rogerson, *de Wette*, 111.

De Wette and Rogerson, and so many others, agree here. Historical investigation of the Bible must be done by historical criticism, and that has little or
nothing to do with theology which must stay away from this operation lest it
contaminate it.[92] The question of what might be at stake in particular philosophies from a theological point of view is not even raised. This, I suggest, is a
good example of what MacIntyre describes as the classic modern *liberal* move,
setting up what MacIntyre rightly calls 'a fictitious objectivity'[93] which
obscures the tradition in which historical criticism is situated and thereby
makes critical evaluation almost impossible. MacIntyre articulates this as
follows:

> There is no way to engage with or to evaluate rationally the theses advanced in con-
> temporary form by some particular tradition except in terms which are framed with
> an eye to the specific character and history of that tradition on the one hand and the
> specific character and history of the particular individual or individuals on the other.
> Abstract the particular theses to be debated and evaluated from their contexts within
> traditions of enquiry and then attempt to debate and evaluate them in terms of their
> rational justifiability to *any rational person*, to individuals conceived of as abstracted
> from their particularities of character, history and circumstance, and you will
> thereby make the kind of rational dialogue *which could move through argumentative
> evaluation to the rational acceptance or rejection of a tradition of enquiry effectively impossible.*
> Yet it is just such abstraction in respect both of the theses to be debated and the per-
> sons engaged in the debate which is enforced in the public forums of enquiry and
> debate in modern liberal culture, thus for the most part effectively *precluding the voices
> of tradition outside liberalism from being heard.* Consider the ways in which this is so in
> the modern university.[94]

One of the effects of postmodernism is that we have become increasingly
aware that the above way of understanding historical criticism – and many
other issues – is itself traditioned and has its own 'prejudices,' to use
Gadamer's term. And in the view of Gadamer those prejudices are not neutral
but are specifically oriented against the Bible as scripture. If Gadamer is right,
then biblical criticism has been philosophically in the extraordinary position
of refusing to allow theological/Christian influence on its enterprise while
making room for traditions and ideologies often antithetical to Christian
belief. The results are then to be understood as truth falling where it may and
theologians being compelled to work with *this* data for their theological
constructions.

---

[92] In biblical studies this view has remained influential despite 'the crisis of historicism'
in neo-orthodoxy. See footnote 56 in Howard, *Religion*, 175, 176.
[93] MacIntyre, *Justice*, 399.
[94] Ibid., 398, 399. Emphasis mine.

As some Christian biblical scholars and theologians have become aware of this the recognition has grown that we need to reconcile biblical studies with theology. Stephen Fowl, in the introduction to his reader, *The Theological Interpretation of Scripture*, notes, for example, that a result of historical criticism is that scholarly reading of the Bible has been separated off from theological reading. Thus, while most biblical scholars still identify themselves as Christians, they have to check their theological convictions at the door when they enter the academy.[95] Consequently, some scholars are calling now for a theological hermeneutic in biblical studies. Fowl defines a theological hermeneutic as one which is informed by and informs theological interests and practice. For Fowl, theological interpretation is distinct from biblical theology and will have the following four characteristics:

- it will take pre-modern interpretation seriously.
- it will shape and be shaped by the concerns of Christian communities seeking to live *coram Deo* rather than by the concerns of those whose primary allegiance is to the academy.
- it will try to resist the fragmentation of theology
- it will be pluralistic in its interpretative methods and will even use the interpretative strategies of modernity to its own ends.

Brevard Childs has long argued that his canonical hermeneutic is *theologically* motivated. More recently, amid the twentieth-century renaissance of trinitarian theology, there have been calls for a trinitarian theological hermeneutic for biblical interpretation.

The trinitarian aspect is not to the foreground in Francis Watson's creative and very stimulating *Text, Church and World: Biblical Interpretation in Theological Perspective*, although it is so in his later work. However, in *Text, Church and World* Watson is quite clear in his proposal for *a theological hermeneutic* in biblical interpretation. He says:

> The text in question is the biblical text; for the goal is a theological hermeneutic within which an exegesis oriented primarily towards theological issues can come into being. This is therefore not an exercise in general hermeneutics . . . the hermeneutic or interpretative paradigm towards which the following chapters move is a theological rather than a literary one, and the idea that a literary perspective is, as such, already 'theological' seems to me to be without foundation.[96]

Indeed, his entire text is directed towards the 'attempt to formulate in more systematic fashion some of the elements of a *theological hermeneutic*, intended as a framework within which exegesis may proceed'.[97]

---

[95] Fowl, *Interpretation*, xiii, xiv.

[96] Watson, *Text*, 1.

[97] Ibid., 221.

For Watson, 'theological' implies a preparedness to work as a biblical scholar within a determinate form of ecclesial discourse in the sense of faith seeking understanding: the tradition of self-critical reflection that emerges from the claims to truth inherent in Christian faith. I must be content here to outline the broad parameters of Watson's theological hermeneutic. As I understand it there are some five or so main pillars to this hermeneutic.

First, a theological biblical hermeneutic means that our focus will be on the final form of the biblical text. This involves something of a paradigm shift from the historical-critical approach. Literary- and communal-usage reasons can be given for this but the most compelling is that the final form of the text is the most suitable for theological use.

Secondly, a theological hermeneutic in biblical interpretation will mean that exegesis is oriented towards specifically theological questions.

Thirdly, a theological hermeneutic will not deny the possibility of criticizing the biblical text. Watson focuses in particular on feminist critique of the Bible and the patriarchal elements in the Bible. For Watson it is of critical important that we develop a theological hermeneutic which equips us to critique patriarchy:

> there has gradually come to light a new dimension of the oppressive law whose presence within these texts and the interpretive traditions they have generated is such a crucially important hermeneutical factor. The oppressive law is . . . the law of patriarchy . . . If 'holy scripture' does not also offer the theological basis for resisting the law of the Father, then this concept should be rejected as an irredeemable ideological construct, however propitious the current climate may otherwise seem for its rehabilitation.[98]

Watson justifies this freedom to criticize Scripture in terms of his law/ gospel distinction which he derives from Luther:

> The duality in Christian experience represented by the law/gospel distinction becomes hermeneutically significant when interpreted as a twofold relation to the biblical text: for the twofold relation to God as the harsh judge to be feared and as the merciful redeemer to be loved is textually mediated. It is holy scripture that both repels and attracts, and a simple, undivided affirmation of its entire content is therefore a sign that one is deceiving oneself.[99]

Fourthly, a theological hermeneutic will not be unhappy to draw on secular insights. Because the church operates in the world, even though a theological hermeneutic will be ecclesial, 'It follows that any correct apprehension of Christian truth or the praxis that must accompany it will occur only through

---

[98] Ibid., 156.
[99] Ibid., 232.

the mediation of a discourse that is not in itself distinctively Christian.'[100]
Watson justifies this drinking at the secular well through the doctrine of the
Spirit at work in the world as outlined by John Owen:

> The sphere of creation-redemption encompasses the whole world, and the indwell-
> ing creator Spirit may also act as the redeemer Spirit, redemptively present in all
> goodness, justice and truth. To permit disclosures of goodness, justice and truth
> originating outside the community to impinge upon the interpretation of the sacred
> texts is not to contaminate them.[101]

Fifthly, a theological position can itself function as a hermeneutic. Watson
shows how bringing the following presuppositions to the biblical text in exegesis can be illuminating: (1) the presupposing of a non-logocentric understanding of the divine Word, (2) a Christology according to which Christ
transforms the whole of creation, and (3) the fundamental importance of love
of one's neighbour. In this respect the relation between exegesis and theology
is a manifestation of the hermeneutic spiral: exegesis of individual biblical texts
presuppose some sense of the whole (an interpretation of the basic content of
Christian faith). Yet this sense of the whole is not imposed from the outside but
itself arises at least partially from prior exegesis.

Sixthly, such a theological hermeneutic will be practised in community.

Most recently Kevin Vanhoozer pleads for a trinitarian hermeneutic in his *Is
There a Meaning in This Text?* Vanhoozer argues that all hermeneutics is theological in that it rests on beliefs about God, the world, and so on, and it would
help if literary critics and philosophers were to make their 'implicit theologies
explicit'.[102] Contra Watson, Vanhoozer argues for a general hermeneutics that
is trinitarian. Vanhoozer does not want to obscure the difference between the
Bible and other books, but he does want to assert that '*the best general hermeneutics is a trinitarian hermeneutics.* Yes, the Bible should be interpreted "like any
other book," but *every* book should be interpreted with norms we derive and
establish from trinitarian theology.'[103] The Trinity thus serves à la Kant as a
transcendental condition, a necessary condition for the human experience of
meaningful communication. Vanhoozer uses speech-act theory to develop his
theory:

> Speech act theory serves as handmaiden to a trinitarian theology of communication.
> If the Father is the locutor, the Son is his preeminent illocution. Christ is God's
> definitive Word, the substantive content of his message. And the Holy Spirit – the

---

[100] Ibid., 9.
[101] Ibid., 240.
[102] Vanhoozer, *Meaning*, 455.
[103] Ibid., 456.

condition and power of receiving the sender's message – is God the perlocutor, the reason that his words do not return to him empty (Isa. 55:11). The triune God is therefore the epitome of communicative agency: the speech agent who utters, embodies, and keeps his Word. Human speakers, created in God's image, enjoy the dignity of communicative agency, though as sinners their speech acts (and interpretations) are subject to all the imperfections and distortions that characterize human fallenness.[104]

There are thus a variety of theological and trinitarian approaches to biblical hermeneutics being proposed. In their insistence that we need a Christian starting point for a biblical hermeneutic I find these approaches thoroughly refreshing. However, in terms of this chapter the question is the extent to which these are adequate responses to the crisis in which biblical interpretation finds itself, and in terms of this chapter whether they sufficiently take *philosophy* into account. Do they adequately chart that largely uncharted area between philosophy and theology?

Theology and Philosophy . . . and Biblical Interpretation

I do not want to detract from the exciting possibilities that these theological proposals open up. I am keen to engage them precisely because they are so creative and exciting. And it is hard to see how a Christian could object to taking Father, Son and Spirit as a starting point.[105] However, I am still not sure that these theological proposals adequately deal with the *philosophical* challenge that modernity presents. Indeed, if one probes these proposals it appears that different understandings of the relationship between philosophy and theology underlie them.

Hints of diverse underlying paradigms are as follows: Vanhoozer speaks of speech-act theory as *the handmaiden* to a trinitarian theology of communication. Is this philosophy as the handmaiden of theology making its appearance?[106] Watson wants a theological (trinitarian) biblical hermeneutic but not a general trinitarian hermeneutic like Vanhoozer. He denies that a literary perspective, for example, is already theological, and maintains a principle of correlation.[107] Jon Levenson discerns like few others the radical

---

[104] Ibid., 457.

[105] For an assessment of trinitarian theology, see Bartholomew, 'Healing'.

[106] Cf. Vanhoozer, 'Christ and Concept', 140.

[107] See Michalson, *Kant*, 128–130, for an important description of how 'Kant's own moral hermeneutics is in many ways the model for the correlative enterprise, which animates the powerful tradition linking Schleiermacher and Tillich and establishes such concepts as the "experience of absolute dependence" and "ultimate concern" at

implications of historical criticism for the 'Hebrew Bible' and the 'Old Testament', but still holds out hope that somehow a literary and a historical-critical approach will together lead to a larger truth![108] These clues suggest that the philosophical challenge of modernity may not yet have been sufficiently faced in biblical hermeneutics and I would plead for biblical scholars and especially those proposing a theological hermeneutic not only to make their religious presuppositions conscious but also to clarify their view of how theology relates to philosophy in terms of biblical study.

This is no easy task. But to chart these largely uncharted waters effectively we urgently need an understanding of the different possibilities and some insight into how these impact biblical interpretation – we need a typology. In this final section I make some preliminary suggestions in this direction, which will need to be followed up in detail elsewhere. Some time ago Kevin Vanhoozer wrote a creative chapter called 'Christ and Concept: Doing Theology and the "Ministry" of Philosophy.' Vanhoozer's chapter alerts one to the issues that need attention in such a project. For example, what is rationality and does it function differently in different disciplines? What is theology? What is philosophy? How have scholars related these disciplines historically? In this chapter Vanhoozer, leaning on Niebuhr, Gilson and Frei develops a fivefold typology of the relationship between theology and philosophy:[109]

1   Christ subsumed under concept (Kant, Hegel, Buri)
2   Christ grounded on concept (Justin Martyr, Tillich, Tracy)
3   Christ in dialogue with concept (Aquinas, Schleiermacher, Bultmann)
4   Christ the Lord of concept (Barth, Frei, Lindbeck)
5   Christ the contradiction of concept (Luther, Wittgenstein)

Vanhoozer critiques all of these and then outlines his *Chalcedonian view* of the theology-philosophy relationship.[110] He argues for a 'fallibilist' concept of rationality which takes rationality to be about the way we solve problems. Vanhoozer argues in this way for the individual integrity, the relative autonomy and the mutual accountability of theology and philosophy.

---

the center of the dialogue between theology and modern culture' (129). Palmer, *Hermeneutics*, 80, 81, notes 'how decisive is our underlying theory of knowledge and our theory of the ontological status of a work, for they determine in advance the shape of our theory and practice in literary interpretation'.

[108] See Levenson, *The Hebrew Bible*, xiv, xv, and Bartholomew, 'Review of Levenson'.

[109] Frei, *Types*, 19–69, is indicative of the sort of direction I have in mind in this section. Frei examines the relationship between theology and philosophy, develops a typology of five types of theology, and then looks at their implications for biblical interpretation.

[110] Vanhoozer, 'Christ and Concept', 130–142.

I cannot outline Vanhoozer's argument in detail here. His chapter itself alerts us to the complexity of the issues involved, and Vanhoozer himself notes that, as with the Chalcedonian formula, it is hard to express the theology-philosophy relationship with precision.[111] What makes me cautious about Vanhoozer's typology are the terms in which he frames the typology: namely that theology is referred to as Christ, and philosophy as concept. Even allowing for the nuanced argument in his chapter, it seems to me that here and elsewhere the quintessentially modern distinction between faith and reason or theology and philosophy is assumed and remains somewhat restlessly present throughout.[112] Is not all theology conceptual, and is reason ever detached from some faith? If MacIntyre is right, as I think he is, that rationality is always traditioned,[113] then the danger with this sort of typology is that it never entirely escapes from the liberal notion of 'objectivity'.

I propose[114] that we think in terms of the following main ways of philosophy being related to theology:

(1) Theology *subservient to* philosophy – for example Kant, and as we have seen, much historical criticism. If theology has a place here it is as a suburb of philosophy. De Wette's early hermeneutic typifies the implications of this type of approach for biblical interpretation, although as his hermeneutic develops the tensions in it drive it towards (2) below. However, the overarching framework remains Kantian. Some of the postmodern work on the Bible fits firmly in this category. Often it lacks any theological interest and in a strongly secular way simply applies postmodern philosophy and critical theory to the Bible.

(2) *Double truth* – theology and philosophy are different but equally important ways of getting at truth and we need both. This approach takes diverse forms. Some argue that theology and philosophy have different *objects* – theology deals with the events of faith while philosophy deals with concepts and interpretation. Others argue that theology and philosophy may overlap in their objects but have different means (faith and revelation vs. universal experience and reason) of studying these objects. This view manifests itself in John Paul II's *Faith and Reason*. John Paul II compares faith and

---

[111] Ibid., 141.

[112] An example of this is Vanhoozer's comment about philosophy and theology that 'Each undertakes to construct a worldview, but only for one is the worldview shaped by a Word-view' (*'Christ and Concept'*, 134).

[113] *Whose Justice? Which Rationality?* The nature of rationality is a huge issue, and naturally requires extensive discussion.

[114] In a most preliminary fashion, merely so as to give an idea of how this might help discern the impact of these issues on biblical interpretation. I hope to develop this in detail elsewhere.

reason (theology and philosophy) to the two wings of a bird; for it to fly properly both are required.[115]

Milbank traces the separation of theology and philosophy back, in particular, to Duns Scotus,[116] arguing that it was he who first radically separated the two. The epistemological reason-revelation duality that stems from this, 'far from being an authentic Christian legacy, itself results from the rise of a questionably secular mode of knowledge'.[117] It is, indeed, hard to see how one can consistently maintain that theology and philosophy deal with different *objects*. Clearly philosophers might choose to reflect on the events of faith too. And the problem with seeing the means as different is that theology too is rational and philosophy is not exempt from a view of religion and an underlying worldview. Issues of epistemology, ontology and anthropology are present in theology as in philosophy.

The danger inherent in the double-truth approach is that of *eclecticism*, in which conflicting perspectives sit in uneasy tension with each other. Interestingly, John Paul II warns in this respect of

> the approach of those who, in research, teaching and argumentation, even in theology, tend to use individual ideas drawn from different philosophies, without concern for their internal coherence, their place within a system or their historical context. They therefore run the risk of being unable to distinguish the part of truth of a given doctrine from elements of it which may be erroneous or ill-suited to the task at hand.[118]

Biblical interpretation is riddled with double truth approaches to the philosophy-theology relationship. Plantinga, for example, shows, in his 'Two (or More) Kinds of Scripture Scholarship' how readily biblical scholars work on the Old Testament with unchristian assumptions built into their historical methodologies.

(3)   *Theology alone* (= Christ against culture[119]) – Tertullian, 'What has Jerusalem to do with Athens?', is the great early representative of this view. The effect of this approach is, of course, the Trojan-horse syndrome. Despised and unacknowledged, philosophy remains at work in the discourse. Few of the contem-

---

[115]   *Faith and Reason*, 3. There is a tension in *Faith and Reason*, I think, between the unity of truth and a nature-grace distinction between philosophy and theology. This is unfortunate because Catholic theology this century has made significant advances in overcoming this tension. See, Milbank, *Theology*, 210–232.

[116]   'Knowledge', 23. This is, however, a much contested view.

[117]   Ibid., 24.

[118]   *Faith and Reason*, 127.

[119]   The categories connect with Niebuhr's Christ-culture categories in his *Christ and Culture*.

porary proponents of a theological hermeneutic would argue for this understanding of the theology-philosophy relationship. However, the danger of a theological hermeneutic which fails to negotiate its relationship with philosophy, will surely be similar. Philosophical subtexts will continue to shape the discourse but in a relatively unconscious way. One suspects that much evangelical biblical interpretation is vulnerable in this respect.

(4) *Christ the clue* to theology and philosophy (= Christ the transformer of culture) – I am using here Lesslie Newbigin's seminal insight, argued *inter alia* from his exegesis of John's Gospel chapter 1, that Christ is the clue to the whole of creation.[120] This does not mean that revelation delivers all we need in a kind of instant package, but it does insist that in our pursuit of (all) truth we go astray if we are not guided by that clue which is Christ. According to this view theology *and* philosophy are academic disciplines which are both traditioned. That is, they *both* depend on and presuppose views of who we are and the nature of our world, so that their rationalities are always particular. This approach insists that if Christ is the clue to creation then he is the clue to all of creation and not just to theology. It insists that 'faith seeking understanding' is not the peculiar terrain of theology but should be true of all academic research.[121]

Nowhere have I seen the 'autonomy' of philosophy challenged so strongly in recent days as in Milbank's 'Knowledge'. In his quest for a radical orthodoxy Milbank discerns the fundamental importance of subverting the autonomy of philosophy and he invokes the neglected 'radical pietist' tradition of Hamann and Jacobi in this respect. 'Hence there can be *no* reason/revelation duality: true reason anticipates revelation, while revelation simply is *of* true reason which must ceaselessly arrive, as an event, such that what Christ shows supremely is the world as really world, as creation.'[122]

From this perspective, in my opinion, a biblical hermeneutic has theological and philosophical dimensions and both need to be informed by faith seeking understanding.[123] Such an integrally Christian hermeneutic/s will not solve all exegetical problems but will, as Stephen Neill said of a theology of history, hold the ring within which *solutions may be found.*[124] At the very least, it

---

[120] Newbigin, *Light*, 1–11.

[121] I am not aware that Newbigin wrote about the relationship between philosophy and theology and biblical interpretation. However his 'The Word in the World', in *Foolishness*, 42–64, and his attention to a theology of history in *Gospel* are highly relevant to biblical hermeneutics.

[122] Milbank, 'Knowledge', 24.

[123] I have attempted to outline the possible contours of such a hermeneutic in *Reading Ecclesiastes*.

[124] Neill and Wright, *Interpretation*, 366. In *Reading Ecclesiastes*, 207–226, I have tried to map out the shape such a biblical hermeneutic might take.

is worth noting, that had de Wette been open to such an integral model, and had he read a text like Wolterstorff's *Reason within the Bounds of Religion*, the direction of modern biblical studies might have been very different indeed!

Not all biblical scholars will agree, however, that such a transformational model is the right way forward in biblical interpretation. Yet I think that if we could pursue this type of question, much more of the whole picture of what is going on in biblical interpretation would become apparent. Especially since Wellhausen, much of what drives biblical interpretation has gone underground, as it were. And the great advantage of developing this sort of typology would be to surface the philosophical and theological presuppositions that continue to shape our scholarship, whether we are aware of them or not. Frei, Niebuhr, Vanhoozer and others have done foundational work in this direction and we need to build upon it in relation to biblical interpretation.

Conclusion

I am aware that the uncharted waters that I have drawn our attention to are large, deep and very challenging. Indeed, the goal of this chapter has not by any means been to solve all the problems raised by these uncharted waters, but to point to them, and to get the issue of philosophy firmly on the agenda as we reflect in depth on the crisis of biblical interpretation and work towards an open book once again.

Modernity is a multifaceted creature but, especially in the academy, philosophy has been at its heart. And de Wette is paradigmatic in alerting us to the impact of Enlightenment philosophy on biblical interpretation. The shift in understanding of the relationship between analysis and philosophy that takes place in Kuenen and Wellhausen, whereby philosophy *follows on* from the accumulation of the facts, is hugely significant, and continues to obscure the impact of philosophy in all biblical interpretation and to reinforce the standard narrative of modernity. At its best the postmodern turn foregrounds this philosophical indebtedness that pervades modern biblical interpretation.

Consciousness of this indebtedness and Christian evaluation of it are crucial if we are to hold on to the progress that modern biblical interpretation has made *and* to facilitate a reopening of the Book for our cultures. Personally, I suggest that it is the last type of understanding of the theology-philosophy relationship within which a new opening of the book will really flourish. And I think times are ready for such an integral approach. Recent decades have witnessed an unprecedented renaissance of Christian philosophy in the USA, and a harnessing of this to the calls for a theological hermeneutic seems to me to be the path of hope and renewal. Charting such a course over these challenging waters will not solve all the problems, but it will, I suggest, hold the ring within which the solutions are to be found.

However, I have by no means made a decisive case for this transformational understanding of the philosophy-theology relationship and biblical interpretation – I have not intended to. My aim in this chapter has been merely to show that modern biblical interpretation is shaped in a thousand ways by philosophy, and that we have to attend to this shaping if we are to understand where we are and where we should move towards if we want to renew interpretation of the Bible as Scripture. I think I have alerted us to a crucial obscuring of biblical interpretation's indebtedness to philosophy via Wellhausen. But here again, there is an immense amount of work to be done – we need to retell the story of biblical interpretation in detail.

And finally, it is important to stress that my agenda is not a negative one. The impact of modern philosophy on biblical interpretation has often been negative, but I agree with Anthony Thiselton that contemporary hermeneutics holds great promise for interpretation of the Bible as Scripture.[125] For that potential to be achieved we will need to attend closely to the relationship between philosophy-theology and biblical interpretation.

> I cannot fail to note with surprise and displeasure that this lack of interest in the study of philosophy is shared by not a few [biblical scholars] . . . I trust most sincerely that these difficulties will be overcome by an intelligent philosophical and theological formation, which must never be lacking in the Church.[126]

Bibliography

Barr, J., *The Semantics of Biblical Language* (London: Oxford University Press, 1961)

—, *Biblical Words for Time* (SBT, First Series, 33; London: SCM Press, 1969²)

Bartholomew, C.G., 'Review of Levenson, J. 1993: *The Hebrew Bible, the Old Testament and Historical Criticism*', *CTJ* 30.2 (1995), 525–530

—, '*Three* Horizons: A Hermeneutics of the Cross / Hermeneutics from the Other End: An Evaluation of Anthony Thiselton's Hermeneutic Proposals', *EuroJT* 5.2 (1996), 121–135

—, 'Post/Late? Modernity as the Context for Christian Scholarship Today', *Themelios* 22.2 (1997), 25–38

—, 'The Healing of Modernity: A Critical Dialogue With Colin Gunton's "The One, the Three and the Many: God, Creation and the Culture of Modernity"', *EuroJT* 6.2 (1997), 111–130

---

[125] Hence the title of Thiselton, Lundin and Walhout's *The Promise of Hermeneutics*.

[126] John Paul II, *Faith and Reason*, 94. 'Theologians' is changed to 'biblical scholars'.

—, 'Babel and Derrida: Postmodernism, Language and Biblical Interpretation' *TynBul* 49.2 (1998), 305–328

—, *Reading Ecclesiastes: Old Testament Exegesis and Hermeneutical Theory* (AnBib, 139; Rome: Pontifical Biblical Institute, 1998)

Beiser, F.C., *The Fate of Reason: German Philosophy From Kant to Fichte* (Cambridge, MA.: Harvard University Press, 1987)

Brett, M., *Biblical Criticism in Crisis? The Impact of the Canonical Approach on Old Testament Studies* (Cambridge: Cambridge University Press, 1991)

Brümmer, V., *Theology and Philosophical Inquiry: An Introduction* (London and Basingstoke: Macmillan, 1981)

Buckley, M.J., *At the Origins of Modern Atheism* (New Haven and London: Yale University Press, 1987)

Carroll, J., *Humanism: The Wreck of Western Culture* (London: Fontana Press, 1993)

Clines, D.J.A., 'Deconstructing the Book of Job', in M. Warner (ed.), *The Bible as Rhetoric* (London and New York: Routledge, 1990), 65–80

—, 'Reading Esther from Left to Right: Contemporary Strategies for Reading a Biblical Text' in idem, S.E. Fowl and S.E. Porter (eds.), *The Bible in Three Dimensions* (Sheffield: JSOT Press, 1990), 31–52

—, 'Haggai's Temple Constructed, Deconstructed and Reconstructed', *SJOT* 7 (1993), 51–77

Clouser, R., *The Myth of Religious Neutrality: An Essay on the Hidden Role of Religious Belief in Theories* (Notre Dame, Indiana and London: University of Notre Dame Press, 1991)

Cook, A., *History/Writing* (Cambridge: Cambridge University Press, 1988)

Derrida, J., *Of Grammatology* (Baltimore and London: The Johns Hopkins University Press, 1997³)

—, 'The Time of a Thesis: Punctuations' in A. Montefiore (ed.), *Philosophy in France Today* (Cambridge: Cambridge University Press, 1983), 34–50

—, *Acts of Literature* (New York and London: Routledge, 1992)

Dirksen, P.B., and A. van der Kooij (eds.), *Abraham Kuenen (1828–1891): His Major Contributions to the Study of the Old Testament* (Leiden: E.J. Brill, 1993)

Fowl, S.E., *The Theological Interpretation of Scripture: Classic and Contemporary Readings* (Oxford and Cambridge, MA.: Basil Blackwell, 1997)

Frei, H., *Types of Christian Theology* (New Haven and London: Yale University Press, 1992)

Fuchs, W.W., *Phenomenology and the Metaphysics of Presence* (The Hague: Martinus Nijhoff, 1976)

Gadamer, H., *Truth and Method* (London: Sheed & Ward, 1989²)

Giddens, A., *Modernity and Self-Identity: Self and Society in the Late Modern Age* (Cambridge: Polity Press, 1991)

Gilkey, L., 'Cosmology, Ontology and the Travail of Biblical Language', *JR* 41 (1961), 194–205

Greenstein, E.L., 'Theory and Argument in Biblical Criticism', *HAR* 10 (1986), 77–93

Harrisville, R.A., and W. Sundberg, *The Bible in Modern Culture: Theology and Historical-Critical Method from Spinoza to Käsemann* (Grand Rapids: Eerdmans, 1995)

Hayes, J.H., and F.C. Prussner, *Old Testament Theology: Its History and Development* (London: SCM Press, 1985)

Howard, T.A., *Religion and the Rise of Historicism: W.M.L. de Wette, Jacob Burckhardt, and the Theological Origins of Nineteenth-Century Historical Consciousness* (Cambridge: Cambridge University Press, 2000)

Iggers, G., 'Historicism: The History and Meaning of the Term', *Journal of the History of Ideas* 56 (1995), 129–152

John Paul II, *Faith and Reason* (London: The Incorporated Catholic Truth Society, 1998)

Kearney, R., 'Jacques Derrida' in idem, *Dialogues With Contemporary Thinkers: The Phenomenological Heritage* (Manchester: Manchester University Press, 1984), 105–126

Kermode, F., *The Genesis of Secrecy: On the Interpretation of Narrative* (Cambridge, MA.: Harvard University Press, 1979)

Kooij, A. van der, 'The "Critical Method" of Abraham Kuenen and the Methods of Old Testament Research Since 1891 up to 1991' in idem and P.B. Dirksen (eds.), *Abraham Kuenen (1828–1891): His Major Contributions to the Study of the Old Testament* (Leiden: E.J. Brill, 1993), 49–64

Kraus, H.-J., *Geschichte der historisch-kritischen Erforschung des Alten Testaments* (Neukirchen-Vluyn: Neukirchener Verlag, 1988[4])

Kuenen, A., 'Critical Method', *Modern Review* 1 (1880), 461–488, 685–713

Levenson, J.D., *The Hebrew Bible, the Old Testament, and Historical Criticism* (Louisville: Westminster / John Knox Press, 1993)

Lyon, D., *Postmodernity* (Buckingham: Open University Press, 1994)

MacIntyre, A., *Whose Justice? Which Rationality?* (London: Duckworth & Co., 1988)

Mandelbaum, M., *History, Man, and Reason: A Study in Nineteenth-Century Thought* (Baltimore and London: The Johns Hopkins University Press, 1971)

McGrath, A., *The Making of Modern German Christology 1750–1990* (Leicester: Apollos, 1994[2])

Michalson, G.E., *Kant and the Problem of God* (Oxford: Basil Blackwell, 1999)

Milbank, J., *Theology and Social Theory: Beyond Secular Reason* (Oxford: Basil Blackwell, 1990)

—, 'Knowledge: The Theological Critique of Philosophy in Haman and Jacobi' in idem, C. Pickstock and G. Ward, (eds.), *Radical Orthodoxy* (London and New York: Routledge, 1999), 21–37

Moore, S.D., *Literary Criticism and the Gospels: The Theoretical Challenge* (New Haven and London: Yale University Press, 1989)

—, *Mark and Luke in Poststructuralist Perspective* (New Haven and London: Yale University Press, 1992)

—, *Poststructuralism and the New Testament: Derrida and Foucault at the Foot of the Cross* (Minneapolis: Fortress Press, 1994)

Neill, S., and N.T. Wright, *The Interpretation of the New Testament: 1861–1986* (Oxford: Oxford University Press, 1988)

Newbigin, L., *The Light Has Come: An Exposition of the Fourth Gospel* (Grand Rapids: Eerdmans; Edinburgh: Handsel, 1982)

—, *Foolishness to the Greeks: The Gospel and Western Culture* (London: SPCK, 1986)

—, *The Gospel in a Pluralist Society* (Grand Rapids: Eerdmans; Geneva: WCC, 1989)

Nicholson, E., *Interpreting the Old Testament: A Century of the Oriel Professorship* (Oxford: Clarendon Press, 1981)

—, *The Pentateuch in the Twentieth Century: The Legacy of Julius Wellhausen* (Oxford: Clarendon Press, 1998)

Niebuhr, H.R., *Christ and Culture* (New York: Harper Torchbooks, 1951)

Palmer, R.E., *Hermeneutics: Interpretation Theory in Schleiermacher, Dilthey, Heidegger, and Gadamer* (Evanston: Northwestern University Press, 1969)

Perlitt, L., *Vatke und Wellhausen* (BZAW, 94; Berlin: Alfred Töpelmann, 1965)

Plantinga, A., 'Christian Philosophy at the End of the 20th Century' in S. Griffioen and B.M. Balk (eds.), *Christian Philosophy at the Close of the Twentieth Century* (Kampen: Kok, 1995), 29–53

—, 'Two (or More) Kinds of Scripture Scholarship', *Modern Theology* 14.2 (1998), 243–278

Ratzinger, Cardinal J., 'Biblical Interpretation in Crisis: On the Question of the Foundations and Approaches of Exegesis Today' in R.J. Neuhaus (ed.), *Biblical Interpretation in Crisis: The Ratzinger Conference on Bible and Church* (Grand Rapids: Eerdmans, 1989), 1–23

Reventlow, H.G., *Problems of Old Testament Theology in the Twentieth Century* (London: SCM Press, 1985)

—, *Problems of Biblical Theology in the Twentieth Century* (London: SCM Press, 1986)

Rogerson, J.W., 'Philosophy and the Rise of Biblical Criticism: England and Germany' in S.W. Sykes (ed.), *England and Germany: Studies in Theological Diplomacy* (Studies in Intercultural History of Christianity, 25; Frankfurt: Peter Lang, 1982), 63–79

—, *Old Testament Criticism in the Nineteenth Century: England and Germany* (London: SPCK, 1984)

—, *W.M.L. de Wette: Founder of Modern Biblical Criticism: An Intellectual Biography* (JSOTSup, 126; Sheffield: Sheffield Academic Press, 1992)

Scholder, K., *The Birth of Modern Critical Theology: Origins and Problems of Biblical Criticism in the Seventeenth Century* (London: SCM Press; Philadelphia: Trinity Press International, 1990)

Thiselton, A.C., 'Semantics and New Testament Interpretation', in I.H. Marshall (ed.), *New Testament Interpretation: Essays on Principles and Methods* (Exeter: Paternoster, 1977), 75–104

—, *The Two Horizons: New Testament Hermeneutics and Philosophical Description* (Carlisle: Paternoster; Grand Rapids: Eerdmans, 1980)

—, *New Horizons in Hermeneutics* (Grand Rapids: Zondervan, 1992)

—, 'Communicative Action and Promise in Interdisciplinary, Biblical, and Theological Hermeneutics' in R. Lundin, C. Walhout and A.C. Thiselton, *The Promise of Hermeneutics* (Carlisle: Paternoster; Grand Rapids: Eerdmans, 1999), 133–239

Toulmin, S., *Cosmopolis: The Hidden Agenda of Modernity* (Chicago: University of Chicago Press, 1990)

Vanhoozer, K.J., 'Christ and Concept: Doing Theology and the "Ministry" of Philosophy' in J.D. Woodbridge and T.E. McComiskey (eds.), *Doing Theology in Today's World* (Grand Rapids: Zondervan, 1991), 99–145

—, *Is There a Meaning in This Text?* (Grand Rapids: Zondervan, 1998)

Watson, F., *Text, Church and World: Biblical Interpretation in Theological Perspective* (Edinburgh: T. & T. Clark, 1994)

Westphal, M., 'Christian Philosophers and the Copernican Revolution' in idem and C.S. Evans (eds.), *Christian Perspectives on Religious Knowledge* (Grand Rapids: Eerdmans, 1993), 161–179

Whybray, R.N., *The Making of the Pentateuch: A Methodological Study* (JSOTSup, 53; Sheffield: JSOT Press, 1987)

Wolterstorff, N., *Reason Within the Bounds of Religion* (Grand Rapids: Eerdmans, 1984)

Wood, A.W., 'Rational Theology, Moral Faith, and Religion' in P. Guyer (ed.), *The Cambridge Companion to Kant* (Cambridge: Cambridge University Press, 1992), 394–416

2

Scripture Becomes Religion(s): The Theological Crisis of Serious Biblical Interpretation in the Twentieth Century★

Christopher R. Seitz

Introduction

I will begin by making several preliminary remarks, in an effort to bring some focus to what could otherwise be an enormous and unwieldy topic.

The conference is using the title 'The Crisis in Biblical Hermeneutics' as an organizing rubric. It is undoubted that as the end of the twentieth century arrives, biblical scholars, church members, and the general public could agree that something like a crisis exists. Naturally, they are concerned about this and feel the pressure of it in different ways, and so their reactions differ as well.

I appreciate the use of the term 'hermeneutics' to locate the crisis, but I want to be sure we agree what we mean by that. In the works of Vanhoozer and Wolterstorff, for example, one sees an effort to address topics like divine speech, inspiration, authorship, and so forth.[1] This is done from the perspective of general hermeneutics (the philosophy of language; speech–act theory) and in both cases the engagement is sustained and intelligent. It is less clear to me that, for example, Francis Watson's two recent contributions emerged to address what one might call a crisis in hermeneutics in the same sense one might locate Vanhoozer's and Wolterstorff's efforts.[2]

A good way to illustrate the difference is by noting how a long-standing problem of relating the two testaments of Christian scripture is seen as central,

---

★ This chapter will appear in my book *Figured Out* (Westminster John Knox Press)
[1] Vanhoozer, *Meaning*; N. Wolterstorff, *Divine Discourse*. See also the work of S.E. Fowl, *Engaging Scripture*.
[2] *Text, Church and World; Text and Truth;* see also my review, 'Christological Interpretation' and his response in *SJT 52 (1999), 209–32.*

or not. Hermeneutics as a science of reading and interpretation could simply speak about matters of authorship, reader, text, inspiration, divine speech, and so forth, in the manner of Vanhoozer or Wolterstorff, and never address the difference between Old and New Testaments on historical, theological, canonical, genre, or specified readership grounds. The Bible would be one big book, whatever its internal differences, and the problems of talking about author or reader or text could go on in general terms without regard for the divide separating two distinct literatures (Old Testament or Tanak, and New Testament). And one could still plausibly argue that a hermeneutical crisis existed and buffeted the field, and not be wrong about this.[3]

When one looks at the discipline of formal biblical studies, however, from the mid-nineteenth century through to the post-war years, in British, North American, and continental contexts, it would be difficult to speak of a hermeneutical crisis as we may now mean it, and yet crisis there was and crises there have been.[4] This *series* of crises focused not on general hermeneutics (text, reader, author, world), but on quite specific matters: the historicity of individual writings; literary methods and their compatibility; dating texts properly; social-historical reconstruction; the history of religion, and so forth. Always sitting close to these questions were serious subsidiary or even more up-front concerns. Is there a unity to Christian Scripture? How is the Old Testament Christian Scripture? In what way does the New Testament function as scripture, especially given its fourfold gospel record and what would come to be known as 'quests of historical Jesus' behind this fourfold account?

These questions – even when covered up with matters of historical and literary science so detailed as to numb the mind – persisted and were never completely banished from the field. It is proper, in my judgment, to call these theological, and not just hermeneutical questions. For they have to do with the way in which the testaments, each in its own specific historical and canonical way, bear witness to God. In the middle of the previous century and for many decades into our own, these questions did not just hover near the fray; rather, they were first-order questions demanding first-order answers if the discipline

---

[3] The distinction I am drawing here is seen at once when one looks at the older German works of Westermann or Reventlow, and compares these with Vanhoozer and Wolterstorff. In these earlier volumes, one cannot talk about hermeneutics without the difference between the two testaments of Christian Scripture being registered as of historical and theological significance, in the nature of the thing. See Westermann (ed.), *Essays on Old Testament Hermeneutics*, Reventlow, *Problems of Old Testament Theology*, followed by *Problems of Biblical Theology*.
[4] See the fine essay of Craig Bartholomew in this volume, where the philosophical problems of nineteenth century biblical interpretation are examined. What is striking is how *conscious* the field once was of its philosophical presuppositions, even as it was a self-consciously *historical* discipline.

was to have any integrity as an historically oriented one still tuned to the life of the church and an inherited intellectual history. What may have happened in recent years is that the central theological questions receded as the discipline, historically oriented as it has been, simply never ceased to find new historical questions to occupy itself with, and chose to focus on them as though the theological matters would somehow fall into place when all was said and done.[5] Qumran and Nag Hammadi freshly enriched our historical and comparative resources, and we should not have been surprised that yet another quest for 'historical Jesus' would give New Testament scholars something to preoccupy themselves with, in line with previous inquiry (so, e.g., Borg, Crossan, Meier, Wright, Johnson, Bockmuehl, Witherington, and many others).[6]

The turn to hermeneutics as a general discipline, then, has not so much offered a resolution of older theological questions, historically considered, as it has changed the subject. One may wish to judge that a good thing, but in so doing there would have to be an admission that what has counted in the history of biblical studies for the past century and a half as central was misguided from the start. The field posed the wrong questions, it would have to be concluded, and therefore got wrong answers and ended up in its present desuetude – call it a 'hermeneutical crisis' – as a consequence. A cursory comparison with Westermann's *Old Testament Hermeneutics* volume, produced at a period of general critical (methodological) consensus, shows an array of concerns untouched in recent hermeneutical discussions. Any accounting of our present crisis is obliged to say why this is so.

A Brief Word about my Chapter's Title

The title for this chapter should reveal several things:

First, the overview will be historical. That is, it will seek to examine biblical studies in the twentieth century in order to make general classifications, as a new century (and millennium) arrives. Because the mid– to late– nineteenth century witnessed the battle over the 'new science' of biblical criticism in intense form in Britain, the survey must begin there.

---

[5] *Hermeneia – A Critical and Historical Commentary on the Bible* utilizes a common preface for all its volumes, written by F. Moore Cross and H. Koester, in which it is said: 'The editors of *Hermeneia* impose no systematic-theological perspective upon the series (directly, or indirectly by selection of authors). It is expected that the authors will struggle to lay bare the ancient meaning of a biblical work or pericope. In this way the text's human relevance *should become transparent, as is always the case in competent historical discourse*' (emphasis added).

[6] For a critical appraisal, see the 1998 issue of *Ex Auditu* on 'The Theological Significance of the Earthly Jesus.'

Second, the area of my interest is what will be called, with all appropriate overtone, 'serious biblical interpretation.' By this is not meant hymnody, or sermons, or church debates over interpretation, or intramural (denominational) uses of scripture (lectionaries; Roman Catholic encyclicals; heresy trials at seminaries; the scriptural defence of gay Christianity; popular church journals and newspapers), even as one might argue these are in some ways more manifest markers of scripture's hold on our century than 'serious biblical interpretation.' By 'serious biblical interpretation' is meant academic formulations and debates about scripture. As we shall see, in the late nineteenth century the integers Watson has named 'text, church and world' were still spinning on one axis, and scholars in the academy had yet to discover they could carve out their own special domain of inquiry. Sequestration or retreat into specialization were not serious options in the nineteenth century. Pusey's defense of Daniel's authorship engaged 'text, church and world' with just as much seriousness as something later to be called specialized 'academic discourse.'[7]

Third, the phrase 'theological crisis' means those aspects of biblical studies manifestly connected to constructive and normative statements about God and the nature of God, whether Jewish or Christian in origin.

Finally, 'scripture becomes religion or religions' refers to what I will argue is a disfigurement of scripture in the name of relating the testaments developmentally. This has been the hallmark of the twentieth-century 'serious biblical interpretation.' One sees an emphasis on what will be called here *testamentalism*, that is, a decision that gradualness, process in religious growth and understanding, tradition-historical development, or some such historical index is central to comprehending the unity of Christian Scripture in the light of an otherwise incontrovertible and manifest diversity.[8] The present turn to general hermeneutics, to the degree that it seeks to work with scripture independently of testamentalism, ignores a very real problem that must be faced. Christian Scripture is twofold in its very essence. This character cannot be undone, or ignored, or historicized, for the twofoldness is part and parcel of serious theological convictions, convictions which Jews and Christians share but which also divide them. These divisions are not anthropological or religious alone, but belong to the nature of the God confessed, as he is seen to be disclosed by canonical scriptures, the first testament of which is shared by both groups.[9]

It will be argued here that testamentalism is, in the nature of the thing, an interest in *religion*, even when that interest proceeds to inquire about normative

---

[7] See the discussion and bibliography below.

[8] The influence of Lessing and the notion of 'the education of the human race' was instrumental, in the same manner as continental Hegelianism encouraged the 'history-of-religion' orientation of the age.

[9] See the author's *Word Without End*. Also, van Buren, 'On Reading Someone Else's Mail', 595–606; Levenson, *Hebrew Bible*; Childs, *Biblical Theology*.

'God statements,' as central to what makes scripture unique and worthy of the denotation. Ironically, the twentieth century had already at its inception inherited a religious outlook and, for all the diversity of approaches that emerged over the next hundred years, it never really offered any genuine alternatives to the religious orientation of the mid– to late– nineteenth century. Several notable exceptions prove the rule.

For this reason our inquiry will begin with the transition from Pusey to Gore. In the judgment of this chapter, permutations in approach in the twentieth century still operate within the range established by the work of these two figures of the nineteenth century.

Pusey in the Lion's Den

Childs remarks in the section of his *Introduction* on Daniel that S.R. Driver's commentary of 1900 'broke the back of the conservative opposition.'[10] What is meant by this? At the threshold of the twentieth century, how was the back of opposition broken and what had it amounted to?

In his treatment of Daniel,[11] Pusey is clearly offended by (at least) four things in Daniel interpretation. One reads the polemic from Pusey today and cannot miss the seriousness of the scholarship deployed and the level of concern for proper interpretation. It is hard to imagine a debate comparable to it in the twentieth century for sheer comprehensiveness of concern.

Pusey is concerned about continental Daniel scholarship and its British counterpart. to such an extent that Childs can accurately conclude, 'Pusey was willing to rest the validity of the whole Christian faith upon the sixth-century dating of Daniel' (*Introduction*, 612). I am not interested here in the arguments for the sixth-century date of Daniel. I am interested in why Childs's characterization is accurate (which I believe it is).

The four areas of concern manifested in Pusey's writing on Daniel relate to (1) piety, or true, expressly Christian, believing; (2) a religious conception, involving prophecy and how it works; (3) the New Testament as interpreter of the Old; and (4) Pusey's appeal to what he calls 'Our Lord.' Pusey is concerned about text, church, and world. His interlocutors are not sequestered in one academic domain, but are conceivably every interested person (this is clear in his footnotes and manner of citing opponents: the debate went on at this period in popular journals and newspaper articles).

Pusey's project is the opposite of what now counts for academic specialization, a fact made all the more ironic when one sees the erudition and almost

---

[10] Childs, *Introduction*, 612.
[11] Pusey, *Daniel*.

impenetrable rationalism deployed by him. If one piece of argument cannot be integrated with another in a much larger universe of meaning, then the whole thing is foul. 'Text' for Pusey is the Old and New Testaments of one Christian Scripture. The non–specialized comprehensiveness of his concern is most obvious in the rhetorical totalitarianism he deploys. He speaks of the debate over the dating of Daniel in this way: 'it admits of no half-measures. It is either Divine or an imposture.'[12] Or, 'The writer, were he not Daniel, must have lied on a most frightful scale. . . .'[13] Here one sees the absolutely moral nature of the debate, and one can say this without thereby declaring Pusey right or wrong. Nor was he an isolated figure who happened to have had a bad temper and a ready pen.

Theology, in this realm of Daniel disputation, involved matters in front of the text (piety leading to proper belief), a religious conception (prophets predict things miraculously), the interrelationship between texts (how the New Testament hears the Old, at once confirming and constraining its literal sense), and a specific doctrine of Christ (he tells the truth and is a privileged witness, not to God, but to proper biblical interpretation for the church and world). Theology is not a doctrine about God as the Old Testament discloses this, in the primary sense, but is a discipline arising from core, unimpeachable religious truths concerning prophecy, Jesus, the believing heart, and the New's hearing of the Old Testament as determinative and totalizing. In other words, Daniel's theological truth had to cohere with a wide range of religious concepts imported from the New Testament, or it failed as Christian Scripture to be a reliable vehicle of God's truth. Pusey felt he was arguing in defense of the literal sense of Daniel, but there was much more on the table.

If any part of this bundle of religious convictions is disturbed, then a threat is felt for which there can be no remedy. Striking here is not so much whether Pusey's view could be sustained (Driver did indeed 'break the back' of an opposition for which Pusey was representative, and the Maccabean dating of Daniel's later chapters was generally accepted in the twentieth century). Could a satisfactory position be set forth which adjusted Pusey's dating scheme without sacrificing his bundle of religious convictions? Pusey was facing a view of Daniel, in British and continental scholarship, without obvious precedent, and where precedent was available (Porphyry and eighteenth-century Deist revivals), it tended to manifest, to his mind, the same irreligion he credited to his nineteenth-century interlocutors.

It is not easy to shift this debate in the late nineteenth century into the realm of a *general hermeneutical crisis*. All sorts of manifestly religious notions inhabit the debate. When Pusey speaks of unbelief, and other matters of impiety in front of

---

[12] ibid., 75
[13] ibid.

the text, he is not talking about options of a hermeneutics of either suspicion or assent.[14] When he speaks of 'our Lord' one cannot properly imagine the after-shocks of Renan, with whom he is familiar, as these registered in waves of quests in the twentieth century culminating in 'the Jesus seminar.' When he speaks about the New's hearing of the Old, one cannot draw a straight line to the general concerns of hermeneutical appraisals of 'text' by Wolterstorff or Vanhoozer. And yet one senses that in this debate much more is at stake than the dating of Daniel. Christian faith, insofar as it is reliant on Scripture's two-testament presentation, is under massive and unprecedented assault. Pusey is standing on a faultline of enormous proportions.

The Transition to Gore

I was struck by a passing remark made at the Theology Seminar at the University of St Andrews, that for all of hindsight's classification of the Tractarians together with succeeding Anglo-Catholic generations, Pusey would have found unrecognizable (or offensive) Gore's 'catholic' view of scripture.

It will be important to read Gore's views on scripture very closely. For in him we see emerging the lineaments of a completely twentieth-century position on scripture. The transition from Pusey to Gore is, however, not surprising. Above all, it is Pusey's attachment of theology to general religious concepts, together with an incipient testamentalism, that paved the way for Gore's full accommodation of continental biblical scholarship, buttressed in his own inimitable way by appeals to the Fathers, church tradition, and Anglo-Catholicism's special mixture of piety, ritualism, and Hegelian idealism.

Gore's views on scripture are provided in his contributions to *Lux Mundi*, in prefaces and in his original essay on the Holy Spirit.[15] This alone is worthy of reflection. That is, *Lux Mundi* offers no independent essay on Scripture. *Lux Mundi* purports to be a book about 'The Religion of the Incarnation' and within such a universe, where religion is manifestly central, one cannot talk about Holy Scripture without beginning with general, anthropologically con-ceived, notions of inspiration which will in turn, it follows, give rise to, or find formal expression within, scripture.

It is obvious that Gore's essay was one of the more, if not the most, contro-versial of the volume (he says so himself in subsequent prefaces), though it was not clear at this period that the culprit was the innocent-sounding 'Religion of

---

[14] See the assessment of Stuhlmacher and his challenge to a 'hermeneutics of suspicion' in Seitz, ' "And Without God in the World." A Hermeneutic of Estrangement Over-come,' *Word Without End*, 41–50.

[15] Gore, *Lux Mundi: A Series of Studies in the Religion of the Incarnation*.

the Incarnation' approach. Lindbeck's recent classifications (cognitive/propositional, experiential/expressive, linguistic) would clearly find a 'Religion of the Incarnation' approach located in the second category, and I suspect Gore would have inhabited that realm with pride.[16] The category of experience, in this instance seen from the standpoint of certain theological convictions about the Holy Spirit, is what guides Gore's reflections on the Bible.[17] There is a measure of overlap, here, between Gore and Pusey. What counted for 'unbelief,' however, in Pusey, has become much less sharply profiled in Gore's own expansive treatment. Indeed, Gore concludes the essay on a much more optimistic note, regarding the insights of the biblical criticism gaining such strength in his day. Yet even here, we find the same language as in Pusey, when Gore speaks of being able to distinguish between 'what is reasonable and reverent, and what is highhanded and irreligious' (361).

At the end of the day, however, Pusey's concern for comprehensiveness has been replaced by admission that 'in all probability there will always remain more than one school of legitimate opinion on the subject (of inspiration)' and that it is better to speak of what can 'without real loss be conceded,' not what one might accept on the grounds of what he terms 'irrationality' (361). One should be able to see here the slippery slope of an appeal to experience (in this case, not within but in front of scripture) as words like 'irrational' are made to sit astride 'reverent' with very little in the way of clarification as to when one is being one and not the other.

Testamentalism

For Pusey, the scriptures in their entirety required a consistent view of prophecy and miracle, on the one hand, and on the other, the record of the second testament was used as a guide to the proper interpretation of the first. What Jesus said about Daniel in the narratives of the New Testament was

---

[16] Lindbeck, *The Nature of Doctrine*. See also, Thiemann, *Revelation and Theology*. For a different take on 'the expressionist (Romantic) view' see Wolterstorff, *Divine Discourse*, and a further response by Lindbeck, 'Postcritical Canonical Interpretation, 26–51.

[17] 'The appeal to "experience" in religion, whether personal or general, brings before the mind so many associations of ungoverned enthusiasm and untrustworthy fanaticism, that it does not easily commend itself to those of us who are most concerned to be reasonable. And yet, in one form or another, it is an essential part of the appeal which Christianity makes on its own behalf since the day when Jesus Christ met the question "Art thou He that should come, or do we look for another?" by pointing to the transforming effect of his work' (315). This is how the essay begins, and the paragraphs which follow proceed along a similar path.

indispensable, indeed central, for how we were to read and interpret Daniel. The Old Testament's *per se* voice had to be consistent with its voice *in Novo receptum*.

This is the first place where the testamentalism of Gore differs from that of Pusey. In Gore's universe, the expectation of intratestamental congruence (even one where the New's hearing of the Old creates a potential imbalance) has been replaced with a decidedly Hegelian appeal to gradualness as the means to comprehend the scriptures' unity. In this universe, the Old Testament has a *per se* voice detachable from the New Testament, but it must be assessed within a larger developmental schema designed with criteria for what counts for a maximal convergence of spirit and reality. Gore uses this Hegelian dialectic and glosses it with his understanding, not of spirit (Geist) in general, but of the Christian Holy Spirit. The consequences for a unified Christian scripture are enormous.

After describing a split between spirit and flesh, faith and experience, and yet the church's need 'for unity in all things,' it would be necessary for Gore to account for the fact that the Old Testament, in his words, 'presented a most unspiritual appearance' (328). He therefore speaks of 'the gradualness of the Spirit's method' as the response given by 'the Church' (he does not cite his sources here) to the problem of Old Testament religion. The frankness of his assessment is startling: 'It is of the essence of the New Testament, as the religion of the Incarnation, to be final and catholic; on the other hand, it is of the essence of the Old Testament to be imperfect' (329).

Two things should be noted here. First, Gore collapses the entire New Testament into a category of religion, thereby making an enormous form-critical assumption about the character of the New Testament as a canonical document; and second, insofar as it has a religion, it is a higher religion, 'final and catholic.' Throughout the essay, Gore speaks of the 'Jews' in the Old Testament and of the distinctiveness of their race. This anachronism is to be explained as consistent with the Hegelianism of his schema, whereby one religion gives way to another, and the scriptures are records of religions differentiated by the testaments.[18]

When at another point when Gore ponders the special character of the religion of the Old Testament Jews (*sic*), over against other races, he wants to emphasize that all peoples have their inspired thoughts and inspired individuals. What is special about 'the Jews' of the Old Testament is that 'the inspiration is both in itself more direct and more intense' (342). The graded character of inspiration fits nicely with the notion of a gradual movement from Old Testament religion to higher Incarnation (New Testament) Religion. Revelation comes in different grades and intensities.

---

[18] Compare the language in the title of the popular, critical treatment of the day, 'The Old Testament in the Jewish Church' by W. Robertson Smith.

One potential problem in this schema is how to account for the movement from New Testament Religion to the church as a post-biblical reality. On the continent, Hegelianism was given a maximal freedom at this juncture. The New Testament scriptures could not be conflated with a single religion, just as surely as the Old Testament scriptures did not reflect one religion either. Many religions existed within the New Testament, and some of these evolved in positive directions, so the theory held, and others less so. 'Early Catholicism,' for example, was seen as a retrograde development. Measured against Pauline Christianity, James was found wanting, and this was so for a whole host of reasons. This is too familiar territory to require detailed comment.

This is where, with hindsight, one can see that Gore was prepared to sacrifice the Old Testament as scripture on an altar of religious gradualness, because he thought the New Testament and creeds presented a firewall for Christian faith (his 'Religion of the Incarnation'). He is adamant about this at one juncture. The New Testament and Old Testament represent not just different religions; they have completely different tolerances for the 'idealizing element:'

> We may maintain with considerable assurance that there is nothing in the doctrine of inspiration to prevent our recognizing a considerable idealizing element in the Old Testament history. The reason is of course obvious enough why what can be admitted in the Old Testament, could not, without results disastrous to the Christian Creed, be admitted in the New (354).

'Our Lord'

The ghost of Pusey rumbles at this point, since the New Testament is used, in the case of Daniel, as the chief defense of its miraculous nature. Did not Jesus accept Daniel in a way that criticism was calling into question? How could Gore avoid this problem with his very different accounting of the unity of a two-testament scripture? Was not Jesus himself hopelessly tied up with this 'religion of the Jews,' even in a New Testament record Gore conflates with a 'religion of the Incarnation'? And in that record, according to Pusey, a Jesus appeared who stated that the scriptures of Israel had such and such an authority, not limited to a lower religion evolving into a higher one. In short, Pusey was well aware that Jesus functioned with a distinction between scripture ('it is written') and 'religion' and that in many ways it is this distinction which lies at the heart of Christian theology (whose creeds speak of a death and raising in accordance with scriptural claims, namely the Old Testament as divine word of figural truth, not a 'lower religion' or one with 'more direct or intense' racial inspiration than another). The relationship between the testaments would have to be comprehended on terms other than revelatory intensity or grades of religion, or one would run up against the second testament's differentiation of Jewish religion(s) and the word of the Old Testament as divine word.

Gore's response at this point is breathtaking. He wishes to see maximal, if reverent, use of critical tools to reconstruct the religion of the Jews, en route to the higher religion of the New Testament. A commitment to gradualism will mean far greater tolerance for the Old Testament being recast into this or that critical reconstruction, since the New Testament neither requires nor anticipates such a handling. Yet with such a high view of the New Testament and of what both he and Pusey called 'our Lord,' why was the true picture of Israel's religion, emerging into the light of day as a consequence of nineteenth- century labors, not capable of integration with what 'our Lord' actually said about the scriptures he inherited?

Religious Conception

The answer is to be found in a competing religious conception, which ranks higher for Gore than Pusey's conception of prophecy in his handling of Daniel and 'Our Lord.'

The problem is obvious. If the Religion of the Incarnation is higher than its precedent 'idealization;' and yet the Incarnate One used the scriptures of Israel as an authority over against his (Jewish and Gentile) culture; and in that use he was obviously departing quite radically from the critical theory of the day accepted by Gore; what would prevent one from charging Gore with massive inconsistency? Should not a 'final and catholic' higher religion centered on Incarnation be prepared to let Jesus lead the way in the handling of scripture? Or, has some sort of *Sachkritik* entered upon Gore's otherwise solid New Testament and credal firewall?

The answer Gore gives is predictable, even as it is curious, given the more radical historicism of continental New Testament scholarship. It belongs to the fact of kenosis, of the human limitations taken on by 'our Lord,' that he would not reproduce the findings of the Old Testament science of his (Gore's) day:

> Thus the utterances of Christ about the Old Testament do not seem to be nearly so definite or clear enough to allow our supposing that in this case He is departing from the general method of the Incarnation, by bringing to bear the unveiled omniscience of the Godhead, to anticipate or foreclose a development of natural knowledge (360).

It appears, therefore, that Gore is combining a certain historicism deeply indebted to Hegel (and Lessing), on the one hand, with larger credal convictions he accepts as unimpeachable, on the other. But can these two distinctly different realms of operation be combined? What is demanded, as we saw above, is congruence between the New Testament and the creeds, on historical grounds, and that is the last thing most historians of the day were willing to concede. And, indeed, Gore does not establish this in his argument. Rather, he simply *demands* that such and such congruence be in place, for functional reasons. It is a 'fact of supreme importance,' he opines, that there be 'none of the ambiguity or remoteness which belongs to much of (how much of?) the record of the preparation,' or else there would be 'results disastrous to the Christian Creed.' True enough, perhaps, but lacking Gore's appeal to early catholicism, one would see the matter quite differently, and did.

Summary

What is refreshing in examining these figures of the nineteenth century is how directly they treat matters central to the use of scripture in the church and world. There is a concern for both testaments (not one apart from the other in areas of historical specialization). There is a concern for some accounting of the two testaments in one scripture. There is concern for emerging catholic Christianity. We have yet to see any 'Balkanisation' of the discipline.

The other thing that is striking is how very few of these issues were resolved in the twentieth century on the strength of better or harder historical-critical labor. There is a degree of persistence in the questions faced by Gore and Pusey. This reality may have been ignored or considered resolved, but most treatments of biblical hermeneutics in the years that followed demonstrated the resilience and persistence of the four areas of concern in Pusey. This makes it now relatively easy to classify major movement in biblical theology and hermeneutics in the twentieth century.

Essays Catholic and Critical

This 1926 collection establishes the final liberation of Anglican Catholicism from Pusey and his scriptural assumptions.[19] The four concerns of Pusey – piety, the Old Testament *in Novo receptum*, appeal to 'our Lord', and prophecy as religious wonder – are transformed under the hand of Gore, leaving the next generation the simpler task to restate, reframe and consolidate.

On the continent the connection between scripture as 'historical science,' hermeneutics, and theology remained under pressure for clear coordination, in a way that ceased to prove so pressing for Anglo-Catholics. It is not clear whether what presented itself as confidence in historical-critical efforts was in

---

[19] Selwyn (ed.), *Essays Catholic and Critical*.

reality that, or was merely an excuse to leave its subtle or more entrenched problems to the side in a convenient division of labor. The 'infallibility' of scripture is dismissed in a paragraph as 'untenable' due to 'the scientific development of the last century' (99) and now there is full acceptance that 'competent scholars' will never 'reach absolute unanimity as to the various problems which the scriptures present' since it belongs to 'scientific thought that it should always contemplate the possibility of further progress' (100). It is as though a new office has emerged to replace the caricatured papal claims or the unscientific confessionalism of Protestants: Christian scholars making progress at something. At the same time as patristic figuration of the sort practiced, presumably, by an Origen merits the description, 'allegorical interpretations of a rather desperate character' (98), confessional statements, 'can only be regarded as the clear teaching of Scripture if it is admitted that the orthodox Catholic interpretation of the Scriptures on these matters in the first four centuries was in fact the correct one.' Obviously, the appeal to the Fathers over against Rome would have to be selective, and Origen's allegories did not measure up to what was needful in the light of biblical science.

The effort to coordinate historical-critical progress with appeal to the Fathers, against both Roman Catholic claims and Protestant confessionalism, reaches its zenith in *Essays Catholic and Critical*. We are told that authority must be verifiable, never mechanical or merely external, and the term 'oracular' is used to characterize both the claims of the Roman church and a doctrine of scripture likely to have caught Pusey in its grasp. Instead, 'the final appeal is to the spiritual, intellectual and historical content of divine revelation, *as verifiable at the three-fold bar of history, reason and spiritual experience*'[20] (emphasis added). There we find the sort of bold abstraction which is never clarified, except insofar as historical-critical methods, in the hands of progressing competent scholars, are somewhere out there generating this.

Walther Eichrodt

Eichrodt was able to work at the history-of-religions questions posed by criticism on the basis of more thorough comparative resources, more subtle literary methodology, and simply greater time to reflect on the traditional problems of scripture's unified authority in the light of 'the new science.'[21]

At the level of comparative work, he accepted the sort of notion posited by Gore, of something 'more direct and more intense' going on within Israel of

---

[20] Rawlinson, '*Authority as a Ground of Belief*' in ibid., 85–97.
[21] Eichrodt, *Theology of the Old Testament*.

old, and then refined this considerably. Israel, it was argued, was truly in possession of a unique perspective in the realm of 'religion,' over against her ancient
Near Eastern neighbors, and this finding at once enhanced the authority of the
Old Testament for Christians and made it far easier to reconsider something
like continuity across the two testaments, linking them at the level of a shared
'higher religion' (to use the language of *Lux Mundi* and *Essays Catholic and
Critical*).

Central to Eichrodt's understanding was the concept of covenant.
Covenant was the datum establishing continuity between Old and New
Testaments. But what covenant meant for Eichrodt was not chiefly to be
located in the final literary presentation of the Old Testament, where from creation to Noah to Abraham to Moses to David to Zion, and back to creation
again (Isaiah 66) it (covenant) was indeed famously crucial – a cruciality also
registered without further ado in the literal sense of the New Testament.
Rather, covenant was central insofar as Eichrodt was competent to establish
this as an historical reality in Israel early on, and vis-à-vis other historically verifiable religions and cultures in the ancient Near East. This left the way open for
other scholars to challenge the theological centrality of covenant as historically
untenable, and such was the challenge which emerged.[22] The debate between
Eissfeldt and Eichrodt over an independent biblical theology was in large
measure a debate over history-of-religions methods propping up theological
realities or aspirations of literary coherence in scripture's full form.[23]
Bultmann's later challenge to Israel's 'sacred history' was only a mopping-up
effort, seen from this perspective, though a particularly effective one it must be
conceded, due to his rhetorical skills (Socrates drank the hemlock in the same
way as Israel's deliverance could be said to be, without further ado, *pro nobis*).[24]

Gerhard von Rad

The attack on 'sacred history' from Bultmann also had another front toward
which its salvos were directed. This was the tradition-history approach
of Gerhard von Rad.[25] Von Rad explicitly rejected an approach based upon

---

[22] Perlitt, *Die Bundestheologie*.

[23] Eissfeldt, 'Israelitisch-jüdische Religionsgeschichte', 1–12; Eichrodt, 'Alttestamentliche Theologie, 83–91.

[24] Bultmann, 'Significance', 8–35. 'The exodus from Egypt, the giving of the law at
Sinai, the building of Solomon's Temple, the work of the prophets, all redound to our
benefit in so far as these are historical episodes which form part of our Occidental
history. In the same sense, however, it can be said that the Spartans fell at Thermopylae
for us and Socrates drank the hemlock for us' (31).

[25] For our purposes, reference is to his *Old Testament Theology*.

'religion' – of either the 'thick' Eichrodt or the 'thin' Anglo-Catholic versions. Instead, he sought to isolate 'Israel's own explicit statements' about Yahweh (*sic*) by using a very sophisticated combination of literary and form criticism.[26]

What Israel said about YHWH was not self-evident, in terms of the canonical presentation, but would have to be reconstructed using historical tools. Only in this way could one successfully plot the theological movement which governed Israel's history as a people and which in turn gave rise to its literary legacy in the Old Testament. At no point could it be said that the final literary form was itself a setting in order of a previous history of tradition, thus making a qualitative distinction operative between tradition-history and scripture, as a literary reality of theological integrity in its final form. Von Rad knew there was something called a combination of P and J in Genesis, but this combination was not amenable to the same sort of theological reading as P and J themselves.[27] In order for tradition-history to make complete sense, there was a need for the traditions to remain aloof from any literary stabilization in the final form – or better, any stabilization with separate theological integrity.

The reason for this is complex. On the one hand, there was the actual legacy of historical-criticism von Rad sought to honor, and whose inner tensions he sought to reslove (see now Rendtorff's challenge to von Rad and Noth's combination of source and form criticism). On the other hand, tradition-history appeared to represent for von Rad a respecter of historical Israel, unsullied by Christian *Nachinterpretation*.

What this required for von Rad, however, was some sense that the typological potential of traditions was actively moving toward a denouement in the New Testament which did not dishonor his historical 'Israel making explicit statements about YHWH.' Ironically, this required him to believe that tradition-history manifestly misdrew historical data in the name of credenda (Gore's idealizing element) so that an eschatological reality yet to unfold came into play. To my mind, what this meant was that historical Israel was separated – not from a critically reconstructed tradition-history of manifest misdrawing, but – from the final form of her scriptures as theologically relevant. In so doing, he built a bridge of tradition from Old to New Testament which could then not account for the New Testament's own specific hearing of the Old in its final form. In the name of tradition-historical richness, and in the name of respecting 'historical Israel', we got a theology neither the New Testament nor the Judaisms of the day recognized as 'it is written.'

---

[26] Compare my analysis in 'The Historical-Critical Endeavor as Theology' in *Word Without End*, 28–40.

[27] *Genesis*.

From Tradition–History to Unruly Traditions: Walter Brueggemann

In his chapter on 'Authority' for *Essays Catholic and Critical*, W. Knox referred to the collapse of confidence in the Bible as a 'verbally inspired book, to which we can appeal with absolute certainty for infallible guidance in all matters of faith and conduct' – a bloated claim whose only point was to set up the higher-critical vis-à-vis. This consisted of determining 'the exact meaning of its various parts and the authority which they can claim,' a task to 'be discussed by competent scholars' whose results would always be provisional, progress being what it is. Reference to 'various parts' and their exact meanings was, in the decades to follow, to be given a highly theological profile in the tradition-historical, typological method of von Rad.

Walter Brueggemann, together with H.W. Wolff, popularized this tradition-historical approach in a book called *The Vitality of Old Testament Traditions*.[28] The point of the book was to give an equally sharp and an equally theological-homiletical reading of discrete sources, isolated from their narrative location and arrangement in the final form of the Old Testament, and kept strictly separate from one another.

Here we may see the instincts which have recently come to full flower in Brueggemann's effort at theology.[29] Shorn of their historicity, on the one hand, and their capacity for being ranged on a typological trajectory, on the other, traditions in their diversity and in their contradictory manifestations have become the testimony to the unruliness of Israel's God. God has no longer any ontological status, in Brueggemann's estimate, but exists (as it were) strictly in Israel's rhetoric about God, which has likewise refused any effort from within to coordination or coherence; if any is found, it is put there by hegemonic interpreters (excepting, it is supposed, Brueggemann). If ontology and transcendence always mean for Brueggemann tidiness and power/control (there is no engagement with the history of interpretation on this matter, e.g., in the Eastern Church where high doctrines of 'generation' and 'procession' in the Godhead existed, but only sweeping and vast categorizing), then their decided absence from the field of the text is in proportion to God's strangeness and unpredictability. Methodological impasse and crisis and disorder have become in Brueggemann's hands first-order theology. God is as messy and unpredictable as the methodologies of the now not-so-new biblical science.[30]

---

[28] Brueggemann and Wolff, *Vitality*.

[29] *Theology of the Old Testament*.

[30] Brueggemann is forced to footnote his own appeal to rhetoric in this way: 'I have found the issue of speech/reality among the most problematic for my own study. I do not wish to claim that these speech utterances make no assumptions about being, but I do wish to recognize that such assumptions depend upon speech for their

Hermeneutics in the Lion's Den: Pusey Revisited

It has been the argument of this chapter that the mid-nineteenth-century debates give us a glimpse at a comprehensive biblical hermeneutic on the verge of collapse. Matters in front of the text (belief – but not a nineteenth-century version of 'hermeneutics of assent'), in the text (the New Testament's hearing of the Old Testament), in religious conceptuality (prophecy as miracle), and in the text's central subject matter (Jesus Christ as interpreter) all cooperated to produce this comprehensiveness, or the illusion of it, conjured up in the face of attacks without obvious precedent.

These 'attacks' were coming from the new science of biblical criticism. The fragility of the comprehensive universe was likely the consequence of its genuine newness in the history of the church's handling of scripture, but Pusey could not have known that. And indeed his comprehensive picture was closer to the traditional handling of scripture prior to the rise of historical science than the challenger was. Here, with hindsight, Pusey was right to defend his view against the new knowledge and especially against notions of progress inhabiting it. When Gore speaks of the advance of 'natural knowledge' that 'Our Lord' did not foreclose on, by revealing his (Jesus's) awareness of J, E, D, P or the Maccabean date of Daniel 7:12, one is right to wonder what sort of theological defense of the advance of natural knowledge he could muster, genuinely. Under what sort of explicit theological license were we to believe that new science was gaining its proper place in Christian discourse? What is the 'advance of natural knowledge' Jesus did not wish to foreclose on, specifically and theologically defended? To state it differently, what was required was a robust theology of reason, not one brought over from the earlier nineteenth and eighteenth centuries. Could theological accounts of 'reason' keep apace with those mustered for 'criticism'?[31]

In traditional interpretation, concerns raised by Pusey in his defense of Daniel were not handled in the same way, of course. Figuration and allegory

---

establishment as viable, credible claims. While there is an assumed reality outside the text (God), that assumed reality depends on utterance for force, authority, and availability in the community. God in the Old Testament is not a mere rhetorical construct, but is *endlessly in the process of being rhetorically reconstructed*. This is an exceedingly important and dense issue, one I am not able to resolve clearly' (*Vitality*, 65, n. 11, emphasis added). Brueggemann's own rhetoric is unable to sustain his identity as an Old Testament theologian, it would seem from this last sentence; and so too, God's rhetoric is endlessly being reconstructed so that, in respect of his 'being out there' in any meaningful sense, he is available and forceful, but constantly shifting and changing. I am unclear whether this is a statement about ontology or a confession about the limitations of Brueggemann's approach, in the very nature of the thing.

[31] See the trenchant analysis of MacIntyre, *Three Rival Versions*.

stood ready to assure that two testaments of Christian scripture could have something like a unified voice, and yet they did not engage the same forms of rationalism required for defense of the Bible's historicity evidenced in 'Lectures on Daniel the Prophet.' In part, this is because they understood, or were in a position to understand, prophecy differently than Pusey, as well as the relationship of the testaments. It cannot be gainsaid that rules of charity and truth had always been around, and had often provided the main reason why scripture's 'literal sense' was not perceived or obeyed by an interpreter lacking them; that is, Pusey was right to see that something was wrong about the attitude of the interpreter in the mode of new science. He was wrong, however, in my judgment to believe that this was the chief problem.

The Virtuous Reader

This locus is making a comeback in recent days. A prime example is Stephen Fowl's *Engaging Scripture*.[32] Hauerwas and others have flirted with this 'in front of the text' solution to the problem of scripture at the end of a millennium period.[33] Less clear is whether MacIntyre and Milbank can be affiliated with this locus as well.[34] I suspect that the initial reaction to the preface of Pusey, in our times, would be that it is too, well, moralistic or religious. We hear of 'a tide of scepticism' which quickly becomes '[T]he unbelieving school,' 'criticism . . . subservient to unbelief,' 'avowedly infidel,' 'the unbelieving critics,' and so forth. 'Disbelief had been the parent, not the offspring of their criticism; their starting point, not the winning-post of their course.' 'Their teaching was said to be bold. Too bold, alas! it was toward Almighty God.' The examples are too many to list.

I would venture that the problem was not just lack of piety or reverence (Gore's later adaptation). Rather, a thorough misunderstanding of the theological motivations of much continental biblical criticism afflicted English churchmen-theologians. Much nineteenth-century biblical criticism was not an adventure in impiety, but turned on assumptions about the nature of revelation and its (tenuous) relationship to the canon (as a literally shaped and coherent theological product). Wellhausen actually believed that his reconstruction of Israel's religion was necessary if one were to get at the true state of affairs. To be sure, at moments he spoke of manifest manipulation of the truth in the canon's presentation (see his 'P'), but at other places he worked with almost religious awe (e.g. the wonders of Yahwism in the early

---

[32] See note 1 above.

[33] As representative, see Hauerwas, *Character*.

[34] It is difficult to locate his recent volume *The Word Made Strange* in respect of 'radical orthodoxy,' though the links to Hauerwas remain.

period). The Bible's final literary form demanded an accounting such as Wellhausen and others were attempting, in their view, because its presentation was constrained by religious forces which obscured matters and which prevented more obvious, historically tuned, movement from Old Testament to New Testament.

But the more serious problem with this tack can be seen in Gore's accommodation article and in *Essays Catholic and Critical*. Simply define belief in a new way, and Pusey is reduced to being a crank. Suddenly his moral outrage looks like intemperate ranting, and he is closed off from any ongoing discussion.

The problem with the virtuous reader approach can be seen in part in MacIntyre's *Whose Justice? Which Rationality?*' expose.[35] Once scripture's literal sense is open to deconstruction and reconstruction, on such a massive scale, using historical tools, it is no longer obvious what moral outrage might mean. By the time of *Essays Catholic and Critical*, what was immoral was the impeding of human progress. One searches in vain in Stephen Fowl's recent work for any comprehensive, public, agreed-upon statement of what actually counts for virtue, such that we could see it and believe it was under God's providential care as it went about the business of 'engaging scripture.'

'Our Lord'

Gore's solution to this problem of using Jesus as a model for modern biblical interpretation is classic. Jesus cannot be expected to conform to the universe in which modern historical questions are posed. He lived with the conventions of his day.

This is true enough, of course, but what in fact are our options here? Gore makes it sound like we have two. Jesus lives within the constraints of his time and therefore cannot be used to disqualify critical findings. There is the Jesus of his day and there are the findings of scholars working on the Old Testament, of which he knows nothing. Let both go their own way.

To say this is, however, to leave unanswered just what purpose Jesus's use of scripture had for his own time. Gore relieves modern scholarship of having to answer this question, in the name of honoring critical findings which are manifestly not on the horizon for Jesus. But what *is* on the horizon for a Jesus using scripture in the New Testament portrayal? Surely it matters in a 'higher religion' what use is made, by its incarnate Lord, of Israel's scriptures – not in order to give ground for criticism, but more positively, as expressive of assumptions Jesus may have had about these scripture's capacity to render God and God's word. This is a bottom-line theological concern, and if it cannot be

---

[35] MacIntyre, *Whose Justice?*

coordinated in some meaningful way with newer critical findings, then a problem exists which cannot be ignored with appeals to kenotic accommodation or credal truth.

Pusey saw what was at stake, I believe, in divorcing Jesus from any positive, theologically constructive account of Israel's scriptures as the word of God and not just as an evolving lower religion. The problem was that this involved, for Pusey, a hermeneutical gamble over conceptions about prophecy and the proper relationship between the testaments. '[S]uch definite prophecy as the minuter prophecies in Daniel, the foreground of more distant and larger prophecy, is in harmony with the whole system of prophecy, as well in the Old Testament as in the prophecies of our Lord' (xii). As he himself put it, '[m]en, then, had no choice between believing all and disbelieving all' (xi). Well, Gore gave them another choice but in so doing he dismissed as essential an account of the theological force of the Old Testament, not just on 'our Lord' but on the church catholic. By the time of *Essays Catholic and Critical*, no one even felt the loss anymore, as scripture became religions and religiosity and church theologians could annex the field of critical biblical scholarship and wait as it produced its findings and made its progress.

Daniel Revisited: The Fresh Approach of B.S. Childs

Childs conceded that with S.R. Driver's 1900 commentary, Daniel scholarship slipped out of Pusey's range of fire. Yet Childs did not offer one more historically sophisticated interpretation himself.[36] It is hard to know what Pusey would have made of it. If Pusey would not have recognized Gore's use of scripture, it does not necessarily follow that Childs's effort would similarly disappoint him. This is not for reasons of proper piety, though many have seen an introduction to the Old Testament 'as scripture' defined in such a way.[37] Rather, Childs produced a reading of Daniel, and other books, which once again fitted it into a comprehensive view of scripture and Christian theology, but did not do so on terms Pusey had once felt were necessary, indeed obligatory.

Childs has asked an important question. Not, did the final chapters belong to the Maccabean period? They manifestly did. Rather, how was a reader, later than the Maccabean details to which the book had been so acutely attached, meant to hear Daniel's ongoing word? This small shift amounted to raising a question, not about religion, but about *scripture* as a vehicle of God's dynamic word. At once a connection to a *Wirkungsgeschichte* which included the New

---

[36] *Introduction*, 608–23.

[37] See, e.g., the manner of analysis deployed by Davies, *Bible*.

Testament and 'our Lord' opened up. In other words, a book of Daniel manifestly outfitted with Maccabean-era dress, as the critical reading insisted, might still end up a fraud, but on different grounds: the grounds of false prophecy or non–prophecy. For why did Daniel's pseudepigraphic additions not prove accurate? Or, even if partly fulfilled, had the book become nothing more than a tribute to something that happened (at least partially) in the past, and in that sense was not prophecy in the proper sense at all? This was the effect of having its eschatological character voided through historicizing, in the name of highlighting a Maccabean setting which generated *vaticina eventu* which themselves proved false as time passed.

Childs was, however, asking a question about how Daniel continued to function as a vehicle of God's word. Ironically, historical labors had given greater and greater focus to referentiality, but stopped short of asking another historical question, tied to the history of reception. That stopping short was not accidental, but was the logical consequence of locking a book into an historical setting, and letting it only describe a moment in religious history now past.

Childs's, appeal to 'scripture' in some sense opened the way for a different understanding of prophecy, in larger terms. Prophecy had in 'the new science' become speech to contemporaries (forth-telling). Predictions, where they did appear, became prophecies after the event, and they belonged, in terms of composition, to the periods in which their message was hoped for, or regarded as about to be fulfilled. Much nuance was required to keep this distinction fluid (and one need only look at Isaiah scholarship for the bulk of this century to see how complicated the nuancing became). Forthtelling was settled into one phase of religious or tradition-history, while the foretelling *vaticina ex eventu* found their (later) home in the same trajectory. Daniel took it hard, because in its case, the book was chopped into two with almost no way to link the halves – no matter that Daniel was not even prophecy in any typical sense, and indeed was regarded by von Rad as wisdom[38] and by the traditional Hebrew division as one of the Writings.

---

[38] I can only quote selectively. 'It is important to notice how the book was reinterpreted. The belief in the coming of a new age, which would be ushered in by God, was not separated from the end of the fourth kingdom and then projected into the future, as one might have expected. Rather, the original sequence of the destruction of the last world power and the immediate entrance of the kingdom of God was unaltered. Then both the period of the fourth kingdom and the coming of God's Kingdom were projected into the future to mark the end of the age. Obviously a major hermeneutical move in respect to the biblical text had been effected. The description of the 'period of indignation' which reflected the policy of Antiochus against the Jews was now understood typologically. Antiochus had become a representative of the ultimate enemy, but

So long as the biblical books were divided up along lines like this, and fitted into a general religious history, leaning toward, corrected by, aborted into, the religion of the New Testament, the expectation disappeared that such books could actually function as scripture in their own literary presentation.

Childs succeeded in connecting the two halves of Daniel by deploying a midrashic approach. Later chapters were serial efforts to hear earlier parts of the book, especially chapter two. Though Daniel appeared as a figure in these later chapters, as he had in the first chapters, what was at issue was God's prior word pressing for fulfillment, beyond the moment of its original utterance, or seeming reception, and this high view of God's word did not require anything more than obedience to it – even when it seemed, for it could only seem, to remain unfulfilled. Having joined the two halves of the book, not on a prophecy-fulfillment model overly constrained by historicism, but by attention to the dynamic of God's accomplishing word, the way was also open to continue to see Daniel as scripture beyond the timetables at the end of the book and long after the details of Maccabean persecution were past and gone.[39]

Too much attention to locating Daniel in distant phases of a religious history, as well as defense of locating him in exile as a predictor of major divine endowment (Pusey), meant that Daniel as scripture forfeited its capacity to declare God's word from within but also outwith the circumstances of its composition – as understood by critical theory or a defense of prophecy as miracle.

Conclusion: 'Too "bold," alas! it was toward Almighty God'

Figural interpretation has assumed there is a surplus of intended meaning in every divine revelation. This assumption has a basic theological grounding, involving a doctrine of providence and sovereignty. God remains custodian of the word he speaks, and can by the Holy Spirit effect things through a word delivered once upon a time, heeded or unheeded, at yet a later time.[40] When

---

he himself was not the fulfilment of the vision . . . For the reader of the canonical book Daniel still spoke prophetically of the end of the age. He still called upon Israel "to discern the times" and to endure trial for the sake of the coming kingdom.' *Introduction,* 619–20.

[39] See his treatment of Daniel in vol. 2 of *Old Testament Theology.*

[40] The book of Isaiah is the exemplar for this. See my essay '"Of Mortal Appearance": Isaiah as a type of Christian Scripture' in *Ex auditu* (1998).

Christians confess God raised Jesus from the dead 'in accordance with the scriptures,' they do not mean that Isaiah predicted the empty tomb, but rather that God's word to Israel was figured in such a way as to accord with God's wrath and raising vis-à-vis his son.

Where Pusey was right to take umbrage involved not so much the emergence of a competing religious system, over against the one into which he had fitted Daniel and assumed had all likewise before him. Pusey believed that the dissection of Daniel into two halves made Daniel a fraud and a liar, but he also felt – more intuitively – that something was being said about God himself that was wrong. One would search in vain for a distinct or sustained articulation of this concern. My view is that this has to do with a peculiarly Christian attitude, the consequence of Christian possession of a two-testament canon in which claims about Jesus and 'final religion' would appear to tolerate any loose or confused or domesticating handling of the oracles of God entrusted to the Jews, that is, the Old Testament. In the preface to his lectures on Daniel we see, for the last time I suspect in western Anglicanism, a sincere concern that critical method, as a method of constructing religions, is somehow (it is not entirely clear in Pusey) an attack on the one who raised Jesus from the dead and who gave to him his own name, the name above every name (YHWH). This is not an attack on an evolving religion, which Gore's Hegelianism could tolerate better than Pusey's piety. It was an attack on the capacity of the Old Testament to render God and his word as normative for Christian believing.

When Reventlow can classify Miskotte and van Ruler in a separate category in his bibliographic survey of biblical theology, and label it 'The superiority of the Old Testament,' we should see how far the criticism Pusey worried about had advanced.[41] 'Superiority of the Old Testament' is of course nothing of the kind for these two Christian interpreters. Rather, both acknowledge in a way never fully lost in Dutch scholarship (see, e.g., Vriezen[42]) that the Old Testament is a theological book in the most basic sense of the word. That is, it speaks of God as God is, and does this through its own literary form, without necessity of the construction of religious history. Such a history was meant to connect the testaments in some way, but ironically it produced an Old Testament nowhere heard in the New, with a Hebrew G/god en route to finalization or correction in New Testament religion.

But the New Testament is clear even when New Testament and Old Testament scholars are not. 'If they do not believe Moses and the Prophets, they will not be convinced if someone were raised from the dead.' That is a statement of fact having to do with Christian theological convictions about a two-testament scripture, and its capacity, indeed design, for identifying God and allowing him

---

[41] Reventlow, *Problems of Biblical Theology*, 54–64. Barth is also included in this section.
[42] 'Old Testament', 79–96.

to speak for himself. The Bible has been 'figured out' in the last centuries, and there can be little wonder we have a crisis in hermeneutics. The crisis in hermeneutics is in reality a crisis involving God's providence, a proper ecclesiology and doctrine of the Holy Spirit. But that is an essay for another occasion.[43]

Bibliography

Abraham, W.J., *Canon and Criterion in Christian Theology: From the Fathers to Feminism* (Oxford: Clarendon Press, 1998)

Brueggemann, W., *Theology of the Old Testament: Testimony, Dispute, Advocacy* (Minneapolis: Fortress Press, 1997)

Brueggemann, W., and H.W. Wolff, *The Vitality of Old Testament Traditions* (Atlanta: John Knox Press, 1975)

Bultmann, R., 'The Significance of the Old Testament for Christian Faith' in B.W. Anderson (ed.), *The Old Testament and Christian Faith: A Theological Discussion* (New York: Harper & Row, 1963), 8–35

Buren, P.M. van, 'On Reading Someone Else's Mail: The Church and Israel's Scriptures' in E. Blum, C. Macholz, and E. Stegemann (eds.), *Die hebräische Bibel und ihre zweifache Nachgeschichte: FS R. Rendtorff* (Neukirchen-Vluyn: Neukirchener Verlag, 1900), 595–606

Childs, B.S., *Introduction to the Old Testament as Scripture* (Philadelphia: Fortress Press, 1979),

—, *Biblical Theology of the Old and New Testaments: Theological Reflection on the Christian Bible* (Minneapolis: Fortress Press, 1992)

Davies, P.R., *Whose Bible Is It Anyway?* (JSOTSup, 204; Sheffield: Sheffield Academic Press, 1995)

Eichrodt, W., 'Hat die alttestamentliche Theologie noch selbständige Bedeutung innerhalb der alttestamentlichen Wissenschaft?' *ZAW* 47 (1929), 83–91,

—, *Theology of the Old Testament*, 2 vols. (London: SCM Press, 1961, 1967)

Eissfeldt, O., 'Israelitisch-jüdische Religionsgeschichte und alttestamentliche Theologie', *ZAW* 44 (1926), 1–12

Fowl, S.E., *Engaging Scripture: A Model for Theological Interpretation* (Oxford: Basil Blackwell, 1998)

Gore, C., *Lux Mundi: A Series of Studies in the Religion of the Incarnation* (London: J. Murray, 1889)

Hauerwas, S., *Character and the Christian Life: A Study in Theological Ethics* (San Antonio: Trinity University Press, 1985)

---

[43] See above all, Radner, 'Absence, 355–94; and recently, Abraham, *Canon and Criterion.* I have unfortunately come too late to include reference upon the very important book by Frances Young, *Biblical Exegesis.*

Levenson, J., *The Hebrew Bible, the Old Testament, and Historical Criticism: Jews and Christians in Biblical Studies* (Louisville: Westminster / John Knox Press, 1993)

Lindbeck, G.A., *The Nature of Doctrine: Religion and Theology in a Postliberal Age* (Philadelphia: Westminster Press, 1984),

—, 'Postcritical Canonical Interpretation: Three Modes of Retrieval' in C.R. Seitz and K. Greene-McCreight (eds.), *Theological Exegesis: Essays in Honor of Brevard S. Childs* (Grand Rapids: Eerdmans, 1999), 26–51

MacIntyre, A., *Whose Justice? Which Rationality?* (London: Duckworth & Co., 1988)

—, *Three Rival Versions of Moral Enquiry: Encyclopaedia, Genealogy, and Tradition* (London: Duckworth & Co., 1990)

Milbank, J., *The Word Made Strange: Theology, Language, and Culture* (Oxford: Basil Blackwell, 1997)

O'Neill, J.C., *The Bible's Authority: A Portrait Gallery of Thinkers from Lessing to Bultmann* (Edinburgh: T & T Clark, 1991)

Perlitt, L., *Bundestheologie im Alten Testament* (WMANT, 36; Neukirchen-Vluyn: Neukirchener Verlag, 1969)

Pusey, E.B., *Daniel the Prophet* (Oxford, 1864)

Rad, G. von, *Old Testament Theology*, 2 vols. (Edinburgh: Oliver & Boyd, 1962, 1965)

—, *Genesis: A Commentary* (OTL; Philadelphia: Westminster Press, 1972)

Radner, E., 'The Absence of the Comforter: Scripture and the Divided Church' in C.R. Seitz and K. Greene-McCreight (eds.), *Theological Exegesis: Essays in Honor of Brevard S. Childs* (Grand Rapids: Eerdmans, 1998), 355–394

Rendtorff, R., *The Old Testament: An Introduction* (London: SCM, 1985)

Reventlow, H.G., *Problems of Old Testament Theology in the Twentieth Century* (Philadelphia: Fortress Press, 1985)

—, *Problems of Biblical Theology in the Twentieth Century* (Philadelphia: Fortress Press, 1986)

Seitz, C.R., *Word Without End: The Old Testament as Abiding Theological Witness* (Grand Rapids: Eerdmans, 1998)

—, 'Christological Interpretation of Texts and Trinitarian Claims to Truth: An Engagement with Francis Watson's *Text and Truth*', *SJT* 52 (1999), 209–226

Selwyn, E.G. (ed.), *Essays Catholic and Critical* (London: SPCK, 1926)

Smith, W.R., *The Old Testament in the Jewish Church: A Course of Lectures on Biblical Criticism* (London: A. & C. Black, 1881)

Snodgrass, K. (ed.), *Ex auditu: An International Journal of Theological Interpretation of Scripture. XIV: The Theological Significance of the Earthly Jesus* (Allison Park, PA: Pickwick Publications, 1998)

Thiemann, R.F., *Revelation and Theology: The Gospel as Narrated Promise* (Notre Dame: University of Notre Dame Press, 1985)

Vanhoozer, K.J., *Is There a Meaning in This Text? The Bible, the Reader, and the Morality of Literary Knowledge* (Grand Rapids: Zondervan, 1998)

Vriezen, T.C., 'The Old Testament as the Word of God, and Its Use in the Church,' in idem, *An Outline of Old Testament Theology* (Oxford: Basil Blackwell, 1958), 79–96

Watson, F., *Text, Church and World: Biblical Interpretation in Theological Perspective* (Edinburgh: T. & T. Clark, 1994)

—, *Text and Truth: Redefining Biblical Theology* (Edinburgh: T. & T. Clark, 1997)

—, 'The Old Testament as Christian Scripture: A Response to Professor Seitz', *SJT* 52 (1999), 227–232

Westermann, C. (ed.), *Essays on Old Testament Hermeneutics* (Atlanta: John Knox Press, 1963)

Wolterstorff, N.P., *Divine Discourse: Philosophical Reflections on the Claim that God Speaks* (Cambridge: Cambridge University Press, 1995)

Young, F.M., *Biblical Exegesis and the Formation of Christian Culture* (Cambridge: Cambridge University Press, 1997)

3

The Social Effect of Biblical Criticism

Walter Sundberg

Social Effect as Criterion

'What book would you recommend,' I asked a young colleague in New Testament, 'that explains contemporary biblical criticism to beginning theological students?' She suggested *To Each its Own Meaning*, a handy collection of essays that covers the scholarly landscape in biblical studies. The book includes articles on everything from source, form, and redaction criticism to canonical, social scientific, and rhetorical approaches, to more recent methods such as reader-response criticism and feminism. Typical of the textbook genre, the collection takes a positive approach to all positions. It affirms each method of criticism as a valid contribution to biblical studies. Competing methods represent not confusion, but 'diveristy' – a decided virtue in contemporary academia. The concern for diversity extends to the choice of contributors. The editors, Steven L. McKenzie and Stephen R. Haynes, proudly describe the authors of the essays in terms of their personal identies: 'Four are women and nine are men. Seven are Hebrew Bible / Old Testament scholars, and six work primarily in New Testament. Three are from Roman Catholic backgrounds, one is Jewish, and nine represent a variety of Protestant denominations.' As if this were not enough, the editors employ age distinctions in their selection: 'in the interest of balance, some younger scholars were assigned chapters on more traditional methods, while more established scholars were asked to write chapters on newer methods.'[1]

Older readers might consider this argument overly scrupulous in its concern for inclusiveness. To many theological students born in the 1970s,

---

[1] McKenzie and Haynes, *Meaning*, 5–6.

however, it makes perfect sense. They have been raised under an educational philosophy that posits an essential connection between the 'accidents' of gender, race and ethnicity and the 'substance' of ideas. 'Diversity' has become an ethical imperative in the contemporary university. Its purveyors believe that it is best secured by attending to the physical characteristics and social circumstances of scholars. It teaches theological students, especially if they are members of mainline denominations in America or territorial churches in Europe, to accept variety in theology as a blessing.

In this intellectual milieu, it is impossible for a single school of thought to command theology. Powerful theological movements such as existentialism and neoorthodoxy may have inspired the first two generations of pastors and theologians in this century (a 'generation' understood in its traditional definition of thirty-three years) but they have had only marginal impact on this third and last generation of the century. Even such notions as 'Old Testament theology' and 'New Testament theology' (let alone 'biblical theology'), that dominated the theological curriculum in biblical studies into the early 1970s, have fallen by the wayside. The Bible is now commonly understood to be the product of disparate communities of the past. For scripture to be relevant, it must be allowed to speak in various ways to different communities of the present, each of which has its own legitimate needs. No single theology represents the voice of the past or the needs of the present. No religious community may claim privileged access to the content of the Bible. There are as many theological ideas as there are groups and individuals. To demand uniform opinion is wrong.

This situation entails important changes for the discipline of biblical studies. 'In the last 250 years,' write Stephen E. Fowl and L. Gregory Jones, 'debates about the meaning of a text have tended to dominate biblical interpretation.'[2] It was believed that if we only had the proper method of biblical criticism we would find the objective meaning of a specific passage. The fact is that there is neither a proper method nor a single meaning. Does this mean that there is 'no king in Israel' and the people do 'what is right in their own eyes' (Judg. 21:25)? Not quite. Fowl and Jones argue that common ground for debate among biblical scholars can be found. What determines biblical interpretation is the 'interpretive interest' of the exegete and the community of discourse to which the exegete belongs. For example, if the opening chapters of Genesis are placed before 'a physicist, a Marxist, a psychoanalyst, a Christian advocate of "creation science" and an Augustinian Christian,' what will happen? 'The interpreters will only clarify and perhaps resolve their differences to the extent they can articulate more precisely what their interpretive aims are when they read the Bible.'[3] Meaning is not merely a function of what works for the interpreter, but

---

[2] Fowl and Jones, *Reading*, 14.
[3] Ibid., 15–16.

a 'social activity' that 'is subject to the political arrangements in which people interpret' and ideas are 'confirmed, constrained, and determined.'[4] Each interpreter is responsible to a specific political community with its values and strictures. 'Thus there is no interpretive practice which is free of some kind of political presumptions. Hermeneutics is inevitably, though not restrictively, a "political" discipline.'[5] By examining the political arrangements that influence the interpreter, Fowl and Jones argue that different exegetical interests can be measured according to their social effect. The social effect of scholarly ideas is a criterion of judgment that everyone understands.

The Crisis in Biblical Interpretation

I propose in this essay to follow Fowl and Jones by attempting, in very general and admittedly sketchy terms, to analyze the social effect of contemporary biblical criticism. I believe that such an analysis can contribute to an understanding of the proposed assignment of the Scripture and Hermeneutics Seminar: namely, to examine the present 'crisis' in biblical interpretation.

This begs the question, however, as to whether or not there is a crisis. This was a matter in dispute at the Seminar meeting at Cambridge University in September 1999 and it is easy to understand why. Many biblical scholars perceive no threat or difficulty in the variety that characterizes biblical interpretation today. Since the seventeenth century, scholars have been willing and eager to read the Bible as an historical text subject to the same canons of criticism that are applied to historical documents generally. To read the Bible critically is to subject its putatively factual material and literary structure to independent investigation in order to test their truthfulness and to discern their original historical meaning or meanings. It further requires the study of the accumulation of meanings that have accrued to biblical texts over time and across cultures. This task naturally and inevitably leads one to recognize that scripture is subject to different interpretations of the widest possible sort. It is no surprise that there is diversity in biblical scholarship. Why should this be perceived as a crisis?

Besides, consider what modern biblical scholarship has achieved. Our knowledge of the historical backgrounds of the Old and New Testament is far beyond what was known in any previous age of Judeo-Christian culture. We have penetrated the mystery of text formation and understand the subtleties of biblical vocabulary. To be sure, the quest for a single, original meaning of biblical texts has been abandoned by many in the discipline. But this should not blind us to the fact that, despite diversity in interpretation, there is a significant

---

[4] Ibid., 16–17.
[5] Ibid., 16.

degree of consensus that prevails in contemporary biblical studies. This consensus covers such important matters as the definition of biblical genres, the dating of many biblical books, and even the theological profiles of at least portions of the literature in both Testaments. Modern biblical criticism is practiced across national and confessional boundaries. Bibliographical research is conducted openly and efficiently at an international level. Protestant, Catholic, and Jew share a common body of scholarship. Such achievements are usually not part of the profile of a discipline in crisis.

Despite these remarkable and undeniable achievements of biblical scholarship, I still believe there is a crisis in biblical interpretation and that this crisis is serious. It is a crisis most keenly felt among those who are concerned to retain a vital connection between the Bible and the religious communities that treat the Bible as divine word. That contemporary biblical scholarship denies that a unified perspective on the meaning of scripture may be obtained may pose little threat to those ensconced in academia and beholden only to the canons of secular scholarly research. But it is a serious problem for any community of faith that reveres the Bible as the authoritative source of divine revelation and assumes that its fundamental meaning is clear to the average believer and enduring across the ages. This crisis is not anything new. It is part of a chronic pattern of dispute that has characterized modern biblical criticism from its origin over three centuries ago. For a significant number of believers, many of whom are not only well grounded in modern biblical scholarship but are professionally engaged in the discipline, the ultimate effect of biblical criticism is to assault faith rather than support it.

A striking illustration of this problem is Eta Linnemann, student of Rudolf Bultmann and author of a celebrated study on the parables of Jesus, who became a born-again Christian and left her academic post. In a book that garnered quite a bit of attention in conservative evangelical circles, Linnemann claims that any form of critical method is 'perversion.'[6] She recounts in dramatic fashion how she abandoned the discipline after realizing the personal cost she paid as a biblical scholar. 'What I realized,' she writes,

> led me into profound disillusionment. I reacted by drifting towards addictions which might dull my misery. I became enslaved to watching television and fell into a state of alcohol dependence. My bitter personal experience finally convinced me of the truth of the Bible's assertion 'Whoever finds his life will lose it' (Matt. 10.39).[7]

It is easy to dismiss such testimony as extreme and intellectually irrelevant. But I would argue that Linnemann witnesses to a negative social effect of biblical studies that is felt by more pastors and scholars than is often acknowledged:

---

[6] Linnemann, *Criticism*, 116.
[7] Ibid., 18.

namely, the alienation from the security of traditional faith. This alienation must be taken into account in any responsible analysis of the discipline as a whole. The fact is that the relationship of biblical criticism and the church is characterized by deep-seated theological and doctrinal conflict over fundamental presuppositions of thought. A generation ago Gerhard Ebeling made the following assertion:

> [Historical criticism] is indeed all out to justify its existence as an independent theological discipline by discovering more and more new and increasingly radical theories of an anti-traditional kind . . . The impulses which lead to real advance in the development of this discipline are without question those which sharpen the tension with traditional dogmatics.[8]

The same observation could be made today.

The social effect of what Ebeling calls this 'tension' between biblical studies and the church is my subject in this chapter, a subject I propose to explore by attempting to evaluate what Fowl and Jones call 'the interpretive interest' of biblical interpreters. I believe that an examination of the political presumptions of biblical scholars allows us to gauge what are often the unexamined intellectual assumptions of biblical criticism which, in turn, help to explain why biblical criticism so often has a deleterious effect in the church. While such an analysis is offered in no way as a solution to the present crisis, I believe it can provide an important perspective on the crisis.

Political Evaluation

Consider the example of the typical biblical scholar employed in a secular university (I choose this example because I believe that the university biblical scholar is the dominant force in contemporary biblical studies). What does even a cursory political analysis of this type of professional teach us? It appears that such a scholar, ensconced in a secular academic environment, is free to pursue intellectual curiosity wherever it might lead. One would think that this situation is ideally suited to serve the radical pluralism of contemporary biblical studies. In fact, however, the demand to publish and the desire to obtain tenure involve the academic exegete in a highly political context that operates with its own beliefs, taboos, and tests of loyalty. The scholar seeking a permanent job is pressured to conform to the conventional wisdom of book editors and colleagues. This usually means treating scripture as one ancient text among others. Neither the biblical claim to unique revelation nor the Bible's supernaturalistic

---

[8] Ebeling, *Word*, 88.

worldview may be assumed as a matter of intellectual judgment. The belief that the Bible validates the traditions of living religious communities or that it answers spiritual needs of modern people is studiously ignored.

If these secular presuppositions of biblical scholarship are true, if the Bible is essentially an artifact of ancient religion, then it is legitimate to ask why scripture should hold a place of privilege in university religion departments? Why, for example, should a department of ten people have three or four scholars in biblical studies? 'In an era of multiculturalism and budgetary constraint,' observes Jon D. Levenson, no argument meant to insure special treatment for the Bible can possibly be convincing:

> Should the [argument] substitute a cultural for a religious motivation and center on the importance of the Bible in Western civilization, then, in the current climate, a defense of the importance of the West, at least for American students, is imperative. This is, of course, ironic in the light of the tendency of historical criticism to think of itself as transcending particularism and debunking claims of privilege.[9]

Levenson, who is a committed Jew as well as a Harvard Professor, faces the biblical scholar with the actual political situation of academic work. He believes that a secular defense of scripture's special status is impossible to make. The present situation of biblical studies in the university is indeed ironic. The enjoyment of scholarly privileges in universities by biblical scholars depends on 'the residual momentum of religious belief.' But religious belief is the very thing that is discounted by biblical scholars. This makes academic biblical criticism, in Levenson's harsh judgment, 'parasitic.'[10] While it may accomplish many things, biblical studies cannot create the religious traditions out of which it was born.

Levenson is not alone in making this argument. Luke Timothy Johnson, a Roman Catholic scholar at the Candler School of Theology, Emory University, calls attention to 'a crisis in pedagogy concerning the New Testament.' This crisis

> has little to do with constraints imposed on scholars from the outside. It has much to do with the emptiness of biblical scholarship apart from communities for whom these ancient texts have real-life significance and the inadequacy of the historical critical method to meet the questions of significance posed by our culture today.[11]

Johnson decries what he calls the 'Jesus business in America.' An academic cottage industry has developed, exemplified by the notorious Jesus Seminar,

---

[9] Levenson, 'Bible,' 33; see Harrisville and Sundberg, *Bible*, 267–269.
[10] Levenson, 'Bible,' 33.
[11] Johnson, *Jesus*, 75f.

which profits by marketing provocative portraits of 'the historical Jesus.' The keys to its success are the rejection of traditional faith and a preoccupation with the politics of the left. Jesus is redefined as 'countercultural sage' (Marcus Borg), or oppressed 'peasant' (John Dominic Crossan). He is measured according to various liberationist agendas that treat the church, like all established institutions, with suspicion. Radical biblical scholars make a distinction between Jesus and Christianity that is 'ideologically exploited.'[12] While Albert Schweitzer may have exposed the intellectual weaknesses of the quest for a culturally acceptable Jesus nearly a century ago, this does not stop the effort today. Controversial 'Jesus books' sell. They create favorable publicity and income for the scholars who write them.

Biblical Criticism and Mainline Churches

Insofar as this type of scholarship has an influence on seminary education and church life, its social effect can be disruptive. This disruption is felt strongly in liberal and mainline churches where modern criticism of the Bible carries the most weight. Modern criticism calls into question the traditional understanding of the authority of scripture that the majority of active laity hold dear. It can make clergy more beholden to the canons of the academy than to the confessional traditions of their churches. Ironically, the effort to accommodate the Bible to modern notions of truth often serves more to drive members away from the church than to make the church socially acceptable:

> The result has been paradoxical, although perhaps predictable. The churches representing this stance (mainline Protestants and post-Vatican II Catholics) do not see themselves marginalized culturally or intellectually, but they do find themselves in decline. To the degree that this form of Christianity has assimilated itself to the dominant ethos, reasons for anyone joining it are harder to come by.[13]

Johnson's claim is by no means a reckless charge, but has the support of the majority of contemporary religious sociologists. Since Dean M. Kelley's pioneering study *Why Conservative Churches are Growing* (1972), it is widely recognized that liberal churches lack impetus because they deliver a confused message. Characterized by suspicion of strict dogmatic belief, rejection of any doctrine of the infallibility of scripture, and accommodation to cultural trends, these churches thought they had found a secure path into the modern world. Instead, what they appear to have discovered is a dead-end. Ironically, it is evangelical churches that refuse to reconcile themselves to modernity which

---

[12] Ibid., 65; see also 39–50.
[13] Ibid., 64.

are growing in numbers. Dogmatic in belief, strict in their demands on behavior, and especially affirming the strict authority of scripture as divine word, these churches successfully carry out the indispensable function of religion: to explain the meaning of life unambiguously to adherents.

The Scottish sociologist Steve Bruce is among those who have confirmed Kelley's thesis. He concentrates his study on the predicament of liberal churches in western society. Bruce defines liberal churches by their tendency to regard 'human reason as paramount' and to theologize 'from the agenda of the secular world.'[14] Basic to their belief is the acceptance of modern pluralism. If pluralism is an accepted value, how do liberal churches define their core beliefs and boundaries of membership? The answer is that they cannot. This inability is a serious flaw. It goes against the fundamental nature of religion which 'is concerned with certainty. It is about discovering the Archimedean point which allows us to escape the ambiguity and confusion of the mundane world.'[15] The 'profile' of liberal churches is out of sync with the 'product' they offer. One cannot sell certainly with uncertainty.

The inability to market their product hampers liberal churches from recruiting active supporters, whether by evangelization or socialization of the young. Why should adults commit themselves to something vague and dissatisfying? How can children understand the beliefs of a group that lacks conviction? Bruce is especially effective in describing the social effect of the liberal interpretation of the Bible versus conservative exegesis on the Christian education of the young:

> The socialization of young children necessarily involves bowdlerizing and simplifying. The virtue of conservative Protestantism is that it survives such treatment better. Children can understand and believe in a God with the white beard who actually did make the world in six days and who dictated the Bible, to faithful stenographers. Apart from anything else, conservative Protestantism has the advantage that its treatment of the Bible, as containing true stories of miraculous occurrences, makes for appealing presentation to children. Because conservative Protestantism is realistic and dogmatic, what is left after it has been reduced to the level of the comic book is still consistent with the mature product. When it suffers the same translation, liberalism appears either empty or uncertain and ambiguous.[16]

This central matter of the weakness of Christian education in liberal churches has received a good deal of attention by religious sociologists in recent years. For example, Grace Davie of the University of Exeter, following data compiled by Daniele Hervieu-Leger, asserts that the decline of religious sensibility

---

[14] Bruce, *House*, 102.
[15] Ibid., 123.
[16] Ibid., 139.

in European societies, is not so much due to the increase of rationalism as to the fact that these societies 'are less capable of maintaining the meaning that lies at the heart of religious existence.'[17] We are in danger, she says, of creating 'amnesiac societies,' characterized by 'a dramatic generation by generation drop in religious knowledge. An ignorance of even the basic understandings of Christian teaching is the norm in modern Europe, especially among young people; it is not a reassuring attribute.'[18] Is this predicament caused by the practice of biblical criticism in liberal churches? Such a bald claim of cause and effect would be too simplistic. Many factors come into play that affect the status and authority of the church in modern society. But in so far as the catechizing of the young is a contributing factor to the decline of liberal churches, the way in which the Bible is interpreted by the clergy and passed on is an essential factor. The practice of biblical criticism deeply affects catechism and does so largely in negative terms.

A Pattern of Conflict

Plus ça change . . . The more things change, the more they remain the same. The contemporary debate on the social effect of biblical criticism is nothing new. The history of the discipline reveals a long-standing pattern of conflict between academic biblical criticism and defenders of the church. Allow me three examples from the twentieth century.

(1) Nearly thirty years ago, James D. Smart, then newly retired as Professor of Biblical Interpretation at Union Theological Seminary in New York, declared that, 'the average scholar does not appreciate how devastating his critical analysis can be to the preacher.'[19] Smart lamented that pastors think of the Bible as a specialized text requiring analysis by professional exegetes. This viewpoint discourages reading the Bible spontaneously and devotionally. It makes pastors fear sharing the conclusions of critical study with their parishioners because they believe such information contradicts articles of faith. The social effect of modern biblical criticism removes the Bible from the daily life of Christians. This is why there is 'a strange silence of the Bible in the church.'

(2) Over a half-century before Smart, Karl Barth spoke in a similar manner. Barth asserted that the type of professional biblical criticism taught in the university has a negative social effect on the parish pastor who is charged with the responsibility to preach. To read the Bible rightly, one must reject the fundamental academic assumption that the Bible is an historical text like any other.

---

[17] Berger, *Desecularization*, 80.
[18] Ibid., 83.
[19] Smart, *Silence*, 70.

In the Bible, said Barth writing in 1916, we find something different: 'words and experiences which seem at first sight to be nothing but riddles. We do not read the like either in the daily papers or in other books.' The beginning point for the preacher is to ask the question: 'What lies behind?'[20] To ask this question means not the strange silence of the Bible but the recognition that 'within the Bible there is a strange, new world, the world of God.' This world makes the utmost demands: 'If we wish to come to grips with the contents of the Bible, we must dare to reach far beyond ourselves. The Book admits of nothing less.'[21] Two years later, Barth published his first edition of *The Epistle to the Romans*. In the Preface, he staked his ground on the social effect of biblical criticism:

> The historical-critical method of Biblical investigation has its rightful place: it is concerned with the preparation of the intelligence – and this can never be superfluous. But, were I driven to choose between it and the venerable doctrine of Inspiration, I should without hesitation adopt the latter, which has a broader, deeper, more important justification. The doctrine of Inspiration is concerned with the labour of apprehending, without which no technical equipment, however complete, is of any use whatever.[22]

(3) John Gresham Machen echoed Barth's view of biblical criticism in the fundamentalist-modernist controversy that raged in America during the years following the First World War. According to Machen, what the church faces in modern biblical criticism is nothing less than the rival religion of 'naturalism' or 'paganism' that claims the world to be a self-enclosed process in which there is no place for miraculous divine intervention.[23] Scripture is reinterpreted as the symbolic quest for personhood: 'the highest good of human existence [is] the healthy, harmonious and joyous development of existing human faculties.'[24] Confessing Christians are obligated to stand against this view, no matter what their differences. Reformed, Lutheran, and Roman Catholic Christians may separate over important doctrinal matters concerning the authority of scripture, the sacraments, human will, and priestly authority. But they are compelled to speak with one voice in affirming the New Testament testimony 'not to inner spiritual facts,' but to 'what Jesus had done once and for all in His death and resurrection.'[25]

Upon the resurrection depends the truth or falsehood of Christianity: 'if Christ has not been raised, then our proclamation has been in vain and your

---

[20] Barth, *Word*, 29.
[21] Ibid., 33.
[22] Barth, *Epistle*, 1.
[23] Machen, *Christianity*, 148.
[24] Ibid., 65.
[25] Ibid., 53; see also 53–68.

faith has been in vain' (1 Cor. 15:14, NRSV). Liberalism avoids the question of truth or falsehood by interpreting the resurrection as a subjective, emotional experience. This is an illegitimate redefinition of the central event of the faith. It is the denial of a common understanding of what 'resurrection' means by ordinary folk as they engage in the plain reading of the Bible.[26] This false use of language means that liberal biblical criticism is religiously deceitful.[27]

The social effect of the fundamentalist-modernist controversy in America was enormous. European readers may not fully appreciate the depth and extent of the controversy. From the heresy trial of Charles Augustus Briggs in 1891 to the Scopes trial of 1925 and the split of the Princeton Theological Seminary faculty in 1929, the controversy wreaked havoc in the church. It alienated evangelicals in mainline churches from their denominational leaders. It fostered suspicion between ordinary Christians and theological professors at church colleges and seminaries. Surveying the wreckage at the end of the 1920s, the distinguished journalist and social commentator Walter Lippmann attempted to analyze the consequences of the debate. In *A Preface to Morals* (1929), one of the most highly regarded books of its day and still considered a classic interpretation of American culture, Lippmann took the side of Machen. Although a secular critic and nonbeliever, Lippmann believed that Machen was right on the matter of the social effect of liberal biblical criticism. To separate the ideas and values of Christianity from external events goes against the fundamental nature of religious belief. 'There is gone that deep, compulsive, organic faith in an external fact which is the essence of religion for all but that very small minority who can live with themselves in mystical communion or by the power of their understanding.'[28] Because the fundamentalist understands the essential connection between religion and historical externality, he 'goes to the very heart of the matter.'[29]

I do not believe that the pattern of conflict I am describing here between modern biblical criticism and scholars who see their primary allegiance to the church shows any signs of abating. The point of view taken by Smart, Barth, and Machen in the previous generation finds a clear echo today in the criticisms of scholars such as Luke Timothy Johnson or a host of religious sociologists. This conflict has simply become part of the social fabric of existence in which Christians in mainline denominations and territorial churches in Europe live. That a Jewish scholar like Jon D. Levenson has entered the fray shows that the conflict is not confined to the Christian church.

---

[26] Ibid., 112.
[27] Ibid., 111.
[28] Lippman, *Preface*, 32f.
[29] Ibid., 33.

From time to time, I read Søren Kierkegaard's bitter and ironic parable of the money gift to my students:

> Suppose that it was said in the New Testament – we can surely suppose it – that it is God's will that every man should have 100,000 dollars. Do you think there would be any question of a commentary? Or would not everyone rather say, 'It's easy enough to understand, there's no need of a commentary, let us for heaven's sake keep clear of commentaries – they could perhaps make it doubtful whether it is really as it is written. (And with their help we even run the risk that it may become doubtful.) But we prefer it to be as it stands written there, so away with all commentaries!'
>
> But what is found in the New Testament (about the narrow way, dying to the world, and so on) is not at all more difficult to understand than the matter of the 100,000 dollars. The difficulty lies elsewhere, in that it does not please us – and so we must have commentaries and professors and commentaries, for it is not the case of 'risking' that it may become doubtful to us, for we really wish it to be doubtful, and we have a tiny hope that the commentaries may make it so.[30]

The usual reaction this parable gets in the classroom is that students laugh a knowing laugh, deep from the belly. This laugh has as much to say about the social effect of biblical criticism as any historical example – which is exactly what Kierkegaard intended by the parable. The existential situation of many mainline seminarians is that they begin theological education inspired to serve the Lord, only to have their personal faith hammered in the classroom. This can be a good thing. Faith ought to be tested. But the testing that comes with contemporary biblical criticism bears a definite and, at times, enormous social cost. Many students go into the ministry wounded by their academic experience and weakened in their ability to offer a vigorous witness to the truth they hold.

Presuppositions

Between biblical criticism and faith, then, there persists, in the famous phrase of Lessing written over two centuries ago, 'the ugly, broad ditch.'[31] Why is this? I would argue that it is because biblical criticism holds to a set of philosophical presuppositions, originating in the Enlightenment, which inexorably brings it in opposition to the church. Individual biblical scholars may embrace these presuppositions, ignore them, or try to resist them as they go about their work. But the discipline as a whole cannot escape them. These presuppositions involve deep-rooted assumptions or modes of thought that exercise

---

[30] Kierkegaard, *Years*, 334f.
[31] Lessing, *Writings*, 55.

extraordinary influence on academic and religious perceptions. They affect the understanding of reality and religious speech. They carry the weight of long historical practice. They are usually of such inescapable force that they place limits on the possibilities of dialogue with an opposing point of view. To examine these philosophical principles of the discipline of biblical studies is a central theological task. As Cardinal Joseph Ratzinger has said:

> At its core, the debate about modern exegesis is . . . a philosophical debate. Only in this way can it be carried on correctly. Otherwise it is a battle in a mist. The exegetical problem is identical in the main with the struggle for the foundations of our time.[32]

These presuppositions may be described in many ways but Luke Timothy Johnson illustrates them simply and directly when he cites the ancient debate between Protagoras and Plato. Man, said Protagoras, is the measure of all things. God, said Plato, is the measure of all things. Biblical criticism tends towards the Protagorean position; religion sides with Plato. 'The distance between the two starting points is enormous and perhaps unbridgeable.'[33]

What are the particulars of the Protagorean position in biblical studies? Modern biblical criticism has in large part proceeded with three assumptions. The first is to read the Bible *utsi Deus non daretur* – as if there were no God. This equates the Bible with other ancient texts produced by Sumer or Greece or Rome. A key effect of this assumption is to place the scholar at the center of interpretation. Only the expertise of the trained professional can make an ancient document accurately understood. It is this assumption, I think, that has the most to do with making humanity the measure of all things in biblical studies. It defines the standard of truth by a hermeneutic that relies on the perceived thought-world discovered and affirmed by the modern self. The modern individual – it is believed – is enfranchised by natural right to exercise the unassailable authority of his own experience to judge between custom and truth and discover rational, humane, and applicable insights in scripture for the present day.

Secondly, since the time of Spinoza, biblical scholars have made an important distinction between 'truth' and 'meaning.' Among biblical scholars, the notion of 'truth' has been variously defined as universal reason (eighteenth century), historical method (nineteenth and twentieth centuries) or, as is the case with some scholars today, it is bracketed out as philosophically or epistemologically unknowable so that one is left only with the 'text.' But the driving force of the discipline of biblical studies has been to seek 'truth' first and

---

[32] Ratzinger, 'Crisis,' 14.
[33] Johnson, *Jesus*, 59.

foremost in the historical facts that stand behind the scriptures and are assumed to be, in some way, different from the text. This desire to obtain that which is judged to be 'fact' in the Bible arises out of what Van Harvey has called 'an almost Promethean will to truth' that is essential to the heritage of modern biblical scholarship. As he says: 'Only when the question "What really happened?" was consistently and radically posed, did it become clear how much of what was previously accepted as fact was, in truth, fiction; how many long-trusted witnesses were actually credulous spinners of tales and legends.'[34] This assumption is the heart of historical consciousness.

Separating 'truth' from the text leads to the use of the crucial category of 'meaning.' With remarkable consistency across three centuries, biblical critics understand 'meaning' as the cultural expressions and artifacts of specific peoples bound to time and place. This important category allows the biblical critic to explain epiphanies of the divine, prophecies, miracles, and the like as first and foremost phenomena of ancient belief. If the Bible is a book of 'meanings,' however, it loses its role in society as what Hans Frei calls a 'strongly realistic' narrative; that is to say, a narrative that is 'at once literal and historical, and not only doctrinal or edifying.'[35] If scripture as a text of 'meaning,' is removed in some way from 'truth' or at least is seen to bear a complicated and problematical relation to truth, then its role in church and society as a public authority is deeply and adversely affected.

The third assumption of modern biblical criticism is the suspicion of the institutional church. This assumption, of course, has deep Protestant roots. But it took its recognizable modern form beginning in the seventeenth century when many influential intellectual figures, both inside and outside the church, recoiled from the brutalities of religious warfare and the excesses of religious prejudice in early modern Europe. Pioneering biblical critics worked against this prejudice by exposing the traditional use of scripture for dogmatic purposes as ideologically motivated. In doing so they sought to neutralize the harsh political use of the Bible in society; that is to say, they set out to reduce its role in church and society as a public authority. In this endeavor, they were largely successful.

As a practicing church historian and seminary professor, I acknowledge that these philosophical presuppositions of modern biblical criticism are the operating assumptions under which I do my work. But I must also say that I cannot give them an unqualified allegiance. I am tempted to say with Karl Barth that these principles have their 'rightful place,' that they serve 'preparation of the intelligence . . . that can never be superfluous,' but that I need something 'which has broader, deeper, more important justification.'[36] And

---

[34] Harvey, *Historian*, 4.

[35] Frei, *Eclipse*, 1.

[36] Barth, *Epistle*, 1.

that something is faith. I do not want to make this an either/or proposition. My allegiance to scholarship and faith is a genuinely divided one. I know that the Bible is subject to the best judgment of trained scholars who must follow insights wherever they lead, but I also believe that it is the inspired word of God. I know that the Bible must be interpreted according to the dictates of historical consciousness, but I also believe that it transcends history as a sure witness to the true God. I know that the church has abused its authority in society, but I also believe that it is 'one, holy, catholic, and apostolic.' This is the tension in which I, along with many others, live. At any given time and for any number of reasons, this tension can break out into a crisis between biblical scholarship and faith that reveals 'the ugly, broad ditch.' The persistence of this tension is an essential part of the social effect of biblical criticism in the life of the believing community and especially among those of us who are members of liberal churches. *This is the enduring crisis of biblical interpretation.*

What then shall we do? The best policy, I believe, is to teach biblical criticism, but also to teach the tumultuous history of biblical criticism. The former provides undeniable insights into the scriptures; the latter is a key to the fractious history of the modern church in the west. If this teaching is done right it can lead to a creative use of the situation of chronic crisis in biblical interpretation that appears to be the lot of liberal churches in the west.

To teach biblical criticism opens believers to the insights of critical thought into the bone and sinew of scripture as an historical document. The knowledge gained from this study is immeasurable. Among its benefits is that it chastens the dogmatic tendencies of believers by facing them with the limitations and uncertainties of the biblical record. It is not our lot to have perfect security in faith on this earth. We see through a mirror darkly and there is no prospect that this situation will change before the eschaton. However much this acknowledgment of uncertainty in faith may cost liberal churches in attracting and retaining members, it is a cost that must be paid.

On the other hand, *to teach the history of biblical criticism*, and especially the story of its social effect in the church, informs believers that the discipline of biblical criticism comes with a price tag; above all, the way it exacerbates the demonstrated weaknesses of liberal churches in modern society. While, as I have just said, this cost may not be able to be avoided, the fact *that there is a cost* needs to be known better than it is. The way we practice biblical criticism contributes to this cost. Above all, the examination of the theological and philosophical foundations of biblical criticism contributes to the study of Christian theology at the deepest level of its conflict with both contemporary academic culture and secular modernity. The types of battles we see today over such highly publicized ventures as the Jesus Seminar are the important battles for theology to wage. They force us to measure carefully our allegiance to the academy by our prior commitment to the church.

Bibliography

Barth, K., *The Epistle to the Romans*, tr. E.C. Hoskyns (London: Oxford University Press, 1933)

—, *The Word of God and the Word of Man*, tr. D. Horton (New York: Harper & Row, 1957)

Berger, P.L. (ed.), *The Desecularization of the World: Resurgent Religion and World Politics* (Grand Rapids: Eerdmans, 1999)

Bruce, S., *A House Divided: Protestantism, Schism and Secularization* (London and New York: Routledge, 1990)

Ebeling, G., *Word and Faith*, tr. J.W. Leitch (Philadelphia: Fortress Press, 1963)

Fowl, S.E., and L.G. Jones, *Reading in Communion: Scripture and Ethics in Christian Life* (Grand Rapids: Eerdmans, 1991)

Frei, H.W., *The Eclipse of Biblical Narrative: A Study in Eighteenth and Nineteenth Century Hermeneutics* (New Haven: Yale University Press, 1974)

Harrisville, R.A., and W. Sundberg, *The Bible in Modern Culture: Theology and Historical-critical Method from Spinoza to Käsemann* (Grand Rapids: Eerdmans, 1995)

Harvey, V.A., *The Historian and the Believer: The Morality of Historical Knowledge and Christian Belief* (New York: Macmillan, 1966)

Johnson, L.T., *The Real Jesus: The Misguided Quest for the Historical Jesus and the Truth of the Traditional Gospels* (San Francisco: Harper Collins, 1996)

Kierkegaard, S., *The Last Years: Journals, 1853–1855*, ed. and tr. R.G. Smith (London: Collins, 1965)

Lessing, G.E., *Lessing's Theological Writings*, ed. H. Chadwick (Stanford: Stanford University Press, 1956)

Levenson, J.D., 'The Bible: Unexamined Commitments of Criticism', *First Things* 30 (February 1993), 24–33

Linnemann, E., *Historical Criticism of the Bible: Methodology or Ideology?*, tr. R.W. Yarbrough (Grand Rapids: Baker Book House, 1990)

Lippmann, W., *A Preface to Morals* (New York: Macmillan, 1929)

Machen, J.G., *Christianity and Liberalism* (Grand Rapids: Eerdmans, repr. 1946)

McKenzie, S.L., and S.R. Haynes, *To Each its Own Meaning: An Introduction to Biblical Criticisms and Their Application* (Louisville: Westminster / John Knox Press, 1993)

Ratzinger, Cardinal J., 'Biblical Interpretation in Crisis', *This World* 22 (1988), 3–19

Smart, J.D., *The Strange Silence of the Bible in the Church: A Study in Hermeneutics* (Philadelphia: Westminster, 1970)

4

A Response to Walter Sundberg

John Riches

Walter Sundberg has produced a bold and intriguing paper which offers an analysis of the difficulties which, he thinks, biblical criticism is responsible for in the church. Only in the last paragraph does he propose a solution: teach biblical criticism, because of the undeniable insights into the scriptures which it provides; teach 'the tumultuous history of biblical criticism' which is 'the key to the fractious history of the modern church in the west'. At least then people will be warned that they are playing with fire.

This conclusion comes as more than something of a surprise. The general tenor of the chapter is profoundly critical of and unsympathetic to biblical criticism and to the attitudes and assumptions which, it is claimed, biblical scholars hold. In summary these are the following:

(1) Biblical scholars believe that the bible was produced by disparate communities of the past; (2) they treat the Bible like any other ancient book which can properly be interpreted only by specialists; (3) they do not see it as a book with any particular relevance to people today, but read it in a distancing manner as a collection of cultural 'meanings' from the past (though Sundberg also notices that biblical scholars like Stephen Fowl think that interpretation is a political activity, where interpretation is 'determined' by '"the interpretive interest" of the exegete and community of discourse to which the exegete belongs'); (4) they water down and confuse the plain sense of the scripture (about the narrow way, dying to the world and so on, see Søren Kierkegaard); (5) they read it *etsi deus non daretur*, (6) they distinguish truth and meaning, being uninterested in the former, seeking only to describe 'cultural expressions and artifacts of specific peoples bound to time and place'; (7) they are profoundly suspicious of the institutional church.

Such modes of reading the Bible have a profoundly deleterious effect on the majority of lay people who like to take their religion with a large dose of certainty. Liberal readings produce vagueness and uncertainty about core beliefs and (in consequence?) about where the boundaries of the religious community are, about, that is, definitions of rules and standards of membership. Such vagueness and diversity of opinion is inimical to orthodoxy, which Walter understands as uniformity of opinion, to the education of the young, who like their religion simple (God as an old man with a beard) and to the evangelization of adults who want certain truth to live by.

Nevertheless, we are told, biblical criticism is not all bad: its achievements are 'undeniable'; 'Our knowledge of the historical background' is far better than ever before; 'we have penetrated the mystery of text formation and understand the subtleties of biblical vocabulary'. Even though many have abandoned the quest for a single, original meaning of biblical texts, there is still a considerable degree of consensus in contemporary biblical studies.

So it appears that it is all right to have the acceptable bits of biblical criticism, while keeping up one's guard against the unacceptable bits. Awareness of the history of effects of historical criticism should help to keep us alert.

Let me first say what I agree with. I think it is true that many students, particularly those from a broadly conservative evangelical background 'have their personal faith hammered in the classroom' and that a number of them then go on to become teachers of New Testament, teaching it much as they might if they were a member of a classics department, taking occasionally a malicious pleasure in attacking the personal faith of some of their students. I think it is true that many ministers and pastors are reluctant to share the readings of scripture which they have been taught in the classroom and prefer to fall back on what they were brought up on or indeed are further trained in by ministerial associations. But this is about as much as I do agree with.

For I believe that the reason why people's personal faith is 'hammered' by biblical criticism is because biblical criticism draws their attention to *aspects of the biblical texts* which, quite simply, are unreconcilable with some, though by no means all, of their inherited beliefs. Close reading of a pericope in a *Synopsis* will serve to raise a number of quite fundamental issues for many conservative evangelical Christians. Those who have been taught that the Gospels were written by eye-witnesses will be confronted with clear evidence of literary dependency; those who believe in the inerrancy of scripture will have to weigh that belief against the evidence of different and sometimes contradictory editorial presentations of the same incident. In this sense, it is true that biblical criticism is a child of the Enlightenment: that it has no choice but to accept that the deists were successful in their attack on what they called 'bibliolatry', doctrines of the inerrancy and authority of scripture developed in Lutheran and Calvinist orthodoxy. This did indeed remove a considerable element of certainty from

Christian faith,[1] as of course it was intended to.[2] So the first question I have for Walter is how far he thinks the assured results of biblical criticism should lead to a modification and reformulation of popular evangelical faith?

Further, I would like to raise some questions about the way he talks about biblical/historical criticism as if it were a simple and consistent set of methods, assumptions and beliefs, which came into being after the Thirty Years War. Deist criticism was largely rationalist: it looked for contradictions in, for example, the accounts of the resurrection or for immorality in the behaviour of the biblical characters (e.g. David), as it attacked accounts of miracles or the immorality of particular Christian doctrines. Historical criticism properly so-called is a somewhat later development and reaches its first flowering with Baur's *Church History*.[3] Baur drew freely on the methods of modern historiography and did indeed seek to provide an account of the development of religious consciousness in early Christianity, which was not supernaturalist but, broadly, Hegelian. But, long before this, much of the stock in trade of the biblical scholar had been developed, receiving a crucial impulse at the time of the Reformation. It was Luther, tormented by the received interpretations of Romans 1:17 who beat on the text to discover what Paul intended.[4] And he discovered the meaning of the offending genitive, 'the righteousness of God' by observing good humanist practice, that is, by considering the context in

---

[1] For a good description of the theological positions of this period, see Aner, *Theologie der Lessingzeit*. See also my 'Lessing's Change of Mind' and 'Lessing as Editor of Reimarus': Sixth International Congress on Biblical Studies, Oxford 3–7 April, 1978. The classic treatment of the British deists is Leslie Stephen's *History of English Thought in the Eighteenth Century*.

[2] Wise church leaders, like Bishop Butler, realized that loss of such certainty was appropriate: 'Probability', he wrote, 'is the guide of life.' Such views need to be read in conjunction with the extraordinarily sensitive analysis of the place of certainty in faith offered in J.H. Newman's *Essay in Aid of a Grammar of Assent*. Newman argues that the simple assents of simple faith, which can have extraordinary power in people's lives, may also themselves be 'assented to' as the result of prolonged reflection and study, where the mind is led by a series of complex inferences to certitude, 'assenting to the assent'. Butler certainly disliked enthusiastic forms of religious certainty, but distaste with certainty in religion went deeper than that. Religious certainties – Catholic, Lutheran and Calvinist – had inflicted appalling damage on Europe, of which the main occasion was the Thirty Years War, when about a third of the population of Central Europe died. If we are to pay attention to the history of biblical interpretation, then this example of the consequences of overconfidence in one's understanding of the Bible should be given prominence.

[3] Baur, *Church History*.

[4] Preface to the Latin Writings, *Luther's Works, vol. 34*.

which it was used. There is, that is to say, nothing rationalist or specifically linked to the Enlightenment in using the methods of secular scholarship to discover the meaning of the biblical text. My second question then is: would it not be better to abandon talk of biblical or historical criticism as some kind of ideological creation of the Enlightenment, which is by nature opposed to orthodox, supernaturalist forms of Christianity (though the tools of historical method were certainly used against such forms of orthodoxy) and instead view it as a set of tools which are available to us for study of the text, its historical context and formation (and indeed its subsequent history of use?) which may indeed encourage us to look at what is there, regardless of (or at least in despite of) our pre-judgements about what kind of text it is?

If we allow that scholarly expertise can play an important part in the unlocking of the meaning of scripture, then indeed certain questions follow which will be important for the interpretation of the Bible within a church context. What is the role of the 'scholarly reader' in relation to the 'ordinary reader'. How should we as trained readers 'read with'[5] others in the church so as not to inhibit their ability to find in the text that which is life-giving? I would like to ask Walter as a church historian at Luther Seminary why it is that this question has troubled Lutherans so little? Why have they accepted Luther's doctrine of the preaching office so readily, without consideration of its relation to lay Christians' understanding of the *plain* meaning of scripture? Is it because they had hidden doubts about its plainness and clarity? Or because they feared the diversity of readings which even a close and responsible reading of the text would throw up among different people in different situations at different times, as indeed any history of the interpretation of a particular biblical text will clearly demonstrate?

Does not this raise very special questions for the Bible Society? The Bible Society saw its role as being to provide translations *without notes or commentary* to any who wanted them. What in fact has happened is that the diffusion of the scriptures in the vernacular across Africa and other continents has led to the growth of a great variety of indigenous churches which have rejected or significantly modified the teaching of the mainline churches. What does this say, not so much about our doctrines of revelation and the authority of scripture but about our doctrines of its clarity, of scripture as *se ipse interpretans*?

One way of saving the doctrine of the clarity of scripture would be to abandon the tight insistence on uniformity of belief as a mark of orthodoxy. Why should not different people hold different beliefs at different times and different places, all of which are 'orthodox' in the sense that they express the

---

[5] See Upkong, 'Parable', 196, in *Semeia* 73 (1996), '*Reading With*': *An Exploration of the Interface between Critical and Ordinary Readings of the Bible. African Overtures.*

will of God for those communities at those times? Reading the Bible in community means listening carefully to the text, allowing it to inform the community's understanding of its situation and to help it to see its way forward, to discern God's presence and will for them in that situation. Different texts will speak differently to different peoples. Exodus texts have spoken powerfully to the poor and oppressed of Latin America. For communities in inner city areas where social cohesion has been seriously eroded, psalms of exile have had a message of comfort and hope. The story of the laying of the foundations of the new Temple in Ezra and of the great shout of weeping and joy which went up, resonates strongly with communities in Mozambique attempting to reconstruct their lives after the long and devastating civil war.

Walter's final recommendation is to teach 'the tumultuous history of biblical criticism' which is 'the key to the fractious history of the modern church in the west'. Is the suggestion that it is biblical criticism which is responsible for all the divisions in the church in the west? But how can a biblical criticism which is defined as having its origins after the Thirty Years War be held responsible for, say, the present fractious history of the church in Northern Ireland? The various parties there at least are in no doubt that their divisions have their roots in the conflicts of the seventeenth century. And the certainty with which they hold to their beliefs is one of the most frightening things about the situation. Some sense that there are and always have been varying views about the truth of things, and a willingness to compromise and settle for less than the highest expression of the truth for the sake of peace might advance things rather more speedily than more certainty. Historical criticism with its carefully qualified judgements may seem impossibly vague and indecisive to the young and those who seek firm convictions and certainties by which to live. But it may also encourage a more mature form of faith. The social effects of conflicting orthodoxies can be a good deal more fractious than those of supposedly vague liberalism.

I would advocate the study of the history of biblical interpretation (as opposed to just the history of biblical criticism) for quite different reasons. Firstly, because it shows what Ulrich Luz has called the *Sinnpotential* of texts. Texts are 'reservoirs of meaning' and the history of interpretation can show how responsible interpreters have drawn on their potentiality to construct their own readings and make sense of their own lives. It shows the rich and creative diversity of forms of life (as opposed to uniformity of life and practice) which has flown from the embodiment of different understandings of the texts in particular communities at particular times. But the history of interpretation will also throw up readings of the Bible which have been oppressive (cf. colonial readings of the conquest traditions, apartheid readings, uses of the Bible in defence of slavery) or which have been the ground for oppressive behaviour towards those with other opinions (consider the mainline Reformation churches' treatment of the Radical Reformation whose various readings of the Sermon on the Mount Luz documents in his Matthew commentary).[6] Such a history teaches caution about the confidence with which we hold our own views about the Bible's meaning; it should encourage us to develop a sense of discernment for those readings which have been genuinely life-giving and those which have brought death. So my question to Walter here is a more specific one: does not the history of the interpretation of the Sermon on the Mount, specifically of the profound disagreements between mainline and radical reformers over questions of arms bearing and oath-taking indicate the great difficulty of coming to a uniform understanding of the meaning of scripture, with or without the benefit of biblical criticism? Could biblical criticism help here? Which side would it favour?

Lastly, I confess myself more than a little puzzled by what Walter has to say firstly about Kierkegaard and secondly about the suspicion of the institutional church, and would like to know how the two sets of statements relate. Let me start with the second point: it is a fact of evangelical history that it starts with a profound protest against the Babylonian captivity of the church which is at the same time an attempt to liberate the church from such captivity. One might say, then, that there is in Protestantism a deep-seated suspicion of the institutional church, precisely because of its proven propensity to be corrupted and seduced by the world. True church exists properly, on at least some Lutheran views, only where the Word is preached and heard (interestingly, structurally not unlike some Orthodox views that the church is there where the Spirit is called down on the elements at the *epiklesis*). This is what one might call an actualizing view of the church, as opposed to views which see the church as a *given*, as in some sense an extension of the incarnation. Certainly on such actualizing views, the corruption of the 'visible', institutional church should come as no surprise, nor the fact that it has misused its power and manipulated people's fear. Does the fact that the churches have now largely lost power in Europe, and therefore are no longer in a position to misuse it, mean that we need no longer be on our guard against this kind of institutional corruption? Are there not other, perhaps more subtle forms of corruption: lack of vision, smallness of mind, craven holding on to the old ways of doing things, even, dare one say, a desire for certainty rather than the boldness of faith that Luther called for?

But given Walter's defence of the institutional church, I am puzzled about his appeal to Kierkegaard. For the same sense of sharp protest against the dominant, offical, institutional church which we saw in Luther runs through the writings of Kierkegaard, who is filled with a sense of abhorrence of the embourgeoisement of the Danish church. Who are the butt of his parable? Not

---

[6] *Das Evangelium nach Matthäus.*

liberation theologians with their historical reconstructions of a radical Jesus and their 'preoccupation with the politics of the left' and their 'liberationist agendas which treat the church, like all established institutions, with suspicion'.[7] Rather, people who could see the plain sense of scripture if it were in their own financial, commercial interest, but who look for help from the commentaries and professors to mask the sense of scripture, when it demands of them that they abandon wealth, possessions, security, family and marriage (cf. Kierkegaard's own painful relationship with Regine Olsen). Now in what sense is that an attack on historical biblical criticism? Were Danish professors of the mid-nineteenth century ardent practitioners of the historical critical method? Or were they advocates of a kind of Lutheranism which supported the institutions of the Danish state and encouraged a rather unhealthy religious introspection? Were the commentaries which he refers to all that different from those of Luther and Calvin which argued that the antitheses of the Sermon on the Mount were to be seen as complementary to the Old Testament law and that therefore we should not adopt a radical view on wealth and military service. Of course, *those who so wish* could very well use historical enquiry to argue some such view (as Walter has hinted, all interpretation, including historical interpretation of texts, is a political business). But it is certainly not the case that biblical/historical criticism *must* lead to such a weakening of the demands of the gospel.

To the contrary, the careful historical reading of the Sermon on the Mount in Luz's commentary on Matthew suggests strongly that it is the Radical Reformation which came closest to the sense which it would have had for Matthew's own community (even allowing that there is in the Sermon a certain tendency towards interiorizing the demands of the gospel). Similarly, Ernst Käsemann, in his understanding of the 'righteousness of God'[8] proposed a sense that challenged the quietism of much German Lutheranism, which saw God's righteousness as a gift of an alien righteousness, whereas Käsemann saw it as the power of God, setting his world to rights and drawing people into its service, as instruments of his righteousness. Again, this view was arrived at historically, through the investigation of contemporary Jewish texts (1QH). Would Kierkegaard have sneered at such commentaries and professors?

To conclude: biblical criticism is a complex phenomenon. It is clear to me that critical historical study of the text has seriously undermined some of the

---

[7] The polemic seems to widen here to embrace those who reject some kind of notion of 'orders of creation' (traditionally: nation, state, church, family) which is here extended to include 'all established institutions'. What might this include: banks, armies, universities, transnational companies, anything that is a recognized organ of our societies?

[8] E. Käsemann, 'Gottesgerechtigkeit bei Paulus', *EVB* 2 (1960), 181–93.

doctrines of the authority and inspiration of scripture of Lutheran and Calvinist orthodoxy of the seventeenth and eighteenth centuries. It can, however, be used to support some traditional Christian readings of scripture, just as it can be used to attack others. What it does not do is to establish the one true meaning of scripture, though it may indeed make some views a great deal more tenable than others! It is a set of tools, which can be used to make us more aware than we might otherwise have been of just what is there in scripture, with all its luminous clarity in some places, and its ambiguities, gaps and inconsistencies in others. It can too – if we widen the scope of historical enquiry to include the history of its reception – make us much more sharply aware of the ways in which subsequent readers have filled in those gaps, resolved the ambiguities and inconsistencies, drawing on their own antecedent beliefs and moulding the texts to their own experience. In this it illuminates what we have only lately come to recognize, that the meaning of texts is not purely a function of the linguistic symbols of which they are composed, but is something which readers have to construct for themselves as they bring their own questions and prejudices to bear on the text. And once we recognize this truth about the reading process, we should not be surprised to discover that different communities at different times, reading the texts prayerfully and attentively, nevertheless read them rather differently. Diversity of interpretation is an (almost) inevitable concomitant of a religion of the book. Only a refusal to translate and the exercise of a strict central control on access to the text and authorization to interpret could possibly ensure otherwise, and the Lutheran Reformation (and the invention of the printing press) effectively put paid to all such attempts within Christianity. The task of biblical hermeneutics, may I suggest, is then not to work out strategies for the recovery of a long-lost uniformity, but to assist in the discernment of legitimate diversity.[9]

See Addendum p. 367 for Bibliography.

---

[9] I have attempted to develop some of these themes a little further in *The Bible: A Very Short Introduction.*

5

Confessional Criticism and the Night Visions of Zechariah

Al Wolters

Introduction

One of the hallmarks of biblical scholarship in the last two centuries has been the chasm which has opened up between 'critical' readings of the Bible and religiously committed readings. As a result, there is often very little connection between what a scholarly commentary has to say about a given biblical pericope, and what that same passage is taken to mean in a sermon, or in a believer's private devotions. The split between 'knowledge' and 'belief,' a significant epistemological legacy of the philosophy of Immanuel Kant, has given rise to this dramatic divorce in the field of biblical studies.

It is one of the welcome features of contemporary postmodernism that it challenges this Kantian legacy. The tradition of mainline historical criticism, which strove to make itself immune from any non-rational factors, notably religious commitment or 'theology,' is now widely recognized to be a characteristic product of the *modernism* associated with the Enlightenment project, which equated true 'knowledge' with *Wissenschaft* – with an historically unsituated and religiously uncommitted rationality which unerringly points to a universally valid truth – and which was quite unaware of its own unfounded claims to epistemological power. Within this universe of discourse, *Kritik* came to mean investigation and analysis of the biblical writings which resolutely sought to bracket all 'dogmatic' assumptions about inspiration, prophetic prediction or God's action in history. To be 'scientific' meant to be 'critical,' and this in turn meant to be *voraussetzungslos*, 'without presuppositions.'

But postmodernism has given wider currency to the insight that it is impossible to be *voraussetzungslos*, and it has thus helped to create an intellectual climate in which the chasm between knowledge and belief can be more plausibly bridged – or rather, shown to rest on false premises. In this chapter I would like to propose a provisional sketch of an integrated approach to biblical exegesis and interpretation which does not presuppose a Kantian separation of knowledge and belief. Specifically, I will attempt to do three things: (1) to draw up a representative list of the main dimensions or approaches of biblical interpretation, (2) to arrange these approaches in an order of basicality, that is, in a sequence in which the earlier is necessarily presupposed in the later, and (3) to explore the proper interrelations among these various dimensions of interpretation. This is obviously an ambitious project, and this chapter cannot hope to give more than an incomplete, provisional, and tentative sketch. Its chief concern will be to probe the hermeneutical issues with a different set of assumptions, and to do so in a way which stays in close contact with the actual working world of the biblical scholar.

I have chosen to call my approach 'confessional criticism.' By 'confessional' I mean 'rooted in the classical Christian confession of Scripture as the Word of God.' (I prefer to avoid the term 'theological,' since it tends to obscure the crucial difference between existential religious commitment and theoretical reflection about such commitment.) By 'criticism' I mean simply 'scholarly analysis,' thus reclaiming for this term the meaning it had in biblical studies before the widespread adoption of the Kantian split. It is very telling that this era of biblical interpretation is often referred to in somewhat dismissive terms as 'pre-critical,' since the heirs of the Enlightenment tend to claim exclusive rights to genuine *Kritik*. Consequently, within the discourse of what has become known as 'historical criticism,' a term like 'confessional criticism' is an oxymoron. I use the term deliberately in order to highlight this clash of assumptions.

In order to ground my discussion in the concrete details of the work of biblical interpretation, I have chosen to focus on a specific section of Scripture, namely the so-called 'night visions' of Zechariah. This refers to the central section of the first major division of the book of Zechariah, and consists of the eight visions plus commentary which comprise the bulk of the first six chapters (1:7 to 6:8). These are visions which the prophet received 'on the twenty-fourth day of the eleventh month, the month of Shebat, in the second year of Darius' (1:7), that is, on February 15, 519 BC. In quick succession, the prophet describes seeing eight arresting scenes: mounted scouts who report on a global reconnaissance mission, four horns which are destroyed by four smiths, a surveyor who is prevented from measuring the dimensions of Jerusalem, the high priest Joshua who is reclothed in clean garments, a menorah which is fed oil from two adjacent olive trees, a flying curse-scroll which destroys the homes of sinners, a woman called Wickedness who is flown to Babylon, and four spirit-chariots which go out from the presence of God.

Nine Levels of Biblical Interpretation

To begin with, then, let me briefly list nine representative dimensions or levels of biblical interpretation, and single out one or two illustrations of each from the section in Zechariah dealing with the night visions. The dimensions I have chosen are textual criticism, lexicography, syntax, diachronic literary analysis, synchronic literary analysis, historical analysis, ideological criticism, redemptive-historical analysis, and confessional discernment.

Textual criticism

Clearly, the most basic level of interpretation is the establishment of the text on which the rest of the interpretation is to be based. Scholars tend to differ widely in the degree of confidence which they have in the textual reliability of the Masoretic Text, and therefore in their readiness to propose divergent readings as preferable to the MT. In the case of Zechariah's night visions, there are scholars like Rignell who do not accept a single emendation to the traditional Hebrew text.[1] On the other hand, the translators of the New English Bible (1970) accepted twenty-one departures from the MT in this section.[2] Clearly, there is a great deal of scope for discretionary judgment in textual criticism. Most contemporary commentators and translators fall somewhere between the extremes represented by Rignell and the NEB, with a marked tendency toward a more conservative position in recent years. This conservative trend is especially marked in the very thorough discussion of the text-critical issues found in the final report, edited by Dominique Barthélemy, of the Committee for Textual Analysis of the Hebrew Old Testament established by the United Bible Societies. It surveys twenty-nine different proposals to emend the MT in Zechariah 1:7–6:8, but favors only one of them, the reading עֵינִי, 'my eye,' instead of עֵינוֹ, 'his eye,' in Zechariah 2:12 (English 2:8).[3] However, this single exception is one of the *tiqqunê soperim*, 'corrections of the scribes,' in the Hebrew Bible, where the Masoretic tradition itself informs us that the former reading was original.[4]

---

[1] Rignell, *Nachtgesichte*, 248.
[2] Brockington, *Hebrew Text*, 264–266.
[3] Barthélemy *Critique textuelle* 3, 935–962.
[4] See Tov, *Textual Criticism*, 64–67.

For our purposes we will highlight two places where the text is still frequently emended. One is found at the beginning of 2:12 (English 2:8), where a literal rendering of the MT would be 'For thus says the Lord of hosts, after glory he sent me (אחר כבוד שלחני) to the nations which plundered you.' The words translated 'after glory he sent me' are perfectly straightforward taken by themselves, but make little sense in the context. Wellhausen's proposal to simply delete them[5] has been followed by a number of scholars, most recently by Alonso Schökel in the *Biblia del Peregrino*,[6] and Reventlow.[7] Other scholars have suggested a whole series of different conjectural emendations, notably Sellin's אשר כבודו, which is followed in the first edition of the Jerusalem Bible ('he whose glory has sent me'). None of these emendations has been able to command widespread assent.

Our second example is found in 5:6, where according to the MT the interpreting angel says of the ephah containing the woman: 'This is their eye (עינם) in all the land.' 'Their eye' is usually emended to 'their iniquity' (עונם), a small change which is supported by the Septuagint and by verse 8, where the angel says of the woman in the ephah, 'This is wickedness (הרשעה).'

Lexicography

Once the words of the text have been established in textual criticism, the lexical meaning of the words has to be determined by 'lexicography,' or lexical semantics. Usually this is not a problem, since most lexemes in any given passage in the Hebrew Bible are well known, and their meanings firmly established. However, there is also a significant proportion of biblical Hebrew words whose senses must be guessed at. In the history of Hebrew lexicography it frequently happens that such semantic guesses begin to acquire a spurious authority, simply through being repeated in authoritative dictionaries. I have often made the discovery, when tracing the lexicographical history of a word in biblical Hebrew, that the standard meaning assigned to it in contemporary lexica and commentaries goes back to an educated guess first made a few hundred years ago, often in the sixteenth century.[8] In short, it is my judgment that biblical scholars often assign too much authority to tradition in matters lexicographical.

The following is a partial list of Hebrew words or expressions, drawn from the section in Zechariah that concerns us, which illustrates this general trend.

---

[5] Wellhausen, *Die kleinen Propheten*, 180.

[6] The *Biblia del Peregrino* is a revision of the *Nueva Biblia Española*, both prepared under the general supervision of Luis Alonso Schökel.

[7] Reventlow, *Haggai, Sacharja und Maleachi*, 48.

[8] See for example Wolters, 'The Meaning of *kîšôr*.'

In each case the commonly accepted meaning of a lexical item is a medieval or modern guess which has acquired authority through much repetition. They are not necessarily mistaken, but in the present state of our knowledge they are no more plausible than a number of alternative guesses:

(1) גלה (4:2,3), 'bowl.'
(2) ידה (2:4), 'cast down.'
(3) כפי (2:4 [English 1:21]), 'so that.'
(4) מוש (3:9), 'remove.'
(5) מצלה (1:8), 'glen' or 'deep.'
(6) פוץ (1:17), 'overflow.'
(7) צנתרות (4:12), 'pipes.'
(8) שרקים (1:8), 'sorrel.'

I would single out for special mention the *hapax legomenon* צנתרות in 4:12. This is part of the description of the golden menorah in the fifth vision, and has been taken since the sixteenth century to refer to pipes which convey oil to the menorah's lamps from a 'bowl' (*gullâ*) situated above them. The meaning 'pipes' was suggested by the word's similarity to צנור, which was also taken to mean 'pipe.' This explanation has persisted into the twentieth century (see the first edition of Koehler–Baumgartner[9]), but is clearly on very shaky ground. Not only is the meaning of צנור itself disputed, but an infixed *taw* after the second radical appears to have no parallel in Hebrew (or generally Semitic) word-formation elsewhere.

Although dozens of other proposals have been made for the meaning of צנתרות (e.g. 'candle snuffers,' 'faucets,' 'funnels,' 'mountains'), none has been able to dislodge 'pipe' from its position of preeminence in modern lexica, commentaries, and versions. Yet it remains a very implausible suggestion. The truth is that we simply do not know what the word means.

In my own opinion, the most plausible guess is that צנתרות means '(oil-)pressers,' and that the sentence in which it occurs can be translated: 'What are the two olive twigs that are in the hands of the two pressers of "gold"?' My proposal is still a guess, but it can be supported by better arguments, I believe, than any of the alternatives. If it is correct, it is tempting to see in צנתרות an early corruption of צהורות (cf. צהר hiphil, 'to press out oil').

My point in adducing these examples is simply to underscore the point that on the lexicographical level of interpretation, as on the text-critical, there is a good deal of uncertainty. Much depends on an individual interpreter's judgment.

---

[9] Köhler and Baumgartner, *Lexicon*, s.v.

Syntax

When the text has been established, and the meanings of the individual lexical items determined, it is necessary to put them into syntactical relation with each other. Once again, this level of interpretation is usually not problematic, since the rules of Hebrew grammar in most cases do not allow for significant ambiguity. However, there are also many exceptions.

A particularly striking example is furnished by the simple three-word sentence in Zechariah 2:12 (English 2:8) which we have already discussed: אחר כבוד שלחני. If we accept the MT as it stands, this apparently simple sentence proves to be highly ambiguous on the syntactical level. I have noted the following eight construals which have been put forward in the history of interpretation. In order to highlight the syntactical differences, I have given the Latin equivalent in each case:

(1) 'After glory he sent me'
     E.g. King James Version: 'After the glory hath he sent me'
     Latin: 'Post gloriam misit me' (= Vulgate)
(2) 'Achar Cabod [= the archangel Michael] sent me'
     E.g. Grotius: 'Michael vocatur אחר כבד (sic)'[10]
     Latin: 'Achar Cabod misit me'
(3) 'Afterwards Glory [= God] sends me'
     E.g. Neumann, as cited by Köhler: 'einst sendet Glorie mich'[11]
     Latin: 'Postea Gloria mittit me'
(4) 'Afterwards: glory! He sent me'
     E.g. Louis Segond in *La Sainte Bible*: 'Après cela, viendra la gloire! Il m'a envoyé'[12]
     Latin: 'Postea: gloria! Misit me'
(5) 'After the glory [= vision] which he sent me'
     E.g. Mitchell: 'After the glory (vision) which he sent me'[13]
     Latin: 'Post gloriam quam misit mihi'
(6) 'With glory he has sent me'
     E.g. Junker: 'Mit (seiner) Herrlichkeit hat er mich gesandt'[14]
     Latin: 'Cum gloriā misit me'
(7) 'The back of the glory sent me'
     E.g. North: 'L'arrière de la gloire m'a envoyé'[15]
     Latin: 'Dorsum gloriae misit me'

---

[10] Grotius, *Annotationes*, 549.
[11] Köhler, *Weissagungen*, 99.
[12] *La Sainte Bible*.
[13] Mitchell et al, *Haggai, Zechariah*, 142.
[14] Junker, *Die zwölf kleinen Propheten II*, 128.
[15] North, *Exégèse pratique*, 33.

(8)   'After Glory had sent me'
       E.g. Hanhart: 'nachdem die Herrlichkeit mich gesandt hatte'[16]
       Latin: 'Postquam Gloria miserat me'

The syntactical ambiguity of this clause is further complicated by its connection with the phrase which follows: 'to the nations which plundered you.' Should this be construed with 'sent me' or (taking the debated three words as a parenthesis) with the preceding 'Thus says the Lord'? Both readings have found their defenders.

It is clear that, in wrestling to make sense of the MT in its context, commentators have exercised considerable ingenuity, exploring every syntactical possibility, however remote.

Diachronic literary analysis

On the basis of the results achieved on the text-critical, the lexicographical, and the syntactical levels of interpretation, it is possible to proceed to 'diachronic literary analysis.' By this term I mean all the critical methodologies which seek to trace the prehistory of the canonical text as it stands. It includes such approaches as source criticism, redaction criticism, and tradition history. The basic strategy is to analyze the text into disparate elements, to determine as nearly as possible the various dates and authors to which these disparate elements can be assigned, and then to reconstruct the historical process by which they finally yielded the canonical shape of the text.

It is impossible to give an overview in short compass of the various ways in which this kind of approach has been applied to the night visions of Zechariah. We would have to discuss the basic distinction that has frequently been made between the visions proper and the so-called 'oracles' of 1:16–17; 2:10–17; 3:8–10, and 4:6b–10a, together with their relative dating,[17] and the detailed tradition-historical analysis given by Beuken.[18] For our present purposes we will briefly lay out two more recent examples of diachronic analysis, those by Schöttler and Redditt.

Schöttler analyzes the literary history of the night visions into the following four stages:[19]

(1)   The original 'bottom layer' (*Grundschicht*), consisting of Visions 1, 3, 5, 7 and 8, plus the 'Yahweh words' of 1:14 and 2:14. This stage is dated to 519 BC.

---

[16]   Hanhart, *Sacharja*, 114.
[17]   See for example Petitjean, *Les oracles du Proto-Zacharie*.
[18]   Beuken, *Haggai–Sacharja 1–8*.
[19]   See the chart in Schöttler, *Gott inmitten seines Volkes*, 448.

(2)   The first revision, which added Visions 2 and 4, plus the 'Yahweh words' of 1:15; 2:11; and 4:6b, as well as expansions in 4:10$^+$, 11, 12b ,13 and 14$^+$. This stage is dated to approximately 515 B.C.

(3)   The second revision, which added Vision 6, plus the 'Yahweh words' of 2:10a, 12f.; 4:6a, 7, 10 (4:8f.); 6:8, as well as additional elements of Vision 4. This stage is dated to the mid-fifth century.

(4)   An addendum consisting of the symbolic action components of Vision 4. This stage is dated to the late fifth or early fourth century.

To these four stages Schöttler adds a fifth, but this refers to material before and after the night visions proper. Each stage has its own literary motifs and theological focus.

A somewhat less ambitious attempt to trace the literary prehistory of Zechariah's night visions was recently undertaken by Redditt.[20] He treats the night visions as including the coronation scene of 6:9–15. In his analysis, it is possible to discern basically two literary strata in Zechariah 1:7–6:15, with 'one last touch' being added in 3:8, 10 and 6:11b–13.[21] The first stratum consists of the canonical text minus 3:1–10; 4:6b–10a; and 6:9–15, the only three passages which mention Zerubbabel and/or Joshua the high priest. This first stratum had only seven visions (Vision 4 had not yet been added) and was composed sometime between 539 and 520. It constituted an appeal to the exiles in Babylon to join the Jews who had returned to Jerusalem. A second stratum, consisting of the three Zerubbabel–Joshua passages, was added in January/February 519, resulting in a 'revised and enlarged edition' of the night visions. It focused on the task of rebuilding in Jerusalem, and the necessity for the civil and religious authorities to work together in harmony. It is possible that Zechariah himself was the redactor responsible for this revision. Sometime after this, when it became clear that Zerubbabel was not the messianic Branch that had been predicted, a later redactor reinterpreted the 'Branch' to refer to Joshua instead, and made the requisite changes in 3:8, 10 and 6:11.

Even this brief sampling of work done in diachronic literary analysis makes clear that it is difficult to achieve consensus in this kind of investigation. Although an appeal is constantly made to given features of the canonical text, the results achieved depend in large measure on the ingenuity and imagination of the individual scholar.

Synchronic literary analysis

On this level we are concerned, not with the successive stages which led up to the final form of the text, but rather with that final form viewed as literature.

---

[20] Redditt, 'Zerubbabel, Joshua,' and Redditt, *Haggai, Zechariah, Malachi*, 38–43.

[21] Redditt, 'Zerubbabel, Joshua,' 257.

Strictly speaking we could apply such an approach to a reconstructed earlier stage of the text (for example, the visions in Redditt's first stratum display a regular chiastic structure[22]), but the hypothetical nature of such diachronic reconstructions makes such an approach less attractive. More and more, when biblical scholars speak of 'literary criticism,' they no longer mean *Literarkritik* in the classical sense of source criticism, but the analysis of verbal artistry as embodied in the canonical shape of the text. To the extent that this is so, this fifth level of interpretation rests directly on the first three, and may very well disregard the fourth altogether. The insights of structuralism, form criticism, and rhetorical criticism all contribute to literary analysis on this level. I would argue that figures of speech, wordplays, and intertextual allusions are also 'literary' in this sense.

Perhaps the clearest example of literary artistry in our section of Zechariah is the arrangement of the eight visions themselves. It has often been noted that they display a not-quite-regular chiastic structure. There are thematic and structural correspondences between Visions 1 and 8, between Visions 2 and 7, and between Visions 3 and 6, while Vision 5 (the menorah) fits well as the center of the chiasm. The difficulty is that Vision 4 (the reclothing of Joshua) does not seem to fit the chiastic structure. Furthermore, the internal literary pattern of Vision 4 diverges significantly from that of the other seven.

There are four ways in which the apparent anomaly of Vision 4 within the overall literary arrangement of the night visions has been dealt with. The most common has been to look upon it in diachronic terms as belonging to a later redactional layer. Redditt, as we have seen, is one of the many who have adopted this solution. Alternatively, Visions 4 and 5 (Joshua and the menorah) are grouped together as constituting the center of the chiasm, and representing the religious-civil dyarchy of Joshua and Zerubbabel. A proponent of this analysis is Butterworth, who has devoted an entire monograph to the question of literary structures in Zechariah, and also developed fairly rigorous criteria for recognizing chiastic structures.[23] A third approach is to take Visions 6 and 7 (scroll and ephah) together as a double unit, corresponding to the double unit of Vision 2 (horns and smiths), thus making the reclothing of Joshua the center of the chiasm. This is the tack taken by Kline, and has the further consequence that Vision 5 (the menorah) is construed as the structural analogue of Vision 3 (the surveyor). This reconfiguring of the night visions is part of Kline's larger structural analysis of the book of Zechariah as a whole, in which the 'vision chiasm' of 1:7–6:8 corresponds to the 'burden chiasm' of chapters 9–14.[24]

---

[22] Redditt, *Haggai, Zechariah, Malachi*, 41.

[23] Butterworth, *Structure and Zechariah*, 299; similarly Hanhart, *Sacharja*, 51; and Ollenburger, 'Book of Zechariah,' 737.

[24] Kline, 'Structure of Zechariah.'

Perhaps the most satisfactory treatment is that of Carol and Eric Meyers in their Anchor Bible commentary. Like Butterworth and others, they look upon Visions 4 and 5 as central to the chiasm as a whole, but unlike them they see the Joshua section as a deliberate variation on the pattern of the other seven visions. In fact, they argue that a '7 + 1 pattern' is itself a literary feature of the night visions. They make their case in the context of their larger thesis that Haggai and Zechariah 1–8 originally constituted a single composite work, which displays the 7 + 1 pattern in a number of different ways.[25]

This example illustrates that also on this level of interpretation there is considerable scope for coming to different conclusions.

Historical analysis

This very broad category includes all the ways in which our knowledge of the original historical context of a text illumines (or problematizes) the interpretation of the latter. This includes information drawn from other parts of Scripture, from ancient historians, from archeology, from ancient Near Eastern literature and inscriptions, and from social-scientific reconstructions of ancient society. A few examples of this kind of historical light on the night visions of Zechariah are the following:

Archeological discoveries have shown, not only that lampstands could have multiple lamps (like the menorah of Vision 5), but also that these lamps could have multiple 'spouts' or wick-niches. This has clarified the meaning of 'seven spouts each' (שבעה ושבעה מוצקות) in Zechariah 4:2. As most commentators now realize, מוצקות here does not mean 'pipes' (derived from the root יצק, 'pour'), but rather 'spouts' (derived from the root צוק, 'be narrow').[26] (The dictionary of Koehler-Baumgartner still perpetuates the sixteenth-century guess 'pipes'.[27]) Furthermore, these archeological discoveries show that the formerly common emendation of שבעה ושבעה to שבעה is unnecessary.[28] Each of the seven lamps had seven spouts.

Another notable exegetical advance based on archeological givens is the way the oracle inserted in Vision 5 is illumined by comparison with Akkadian royal building inscriptions. For example, this comparison clarifies the enigmatic expression האבן הראשה of Zechariah 4:7, which turns out to be the Hebrew analogue of Akkadian *libittu mahrītu* , 'former brick,' and refers to the reuse of a brick from a former temple when a new one was built on the same

[25] Meyers and Meyers, *Haggai, Zechariah 1–8*, xliv–lviii.

[26] Möhlenbrink, 'Der Leuchter,' 285; Keel, *Jahwe-Visionen*, 275–280; Meyers and Meyers, *Haggai, Zechariah 1–8*, 235–238.

[27] Köhler and Baumgartner, *Lexicon*, s.v. also *HALAT*, s.v.

[28] Barthélemy, *Critique textuelle 3*, 949–950.

site. The Akkadian parallels also explain other puzzling features of the text, such as the cry חֹן חֵן in the same verse.[29]

However, it is especially the Persian imperial setting in 519 BC which is relevant to the interpretation of the night visions. The horsemen of Vision 1 are likely an allusion to the system of mounted imperial couriers which had been instituted by the Persian Great King,[30] and the divine 'eyes' of Vision 5 may well allude to the imperial agents known as 'the eyes of the King'.[31] I have argued that the phrase 'among the myrtles in the מצלה (shady place)' in Vision 1 alludes to the garden-palace of Pasargadae, where the Great King had his residence.[32]

Of particular historical interest is the great Behistun inscription of Darius I, which was being completed precisely at the time that Zechariah received his visions in early 519 BC, and which recounts the quelling of a series of rebellions which had broken out throughout the Persian empire upon Darius's succession three years earlier.[33] Some commentators relate the subsequent peace to the report of the horsemen in Vision 1: 'We have patrolled the earth, and lo, the whole earth remains at peace' (2:11).[34] It is, however, a matter of exegetical judgment whether this verse should be interpreted as referring to these contemporary political events in the Persian empire. Hanhart, for example, assumes an absence of any connection (*Zusammenhanglosigkeit*) between the contemporary imperial disturbances and the report of the horsemen.[35]

Within a broader world-historical context it is also instructive to note that the night visions of Zechariah are dated to the remarkable period which historians and philosophers have designated as 'the Axial Age' (German *Achsenzeit*), when spiritual and intellectual revolutions were taking place in China (Confucius and Lao-Tze), India (Buddha), Iran (the rise of Zoroastrianism), and Greece (the birth of philosophy).[36] Within this context it is puzzling indeed why the horsemen should report that 'the whole earth remains at peace.' To my knowledge no commentators on Zechariah have made a connection between the night visions and the Axial Age.

The last two examples illustrate that a crucial component of the historical dimension of interpretation is the selection, from among the vast array of

---

[29] Petitjean, *Les oracles du Proto-Zacharie*, 215–263; Laato, 'Zechariah 4,6b–10a.'

[30] Meyers and Meyers, *Haggai, Zechariah 1–8*, 111.

[31] Oppenheim, 'The Eyes of the Lord.'

[32] Wolters, 'Pasargadae.'

[33] Wiesehöfer, *Der Aufstand Gaumatas*, 228–229; Borger, *Die Chronologie*.

[34] So, for example, Baldwin, *Haggai, Zechariah, Malachi*, 96; Van der Woude, *Zacharia*, 37; Meyers and Meyers, *Haggai, Zechariah 1–8*, 37, 115.

[35] Hanhart, *Sacharja*, 68. Cf. Wellhausen, *Die kleinen Propheten*, 179.

[36] Metzler, 'Der Konzept der Achsenzeit.'

potentially significant historical data, of those givens which can be considered exegetically relevant to the text in question.

Ideological criticism

I use this term to refer to all the ways in which an author's 'social location' (especially their race, class, gender, and sexual orientation) is deemed to be significant for the interpretation of that author's writing. It is common in this connection to speak of 'the hermeneutics of suspicion' and the 'deconstruction' of texts. In the case of the night visions of Zechariah, it is chiefly considerations of class and gender which have been brought to bear. (I leave out of consideration Levenson's claim that anti-Semitism was implicit in the Wellhausian depreciation of post-exilic Judaism.[37])

Paul D. Hanson, relying on the insights of the sociology of knowledge, notably the basic contrast between 'ideology' and 'utopia' elaborated by its founder Karl Mannheim, discerns a parallel contrast between 'hierocrats' and 'visionaries' in the post-exilic community.[38] Zechariah, being a priest and a member of the ruling classes, belongs to the former group, and is thus concerned to legitimate the status quo, especially the institutions of temple and priesthood. Thus chapters 1–8 of Zechariah (which essentially go back to Zechariah himself) reflect a hierocratic perspective intent on undergirding the establishment, while chapters 9–14 (by later authors) reflect a visionary perspective. Ironically, therefore, the night visions are not really 'visionary,' they function simply as 'suitable carriers of the propagandistic message of the hierocracy.'[39] For example, Hanson interprets the removal of the high priest Joshua's filthy clothes in Vision 4 as a divine exoneration of the false charges laid by the visionaries against the hierocrats.[40]

While Hanson reads the text with a view to exposing a bias rooted in social class, feminist biblical scholars are alert to bias rooted in gender. One example of a feminist reading of the night visions is found in a programmatic essay by Phyllis Trible, who alludes to Vision 7 in a discussion of passages which are 'much more patriarchal' than usually perceived. She writes: 'Hosea employed female harlotry to denounce wayward Israel in contrast to the male fidelity of Yahweh (Hosea 1–3). Ezekiel exploited the female with demeaning sexual images (Ezek 23; 36:7). Zechariah continued the process by identifying woman with wickedness and envisioning her removal from the restored land

---

[37] Levenson, *The Hebrew Bible*.
[38] Hanson, *Dawn of Apocalyptic*, 211–262.
[39] Hanson, *Dawn of Apocalyptic*, 256.
[40] Hanson, *Dawn of Apocalyptic*, 254.
[41] Trible, 'Overture', 461.

(Zech 5:7–11).'[41] From this perspective, the phrase זאת הרשעה in 5:8 is interpreted to mean that woman is generically identified with wickedness.

It is clear that ideological readings of the biblical text depend on basic assumptions which may themselves be called ideological, and are likely to be vigorously contested. Hanson's sociological analysis of the post-exilic community has been severely criticized,[42] and Trible's interpretation of Vision 7 seems to overlook the fact that feminine abstract nouns, whether positive (e.g. wisdom) or negative, are all personified as women in the Hebrew Bible.

Redemptive-historical analysis

As we move up the ladder of our nine representative levels of interpretation, the role of the interpreter's basic beliefs tends to increase, and to divide interpreters from each other. This becomes especially evident on the eighth level, which looks at a passage from the standpoint of its place within the grand narrative of the Christian canon. That grand narrative climaxes in Jesus Christ as portrayed in the New Testament, that is, as the long-awaited Messiah through whom the God of the Jews offers salvation to all nations – in fact, promises the ultimate restoration of all things. A redemptive-historical reading within this perspective means tracing the connections of any subordinate part of the biblical metanarrative with this center. Those connections may be direct or indirect, explicit or implicit, but they are never completely absent. From a New Testament perspective, even the Old Testament is full of references to Christ.

This is of course especially clear in the messianic passages of the Old Testament. In the case of the night visions of Zechariah, it is almost universally agreed that the צמח or 'Branch' of 3:8 is a messianic title (so already the Targum). Although many commentators take it to refer here to Zerubbabel, many others understand it of the future messianic king,[43] or of both.[44] That future king is then identified within the context of the Christian canon as Jesus Christ.[45]

But it is not only such explicitly messianic passages which are significant for a redemptive-historical reading. If the Old Testament is read in the light of its New Testament fulfillment, many other features of the night visions take on a deeper meaning. We may mention the centrality of Jerusalem and the temple, the theme of God dwelling among his people (2:14), the prospect of all nations

---

[42] For example Carroll, 'Twilight of Prophecy.'

[43] For example Van der Woude, *Zacharia*, 74–75; Meyers and Meyers, *Haggai, Zechariah 1–8*, 203.

[44] So Hanhart, *Sacharja*, 196–198, 223–226.

[45] Unger, *Zechariah*, 65–66; Laubach, *Sacharja*, 51–52.

joining God's covenant people (2:15), the well-known assurance 'not by might, nor by power, but by my spirit' (4:6), and much more. Situated within the overarching biblical narrative of redemptive history (*Heilsgeschichte*), these aspects of the night visions reveal a significance otherwise unnoticed.

Confessional discernment

As explained above, I am using 'confessional' in the sense 'rooted in the confession of the Scriptures as the word of God.' In other words, confessional discernment has to do with the basic belief that God speaks in the Bible, that he conveys a message to believers of all ages by means of the Scriptures. As a distinct level of interpretation, confessional discernment focuses on hearing what God has to say to his people. For most readers of the Bible, both today and in ages past, this is the most important level of interpretation, the *raison d'être* of all other aspects of hermeneutical inquiry. In academic discourse it is usually referred to as 'theological' interpretation, as discerning the 'message' or 'kerygma' of the text. For preachers who have to make sermons, for leaders of Bible study groups, for ordinary believers who read Scripture for their private devotions, this is the pay-off: 'What is God saying to us, to me, in this passage?'

It is necessary, of course, to distinguish between what a text *meant* for its original audience and what it *means* for believers today. That is why it is important to presuppose the redemptive-historical level of interpretation, which alerts the reader to different stages in the unfolding history of redemption. Nevertheless, the past and present meaning of the text are intimately conjoined: the Word of God to the post-exilic Jewish community is simultaneously the Word of God to the community of faith today.

From this perspective the night visions are a dramatic presentation (something akin to a slide show or video presentation, complete with commentary) of what God is like in his dealings with his people. A sampling of spiritual lessons which they convey is the following: God returns in mercy after punishing his people (Vision 1), he defeats the enemies of his people (Vision 2), he promises protection and ample space for Jerusalem (Vision 3), he removes the guilt from his people's representative (Vision 4), he supplies the necessary spiritual resources for his people (Vision 5), he threatens with the curse those who break his commandments (Vision 6), he promises to remove iniquity from the promised land (Vision 7), and he will mete out justice to the nations (Vision 8). Each of these lessons is applied by contemporary believers to their own situations.

The foregoing completes my brief survey of some of the main approaches used in biblical interpretation. I do not claim that the list is exhaustive (I have made no mention, for example, of canonical criticism, or reader-response theories), but I do believe it is representative. It may also be that the description of each level lacks conceptual rigor (are figures of speech a lexicographical or a literary matter?), but for the moment I am more concerned with making a rough inventory than with achieving analytical precision. Clearly the items mentioned under each of the nine headings are also highly selective, but I mean them to serve as examples only.

A final comment about the nine levels we have listed is this: none of them has a high degree of methodological rigor, such that a significant measure of scholarly consensus can be achieved. There are widely divergent results obtained by equally competent biblical scholars on each level. If science is defined by some such criterion as objectivity or public verifiability, biblical interpretation is very far from being scientific. Whatever consensus there is is usually restricted to like-minded schools of scholars for a few decades or generations. It is even debatable whether biblical interpretation can be said to be an 'art,' in the sense in which that word is sometimes contrasted with 'science.' At best we might say that some scholars have become particularly adept at the 'art' of textual criticism, or rhetorical analysis, or some other sub-discipline. The field as a whole has no masters. At every turn, the biblical scholar cannot help but make judgments which are conditioned partially by lack of personal expertise, partially by paucity of relevant evidence, and partially by a wide array of contested background beliefs, many of them of a religious or ideological nature.

In stressing the lack of strict objectivity in the various levels of biblical interpretation, my point is not to deny that there are methodological standards on each level to which the interpreter must be held. In fact, I would argue that the opposite is true. Not every textual emendation is plausible, and not every Christological interpretation is acceptable. My point is rather that both the identification and the observance of the appropriate methodological standards is a matter of judgment and exegetical tact, and the exercise of such judgment and tact is a responsible act which cannot be reduced to a technical, mechanical, or ideologically neutral procedure. As a responsible human act, interpretation is therefore always enmeshed in a whole range of interpretative 'judgment calls.' It's not that there are no rules, it's just that the business of knowing and applying them is necessarily engaged in all the dimensions of being human.

Relationships among the Levels

With the above rough inventory in hand, we proceed to an exploration of the relationships which obtain among the nine levels. One of the most obvious features of the present state of biblical hermeneutics is the divorce between levels 1–7 on the one hand, and 8–9 on the other. A characteristic of most scholarly commentaries today, as compared with their counterparts before the rise of historical criticism, is that redemptive-historical and confessional considerations are conspicuous by their absence. What used to be considered the most important aspect of the study of Scripture – relating the text to the fundamental biblical story, and hearing the Word of the Lord for believers today – is now rigorously excluded from consideration. To do otherwise would be to compromise the academic integrity, the *Wissenschaftlichkeit*, of the commentary in question.

There are exceptions, of course. There are many so-called 'conservative' commentaries which still seek to bridge the gap, which wish to address the question of the contemporary religious relevance of the biblical texts which they treat. And even in mainline commentary series there is today an encouraging trend of including a 'theological' component (a good example is the currently appearing *New Interpreter's Bible*). But it remains true that within the guild of academic biblical studies the most prestigious work is still being done by scholars who explicitly or tacitly agree to exclude 'theological' considerations from their scholarship. Furthermore, those scholars who do still overtly treat the Bible as Scripture, as Holy Writ, tend to be remarkably circumspect, if not downright timid (I include myself in that assessment) in speaking of these texts as the Word of God. With very few exceptions, there is a great dearth today among competent biblical scholars of a robust and confident Christian voice.

As I see it, there are two main reasons for this situation. The first, as I suggested at the beginning of this chapter, is the Enlightenment ideal of autonomous rationality which seeks to exclude all nonrational factors. This led to the influential Kantian split between knowledge and belief, and the equation of the former with an enormously prestigious but rigorously nonreligious *Wissenschaft*. Only the first seven levels of our rough inventory could hope to qualify as genuinely 'scientific' scholarship.

The second reason has to do with the way Christians have construed the relationship between 'nature' and 'grace,' that is, between human life apart from Christ's redemption, on the one hand, and the new life in Christ, on the other. As I see it, within historic Christian orthodoxy there have been four major paradigms for relating these two basic categories of Christian experience. 'Grace' in this sense may be construed as either opposing, crowning, flanking, or renewing 'nature.'[46] In the first three of these paradigms, nature is conceived of as a religiously neutral category, and can be readily combined with the Enlightenment ideal of a religiously neutral *Wissenschaft*. Once this is done, the first seven hermeneutical levels are categorized as 'nature' with respect to the last two as 'grace.' Depending on the operative paradigm, therefore, the two

---

[46] See Wolters, 'Nature and Grace', and Wolters, 'Christianity and the Classics.'

highest levels either 'oppose' academically rigorous biblical studies (that is, stand in dialectical tension with them), or 'crown' them (that is, add a supranatural supplement), or 'flank' them (that is, stand juxtaposed as a parallel but unrelated reality). In other words, by conflating Enlightenment rationality with natural reason, Christian theology has itself aided and abetted the divorce between scholarship and religion – and that not only in other disciplines, but also in biblical studies.

In my judgment, the best way forward in the present crisis is to bring to bear the fourth of the classical nature–grace paradigms, which challenges the very idea of 'nature' as a religiously neutral category, and *a fortiori* the Enlightenment ideal of knowledge divorced from belief. In other words, the relationship between the various hermeneutical levels which I have sketched is not that of two blocks of methodological approaches which can be pitted against each other, or kept rigorously sealed off from each other, but rather that of an intricate interplay of all levels with each other. Among other things, this means that there is also a legitimate direction of influence from the highest levels to the lower ones. In short, it is possible to speak of 'confessional criticism.'

In exploring this thesis, we will look first at the way lower levels affect higher ones ('bottom-up relationships'), and then at the reverse phenomenon ('top-down relationships').

Bottom-up relationships

By speaking of 'levels,' and arranging them in a unilinear sequence, I have already loaded the dice in favor of recognizing the validity of bottom-up hermeneutical relationships. However, I would submit that in large measure such a claim is uncontroversial. We must first determine whether a word is actually in the text (textual criticism) before we assign a meaning to it (lexicography), and we must usually know the meanings of words in a sentence before we can construe their grammatical relationships with other elements in the sentence (syntax). Hanhart's judgment that the אחר of אחר כבוד שלחני in Zechariah 2:12 (English 2:8) is a conjunction (*postquam*) rather than a preposition (*post*) presupposes the lexicographical judgment that *postquam* is a possible meaning of this word, and the text-critical judgment that אחר is actually part of the text. There is indeed an order of basicality which holds among these levels. Furthermore, it seems clear that these three levels together (which we might collectively call the 'philological' levels) are presupposed in all subsequent approaches.

However, as we have seen, the sequence is not quite so obviously unilinear after the third level. Although classical historical criticism might insist that the establishment of a text's literary prehistory (level 4) should be basic to all subsequent analysis, this is an unrealistic expectation if scholars are hopelessly divided with respect to the number, the extent, the date, and the authorship of the various sources and traditions into which the text is analyzed. As a result, it is common nowadays to leap over the fourth level altogether, and base one's synchronic literary analysis directly on the final form of the canonical text, as understood by philological means.

It is not clear whether historical analysis (level 6) presupposes synchronic literary analysis (level 5) or whether it is the other way around. In the examples I chose from Zechariah's night visions, none of the relevant historical data depend for their relevance on the chiastic relationship of the visions among themselves – but the same is true for the reversed order. Perhaps these two levels should be treated as on a par with each other, each resting directly on the levels below.

However, it is not doubtful that ideological criticism (level 7) presupposes historical analysis, since the former depends on the socio-political order which prevails in a given historical period. Thus Hanson's interpretation of the reclothing of Joshua (Vision 4) presupposes his historical reconstruction of the tensions in post-exilic Jewish society. Similarly, redemptive-historical analysis (level 8) presupposes historical analysis *tout court* (after all, the return from exile was also a crucial turning point in the unfolding narrative of God's plan of salvation), although it does not seem necessary for ideological criticism to intervene between these two levels. This seems to suggest that levels 7 and 8 are also in a sense on a par with each other, both directly dependent on level 6.

Finally, it is significant that confessional discernment presupposes redemptive-historical analysis. As mentioned above, the Word of God to his people in Zechariah's time can be appropriately heard as the Word of God to his people today only if the redemptive-historical location of the former is taken into account. For example, the message conveyed in Vision 2, that God will defeat the enemies of his people, is embedded in a redemptive-historical context where this had heavily ethnic and military connotations, but has a much broader application for Christians today.

Needless to say, the effect of judgments made on earlier levels upon those made on later ones is not simply the effect of one level on the next higher. For example, a decision on the text-critical level, say the deletion of אחר כבוד שלחני in Zechariah 2:12 (English 2:8), has potential implications for the interpretation of Vision 3 on each of the subsequent levels. The range of interpretative options on the higher levels is in large part restricted by philological and exegetical choices made lower down the ladder.

For ease of reference I summarize our discussion of bottom-up relationships in the following chart.

9. Confessional discernment
8. Redemptive-historical analysis / 7. Ideological criticism
6. Historical analysis / 5. Synchronic literary analysis
4. Diachronic literary analysis
3. Syntax
2. Lexicography
1. Textual criticism

Top-down relationships

By speaking of 'levels' we have been implicitly using the metaphor of stratification, in which each level 'rests upon' the ones below it, and thus 'presupposes' them. In this way we have suggested that interpretative moves on higher levels depend on interpretative moves on lower levels. Despite debatable issues of exact sequence, I suspect that this general scheme looks intuitively right to most people. It also reinforces the notion that levels 8 and 9 are somehow an 'add-on,' which ought not to interfere with the academically rigorous work of levels 1–7. The higher should depend on the lower, not the other way around.

However, the word 'depend' also suggests another metaphor, namely of something lower 'hanging on' something higher. In fact, it can be shown that interpretative judgments on one level often do 'hang on' decisions made on a higher level. The hermeneutical traffic is not all one way.

The following are some examples, drawn from the illustrative material adduced above, of hermeneutical influence running downward: Consider the fact that commentators are now generally agreed that the מוצקות in the description of the menorah in Vision 5 (Zech. 4:2) means 'spouts' (wick-niches) rather than 'pipes.' This is a change on level 2 (lexicography), but it depends on level 6 (historical analysis), informed by archeological discoveries of actual lamps from biblical times. Furthermore, the level 1 decision not to emend שבעה ושבעה in that same verse depends on level 6 evidence as well, as does the level 2 interpretation of אבן הראשה in 4:7 as 'former brick.' If I am right in my hypothesis that צנתרות in 4:12 does not mean 'pipes' but 'oil-pressers' (a level 2 hypothesis) then this becomes legitimate grounds for entertaining the textual emendation צהורות (a level 1 hypothesis). Similarly, the judgment that Vision 4 does not fit the chiastic literary arrangement of the visions as a whole (level 5) has led Redditt and many others to propose that it belongs to a later redactional stage (level 4). Also, the various efforts to make syntactical sense (level 3) of the difficult phrase אחר כבוד שלחני in 2:12 (English 2:8) has led interpreters to assign widely different lexical meanings to אחר and כבוד (level 2).

This widespread phenomenon of top-down influence also applies to the very highest levels. Trible's judgment that the אשה אחת in Vision 7 (5:7) does not represent a personification of Wickedness (הרשעה) but rather an identification of woman in general with wickedness (a level 2 judgment), is clearly influenced by her feminist perspective (a level 7 matter). Similarly, the historical judgment of many Christian commentators that the messianic title 'Branch' of 3:8 does not refer to the contemporary governor Zerubbabel (level 6), is just as clearly influenced by the redemptive-historical belief (level 8) that the promised Messiah is Jesus Christ.

Finally, an interesting example of how confessional beliefs impinge on the diachronic literary level is found in Rudolph's commentary on 4:12. He argues that this verse must be secondary because otherwise the original text would imply 'the blasphemous thought' that the two sons of oil in this passage feed and fortify Yahweh himself.[47] Along the same line, Keel argues that ביד in this same verse cannot mean 'beside,' as commonly assumed (level 2), because this would yield the 'theological nonsense' (level 9) of making Yahweh dependent on human agency.[48]

The point of these examples is not that the interpretative judgments mentioned are right or wrong, but simply that it is both common and reasonable to have higher-level considerations influence lower-level judgments. The 'intricate interplay' of which we spoke earlier includes movements in both directions, up and down, and gives in-principle legitimacy to the hermeneutical influence of any one level on that of any other.

Thus, to mention another tentative hypothesis of my own, I believe it is legitimate to entertain the possibility that the Hebrew preposition לפני has the unusual sense 'after' in Zechariah 3:8 and 3:9, so that these two texts speak respectively of 'you [Joshua], and your colleagues who will officiate *after* you,' and 'the stone that I have put in place *after* you.' Such a reference to the redemptive-historical *future* is suggested to me, not only by the immediate context (Joshua's colleagues are called אנשי מופת, 'an omen of things to come' [NRSV]), and the history of interpretation (the Targum already understood the 'stone' as a reference to the Messiah), but also by my own Christian belief that the Israelite priesthood foreshadowed Jesus Christ. I am not now arguing that this lexicographical judgment is in fact correct (there are important philological considerations which count against it), but I am claiming that such a possibility should not be excluded simply because it is suggested by my religious understanding of the overall biblical story of salvation.

---

[47] Rudolph, *Haggai-Sacharja*, 109.
[48] Keel, *Jahweh-Visionen*, 310.

A paradox and a danger

However, there seems to be a basic flaw in my argument so far. The widespread in-
cidence of top-down influence in biblical interpretation gives rise to the question of
its relationship to bottom-up influence. There seems to be something paradoxical
about first arguing that the later levels naturally presuppose the earlier, and then
pointing out that the reverse is also true. I would suggest that the paradox can be resolved by distinguishing between an 'order of first reading' and an 'order of second
reading.' The order of first reading is the one which moves from the bottom up, and
works with the traditional, the familiar, and the obvious. Thus it accepts the text as
transmitted in the MT, assigns the most common meanings to the words, connects
them in the most familiar grammatical constructions, entertains the most everyday
forms of literary prehistory, notices the most obvious literary patterns, and so on,
right up to the ninth level, where it understands the divine message in terms of the
most familiar teachings of biblical theology. This is the prior and basic way of reading a text; perhaps it can be called 'naive.' But the order of second reading is the one
that challenges the traditional, the familiar, and the obvious, and in so doing opens
up the possibility of top-down hermeneutical relationships. Recent archeological
discoveries, new insights into the dynamics of gender and class, innovative work in
the Bible as literature, a fresh appreciation of a theme in biblical theology – all can be
the catalyst for reexamining familiar assumptions on a lower level. This is a secondary way of reading, which is necessarily parasitical upon the first, even as it challenges and corrects it; perhaps it can be called 'critical.' The two orders presuppose
each other, and together participate in the dynamics of the hermeneutical circle.

I have called my approach 'confessional criticism' because I want to insist
upon the legitimacy of top-down hermeneutical influence, specifically including the top level of confessional discernment. The Bible is an overwhelmingly
religious book, and the requirement to read it in strictly nonreligious terms is
unreasonable. In fact, I would argue that such a requirement itself reflects a religious prejudice.

To defend the legitimacy of confessional considerations in the hermeneutics of reading the Bible is not, however, to endorse every exegesis inspired by
pious assumptions. There is a hermeneutical danger here. For example, I
would personally want to take issue with what was for centuries the standard
Christian exegesis of the enigmatic words אחר כבוד שלחני in Zechariah 2:12
(English 2:8). In that exegesis the speaker of these words is the Angel of the
Lord, who in turn is equated with Christ, so that 'he has sent me' refers to the
incarnation. From the fourth-century church fathers[49] to the sixteenth-century
Reformers,[50] this was the standard interpretation of these words, and it is still

---

[49] For example Didymus the Blind; see Doutreleau, *Didyme l'Aveugle*a 266–271.
[50] For example Calvin, *Twelve Minor Prophets*, 68–70.

defended today.[51] It strikes me that this reading, apart from being based on what is probably a corrupt text, takes insufficient account of the redemptive-histori-cal distance between Old and New Testament. Nevertheless, I would argue that the mere fact that Christ is brought into the exegetical picture at this point should not *ipso facto* disqualify it from serious consideration.

This illustration highlights the fact that much more needs to be said about the safeguards which must be put in place to avoid the kinds of excesses which have so often been associated with Christocentric readings of the Old Testa-ment in the past. Prominent among such safeguards, I would argue, is a firm sense of the distinction between typology and allegory, and the recognition that the level of confessional discernment necessarily presupposes that of redemptive-historical analysis. The present context is not the place to elaborate on this.

An Illustration: Reading Vision 5

Taking all of the above into account, I propose in conclusion to give an inte-grated illustration of the points I have made, applying them to the vision of the menorah and the olive trees (Zech. 4). I shall give my own fairly literal transla-tion of this chapter, and add a few brief notes illustrative of the nine levels of interpretation:

> **4:1** And the messenger who spoke with me came back and woke me up, the way a man is woken up from his sleep. **2** And he said to me, 'What do you see?' And I said, 'I see a menorah all of gold, with its branchwork on top, and seven lamps on top of that, and seven spouts each for the lamps on top of it. **3** And two olive trees stand over it, one on the right of the branchwork, and one on its left.' **4** And I said in reply to the messenger who spoke with me as follows, 'What do these things mean, sir?' **5** And the messenger who spoke with me said to me in reply, 'Don't you know what these things mean?' And I said, 'No, sir.' **6** And he said to me in reply as follows, 'This is the word of the Lord to Zerubbabel, to wit: 'Not by force and not by power, but by my spirit,' says the Lord of hosts. **7** Who are you, big mountain? Before Zerubbabel you'll be level ground!' And he will extract the former stone amid shouts of 'Hail! Hail to it!' **8** And the word of the Lord came to me as follows, **9** 'The hands of Zerubbabel have laid the foundation of this house, and his hands will com-plete the job. Then you will know that the Lord of hosts has sent me to you people. **10** For who has despised the day of small things? And people will rejoice and see the stone of tin in the hand of Zerubbabel. These seven are the eyes of the Lord; they dart through all the earth.' **11** Then I said to him in reply, 'What do these olive trees mean, on the right of the menorah and on the left of it?' **12** And a second time I said to him in reply, 'What do these streaming olive twigs mean which are in the hands

---

[51] For example Barker, 'Zechariah,' 618.

of the pressers of the "gold" – the ones who express the "gold" out of them?' **13** And he said to me, 'Don't you know what they mean?' And I said, 'No, sir.' **14** And he said, 'These are the two sons of oil who stand before the lord of the whole earth.'

The brief notes which follow are small samples of the kind of integrated interpretation which I am advocating. Needless to say, they are very selective.

Textual criticism

Despite a number of proposed emendations, there is no need to depart from the MT in this chapter.[52] It is possible that the *hapax legomenon* צנתרות (v. 12) is a ghost-word, based on an early corruption of צהורות, but this is not certain. In any case the meaning is not affected.

Lexicography

מוצקות (v. 2) means 'spouts,' not 'pipes' (*pace HALAT*). I interpret גלה (vv. 2 and 3) to refer to the curved upper part of the menorah, consisting of the seven branches (hence 'branchwork'). This interpretation, which is that of Rignell,[53] is to be preferred to the standard rendering 'bowl,' which was first proposed in the sixteenth century. As mentioned above, I interpret צנתרות (v. 12) to mean, not (once again) 'pipes' (another sixteenth-century guess) but '(oil-)pressers,' perhaps originally צהורות. The rendering of חן חן and אבן הראשה (v. 7) and האבן הבדיל (v. 10) follows Laato.[54] ביד (v. 12) should be taken in its usual meaning, not in the otherwise unattested sense 'beside.'[55]

Syntax

Once צנתרות (v. 12) has been understood as 'pressers' the following זהב can be understood as an objective genitive, and the subsequent phrase המריקים מעליהם הזהב as an explanatory gloss in apposition to this construct chain.

Diachronic literary analysis

Wellhausen considered verses 6b–10a to be a 'completely independent piece,' which is intrusive in the present context.[56] He has been almost universally

---

[52] See Barthélemy, *Critique Textuelle*, 949–955.
[53] Rignell, *Die Nachtgesichte*, 146–150.
[54] Laato, 'Zechariah 4,6b–10a.'
[55] So Keel, *Jahweh-Visionen*, 310.
[56] Wellhausen, *Die kleinen Propheten*, 182–183.

followed by nonconservative commentators. However, a good case can be made for retaining these verses in their canonical place.[57]

Verse 12, too, is usually considered secondary. I believe that the new interpretation reflected in the above translation provides grounds for retaining it in its present context.

Synchronic literary analysis

Within the overall literary arrangement of the eight night visions, the vision of the menorah stands, alongside that of the reclothing of Joshua, at the center of the chiastic structure. High priest and menorah call to mind the temple, which also occupies the central position in Zechariah's view of the earthly world.[58]

There are also a number of noteworthy wordplays in this chapter, especially in the very artfully constructed verse 12. The plural of שבלת does not mean just 'twigs' or 'branch-ends' (so most commentators), nor just 'streams',[59] but rather both together. The olive-laden twigs (resembling a full head of grain) at the same time become a stream of oil in the hands of the oil-pressers. Similarly, the participle המריקים not only explicates the meaning of צנתרות but also evokes connotations of 'shining,' 'yellow,' and 'gold.' For a fuller discussion of these and other wordplays in this verse I refer to my essay on 'Word Play in Zechariah.'[60]

Historical analysis

The vision of the menorah is an integral part of the recently renewed efforts to rebuild the temple in Jerusalem. A restored temple would require something resembling the divinely prescribed menorah, which was made of gold, and required a steady supply of virgin olive oil (Exod. 25:31–40; 27:20–21). However, gold was in short supply in the post-exilic community (gold for Joshua's crown had to come from Babylon; see Zech. 6:9–14), as was olive oil (the olive crop had failed the year before; see Hag. 1:11). This was one of the daunting challenges facing Joshua and Zerubbabel, and likely preyed on the mind of the priest Zechariah as well. The vision of the solid-gold menorah and the miraculous olive trees connects directly with this concrete problem in the historical situation of February 519 BC.

---

[57] See the arguments adduced by Van der Woude, *Zacharia*, 81–82; Meyers and Meyers, *Haggai, Zechariah 1–8*, 242, 265–72; Fournier-Bidoz, 'Des mains de Zorobabel.'

[58] Meyers and Meyers, *Haggai, Zechariah 1–8*, lvi.

[59] So Calvin, *Twelve Minor Prophets*, 122; Petersen, *Haggai and Zechariah 1–8*, 235–236.

[60] 'Wolters, Word Play in Zechariah.'

Ideological criticism

It is remarkable how the leadership of the post-exilic community, including not only the prophets Haggai and Zechariah themselves, but also the high priest Joshua and the royal governor Zerubbabel, were apparently galvanized into cooperative action by the prophetic message, and led a formerly reluctant people to become enthusiastic about the temple-building project. Where a hermeneutics of suspicion sees a fierce ideological strife between opposing parties, each contending for their own self-interest, an unsuspicious reading of the canonical text sees a religious revival which inspires the whole community to work together in finishing the long-neglected task of rebuilding the house where God may once again dwell among his people. The vision of the menorah exemplifies this spirit of cooperation. Zechariah the prophet, himself a priest, is the bearer of a message which not only promises divine assistance and future success to Zerubbabel, but also pictures him and Joshua (the two 'sons of oil') as twin agents of the Lord's powerful assistance.

Redemptive-historical analysis

Within the overall sweep of the biblical story, key elements of this vision receive amplified resonance in the later realities of the New Testament which they foreshadow: the promise of the spirit, the building of the temple, the conjoining of the priestly and royal offices. Furthermore, the message of Vision 5 is aimed directly at Zerubbabel, the grandson of the last king of Judah before the exile, and a direct ancestor of Jesus Christ in the Davidic line (Mt. 1:12–13).

Confessional discernment

Taking into account the difference in redemptive-historical location of God's people in Zechariah's day and our own, Christian believers today can appropriate for themselves the well-known words, 'Not by force, and not by power, but by my spirit.' In fact, I would submit that it is not too much to say that this vision teaches the world church today that the whole mountain of seemingly insuperable problems which it faces today, from persecution to consumerism, from modernism to postmodernism, will ultimately become a plain before the Davidic king. God himself will supply the necessary resources to ensure that his temple will be built, and that he will dwell among his chosen people.

★ ★ ★ ★ ★

What I have tried to do in this chapter is to sketch out, in a very incomplete and tentative way, a model of biblical hermeneutics which respects the daunting diversity and complex interdependence of the main dimensions of biblical scholarship, and which does so in a way which challenges the modernist assumptions of classical historical criticism, notably the strict separation of scholarship and faith. It is essentially a plea for *integrality* in biblical studies, an integrality which reflects the fundamentally religious nature of both the Bible and its interpreters.

Bibliography

Alonso Schökel, L.A. (ed.), *Biblie del Peregrino* (Bilbao: Ega/Mensejero, 1993)

Baldwin, J., *Haggai, Zechariah, Malachi* (TOTC; Leicester: Inter-Varsity Press, 1972)

Barker, K.L., 'Zechariah' in F.E. Gaebelein (ed.), *The Expositor's Bible Commentary*. VII. *Daniel-Minor Prophets* (Grand Rapids: Zondervan, 1985), 593–697

Barthélemy, D., *Critique textuelle de l'Ancien Testament*. III. *Ézéchiel, Daniel et les 12 prophètes* (Freiburg, Switzerland: Éditions Universitaires; Göttingen: Vandenhoeck & Ruprecht, 1992)

Beuken, W.A.M., *Haggai-Sacharja 1–8: Studien zur Überlieferungsgeschichte der frühnachexilischen Prophetie* (Assen: Van Gorcum, 1967)

Borger, R., *Die Chronologie des Darius-Denkmals am Behistun-Felsen*, Nachrichten der Akademie der Wissenschaften in Göttingen. I. Philologisch-Historische Klasse (Göttingen: Vandenhoeck & Ruprecht, 1982)

Brockington, L.H., *The Hebrew Text of the Old Testament: The Readings Adopted by the Translators of the New English Bible* (Oxford: Oxford University Press; Cambridge: Cambridge University Press, 1973)

Butterworth, M., *Structure and the Book of Zechariah* (JSOTSup, 139; Sheffield: Sheffield Academic Press, 1992)

Calvin, J., *Commentaries on the Twelve Minor Prophets*. V. *Zechariah and Malachi*, tr. J. Owen (Edinburgh: Calvin Translation Society, 1849; Edinburgh: Banner of Truth Trust, repr. 1986)

Carroll, R.P., 'Twilight of Prophecy or Dawn of Apocalyptic?', *JSOT* 14 (1979), 3–35

Doutreleau, L., *Didyme l'Aveugle: Sur Zacharie* (Sources Chrétiennes, 83–85; Paris: Éditions du Cerf, 1962)

Fournier-Bidoz, A., 'Des mains de Zorobabel aux yeux du Seigneur: Pour une lecture unitaire de Zacharie IV 1–14', *VT* 47 (1997), 537–542

Grotius, H., *Annotationes ad Vetus Testamentum* in *Hugonis Grotii Opera in Tres Tomos Divisa. Tomus Primus* (London: Pitt, 1679)

Hanhart, R., *Sacharja* (BKAT, 14.7; Neukirchen-Vluyn: Neukirchener Verlag, 1990–)

Hanson, P.D., *The Dawn of Apocalyptic: The Historical and Sociological Roots of Jewish Apocalyptic Eschatology* (Philadelphia: Fortress Press, rev. edn. 1979)

Junker, H., *Die zwölf kleinen Propheten*. II. Hälfte: *Nahum Habakuk Sophonias Aggäus Zacharias Malachias* (Bonn: Hanstein, 1938)

Keel, O., *Jahwe-Visionen und Siegelkunst: Eine neue Deutung der Majestätsschilderungen in Jes 6, Ez 1 und 10 und Sach 4* (Stuttgart: Katholisches Bibelwerk, 1977)

Kline, M., 'The Structure of the Book of Zechariah', *JETS* 34 (1991), 179–193

Köhler, A., *Der Weissagungen Sacharjas erste Hälfte, Cap. 1–8* (Erlangen: Andreas Deichert, 1861)

Köhler, L., and W. Baumgartner, *Lexicon in Veteris Testamenti Libros* (Leiden: E.J. Brill, 1953)

Laato, A., 'Zechariah 4,6b–10a and the Akkadian Royal Building Inscriptions', *ZAW* 106 (1994), 53–69

La Sainte Bible. Traduite d'après les textes originaux hébreu et grec par Louis Segond (Paris: Alliance Biblique Universelle, 1959)

Laubach, F., *Der Prophet Sacharja* (Wuppertaler Studienbibel; Wuppertal: Brockhaus, 1984)

Levenson, J.D., *The Hebrew Bible, the Old Testament, and Historical Criticism: Jews and Christians in Biblical Studies* (Louisville: Westminster / John Knox Press, 1993)

Metzler, D., 'A.H. Anquetil-Duperron (1731–1805) und das Konzept der Achsenzeit' in H. Sancisi-Weerdenburg and J.W. Drijvers (eds.), *Achaemenid History. VII. Through Travellers' Eyes; European Travellers on the Iranian Monuments* (Leiden: Nederlands Instituut voor het Nabije Oosten, 1991), 123–131

Meyers, C.L., and E.M. Meyers, *Haggai, Zechariah 1–8: A New Translation with Introduction and Commentary* (AB, 25B; New York: Doubleday, 1987)

Mitchell, H.G., J.M. Powell Smith, and J. Bewer, *A Critical and Exegetical Commentary on Haggai, Zechariah, Malachi, and Jonah* (Edinburgh: T. & T. Clark, 1912)

Möhlenbrink, K., 'Der Leuchter im fünften Nachtgesicht des Propheten Sacharja: eine archäologische Untersuchung', *ZDPV* 52 (1929), 257–286

North, R., *Exégèse pratique des petits prophètes postexiliens* (Rome: Biblico, 1969)

Ollenburger, B.C., 'The Book of Zechariah: Introduction, Commentary, and Reflections' in *The New Interpreter's Bible* (Nashville: Abingdon Press, 1996), 7:735–840

Oppenheim, A.L., '"The Eyes of the Lord"', *JAOS* 88 (1968), 173–180

Petersen, D.L., *Haggai and Zechariah 1–8* (OTL; Philadelphia: Westminster Press, 1984)

Petitjean, A., *Les oracles du Proto-Zacharie: Un programme de restauration pour la communauté juive après l'exil* (Paris: Librairie Lecoffre J. Gabalda; Louvain: Éditions Imprimerie Orientaliste, 1969)

Redditt, P.L., 'Zerubbabel, Joshua, and the Night Visions of Zechariah', *CBQ* 54 (1992), 249–259

—, *Haggai, Zechariah, Malachi* (NCB; Grand Rapids: Eerdmans; London: Marshall Pickering, 1995)

Reventlow, H.G., *Die Propheten Haggai, Sacharja und Maleachi* (ATD, 25.2; Göttingen: Vandenhoeck & Ruprecht, 1993)

Rignell, L.G., *Die Nachtgesichte des Sacharja: Eine exegetische Studie* (Lund: Gleerup, 1950)

Rudolph, W., *Haggai-Sacharja 1–8, Sacharja 9–14, Maleachi* (KAT, 13.4; Gütersloh: Gerd Mohn, 1976)

Schöttler, H.-G., *Gott inmitten seines Volkes: Die Neuordnung des Gottesvolkes nach Sacharja 1–6* (Trier: Paulinus-Verlag, 1987)

Tov, E., *Textual Criticism of the Hebrew Bible* (Minneapolis: Fortress Press; Assen/Maastricht: Van Gorcum, 1992)

Trible, P., 'Overture for a Feminist Biblical Theology' reprinted in B.C. Ollenburger, E.A. Mortens and G.F. Hasel (eds.), *The Flowering of Old Testament Theology* (Sources for Biblical and Theological Study, 1; Winona Lake, IN.: Eisenbrauns, 1992), 445–464 (originally published in *TS* 50 [1989], 279–295)

Unger, M.F., *Zechariah, Prophet of Messiah's Glory* (Grand Rapids: Zondervan, 1963)

Wellhausen, J., *Die kleinen Propheten* (1892; Berlin: Walter de Gruyter, repr. 1963)

Wiesehöfer, J., *Der Aufstand Gaumatas und die Anfänge Dareios I* (Bonn: Rudolf Habelt, 1978)

Wolters, A., 'Nature and Grace in the Interpretation of Proverbs 31:10–31', *CTJ* 19 (1984), 153–166

—, 'Christianity and the Classics: A Typology of Attitudes' in W. Helleman (ed.), *Christianity and the Classics: The Acceptance of a Heritage* (Lanham, MD.: University Press of America, 1990), 189–203

—, 'Pasargadae and the Scene of Zechariah's First Vision.' Paper delivered at the Annual Meeting of the Society for Biblical Literature in Washington DC, November 22, 1993

—, 'The Meaning of *kîšôr* (Prov 31:19)', *HUCA* 65 (1994), 91–104

—, 'Word Play in Zechariah', in S.B. Noegel (ed.), *Puns and Pundits: Word Play in the Hebrew Bible and Ancient Near Eastern Literature* (Bethesda, MD.: CDL Press, 2000), 223–230

Woude, A.S. Van der, *Zacharia* (De Prediking van het Oude Testament; Nijkerk: Callenbach, 1984)

6

A Response to Al Wolters

Rex Mason

Questioning as it does some of the assumptions and methods of traditional critical scholarship, Al Wolters' chapter is itself characterized by meticulous scholarship of the highest order, by a welcome inclusiveness which makes room for a variety of methods and approaches to the biblical text, by a humility and generosity to the work of those with whom he disagrees, and, above all, by an evident passionate concern to open the treasures of the Bible for faith. Grounding theoretical discussion within the particularities of a specific biblical text has also been a most helpful illustration of the values of 'incarnation', and has afforded an excellent platform for his subsequent reflections on the interaction of all the various approaches to the biblical text he discusses and illustrates. I found particularly helpful his insistence on both 'bottom-up' and 'top-down' use of the methods. So this 'response' will be mainly an appreciative reflection on a discussion from which I have profited enormously and have found most helpful in stimulating my own, often confused, continuing thinking about these things.

In general I agree with his ordering of the approaches and also his recognition of a subjective element in all of them. One must first 'establish one's text', as the Germans say, but there is always going to be an interpretative element of subjective evaluation of the various texts and versions which have come to us. Indeed, most scholars would now acknowledge that any attempt to get back to 'the original text' is the pursuit of a chimaera. Lexicography is another vital early element in any interpretation of the text, and Wolters' insistence on questioning some traditional instances of interpreting Hebrew words is greatly to be welcomed. However, here the call is for greater exactness of scholarship, not dispensing with it in despair, since comparative philology as well as the kind of archaeological and 'historical' factors he makes use of in his own exegesis of the night visions are clearly important factors in delivering us from the Humpty-Dumpty syndrome: 'When I use a word it means just what I choose it to mean.' Wolters has also done us a service in reminding us that our syntactical reading of the Hebrew text, especially where its meaning is opaque as it stands, is very largely a matter of the interpreter's individual judgement. It is, indeed, difficult to know what else it could be. Personally, I would have put his point 6, 'Historical Analysis', next in order, for this is still very much in the realm of at least partially 'objective', observable data uncovered by the study of archaeology and other historical knowledge. Even here, however, individual interpretation enters in and the story of so-called 'biblical archaeology' is littered with instances where the archaeologist's own ideological stance has influenced his or her interpretation of artefacts and stratified deposits. Further, some interpreters of the biblical texts, of perhaps a more literalistic historical approach, will see an historical event to be identified where someone else will see a symbolic or typical allusion. Certainly Wolters' fourth, very general, heading, 'Diachronic Literary Analysis' affords the most clearly subjective approach, with the inclusion of source criticism and, above all, redaction criticism and, to some extent, tradition criticism. Where we have only one text before us (as opposed say to the ability to contrast and compare the distinct texts of the books of Kings and Chronicles), attempts to establish an orderly and historical 'development' of that text must be subjective to the point of hazard, as far too much redaction criticism has illustrated all too clearly. And yet, we have to acknowledge that the biblical text as it stands, does contain inconsistencies, obvious 'jointing' and evident variation in theological outlook, even after allowing for the truth that ancient documents may not always be susceptible to the methods and presuppositions of modern rational thought, so that some attempt to account for them must be undertaken if they are not to appear insufferably alien to modern congregations. For, let us remember, members of modern congregations are also the children of 'modern rationalism'. Disillusion felt by many with the diverse and unsatisfactory results of the methods of Wolters' point 4 has made very attractive various attempts at 'synchronic analysis', his point 5. There can be no real argument that such methods were sorely needed to counterbalance the overwhelmingly analytical measures of earlier approaches. This, after all, is the way people read and know a text, and many 'final form of the text' approaches to a biblical book, or to the whole Pentateuch for example, uncover valuable insights into the thoughts and purposes of those who did finally put all this material together. At this point we are greatly indebted to Wolters' 'inclusivist' approach for it must surely be a case of not 'this approach or that one' but 'this approach and all these others'. Yet even here we must not think that all the earlier methods proved prone to subjectivism while synchronic analysis, which blessedly deals with the objectiveness of the given text as we have it, is free of it. The widely varying patternings of the same text by those claiming to discern the literary structure within it is sufficient to disabuse us of any such hope, not least the varying patternings many have seen in the present form of the eight night visions of Zechariah. Indeed, Mike Butterworth's book *Structure and the Book of Zechariah*, which Wolters commends, has the courage to posit a fictional 'Isaiah chapter 67' which he got his computer to compose by drawing arbitrarily a verse from each of the actual sixty-six chapters. This chapter he then subjects to the methods of literary structural analysis and comes up with marvellous examples of literary patternings including a highly complex example of chiasm![1]

My general point arising from all this is not, therefore, to challenge the subjective element in all the traditional approaches used by biblical scholars, but to argue that subjectivism is an inevitable element in all such study, in methods both ancient and modern. But I reject the consequent resignation of some postmodernists in their claim that we can discover no meaning except the meaning imposed upon the text by each reader. I would argue for greater, not less, thoroughness and meticulousness of scholarship. I believe, however, that every one of us needs to be humble in the face of the text and to acknowledge the partiality and incompleteness of conclusions drawn from our own methods. And, above all, I warmly endorse Wolters' insistence on the use of all the weapons in the armoury, in the hope that each will show the limitations and the possibilities of others, and so all will complement rather than compete with each other. This, after all, was a point made long ago by John Barton in his excellent and seminal work *Reading the Old Testament*.

It is in the relation of Wolters' points 8 and 9, 'Redemptive-Historical Analysis' and 'Confessional Discernment', to the other methods that we come to the crunch of his chapter and to one of its greatest values in stimulating thought. It is quite impossible in the time available to respond adequately to his creative and imaginative discussion here, and so I content myself with one or two rather detached thoughts, which, I hope, may continue to stir the debate. None of us who reads and uses the Bible because we believe that God speaks powerfully through it still, awakening and sustaining faith, can be content with the kind of literary and historical analysis to which we would subject any other piece of ancient literature. We shall want to proceed to the kind of exposition for faith, which we often do in the kind of commentary series to which he alludes, in Bible reading notes, in teaching of any kind within the household of faith. If we are being told, however, that all biblical scholarship in this post-Kantian era should be of this confessional kind, I begin to feel a few qualms of uneasiness. Wolters seeks control of unbridled personal and subjective interpretation of the Bible in subjecting confessional criticism to the discipline of 'redemptive-historical' analysis. But this is to impose on the Bible a dogmatic

---

[1] Butterworth, *Structure*.

theological construct which is as much the product of the church as of the biblical writers, apart from the fact that it leaves the old problems of what to do with the Wisdom literature and those books which have little redemption history within them, and what inherent value the Old Testament possesses within itself. Further, it does not take long to remember that many different 'confessions' all claim the authority of the Bible for their beliefs. It is very easy to shape the Bible until it becomes a mould to fit the ideas we pour into it. But how does it then become the judge and controller of all our religious ideas and theological thinking? Of course, the interaction between church and Bible is a complex, two-way and continuously living process. The church has produced the Bible just as the Bible has produced and guided the church. If all biblical interpreters were as sound in their scholarship and controlled in their interpretation as Al Wolters, we should have nothing to fear. But I wonder if his approach may not run the danger of opening and widening a hole in the dyke for other forces within and without the church.

For what it is worth, my own approach is along the lines that all the Scriptures are the product of communities of faith, whether the faith of original writers and speakers, of redactors, tradents, preachers and exegetes as well as of those who recognized the worth in the writings which led to their achieving canonical status. There is a method of approach to the Bible, which Wolters clearly uses but does not mention specifically, a method which might be called 'the history of exegesis'. This recognizes the process of exegesis within Scripture itself as earlier words are taken up and applied in new situations; further, there is the exegesis of those who established the text, the exegesis of the Old Testament within the New, and the continuing process of exegesis in every age since. It is a process, which Brevard Childs observed and exploited so well in his commentary on Exodus.[2] To recognize this growth of Scripture and its understanding within the communities of faith is not to say that all such exegesis was 'correct' (whatever that may mean). But it does recognize that the main point of the Bible is its 'confessional' nature as Wolters so truly emphasizes, and not its geography, its history, its local cultural context or any other incidental matter, important as these may sometimes be to our understanding. To recognize this constant process of interaction between the Spirit of God and the communities of faith allows for the frankly awful things in the Bible. Wolters becomes a little embarrassed by the theme of 'God's judgement of his people's enemies' which he finds as one of the continually relevant theological points of the night visions. But such crude and convenient theology is challenged within other parts of the Old Testament and, most certainly in the New. Since this living process of interaction in interpreting the Bible is between the Spirit and the church, and one of the partners in the process is human, the story is by no

---

[2] Childs, *Exodus*.

means free of error, nor is it one of continuing evolutionary development from the less true to the greater. But there is no need to think it has ended with the closing of the biblical canon. Few Christians today would base their beliefs about slavery on what the New Testament has specifically to say on the subject (its basic theological insights are, of course, quite a different matter), nor would most today feel easy with what it has to say about the position of women within the church. For, just as the Mosaic law had constantly to be expanded and adapted to the needs of new social situations, so sociological, scientific and political developments mean that the church is always having to engage with the ethical teaching of the Bible and its implications over vexed and difficult issues which face us now. And we dare to believe that in this process the Spirit is still interacting with the church as he has done throughout every age of the Bible's development and use.

Yet, in all this, I still believe that the Bible itself has a controlling and authoritative role to play. And I do, therefore, feel it is important at least to attempt to understand what is going on there and just what is being said, so that it may continue to exercise that normative control on all our confessional thinking and development. And while postmodernism has shown us the great difficulty in looking at the Bible without our own particular pair of spectacles on, I still believe it is not entirely impossible. I find that most other classicists and I can agree fairly closely on what Vergil is saying in *The Aeneid*, for example. Why should it be wholly otherwise with the documents, which form our Bible?

Perhaps I am showing my age and encrustedness in ancient ways when I plead, 'Recognize the severe limitations of Kantianism, certainly. But don't jettison Kant entirely.' Otherwise we may end up speaking a good deal of 'cant', although it will be spelled rather differently.

Bibliography

Barton, J., *Reading the Old Testament: Method in Biblical Study* (London: Darton, Longman & Todd, 1996[2])
Butterworth, M., *Structure and the Book of Zechariah* (JSOTSup, 130; Sheffield: JSOT Press, 1992)
Childs, B.S., *Exodus: A Commentary* (OTL; London: SCM Press, 1974)

7

The Philosophy of Language and the Renewal of Biblical Hermeneutics

Neil B. MacDonald

Introduction

'How might the philosophy of language aid the renewal of biblical hermeneutics?' There is no doubt more than one conceivable response to this question. What I attempt to do in this chapter is to outline some answers that the philosophy of language in the analytic tradition could offer from its conceptual resources in response to a specific problem that I take to be typical of the present situation in biblical hermeneutics. The problem is that of typological interpretation and its demise in the wake of theological hermeneutics in the age of Enlightenment or thereabouts. Typological interpretation of the Bible has a long and illustrious not to say diverse history. But amidst all this diversity I take it there is sufficient conceptual similarity, enabling scholars to agree on the following definition: typological interpretation of the Old Testament is based on the 'presupposition that the whole Old Testament looks beyond itself for its interpretation.'[1] Historically this meant that 'types and prophecies of the

---

[1] Barr, *Old and New*, 103–148, esp. 139f. Notwithstanding that some leading scholars in the twentieth century have attempted to distinguish between typology and allegory, e.g. Eichrodt and von Rad, Barr has disputed whether there is any such distinction, preferring to understand typological interpretation as a species of allegorical interpretation, namely the allegorical interpretation of the Old Testament in terms of the history of Jesus Christ. Brevard Childs agrees with Barr on this but criticizes him on the grounds that he has not got to the heart of the theological problem related to biblical typology (Childs, *Biblical Theology*, 13–14). I agree with Childs on this, and one fundamental rationale behind my chapter is that the philosophy of language can get to the heart of the theological problem, which is precisely that of Christian truth-claims.

coming Christ were sought throughout the Old Testament, and with the life of Christ already known to all, they were readily found'.[2] Since there is more than one kind of typological interpretation, I will focus on but one example of it, that of the typological relation between Christ as he is portrayed in the New Testament and Adam as portrayed in the Old Testament book of Genesis, and in particular in Genesis 3. My main objective will be to show how the philosophy of language – and indeed analytic philosophy – might be able to cast new light on the rationality or otherwise of this particular example of typological interpretation. It is central to Christian theology that the Gospels affirm a historical truth-telling narrative that narrates the history of God in Christ going to the cross in order to reconcile the world to Him. Central also is that Christ does this in obedience to the Father – without ever succumbing to temptation. One of the primary tenets of Christian theology is that Christ atoned for sin as it is ascribed to Adam and the rest of the human race in Genesis 3 (however the relation between Adam and the human race is to be understood). Stated in this way, the rationale for the relation is relatively unproblematic, appearing to involve only truth-claims about what it is Christ accomplished, without any presumption that the Old Testament itself contains in some sense a Christological dimension. However, what is more problematic, especially for critical scholarship, is precisely this latter, namely the assertion that the Old Testament – and Genesis 3 in particular – does *itself* manifest a Christological hermeneutic, independent of the New Testament. It is this that I wish to examine. Specifically, in the case of Adam and Christ, I want to argue that it was no less true in the historical context in which Genesis 3 was produced and written that the author of the text was speaking then and there about Jesus Christ – *even if one assumes that this was not part of the author's original intention.*[3] It seems to me that this indeed might well be one way in which one could

---

[2] Barr, *Old and New*, 139f.

[3] Throughout this chapter I use the phrase 'the author's original intention' and its variants as a means of making the assumption, along with mainstream historical-critical scholarship, that Jesus Christ was not part of the author's original intention. This does not mean that it would be irrational to claim that Jesus Christ was part of the author's original intention – in a prophetic sense inspired by the Holy Spirit, for example – but it is not the case with which I am concerned here. The case with which I am concerned is one which takes on board the Enlightenment premise that Christ was not part of the author's original intention – whether it is true or not – and investigates what might and might not follow from it. Specifically, I will be concerned with the question: whether it follows that the author of Genesis 3 could not have been speaking of Jesus Christ then and there even on this premise. I am also aware that the concept of the author's original intention may be an utterly anachronistic one, given the nature of the transmission process behind the literary or redactional layers of the text; but again the point is to assume – for the sake of the argument – the premises of the classic Enlightenment position.

rationally affirm that Paul's assertions about Christ and Adam in Romans 5:12–14 are true, and I would also argue that the same could be said about Mark 1:12ff. and also Matthew 4:1–11 and Luke 4:1–13 as regards the Adam-Christ typology.[4]

Some preliminary remarks. The philosophy of language like analytic philosophy in general is essentially a problem-solving discipline. Hence, the rationale of the chapter is to demonstrate the philosophy of language in action. Why might one think or even expect that the philosophy of language in this sense could help? There are at least two possible answers. The first concerns the impact the philosophy of language has had in its own field. The branch of philosophy known as the philosophy of language concerns itself ultimately with how careful attention to language – semantics, syntax, pragmatics – can be brought to bear on the resolution of fundamental philosophical problems (e.g. the relation between truth-claims and reality), and, as a result, engender new (and even *prima facie* paradoxical) philosophical understandings. In the latter respect, the philosophy of language has had some notable successes in undermining some of our most entrenched philosophical beliefs about what was possible or impossible, rational or irrational. To give one celebrated example, in the 1970s Saul Kripke proved that statements existed which though epistemically *a posteriori* were metaphysically necessary.[5] Hitherto it had been thought that one of the fundamental truths of analytic philosophy was that all *a posteriori* statements were metaphysically contingent and that therefore *a posteriori* necessary statements were impossible (and belief in them irrational). I well remember the excitement that Kripke's proof of his decidedly counterintuitive result generated among both teachers and students in an undergraduate philosophy class back in the seventies (Kripke also argued for the existence of *a priori* contingent truths but this created less of a stir, not least perhaps because such a conclusion was too counterintuitive even for those who now accepted *a posteriori* necessary truths!). Kripke's essentially metaphysical conclusions rode on the back of some radically innovative work in the theory of names and definite descriptions, an area in the philosophy of language that has remained vibrant to the present day. What was also implicit in his work was providing the exception to the rule. Instead of construing philosophy as concerned with imposing general inescapable principles on human thought, as in the manner of Kant, philosophy as practised by such as Kripke has been employed as a wickedly critical subversion of the status quo. However, this, among other things, should not be taken necessarily to mean a rejection of the less modern in favour of the

---

[4] I do not intend to pursue this conclusion in this chapter but I would argue that what I have to say may provide the premises on which to move towards it. For the special significance of Mark 1:12f., see Goppelt, *Typos*, 97–100.

[5] Kripke, *Naming and Necessity*.

more modern. Kripke uses his technical apparatus to reinstate one of Descartes' most famous theses: the duality of mind and body. The relevance of this point should not be lost in a chapter that understands itself as attempting a 'post-critical retrieval of a pre-critical mode of interpretation' (to use a phrase adapted from a recent essay by George Lindbeck).[6]

The second answer to the question why one might think or even expect that the philosophy of language could help is that a precedent already exists for the kind of impact that the philosophy of language might have in biblical hermeneutics. The precedent of which I speak is the impact that philosophy has already had on theological epistemology and in particular the rationality of Christian belief. The Enlightenment challenge to the rationality of Christian belief in God was that unless one had good reason for one's belief one ought to give it up.[7] In this context, the historical consequence of the apparent failure of traditional proofs for the existence of God was precisely a crisis of Christian theistic belief. In the face of the Enlightenment challenge, Reformed epistemologists have sought to reinstate the rationality of such belief on the grounds that belief in God can be justifiably be held to be a *properly basic belief*. Since a properly basic belief is a belief that is rational to hold *without basing it on any other belief*,[8] it is not a belief which one can provide good reason for (in the Enlightenment sense), other than demonstrating the rationality of holding it to be a basic belief.

Typological Interpretation in the Wake of Enlightenment Hermeneutics

The context to the problem of typological interpretation today originates in biblical hermeneutics in the age of the Enlightenment and the subsequent impact it had on future interpretation of the Bible in the nineteenth and twentieth centuries. According to both E.D. Hirsch and Werner Jeanrond, the theologian and biblical scholar Johann Salomo Semler (1725–1791) was the first German Protestant theologian to approach the Bible through the eyes of the historian of religion and of the critical explorer of history.[9] This meant among other things that *the main task of hermeneutics was to understand the texts as their authors had understood them*. As Jeanrond puts it, 'over and against the earlier pre-modern synchronistic text-understanding in the Protestant Orthodoxy, Semler demanded a diachronic reading of the biblical texts: what counts for the

---

[6] Lindbeck, 'Postcritical Canonical Interpretation'.
[7] See Wolterstorff, 'Migration', 38–81.
[8] See Audi, 'Direct Justification', 139–166.
[9] Jeanrond, *Theological Hermeneutics*, 39.

interpreter is the disclosure of the *sensus litteralis historicus* [i.e. the literal historical sense] of the biblical text'.[10] Jeanrond goes on:

> As a result of his historical-critical method of interpretation, Semler's view of the Old Testament differed significantly from that of his hermeneutical predecessors, including Martin Luther. Semler could no longer agree with the typological method of reading the Hebrew Scriptures. He denied that all these texts contained prophecies of Jesus Christ. He went so far as to state that certain Old Testament books contain nothing of the Word of God, such as, for instance, the historical books or *The Song of Songs*.[11]

Jeanrond summarizes Semler's impact as follows:

> Semler's contribution to theological hermeneutics was enormous. He exposed the Orthodox dogmatism and biblicism and demonstrated that a truly scientific theology must develop properly academic, i.e. rational and critical, methods of biblical interpretation. He insisted strongly that Christian theology is not a religious exercise but a rational discourse on Christian religion that operates according to a public and rational methodology.[12]

Semler's conclusion that the main task of critical biblical interpretation was to understand texts as their authors understood them has had ramifications to the present day. It is no exaggeration to say that the fundamental rationale behind the rejection of typological interpretation at the present time is that *such an interpretation was not part of the author's original intention*. This is the view that one finds, for example, in Barr's *Old and New in Interpretation: A Study of the Two Testaments*. For scholars such as Barr, loyal to the canons of the Enlightenment, the problem with typological interpretation was that instead of attending to the actual texts of the Hebrew scriptures and understanding them in accordance with their own communicative intentions,[13] typological interpreters 'forced

---

[10] Ibid., 39.

[11] Ibid., 40.

[12] Ibid., 42.

[13] It is no surprise that the fundamental rationale behind the view Barr holds with respect to typological interpretation is that held by mainstream critical theorists in hermeneutics in general. According to one such theorist, E.D. Hirsch, the reader of a text must be concerned to decode a text with a view to grasping and stating its clearly determined original meaning. See his *Validity in Interpretation*, a work supremely representative of the critical tradition in hermeneutics. To be sure, in his later works he also allows for the *significance* of a text in addition to its meaning (it is the latter which is identical with the author's original intention). But significance seems to be a question of the reader rather than of either the author, the text, or reality (see Vanhoozer, *Meaning*, 259–263).

these texts into the strait-jacket of their own theological presuppositions'.[14] According to Barr's understanding, typological interpretation is precisely that kind of interpretation in which 'the text is construed from the perspective of an outside system brought to bear upon it'.[15] For Barr, the aim of interpretation is to uncover the author's original intention as embodied in the *sensus historicus* and such an aim excludes *a priori* the kind of typological interpretation that one finds in the exegetical work of such as Luther and Calvin. According to such pre-modern exegetes one fundamental interpretative way of reading the Old and New Testament as one unitary continuous historical narrative was to make the earlier stories of the Old Testament figures or types of the later stories of the New Testament and of their events and patterns of meaning.[16] Typology was 'viewed as an extension of the literal sense of historical events in a subsequent adumbration and served to signal the correspondence between redemptive events in a single history of salvation'.[17] It was considered closely akin to prophecy and fulfilment and 'thought to be a major New Testament category in relating to the Old Testament'.[18] In the wake of the Enlightenment, it was deemed necessary to jettison typology and all its attendant apparatus on the grounds of the author's original intention and its immediate historical context.

The Enlightenment position on typological interpretation did not of course go unchallenged. In the twentieth century, in the wake of a resurgence of interest, the reasonableness of typology was affirmed by such as Lampe, von Rad, Eichrodt and H.W. Wolff.[19] Most significantly in our own era, very much in vogue in some areas of biblical interpretation are 'postmodern', 'post-structuralist', or 'intertextual' theories of reading. At their most radical, such readings insist that since all interpretation is misinterpretation, all readings are permissible. Moreover, Stanley Fish, one of the central figures in reader-response theory, has a negative answer to the question embodied in the title of his book *Is There a Text in this Class?* which might seem to validate any and all typological interpretation regardless of the individual merits of the case, in particular, in spite of the author's original intention.[20]

Depending on one's definition of rationality, one could argue that 'postmodern' reader-response interpretation of the Bible affirms the rationality

---

[14] Jeanrond, *Theological Hermeneutics*, 19.

[15] Childs, *Biblical Theology*, 14.

[16] Frei, *Eclipse*, 2ff.

[17] Childs, *Biblical Theology*, 13.

[18] Ibid.

[19] Lampe, 'Reasonableness', 9–38; von Rad, *Old Testament Theology*; idem, 'Typological Interpretation', 17–39; Eichrodt, 'Typological Exegesis', 224–245; Wolff, 'Hermeneutics', 160–199.

[20] Fish, *Text*.

of typological interpretation even though it was not part of the author's original intention. This chapter attempts to affirm the same conclusion though clearly without invoking theories such as Fish's. What I want to offer is a rational 'analytic' justification for what, as I have said before, is 'a post-critical retrieval' of a particular 'pre-critical mode of interpretation'. The rationale takes the following theological shape. Brevard Childs has criticized Barr's analysis – typical of much modern critical analysis – on the grounds that it has failed to get 'to the heart of the theological problem relating to typology'.[21] Childs suggests that 'the issue turns on the nature of the biblical referent and the effort of both the Old and New Testament authors to extend their experience of God through figuration in order to depict the unity of God's one purpose'.[22] He criticizes Barr for failing to 'deal adequately with the theological claim of an ontological as well as soteriological unity of the two testaments'.[23] In his concluding remark on the matter he claims that the 'conformity of the two testaments cannot be correctly understood as merely lying at the level of culture, tradition, and religion'.[24] I have no doubt that Childs is right in what he says. In particular, his rejection of the thesis that the unity of the Old and New Testament is explicable by 'culture, tradition, and religion' is doubtless, among other things, a shot across the bows of reader-response theory.

One of the principal lessons of M.H. Abrams's seminal work *The Mirror and the Lamp* is that any adequate theory of interpretation has to be understood in terms of what can be called 'the hermeneutical matrix': the 'author-text-reality-reader' matrix.[25] Though each category in the matrix constituted one of the categories Abrams deemed necessary for interpretation, Abrams was aware that, historically at least, almost all theories had exhibited a discernible orientation towards one only. Reader-response theory would be an example of a theory that emphasizes the 'reader' category at the expense of the other three. Lest I be accused of seeking to emphasize the 'reality' or 'truth' category in this respect, I should make it clear that, in taking up the train of thought such as one finds in Childs on the importance of the biblical referent (rather than simply reference itself), I am simply seeking to redress a certain imbalance regarding the category of truth in the matter of interpretation, and biblical interpretation in particular. What I want to do in the following section is show how the philosophy of language might demonstrate the central importance of the matter of the truth of Christian truth-claims – matters ontological as it were – as regards the validity of typological interpretation. In particular, in the context of certain

---

[21] Childs, *Biblical Theology*, 14.
[22] Ibid.
[23] Ibid.
[24] Ibid.
[25] Abrams, *Mirror*, 3–29.

fundamental distinctions in the philosophy of language, the question I want to pose is whether it could be rational to affirm a typological interpretation of Genesis 3 even though the Adam-Christ typology was clearly not part of the author's original intention. How might certain tools of the philosophy of language be brought to bear on this question?

The Philosophy of Language: Meaning, Reference and Referents

A working definition of language that I hope is uncontroversial: language is a *system of communication*. First of all it is a *system* of communication in the sense that it has a finite though evolving vocabulary – or words – and in the sense that it has a finite set of syntactic rules that combine the words in grammatical order to give us sentences. The study of this system is the province of *semantics* – lexical meaning – and of *syntax* – grammatical rules. Second, it is a system of *communication* in that the system – or part thereof – is *used* to make many different kinds of communication. By that I mean the many varied uses to which language can be put. This is the province technically of what is called *pragmatics*: the study of language use. Ludwig Wittgenstein listed a number of uses to which language is typically put in his *Philosophical Investigations*: obeying and giving orders, describing the appearances of objects, giving measurements, constructing an object from a description, reporting an event, speculating about an event, forming and testing a hypothesis, presenting the results of experiments in tables and diagrams, making up stories, acting plays, singing songs, guessing riddles, telling jokes, translating from one language to another, asking, thanking, cursing, greeting and praying.[26]

The concepts of meaning and use point to an important distinction in the study of language, one that has taken on philosophical significance in the hands of philosophers in the twentieth century in the resolution and clarification of philosophical problems. The twentieth century has been characterized as the century in which philosophy took a 'linguistic turn'. If philosophy of the seventeenth, eighteenth and nineteenth centuries can be characterized as dominated by the theme of *ideas* – those things that we apparently have in our head and communicate to others – then it is true to say that fundamental to much philosophy in the twentieth century has been the philosophy of *language*.[27] Indeed, with the work of the later Wittgenstein and the so-called neo-Wittgensteinians – most notably in theology that of D.Z. Phillips – the

---

[26] Wittgenstein, *Philosophical Investigations*, §23.

[27] See Hacking, *Language*, for an account of philosophy as an enquiry into ideas and as an enquiry into language.

concepts of meaning and use became central to much philosophy of religious language. Wittgenstein in particular is credited with the saying that for many words in our language their meaning is the use to which they are put. In other words, meaning is reducible to language use. But it may be just as valid if not more illuminating to say that very often the use of language coincides with – is identical with – the system of lexical meaning and syntax that is embodied in that which we call a language and its conventions, which is to say that the phenomenon of language exists objectively prior to its use by us. We, so to speak, come along and use it – use it in ways which coincide with this pre-existing meaning as embodied in the system of semantics, but also use it in ways which do not. Nevertheless, even in the latter case, usage still exploits the pre-existent meaning. What I have in mind here, for example, is the distinction between literal usage of language which coincides with the pre-existent meaning inhering in the system of language itself, and metaphorical usage, where the use is other than the meaning (though more often than not reliant on it). Not every philosopher locates metaphor at the level of use rather than meaning but it is fair to say that this has been the conclusion of some of the most influential philosophers of language.[28]

How should the distinction between meaning and use be accommodated within the 'author-text-reality-reader' matrix? In Abrams's matrix, an author may *use* a *system* of communication – in this case the conventions: semantic, syntactic, generic – to speak about *reality* to the reader. Let me break this down further to hasten the point of relevance for biblical hermeneutics. Let us suppose that the author uses a system of communication to mean (or to refer to) someone or something – the referent – in the 'reality' category. He or she uses the system of communication to mean someone in the real world, for example. He or she says, for instance, 'There's Jones sweeping leaves,' meaning, of course, Jones. If the person turns out to be Jones then one can say that (1) whom he or she meant is identical with whom he or she is in actual fact speaking of. If the person turns out to be someone else – that it turns out in actual fact to be Robinson for example – then one should say that (2) whom he or she meant was other than the person he or she was in actual fact talking of.[29] What is

---

[28] Notwithstanding their disagreements on other matters, Davidson, in his *Inquiries into Truth and Interpretation*, and Dummett, in his *The Seas of Language*, agree that metaphor is a matter of use and not meaning and so strictly speaking there is no such thing as metaphorical meaning. Simile too is a matter of use but a matter where the use coincides with the meaning: Jones is like a pig (simile) means what it literally says: its use coincides with its meaning. In contrast, Jones is a pig (metaphor) does not: it is used to say other than what it means according to our pre-existent system. Used metaphorically it does not mean what it literally says since Jones is not literally a pig!

[29] One can use words and indeed sentences to mean what they mean or one can use words and sentences to mean other than what they mean.

crucial to note is that whether (1) or (2) is true does not depend on who is meant (which is the same in both). Rather it depends on what is in actual fact true. This assertion is of crucial relevance for what I want to say about the importance of Christian truth-claims as regards typological interpretation in the context of the hermeneutical matrix. Let me now look at (1).

The case of (1) takes its point of departure from relatively recent work on the theory of names and of definite descriptions as found in the work of, for example, Keith Donnellan and the philosopher whom I cited in the introduction, Saul Kripke. In an extremely influential article entitled 'Reference and Definite Descriptions'[30] Donnellan brought the distinction between *that whom one means* and *that whom one is speaking about or referring to* – the *referent* of one's utterance – to bear on the theory of definite descriptions. (A definite description is a description that uniquely identifies the individual in question from a range of possible individuals. For example, 'the inventor of bifocals' can be used uniquely to identify the person of Benjamin Franklin as in 'Benjamin Franklin was the inventor of bifocals.') Donnellan distinguished between the 'referential' and 'attributive' uses of a definite description.[31] He gives the example of a person making the claim that 'Jones's murderer is insane,' meaning Smith, when it turns out to be another person, Robinson, who murdered Jones. The person means Smith but is in fact referring to Robinson since in actual fact Robinson is the referent of the definite description 'Jones's murderer' ('the man who murdered Jones') and not Smith. *The actual referent of the description is Robinson even though the description is attributed to Smith.* The point is that the person is speaking of other than whom they originally meant or intended. And the reason this is true is that it turns out to be true that Robinson murdered Jones and not Smith.

Following on from the work of Donnellan, Kripke employs the same distinction between *that which one means* and *that which one is speaking about or referring to* in his theory of names. Kripke writes:

> 'Two men glimpse someone at a distance and think they recognise him as Jones. 'What is Jones doing?' 'Raking the leaves.' If the distant leaf-raker is actually Smith then in some sense they are *referring* to Smith, even though they both use 'Jones' *as a name of* Jones.'[32]

---

[30] Donnellan, 'Reference', 281–304; see also Linsky, 'Reference'.

[31] For the purposes of clarification one should understand that if the person meant is identical with the person spoken of, then it follows that the attributive use of a definite description is identical with the referential use. But if the person actually spoken of is other than the person meant then we say that the attributive use is other than the referential use.

[32] Kripke, *Naming and Necessity*, 25.

Kripke says that though the two mean the person Jones – Jones is part of their original intention – it turns out that they are actually speaking about Smith. Moreover, what makes it the case that they are speaking about Smith is that it turns out to be true that it is Smith who is raking the leaves. The truth-claim that it is Smith who is raking the leaves is true. He is the real referent of the utterance. In other words, those who made the utterance 'There's Jones raking leaves' are speaking of other than whom they originally and intentionally meant. What this example demonstrates, like Donnellan's, is that one can be speaking of other than whom one originally and intentionally meant.

In other words: though a particular person is not part of an author's original intention *it does not follow* that they could not be speaking of this person. *This seems to me to be a conclusion worth stating in juxtaposition to the tradition of theological hermeneutics since the Enlightenment.* It seems to me that the critical tradition in theological hermeneutics originating in Semler and culminating in such as Barr and Hirsch has taken it for granted that if someone is not part of the original intention then it follows that this person cannot be part of the interpretation of the text. According to the philosophy of language this inference is false.

The Adam-Christ Typology

It is of course case (2) that is of greater interest here. Granted that Donnellan's and Kripke's respective examples demonstrate that one could be speaking of someone even though they were not part of the original intention, it is clear that their examples work on the presupposition that the original intention was not satisfied in reality. The individuals in question meant other than whom they spoke of precisely because they held a belief that turned out to be false. They made a mistake because reality was other than they took it to be. If we were to apply this to the case of Genesis 3 we would seem compelled to say that though the author thought he was speaking of Adam – this is what he meant – he was not speaking of Adam, he was in actual fact speaking of Jesus Christ. But surely we don't want to say this? Rather, we want to say that the author of Genesis 3 was *speaking of whom he meant*: that whom he meant and whom he was speaking of were the same, or, in other words, whom he was speaking of was identical with whom he meant, not other than whom he meant. (*Inter alia* this means that we affirm the discrete witness of the Old Testament in this instance.[33])

---

[33] I would suggest that to say that one means Adam but is not speaking about Adam, but rather Jesus Christ, breaks with this commitment. But more than that I would not want to say at present.

I said earlier that whether (1) or (2) above is true does not depend on who is meant. Rather it depends on what is in actual fact true. The general moral transposed to the realm of Christian theology is this: If we understand Christian theology fundamentally as about Christian truth-claims then, in the context of the hermeneutical matrix, it is what turns out to be true Christian doctrine – as opposed to false – that determines whether the author of Genesis 3 is speaking about Jesus Christ or not. One Christian doctrine that would satisfy the criterion is any doctrine that implied that *Adam is included in, encompassed by, incorporated into, the person of Jesus Christ.* For clearly, even though the author of Genesis 3 was speaking of whom he meant it is also true that he was speaking of Jesus Christ, *even though this was not part of his original intention.* The author of Genesis was speaking of Jesus Christ even though he did not mean Jesus Christ, and even though he was also speaking of whom he meant. Included in what was originally meant by 'Adam' (with the definite article) in chapter 3 – 'the man' (and indeed 'the first man') – is the temptation, disobedience and fall of humankind. The constraint of Christian truth-claims becomes precisely that set of doctrines which entail that the first man (whosoever this man is, though it appears he is later given the proper name 'Adam' in Genesis chapter 5) is included in, encompassed by, incorporated into, the person of Jesus Christ.

One such doctrine is affirmed by Karl Barth in the *Church Dogmatics.* I do not argue that it is the only position that succeeds in this respect. I cite it as one possible example, for the purposes of exposition. For Barth the sole point of departure for Christian truth-claims is the resurrection appearances history which, he argues, tell us that, first, the man Jesus reveals himself in the mode of God, reveals himself as the eternal God.[34] To this he adds the claim that, secondly, the result of the man Jesus' self-revelation is that he reveals himself in identity with the one the disciples had encountered in the pre-Easter history as the one who had been crucified, dead and buried.[35] Therefore, according to Barth, God was (ontologically and not merely functionally) in Christ in the pre-Easter history. Or to put it another way, the man Jesus reveals himself as God and therefore is God, the eternal God, and in particular the eternal Son of God. The one the disciples had encountered in the pre-Easter history as the one who had been crucified, dead, and buried reveals himself to be God. Therefore the pre-Easter Jesus is God incarnate. From this Barth makes a further inference:

What became and is in the divine act of the incarnation is, of course, a man. It is the man Jesus of Nazareth. But its object, that which God assumed into unity with

---

[34] Barth, *Church Dogmatics* 4.2, 447.
[35] Ibid., 144–145.

Himself and His being and essence and kind and nature, is not 'a man', i.e. one of many who existed and was actual with all his fellow-men in a human being and essence and nature and kind as opposed to other creatures, but who was and is also this one man as opposed to other men. For this would necessarily mean either that the Son of God, surrendering His own existence as such, had changed Himself into this man, and was therefore no longer the Son of God . . . Or that He did not exist as One but in a duality, as the Son of God maintaining His own existence, and somewhere and somehow alongside this individual man.[36]

Barth's argument is clearly recognizable as an example of classical deductive logic. If God had assumed into identity with himself 'a man' then it would logically follow 'either that the Son of God, surrendering His own existence as such, had changed Himself into this man, and was therefore no longer the Son of God . . . Or that He did not exist as One but in a duality, as the Son of God maintaining His own existence, and somewhere and somehow alongside this individual man.'[37] But since both logical consequences are untenable according to Barth, it must follow that the antecedent proposition from which these consequent propositions follow is false too.[38] It is false that God assumed into identity with himself 'a man'. Therefore it follows that that which God assumed into unity with himself is the 'essence of man'.[39] What Barth means is that God incarnate is God assuming into unity with himself 'man' in the generic sense rather a specific instantiation of the generic sense, i.e. a specific man or individual. It is on these grounds that Barth feels compelled to affirm the distinction between *enhypostatos* and *anhypostatos*. This is the doctrinal apparatus which affirms, in continuity with Alexandrian Christology, that the hypostasis or identity of Jesus Christ *enhypostatized* an essentially *anhypostatic* human nature. In contrast to a position that holds that the Word became a particular human being with their own hypostasis, such a doctrine holds that the humanity of Christ has no independent hypostatic existence apart from

---

[36] Ibid., 48–49.

[37] Ibid., 49. An example of the former position would be that of the neo-Lutheran kenotic Christology of Gottfried Thomasius in which God changed into the man Jesus and in doing so ceased to be God. The fifth century Antiochene theologian Nestorius was charged (probably wrongly) with the latter affirmation.

[38] The principle of logical reasoning is in fact one known as *modus tollendo tollens*: if p then q; not-q; therefore not-p. A simple example would be as follows: if Jones is six feet tall then he is taller than five feet; Jones is not taller than five feet; therefore Jones is not six feet tall.

[39] Barth appears to make the assumption that the two alternatives – God assuming into unity with himself 'a man' or God assuming into unity with himself 'man' in the generic sense – are logically exhaustive. I have not the space to examine whether this assumption is correct. I merely present it descriptively as Barth's argument and assume it as a premise in mine.

the hypostasis that is the Son of God. The terms *anhypostatos* and *enhypostatos* affirm the Chalcedonian formula 'in two natures' but interpret it along lines that preserve the Alexandrian emphasis on the priority of the person of the Son of God and the unity of the Son of God made flesh. To be sure, the humanity of Christ has to have a hypostasis but it does not have to have its own hypostasis. Its hypostasis is the hypostasis that is the Son of God.[40] It is because of this logic that Barth understands the reconciliation of humankind to God as an event accomplished by God himself *for all human beings* in the obedience of the Son of God even unto death on the cross.[41] The movement of God toward the cross is also the movement of 'man' reconciled by God to God:

> The atonement as it took place in Jesus Christ is the one inclusive event of this going out of the Son of God and this coming in of the Son of Man . . . It was God who went into the far country and it was man who returns home. Both took place in the one Jesus Christ. It is not therefore a matter of two different and successive actions, but of a single action in which each of the two elements is related to the other and can be known and understood only in this relationship: the going out of God only as it aims at the coming in of man; the coming in of man only as the reach and out-working of the going out of God.[42]

But since this 'coming in of man' is man in the generic sense, included in man is every man, or more properly, every human being. *And this includes the first man, 'Adam'.* As Barth puts it in *Church Dogmatics* 4.1, Adam is 'first among equals' (*primus inter pares*) as sinful man[43] and is included along with us in the essence of human nature which God assumed into identity with himself in the incarnation and which essence God restores to covenant with himself in Jesus Christ's obedience even unto death on the cross. There is only one human being, Barth argues, who is obedient to God – the man Jesus who is a specific man but only as he is the Son of God. Since humanity is included in Jesus' obedience, it follows that sinful humanity is obedient to God in the person of Jesus Christ. That, in broad outline, is Barth's theology of reconciliation.

---

[40] See Lang, 'Anhypostatos-Enhypostatos', 630–657, for a comprehensive account of the history of the terms.

[41] Barth prefers 'reconciliation' as his primary category for atonement, emphasizing the sense of exchange that is involved in it: it is God who went into the far country and it is fallen man who returns home. Both, as Barth says, took place in the one Jesus Christ (*Church Dogmatics* 4.2, 21).

[42] Ibid., 21. Barth understands 'Son of Man' as man in the generic sense. Jesus Christ 'became and is the Son of Man only because and as the Son of God took human essence and gave it existence and actuality in and by Himself' (ibid., 71).

[43] Barth, *Church Dogmatics* 4.1, 509.

The manner in which this position moves the conclusion that the author of Genesis 3 was speaking of Jesus Christ, even though it was not his intention to speak of him, should be obvious. Since Adam, along with every other fallen human being is included in the person of Jesus Christ (and Barth argues that it is in the person of Jesus Christ that we are united with Adam rather than through the inheritance of original sin from him),[44] it follows that the author of Genesis 3 can be said to have been speaking about Jesus Christ – and this is so (to get back to the main issue) even though it was not part of his original intention, even though he did not mean this at the time.[45] My conclusion? One may make the provisional claim that the philosophy of language – in conjunction with the right kinds of ontological Christian truth-claims – may well provide one particular rational means of affirming one particular example of typological interpretation.

What I hope is that I have had some measure of success in developing Childs's view that typology constitutes 'a theological claim of an ontological as well as soteriological unity of the two testaments' which therefore lies beyond 'the level of culture, tradition, and religion'.[46] I hope I have also done some justice to his thesis that 'the issue turns on the nature of the biblical referent'.[47] It may be this that ultimately justifies what he refers to as 'the effort of both the Old and New Testament authors to extend their experience of God through figuration in order to depict the unity of God's one purpose.'[48]

Have I retrieved in post-critical fashion a particular pre-critical mode of interpretation, namely typological interpretation? Typological interpretation of the Bible as 'a specific kind of allegorical interpretation of the Old Testament', namely a reading of the Old Testament based on the 'presupposition that the whole of the Old Testament looks beyond itself for its interpretation'?[49] Typology 'viewed as an extension of the literal sense of

---

[44] Ibid., 499–511.

[45] Under which conditions would Genesis 3 not be speaking about Jesus Christ? One condition: one would not be speaking about Jesus Christ if Adam is not included in, encompassed by, incorporated into, Jesus Christ. But if Jesus Christ is necessarily (to use Karl Barth's evocative phrase) 'the Son of the God who went into the far country' in order to reconcile humanity to himself then it follows that one would not be speaking about Jesus Christ if no one went this way. Therefore one would not be speaking about Jesus Christ if he had not 'gone into the far country' in order to reconcile sinful humanity to God.

[46] Childs, *Biblical Theology*, 14.

[47] Ibid.

[48] Ibid.

[49] Barr, *Old and New*, 139f.

historical events in a subsequent adumbration and served to signal the correspondence between redemptive events in a single history of salvation'?[50] Have I affirmed a synchronic over a diachronic reading? The answer, I think, is a qualified yes. In particular, if the author of Genesis 3 was speaking of Jesus Christ then and there, as it were, then one might want to say that this implies a synchronic reading (though perhaps my post-critical retrieval refuses to recognize the debate in these terms). But the reading is one that would concur with one of Childs's other principal concerns, namely the discrete witness of the Old Testament, or as another who himself has continued Childs's project has put it, the 'abiding theological witness of the Old Testament'.[51]

Conclusion

Is there a greater moral to my chapter than that the philosophy of language can provide grounds for the rationality of a certain species of typological interpretation? I think there is. The moral of the story is not that philosophy, and the philosophy of language in particular, challenges Hamlet's assertion that 'there are more things in heaven and earth than are dreamt of in your philosophy, Horatio' (though I seem to recall a successful refutation from the mind of Bertrand Russell!). Rather, the moral is that there may well be more in philosophy – and consequently to rationality – than is dreamt of by some theologians and biblical scholars. Theologians and biblical scholars are sometimes unaware of the linguistic distinctions that philosophers deem essential to an understanding of philosophical and especially metaphysical questions, questions of truth. One of the legacies of the 'linguistic turn' in philosophy which began in earnest with Frege, and persisted in Wittgenstein, and later in Quine, Davidson and Kripke, is that it has sought to show that such distinctions matter a great deal as regards extending the limits of rational thought, and that to ignore or neglect them is precisely to limit oneself in the arena of critical argument. Arguably, practitioners of biblical and theological hermeneutics are relatively indifferent or sceptical toward what philosophy, and the philosophy of language in particular, can achieve in the area of biblical interpretation. If so, I think that this state of affairs is gradually changing. I hope to have given some further reasons for thinking that it ought to.

---

[50]   Childs, *Biblical Theology*, 14.
[51]   Seitz, *Word*.

Bibliography

Abrams, M.H., *The Mirror and the Lamp: Romantic Theory and the Critical Tradition* (Oxford: Oxford University Press, 1953)

Audi, R., 'Direct Justification, Evidential Dependence, Theistic Belief' in idem and W.J. Wainwright (eds.), *Rationality, Religious Belief, and Moral Commitment: New Essays in the Philosophy of Religion* (Ithaca: Cornell University Press, 1986), 139–166

Barr, J., *Old and New in Interpretation: A Study of the Two Testaments* (London: SCM Press, 1966)

Barth, K., *Church Dogmatics*, 4 vols. (Edinburgh: T. & T. Clark, 1956–76)

Childs, B.S., *Biblical Theology of the Old and New Testaments* (London: SCM Press, 1992)

Davidson, D., *Inquiries into Truth and Interpretation* (Oxford: Clarendon Press, 1984)

Donnellan, K., 'Reference and Definite Descriptions', *Philosophical Review* 75 (1966), 281–304

Dummett, M., *The Seas of Language* (Oxford: Clarendon Press, 1993)

Eichrodt, W., 'Is Typological Exegesis an Appropriate Method?' in C. Westermann (ed.), *Essays in Old Testament Interpretation* (London: SCM Press, 1963), 224–245

Fish, S., *Is There a Text in This Class? The Authority of Interpretative Communities* (Cambridge, MA.: Harvard University Press, 1980)

Frei, H.W., *The Eclipse of Biblical Narrative: A Study in Eighteenth and Nineteenth Century Hermeneutics* (New Haven: Yale University Press, 1974)

Goppelt, L., *Typos: The Typological Interpretation of the Old Testament in the New* (Grand Rapids: Eerdmans, 1982)

Hacking, I., *Why Does Language Matter to Philosophy?* (Cambridge: Cambridge University Press, 1975)

Hirsch, E.D., Jr., *Validity in Interpretation* (New Haven: Yale University Press, 1967)

Jeanrond, W., *Theological Hermeneutics: Development and Significance* (London: SCM Press, 1994)

Kripke, S.A., *Naming and Necessity* (Oxford: Basil Blackwell, 1980)

Lampe, G.W.H., 'The Reasonableness of Typology' in idem and K.J. Woolcombe, *Essays in Typology* (SBT, 22; London: SCM Press, 1957), 9–38

Lang, U.M., 'Anhypostatos-Enhypostatos: Church Fathers, Protestant Orthodoxy and Karl Barth', *JTS* 49 (1988), 630–657

Lindbeck, G.A., 'Postcritical Canonical Interpretation: Three Modes of Retrieval', in C.R. Seitz and K. Greene-McCreight (eds.), *Theological Exegesis: Essays in Honor of Brevard S. Childs* (Grand Rapids: Eerdmans, 1999), 26–51

Linsky, L., 'Reference and Referents' in C.E. Caton (ed.), *Philosophy and Ordinary Language* (Urbana: University of Illinois Press, 1963), 74–78

Prestige, G.L., *God in Patristic Thought* (London: SPCK, 1952^2)

Rad, G. von, *Old Testament Theology*, 2 vols. (London: SCM Press, 1962, 1965)

—, 'Typological Interpretation of the Old Testament' in C. Westermann (ed.), *Essays in Old Testament Interpretation* (London: SCM Press, 1963), 17–39

Seitz, C.R., *Word Without End: The Old Testament as Abiding Theological Witness* (Grand Rapids: Eerdmans, 1998)

Vanhoozer, K.J., *Is There a Meaning in This Text? The Bible, the Reader, and the Morality of Literary Knowledge* (Leicester: Apollos, 1998)

Wittgenstein, L., *Philosophical Investigations* (Oxford: Basil Blackwell, 1953)

Wolff, H.W., 'The Hermeneutics of the Old Testament' in C. Westermann (ed.), *Essays in Old Testament Interpretation* (London: SCM Press, 1963), 160–199

Wolterstorff, N., 'The Migration of the Theistic Arguments: From Natural Theology to Evidentialist Apologetics' in R. Audi and W.J. Wainwright (eds.), *Rationality, Religious Belief, and Moral Commitment: New Essays in the Philosophy of Religion* (Ithaca: Cornell University Press, 1986), 38–81

8

A Response to Neil B. MacDonald

Mary B. Hesse

I will comment on two main themes in MacDonald's paper. First he argues for the usefulness of techniques of analytic philosophy in approaching problems of biblical hermeneutics, and secondly he applies this to the classic method of *typology*, particularly the view that Adam according to the author of Genesis is a *type* of Christ.

I am not competent to make an informed judgment on his account of various traditional discussions of biblical interpretation, but I want to appauld his effort to take a middle way between two extremes found there. First, the Enlightenment and modernist view is that all texts should be understood as the author intended them, in which case typology has to be abandoned – the author of Genesis 3 cannot have *intended* to speak of Christ. Second, the postmodernist view is that each reader's interpretation of a text is as good as any other, in which case any sort of typological interpretation would do, depending on the reader. I also heartily accept his, and Professor Childs's, further objection to both extremes, namely that they fail to take seriously the *ontological* context within which any sort of typology must be defended. That is to say, whether or not Adam is a type of Christ, and in what sense, must depend on what is understood to be the Christian truth to which both Testaments bear witness.

At this point, however, I begin to have difficulties. Following his aim to use the tools of analytic philosophy, MacDonald introduces Donnellan's influential analysis of meaning and reference, in which a distinction is made between 'what one means' (as purely linguistic) and 'what one is speaking about' (i.e. in reality). I say 'There's Jones in the garden', meaning my friend Jones, but in reality I am mistaken and it is Robinson in the garden. Summarizing MacDonald's point very crudely, he wishes to apply this analysis to say: Genesis 3 meant (intended) to speak of Adam getting up to various things, but in light of Christian truth it is in fact Jesus Christ who was actually being and doing these things (presumably not all but at least some of them) although of course the author could not have intended to say this.[1]

My first difficulty is a general one about analytic philosophy, namely that the examples taken in that genre are usually so uncomplicated that it is initially implausible to suppose that they could throw light on such profound and complex issues as the ontology and typology implied in the Old and New Testaments. One source of my intuitive dismissal of this possibility is the presupposition of practically all current analytic philosophy that (as MacDonald summarizes earlier in his paper) meaning in language is literal and univocal, and forms a pre-existing communication system within which any particular utterance must be understood. It follows from this that extensions, innovations and metaphors which are constantly coined in actual communication, let alone in constructive metaphysics, are not meaningful in this sense. But if anything requires an analysis of such linguistic meaning-changes throughout a complex and difficult text like the Bible, surely the notion of typology above all requires it.

More specifically, the distinction of meaning and reference is something required in the analytic context to bolster the initial presupposition of a pre-existing semantic system which is independent of the truth-value of propositions stated within it. I have difficulty therefore in seeing how this distinction can do more than give us the purely *negative* conclusion that MacDonald correctly draws in his paper. This is that *it does not follow* that Genesis 3 was not speaking truly about Christ when it purports to be speaking about Adam. But neither does it follow that Genesis 3 was not speaking about, say, the Great Khan or Karl Marx. What we need, as MacDonald rightly says, is some (Christian) ontology according to which 'Adam is *included in, encompassed by, incorporated into, the person of Jesus Christ*'.[2] If we had this, then some (but surely not all) the things said about Adam may really be true only of Christ.

This is where the real meat of the problem of typology lies, and it is interestingly explored in the latter part of the paper. Here profound and complex Christologies are introduced, which might give us the doctrine needed to make sense of the typology. More about these in a moment. But the trouble with using examples from analytic philosophy is that they force us at this point to ask niggling questions such as: Do we want to say that Genesis 3 was *mistaken* in purportedly speaking of Adam, as I was mistaken in saying and meaning 'Jones'? Adam was (is) certainly the denizen of a potent myth within which the

---

[1] Note that it is irrelevant to this argument whether Adam was a historical or a mythological figure.

[2] His italics.

notion of a 'mistake' about the real world is not applicable, but he might perhaps also have been a real historical figure who did at least some of the things ascribed in Genesis, and therefore Genesis was not wholly mistaken. Neither of these possibilities detracts from the suggested typology. More importantly, a typology seems to require something in common or analogous between Adam and Christ. What property of Christ is it that was true of him and not (or not only) of Adam in Genesis 3? Again, the Jones/Robinson example does not quite work, because for all we know there may be no properties in common between those two, except that something made me mistake one for the other.[3]

What initially emerges from a naïve reading of Genesis 3 and some other relevant biblical texts, is the *contrast* between Adam and Christ. They are rather antitypes than types: 'As in Adam all die, even so in Christ shall all be made alive' (1 Cor. 15:22) – the important element is the contrast of life and death, although there is also an analogy in that the consequences of the actions of both are for all mankind. But Christ did not fall into temptation, the ground was not cursed for his sake, etc., etc. The only property appealed to by MacDonald on which to base the type, appears to be that (metaphorically) both went into 'a far country', both were *scapegoats*, although it is specifically *not* said of Adam that he, being sinless, atoned for the sin of humankind in his exile. These sorts of question leave Jones and Robinson far behind, and require us to look more carefully at the ontological presupposition that MacDonald identifies as necessary for the Adam/Christ typology to work.

The presupposition is that 'Adam (in the generic sense, i.e. as embodying all humankind) is included in . . . the person of Jesus Christ'. Incidentally, this is surely not a proposition whose meaning can be analysed in terms of a pre-existing structure of English or any other natural language system. Be that as it may, it is a bearer of rich and thought-provoking metaphor and metaphysics. MacDonald cashes it out in terms of two classic Christologies. What he calls the Alexandrian position postulates (I paraphrase here) a substance of Christ which from eternity transforms essential or substantial human nature (the generic Adam) into itself. This seems to imply (from all eternity?) that the Fall, the curse of God, etc., are overcome and discarded as some kind of *accidental* properties of humankind.[4] The other position, which surely has been closer to that of traditional orthodoxy, is that Jesus Christ came as a particular human being, who in his life and death sinlessly atoned for all humankind. In the first case some sense of typology is retained at the cost of an ontology which is difficult to articulate in modern philosophical concepts and sounds very near to heresy. In the second case the sense of 'type' becomes a generalizable analogy between the

---

[3] This possibility even echoes the extreme postmodern view that anything the observer takes to be, is.

[4] This would come very close to saying sin is unreal.

many 'scapegoats' and 'suffering servants' of religious history. Such analogies undoubtedly need rational scrutiny, but analytic philosophy has presuppositions about univocal meaning which prevent it from developing a relevant analysis of the metaphoric language.

Doubtless this argument will go on, and it is in just such considerations that a modern hermeneutics for typology is most urgent and most difficult. If 'typology' has anything to say to a spiritual interpretation of the Bible for the millennium, then these questions have to be addressed in theologically intelligible terms, and analytic philosophy is not going to take us past a first, comparatively trivial step.

9

Renewing Historical Criticism

Karl Möller

Introduction

In his response to the consultation, Brueggemann noted that the problem of historical criticism did not generate great passion among participants, and that that might have been so because all were basically agreed that while historical-critical study of the Bible 'is problematic we cannot do without it'.[1] This view is shared by an increasing number of scholars who would affirm the principal value of historical criticism while at the same time contending that we urgently need to move away from the preoccupation with nothing but historical questions. Seitz, for instance, has protested that historical questions have taken on 'a life of their own, and run today virtually on autopilot',[2] and that, as a consequence, theological questions have receded 'as the discipline . . . simply never ceased to find new historical questions to occupy itself with'.[3] Tragically, one might say, 'entire careers have been spent doing nothing but dating the Yahwist and refining and further refining our look at this author'.[4] The upshot of all this has been the replacement of theology by tradition history so that we are now dealing with 'theology in-the-making' rather than with biblical theology.[5]

Seitz's answer to what he identifies as 'a crisis in approach and method of the most basic sort'[6] involves the deployment of the canonical approach as

---

[1] Cf. Brueggemann's contribution to this volume.
[2] Seitz, *Word*, 10; cf. also 33, 107.
[3] Ibid., 18.
[4] Ibid., 32.
[5] Ibid., 7.
[6] Ibid., 78.

developed by Childs.[7] While not being particularly keen on historical-critical study, which 'plays no positive theological role whatsoever',[8] Seitz does regard it as a necessary preliminary with a preparatory function.[9] Thus, a canonical approach builds upon historical-critical achievements, beginning 'with the recognition that biblical books have diverse origins and a complex history of development before their final shape is achieved'.[10] Commenting on the approach adopted by Childs in his Exodus commentary,[11] Seitz furthermore notes that in Childs's estimate the historical-critical methods 'were not wrong, but were being put to wrong use',[12] a view with which Seitz seems to agree. As far as the future task of historical criticism is concerned, Seitz urges that it should do what it does best. That is to say, it should 'restrict itself to the task of spotting repugnance, of showing how it is that the Bible is not a simple, single-authored document, free of seams and tensions, literary, theological, and logical'.[13]

Let me stress that I share many of Seitz's theological concerns, and that I have profited greatly from engaging with his immensely creative, thought-provoking and often refreshingly radical work. I also have the greatest sympathy for his desire to move beyond the endless preoccupation with historical questions, which has had many detrimental effects on the study of the Old Testament. Indeed, Seitz is absolutely right, in my opinion, to stress the need for a theological reading of the Old Testament that takes the Christian canon, and in particular the fact that we are dealing with an Old and a New Testament, seriously.

After these comments, there is bound to be a 'but'. And there is, but I'm afraid that readers will have to 'linger in the woods' for a little while, as Eco once put it.[14] And while you are enjoying your 'inferential walks', I am going to have a look at two recent works on the book of Amos.

Two Recent Views on the Book of Amos

In a new contribution to the current quest for the composition of the book of the Twelve (XII), Schart recently suggested taking the book of Amos as the point of departure. Building on the work of Wolff and Jeremias,[15] Schart traced

---

[7] Cf. esp. Childs, *Biblical Theology; Introduction;* and *Old Testament Theology.*

[8] Seitz, *Word*, 97.

[9] Ibid., 99.

[10] Ibid., ix.

[11] Cf. Childs, *Exodus*, ix–xvi, for Childs's own programmatic statements.

[12] Seitz, *Word*, 102.

[13] Ibid., 99.

[14] Cf. Eco, *Six Walks*, ch. 3, 'Lingering in the Woods'.

[15] Wolff, *Joel and Amos;* Jeremias, *Amos.*

six redactional layers in Amos,[16] which he then correlated to the remaining material in the XII.[17] Put very briefly, Schart suggested the following redactional development: in a first step, an early collection of speeches in Amos 3–6⋆[18] was expanded by Amos' tradents who thereby created the so-called 'tradent's version' Amos 1–9⋆. At the level of the XII, Hosea⋆ was added at this point. Next, a 'D-layer'[19] was inserted together with other 'deuteronomistic*ish*'[20] additions, i.e. mainly 'D-Micah' and 'D-Zephaniah', thus resulting in the 'D-corpus'. Subsequent redactional stages produced the 'Nahum-Habakkuk-corpus' (addition of the hymnic layer Amos 4:13; 5:8; 9:6; Nah.⋆; Hab.⋆) followed by the 'Haggai-Zechariah-corpus' ('salvific layer' Amos 9:11–15⋆; Hag.⋆; Zech.⋆) and the 'Joel-Obadiah-corpus' (eschatological layer Amos 4:9; 9:12a, 13aβb; Joel; Obadiah). Eventually, after the book of Amos had already reached its final form, the addition of Malachi and Jonah completed the literary growth of the XII.[21]

Gowan has taken an entirely different route in his reading of the book of Amos. Challenging redaction-critical conceptions, Gowan questions (a) whether 'the thought of one individual can be isolated from additions made to it by others' and (b) whether 'it is important to do so'.[22] Given the textual data that has come down to us, he is rightly critical of what he calls the 'biographical approach' noting that

> we have an almost unavoidable desire to gain access to the personality, experiences, and faith of the individuals responsible for the prophetic books, and that desire is so strong that the most responsible scholars have not hesitated to use their imaginations, along with every clue that they can find in the texts of these books, to create biographies they believe to be fair representations of the lives of those prophets.[23]

---

[16] Schart, *Entstehung*, 50–100; cf. esp. his summary on 98–100.

[17] Ibid., 101–303.

[18] The asterisk indicates that not all of the material in the chapters in question is part of that early collection.

[19] The sigla 'D' indicates that the material belonging to this layer is part of or related to the 'deuteronomistic stream of tradition'.

[20] Reacting to Lohfink's criticism of the current tendency towards a 'pan-deuteronomism' (Lohfink, 'Deuteronomistische Bewegung'), Schart is somewhat hesitant to speak of deuteronomistic redactors, preferring instead to refer to a redaction that has close affinities with deuteronomistic conceptions (Schart, *Entstehung*, 46, 156 n. 2).

[21] This is a highly simplified account of Schart's proposals. For a detailed list specifying precisely which parts (or verses) were added at which juncture in the literary development of the XII, cf. *Entstehung*, 316f.

[22] Gowan, 'Amos', 341.

[23] Ibid., 340.

According to Gowan, not only is this general biographical interest misguided, but it is also 'probably far less important to know exactly what the man Amos *said* than many have assumed'.[24] Indeed, Gowan is 'sceptical of all efforts to deduce from the words of the prophets . . . clear standards as to what they could or could not have said'.[25] Instead, he expresses his intent to focus on the book itself, on what he calls the 'Amos tradition'. Noting the possibilities that 'the book of Amos may all have come from him, may be mostly his with a few later additions, or may have been heavily redacted',[26] Gowan is adamant that most, if not all, of its material 'makes good sense against a mid-eighth-century BCE background'.[27] Thus, in stark contrast to Schart who envisaged six redactional stages spanning a few centuries, Gowan claims that 'the utter newness of the message that God had decreed the end of God's people Israel and the distinctive characteristics of style in the book strongly suggest that one writer was responsible for both its basic message and the ways in which it was expressed'.[28]

This estimate quite obviously renders any ongoing search for redactional stages superfluous. Yet what is most striking in Gowan's treatment of the issue is how quickly he moves, in no more than two pages, from noting the various possibilities of how the book may have come into being (i.e. written by Amos, heavily redacted, etc.) to saying that all the material (the 'Amos tradition') does actually make good sense against an eighth-century background *and* that no more than one writer may have been responsible for it all.

Coming to Terms with the Legacy of Historical Criticism

These two examples, chosen more or less at random, typify two of the prevailing ways of dealing with the historical-critical legacy. A third option and one that one feels many today would regard as the best way forward is the route taken by Seitz in saying that historical-critical work is needed but that the approach has no more than a preparatory function. Thus, we are presented, it seems, with a choice of three possible ways ahead:

(1) We can buy into the traditional historical-critical paradigm accepting not only the methods themselves but also that, by and large, the approach has done reasonably well and that the results it has produced over the centuries can be trusted and worked with. This is what Schart has done in taking earlier redaction-critical work, in particular that by Wolff and Jeremias, as the starting

---

[24] Ibid., 341 (my italics).
[25] Ibid.
[26] Ibid.
[27] Ibid., 342.
[28] Ibid.

point for developing his own redaction-critical analysis of the genesis of the XII.

(2) An increasing number of scholars have declared the historical-critical approach bankrupt, impracticable and unhelpful given the tasks the biblical interpreter faces. Thus, Gowan, as we have seen, rejects both, redaction-critical findings *and* the methodological approach itself, questioning whether what redaction critics aim to achieve is possible or even necessary. The whole surge of recent alternative methods (such as New Criticism, poetics or narratology, reader-response theory or reception aesthetics, structuralist criticism and deconstruction as well as 'ideological criticisms', such as feminist or Marxist criticism or liberation hermeneutics) are characterized, by and large, by such an attitude.[29] However, it needs to be pointed out that Gowan's approach differs from many of these recent models for interpretation in that he takes the historical rootedness of the biblical text seriously. Yet what is of interest to us at this point is that he eschews one of the defining interests of historical criticism, namely the quest for the genesis of the text, thus departing markedly from the historical-critical tradition of interpretation.[30]

(3) Finally, there are those who would be uncomfortable with both, a wholesale affirmation as well as a sweeping rejection of historical criticism, claiming that the approach does have its uses and that, while it is problematic, we just cannot do without it, to put it in Brueggemann's terms. We thus have to practise historical criticism but, having done that, we move on to do what really matters, as for instance developing a theological and canonical reading of the Old Testament.

These approaches to biblical interpretation differ substantially. Yet they share a lack of interest in a critical assessment of the aims, presuppositions and methodological procedures of historical criticism. These are either taken for granted, rejected or, somewhat grudgingly, accepted only to be relativized by being augmented, for instance, by a theological reading, which is what *really matters*. But – and this is the 'but' I promised earlier on – while I find myself in general agreement with those who urge us not to get bogged down by the never-ending stream of historical questions, I am not convinced that simply to supplement historical criticism by asking additional questions is the best way forward.[31] Given the severe criticisms that have been

---

[29] To give just one example, Gunn and Fewell stress that they 'do not think that historical-critical analysis, interesting as it might be, is a necessary major precondition of our reading' (Gunn and Fewell, *Narrative*, 11).

[30] Gowan does, however, affirm the value of other types of historical criticism such as form criticism ('Amos', 342).

[31] Of course, neither option one, i.e. to embrace historical criticism unquestioningly, nor option two, simply to ignore it, offers a viable alternative to the approach suggested by Seitz and others.

levelled against the approach in recent years, I believe that there are quite a number of important questions that require clarification if we are ever to come to terms with the legacy of the historical-critical approach.[32]

Criticisms of Historical Criticism

In what follows, I intend to summarize some of the main criticisms that have been levelled against both the theoretical conception as well as the practical methodological outworkings of the historical-critical approach. I shall deal with these under the four headings of philosophical, literary-critical, theological and socio-religious criticisms, but it should be noted that, due to the inter-relation of these areas,[33] the actual arguments brought against biblical criticism frequently address more than one of them. Secondly, as this is intended to be but a brief sketch, it will not be possible to do justice to all the subtleties of the issues discussed.[34]

Philosophical

Starting with the philosophical shortcomings of the historical-critical enterprise, it should be noted, first, that its epistemological positivism has come under sustained attack. For instance, the positivist notions of history and historical inquiry, characteristic of historicism and evidenced by much

---

[32] Looking at Perlitt's study on Vatke and Wellhausen, I was struck by his observation that already in the early years of the twentieth century scholars such as Seeberg had criticized Wellhausen precisely because his focus on history only distracted from a theological understanding of the Old Testament (Seeberg, *Die Kirche Deutschlands*, 332, quoted in Perlitt, *Vatke und Wellhausen*, 157). It is interesting to note that, as the history of biblical interpretation teaches us, the call to focus on theological questions did not do much to shatter the approach advocated by Wellhausen and those following in his footsteps.

[33] For instance, Clines, 'Story and Poem', 117, has rightly stressed that 'the distinction between the Bible as literature and the Bible as scripture is largely artificial'. In similar vein, Alter, *Art of Biblical Narrative*, 19, has called for 'a complete interfusion of literary art with theological, moral, or historiosophical vision'.

[34] For instance, it will not be possible in this context to do justice to the fact that there is no such animal as *the* historical-critical method, as some have insisted that we must (see Bartholomew, *Reading*, 66f., 82f., who criticizes Krentz, *Historical-critical Method*, for neglecting the multifacetedness of historical criticism; cf. also McIntyre, 'Historical Criticism', 374; and Plantinga, 'Scripture Scholarship', 352ff., who distinguishes three types of historical criticism, i.e. 'Troeltschian', 'Duhemian' and 'Spinozistic').

historical–critical work, have been unmasked and subjected to increased scrutiny.[35] A positivist philosophy of history construes the task of the historian as the discovery of 'what really happened'.[36] In defining the objective of historical inquiry along these lines, it is assumed that we can have unmediated access to the facts, i.e. that history writing is an objective exercise that is not tainted by the personal views and interests – or, more generally, the social context – of the historian.

As regards biblical criticism, Sternberg has pointed out that 'source-oriented critics [i.e. historical critics] often imply that they deal in hard facts and consign "aesthetic" analysis to its fate at the none too reliable hands of the literary coterie'.[37] Sternberg rightly calls this a delusion noting that 'the movement from text to reality cannot but pass through interpretation'.[38] Indeed, to entertain the idea that 'history-writing is wedded to . . . factual truth' is to make a 'category-mistake of the first order' in that 'history-writing is not a record of fact – of what "really happened" – but a discourse that *claims* to be a record of fact'.[39]

In a recent article calling for a rethinking of historical criticism, Dobbs-Allsopp has made a similar point in relation to foundationalism. Central to the foundationalist understanding of reality is the belief in 'mind-independent objects'. Given these, 'it logically follows that there is one true and complete description of these brute facts'.[40] In textual interpretation, the construal of the text as a 'mind-independent object' had similar implications, procuring a never-ending search for *the* meaning of the text in question.[41] However, any attempt to produce an objective account of 'the facts as they really are' or to arrive at *the* meaning of a text has always been fated to be unsuccessful, as we

---

[35] E.g. Perdue, *Collapse*, 6f.; and Collins, 'Critical Biblical Theology', 7, who notes that historical criticism 'too is a tradition, with its own values and assumptions'.

[36] As Bartholomew, *Reading*, 109, notes, 'positivism sought to apply its epistemology to all disciplines', which 'meant that methods derived from the natural sciences were extended to other disciplines so that a science of literature analogous to the natural sciences emerged'.

[37] Sternberg, *Poetics*, 16.

[38] Ibid.

[39] Ibid., 25 (my italics). It should be noted that Sternberg also rejects the notion that fiction-writing is opposed to factual truth pointing to the residual of factual truths in, for instance, 'historical novels' such as Tolstoy's *War and Peace*. Thus, he concludes that 'the antithesis [of history-writing and fiction-writing] lies not in the presence or absence of truth value but of the commitment to truth value' (ibid.).

[40] Dobbs-Allsopp, 'Rethinking', 240.

[41] For a rejection of the idea that one only has to develop *the* correct method in order to get at *the* meaning of a text see Barton, *Reading*, 5, who, however, does not discuss the philosophical roots of this quest.

have 'no access to an experience other than that which is already prefigured by the mind'.[42] As Eagleton notes, 'any . . . notion of absolute objectivity is an illusion'.[43] And as this has become increasingly evident, the result has been a 'loss of confidence in the epistemological claims of the Enlightenment to be grounded in objectivity and critical, rational enquiry'.[44] In particular, it has been stressed that all knowledge is socially and culturally determined in that historians or interpreters are themselves deeply 'embedded in their own cultures with all of that culture's attendant prejudices and biases'.[45] However, this then points to a striking inconsistency in historicist thought because, as Dobbs-Allsopp has pointed out,

> part of what motivates historical critics to historicize the biblical texts . . . is the belief that the authors of these texts would have been unavoidably marked by the historical epoch in which they were embedded. The contradiction arises in these critics' failure to realize that they too must be unavoidably marked by their own historical epochs.[46]

In similar vein, focusing on the contingent nature of history (and historical inquiry), Strauss notes that

> historicism asserts that all human thoughts or beliefs are historical, and hence deservedly destined to perish; but historicism itself is a human thought; hence historicism can be of only temporary validity, or it cannot be simply true. To assert the historicist thesis means to doubt it and thus to transcend it . . . Historicism thrives on the fact that it inconsistently exempts itself from its own verdict about all human thought.[47]

Up to this point, we have sketched some of the criticisms levelled against positivist and foundationalist epistemologies and philosophies of history, which, as has been noted, have shaped the historical-critical approach in no small way. However, given the specific nature of the biblical texts, attention needs to be drawn also to the secular character of the historical-critical understanding of history.[48]

According to Krentz, historical criticism has led to the secularization of the

---

[42] Dobbs-Allsopp, 'Rethinking', 243.
[43] Eagleton, *Literary Theory*, 60.
[44] Perdue, *Collapse*, 8.
[45] Dobbs-Allsopp, 'Rethinking', 242.
[46] Ibid., 244.
[47] Strauss, *Natural Right*, 25, quoted in Levenson, *Hebrew Bible*, 116.
[48] Krentz, *Historical-critical Method*, 1. Gadamer, *Truth*, 272, has made it very clear that the Enlightenment critique is directed against the religious tradition of Christianity.

Scriptures.[49] Secular notions are very much to the fore, for instance, in Troeltsch's principles of historical inquiry, put forward in his famous essay on historical and dogmatic method. According to Troeltsch, historical study is characterized by the principles of methodological doubt (historical inquiry can never attain absolute certainty), analogy (all historical events are similar in principle) and correlation (historical phenomena are interrelated by being part of a chain of cause and effect).[50]

Comparing these principles to those at work in traditional religious readings (often termed 'pre-critical'), Collins rightly speaks of 'a clash between two conflicting moralities, one of which celebrated faith and belief as virtues and regarded doubt as sin, whereas the other celebrated methodological scepticism and was distrustful of prior commitments'.[51] Troeltsch's second and third principles, in particular, have been 'troublesome', as they disallow transcendental causation, which, however, is one of the defining features of a traditional Christian understanding of reality.[52] Biblical criticism, by contrast, is 'largely . . . immanentist in its explanations and incapable of appreciating the category of revelation'.[53]

Literary-critical

Turning to the literary-critical censure of historical criticism, one might begin by noting that it is rather telling how the term 'literary criticism' used to be defined in the discipline of biblical studies. Barton opens his discussion of literary criticism by noting that

> people who come to biblical studies after a training in the study of modern literature are usually puzzled by the sense in which biblical scholars use the term 'literary criticism'. For them, 'literary' criticism is simply the study of literature, especially from the point of view of what in French is called *explication de texte* . . . In biblical studies . . . 'literary' criticism is the attempt to divide [the biblical books] up into their component parts, and then to assess the relative ages of these parts, rather as archaeologists date the various strata of a site.[54]

---

[49] Krentz, *Historical-critical Method*, 30.

[50] Troeltsch, 'Methode'.

[51] Collins, 'Critical Biblical Theology', 3, referring to Harvey, *Historian*, 102. Insightful and radical as this sounds, Levenson, *Hebrew Bible*, 119, has rightly pointed out that Collins's statement itself betrays the marks of positivism in that Collins proceeds from 'the unspoken assumption that the axioms of Troeltschian historicism are not "prior commitments" '.

[52] Bartholomew, *Reading*, 67.

[53] Thus Krentz, *Historical-critical Method*, 30.

[54] Barton, *Reading*, 20.

The so-called 'literary turn' in biblical studies has challenged this preoccupation with the genesis of the texts pointing to substantial weaknesses in the historical-critical understanding and study of literature. Again, all we can do in this context is to summarize some of the flaws that have been exposed in recent years.[55]

Barton, notwithstanding his general willingness to draw on the insights advanced by contemporary literary critics, still seeks to defend the source-critical enterprise by appealing to 'observable discrepancies', which are best explained, in his view, by the assumption that the texts in question consist of a number of different sources.[56] Without wanting to deny the existence of such discrepancies in principle or indeed the need for diachronic or 'source-oriented' study in general, it needs to be pointed out that Barton's account raises the question of what we mean by '*observable* discrepancies'. That is to say: observable by whom and on the basis of which (and whose) criteria?[57] That these questions require an answer becomes all the more obvious in the light of Gunn and Fewell's criticism that 'the analysis of sources . . . was basically dependent on aesthetic premises which were often arbitrary and rarely acknowledged'.[58]

Barton's insistence that 'biblical critics did not begin by *deciding* that [for instance] the Pentateuch must be composed from several sources' but that 'the conclusion forced itself upon them, in some cases much against their will'[59] is not an adequate response to this challenge. Again, one wants to ask why it is that certain conclusions '*forced* themselves' upon the critic. These conclusions that Barton wants us to think of as inevitable are in fact determined, as we have seen in the previous section, not only by the object of study but also by the presuppositions (or, more generally, the cultural location) of the investigating scholar. It therefore needs to be considered – very carefully, one is inclined to say – which 'aesthetic unevennesses', 'ideological tensions' and 'factual contradictions' (a) can actually count as such and (b) are of such a nature as to prompt us to think of the text as an agglomeration of sources. As Alter has stressed, 'elements like disjunction, interpolation, repetition, contrastive styles, which in biblical scholarship were long deemed sure signs of a defective text, *may* be perfectly deliberate components of the literary artwork'.[60]

---

[55] Further discussion of these issues (and references to additional literature) can be found in the works mentioned in the footnotes.

[56] Barton, *Reading*, 22.

[57] Cf. the discussion in Möller, 'Presenting', 4–7; see also Bartholomew, *Reading*, 92.

[58] Gunn and Fewell, *Narrative*, 8. See also Sternberg, *Poetics*, 11, who notes that frequently 'anachronistic (and often bizarre) norms of unity, social conduct, world order, convention, value judgment' have been applied to the Old Testament texts.

[59] Barton, *Reading*, 25 (the italics are his).

[60] Alter, 'Introduction', 27 (my italics).

This whole area is a difficult one that is bound to cause much controversy in the years ahead. However, given these difficulties, Sternberg is surely right to emphasize that 'the task of decomposition calls for the most sensitive response to the arts of composition. How else will one be able to tell deliberate from accidental roughnesses and identify the marks of disunity in unity throughout a text whose *poesis* covers the tracks of its *genesis*?'[61]

One effect of the insensitivity to the *ars poetica* characteristic of countless historical-critical readings has been the atomization of the biblical texts. Alter even speaks of the 'hidden imperative "the more atomistic, the more scientific"',[62] which, despite its polemical ring, is not entirely off the mark. In similar vein, Polzin notes that 'traditional biblical scholarship has spent most of its efforts in disassembling the works of a complicated watch before our amazed eyes without apparently realising that similar efforts by and large have not succeeded in putting the parts back together again in a significant and meaningful way'.[63]

Of course, as some older commentaries illustrate, the putting-back-together of the parts occasionally resulted in a different text altogether (here Polzin's analogy breaks down, as it is difficult to imagine that one could do the same with a watch). These practices have rightly come under attack in recent years. Sternberg, for instance, while stressing the need for diachronic study (or 'source-oriented analysis', as he prefers to call it), has criticized 'critics who mix up their quest for the source with the need to fabricate a new discourse'.[64]

One of the reasons for the widespread insensitivity to the *ars poetica* and the resulting fabrication of atomized (or even new) texts is what Gunn and Fewell have described as an 'aesthetic preference for rationalistic, literal reading of literature'.[65] As Perdue has noted, this predilection has its roots in the 'spirit of the Enlightenment' with its preference for reason.[66] One suspects that notions such as these are behind Barton's talk of conclusions that forced themselves upon the critic in that critics were frequently ill-equipped to appreciate the 'literariness' of the texts. As I have argued elsewhere, historical-critical readings of Amos, for instance, are often characterized by a striking literalism that does not allow for rhetorically motivated exaggerations and 'contradictions', which are usually regarded as sure signs of the composite nature of the text.[67] Or, to give

---

[61] Sternberg, *Poetics*, 16.

[62] Alter, 'Introduction', 25.

[63] Polzin, 'Ancestress', 82f.

[64] Sternberg, *Poetics*, 50; see also 7–23 for his perceptive discussion of the relationship of source and discourse.

[65] Gunn and Fewell, *Narrative*, 8.

[66] Perdue, *Collapse*, 10; See also my discussion above, especially the references to positivism and the effects it has had on the study of literature.

[67] Möller, 'Rehabilitation'.

another example, Gunn and Fewell have rightly complained that 'invoking the
notion of ironic writing to account for some apparent contradictions was
usually disallowed'.[68]

Finally, it must not be overlooked that historical critics frequently had only
a limited interest in the literary dimension of the biblical works anyway,
regarding 'them . . . as more or less distorted historical records' thus diverting
attention from the texts as literature.[69] Krentz has made a similar point in noting
that even in attending to 'literary figures' the historical critic's aim usually was
to 'judge the historical usefulness of material, not to achieve a literary appreciation of it *per se*'.[70]

Theological

We have already taken note of Seitz's insistence that Old Testament interpretation, if done from a Christian perspective (which, as a matter of fact, is already
implied by the term 'Old Testament studies'), must abandon its preoccupation
with historical questions and recover an interest in theological interpretation.
Among other things, perhaps even most importantly, this means for Seitz that a
Christian reading of the Old Testament, which he is keen to promote, must
take the Christian canon seriously and read the Old Testament as part of that
canon. Others have made a similar point, arguing for a theological hermeneutic in biblical interpretation. Watson, for instance, notes on the first page of his
Text, Church and World that 'the text in question is the biblical text; for the goal
is a theological hermeneutic for biblical interpretation – that is, a theoretical
framework within which an exegesis oriented primarily towards theological
issues can come into being'.[71]

Thus, from this perspective, historical criticism is accused of neglecting
what matters most to the Christian church, which, as Watson stresses, is the
primary reading community of the biblical text.[72]

However, a theological critique of historical-critical scholarship can also
take a different route. As Levenson has pointed out, there is a type of historical
criticism that builds on a certain Enlightenment critique of religion, which is
akin to, or perhaps even nourished by:

---

[68] Gunn and Fewell, *Narrative*, 8.
[69] Alter and Kermode, 'General Introduction', 3; also Dobbs-Allsopp, 'Rethinking',
235.
[70] Krentz, *Historical-critical Method*, 44.
[71] Watson, *Text*, 1.
[72] Ibid., 3. See also Levenson, *Hebrew Bible*, 123, who calls historical critics a 'secondary
community' that engages 'in second-order reflection upon the primary language of the
religious communities they study'.

a long-standing Christian critique of Judaism, a Protestant critique of Catholicism and Eastern orthodoxy, and a modern Western self-legitimation over against tribal peoples [such as the ancient Israelites]. It is no coincidence that in this model, it is the person whose life is *not* ritualized who has the clarity of vision: only as we break off from ritual communities and transcend their specific performances can we come to perceive the truth. The model does not allow for even the possibility that detachment from ritual performances may decrease one's insight and obscure one's vision. It definitively and nondialectically shifts the locus of truth from the practicing community to the nonpracticing and unaffiliated individual.[73]

This, it should be noted, is not a censure of historical criticism as such. I bring it up nevertheless because, as Levenson has rightly emphasized, historical critics have frequently superimposed their own theological views and preferences on the texts.

Let me stress that, in drawing attention to this issue, I am not suggesting that we need to somehow to rid ourselves of our theological views and preferences. This would be the opposite of what Seitz, Watson and others are arguing for and, as we have already seen above, it would be a futile exercise with no hope of success. What I am suggesting is that we need to cultivate an awareness of our own subjectivity and cultural rootedness. As Long has observed, 'we will be able to be more objective only if we learn to conceal our subjectivity less'.[74] Thus, while it is perfectly legitimate, and indeed inevitable, that we approach texts with preconceived ideas and values, even a particular *Weltanschauung*, it is important that we allow the text to criticize these and, by so doing, to contribute to the re-conceptualization of our position and indeed the reshaping of our own selves. This, I submit, needs to be allowed to happen also to our theological views and beliefs, however Christian (and thus unassailable) we deem them to be.

Socio-religious

Finally, I want to turn to the socio-religious dimension.[75] Levenson begins his trenchant critique of historical criticism by drawing attention to what he calls a double conversion experience, which many students undergo in being converted, first, to an uncritical acceptance of Christian faith, only to be converted again, in the course of their studies, to an acceptance (which usually is equally uncritical, one is tempted to say) of the historical-critical method.[76] Indeed, Levenson quotes Wilfred Cantwell Smith as saying that the courses 'are on the

---

[73] Levenson, *Hebrew Bible*, 115f.
[74] Long, 'Historiography', 166, quoting B.A. Scharfstein.
[75] See also, in this volume, Sundberg's essay on the social effect of biblical criticism.
[76] Levenson, *Hebrew Bible*, 106.

whole calculated to turn a fundamentalist into a liberal'.[77] Given the social character of knowledge, the second conversion is necessary, as the historical–critical approach, like any other worldview, depends on a community that shares a certain set of values and assumptions.[78]

Whereas Levenson is interested primarily in the effects historical criticism has had – and still has – on (religiously committed) academics and their pursuit of biblical studies, Sundberg, in his contribution to the present volume, looks at the devastating social effects of biblical criticism as they manifest themselves in the churches. He notes, for instance, that by eradicating the traditional understanding of the authority of Scripture, historical criticism has driven people away from the churches, which have assimilated themselves to the dominant cultural ethos with the result that they no longer have a distinctive message to offer. Ironically, however, as Levenson has pointed out, historical critics depend for their livelihood 'upon the vitality of traditional religious communities, Jewish and Christian'.[79] After all, it is due to them that the discipline of biblical studies enjoys its privileged place in the academy.

However, to return to the effects biblical criticism has had on the churches and on 'ordinary' readers in general, it has been pointed out that the privileging of the 'original' sources or texts,[80] coupled with the devaluing of the 'final' canonical text, has taken the Bible out of the hands of the non-specialists. Thus, whoever seeks to understand the biblical texts now needs to consult the experts.[81] And as academic scholarship promoted the idea that historical criticism was *the* correct method for getting at *the* meaning of the text,[82] students were led to believe that historical criticism 'was the only "responsible" method' for reading the Bible.[83] All this went together with a 'tendency to denigrate the "ordinary" reader as "non-critical"'.[84] In response to this trend, Alter and Kermode claim that by means of a literary reading 'the *general reader* can now be offered a new view of the Bible as a work of great literary force and authority'.[85]

---

[77] Ibid.

[78] Ibid., 120.

[79] Ibid., 110.

[80] Sternberg, *Poetics*, 13, highlights the extent to which this has dominated biblical scholarship by speaking of 'two hundred years of frenzied digging into the Bible's genesis, so senseless as to elicit either laughter or tears'.

[81] Gunn and Fewell, *Narrative*, 8.

[82] Barton, *Reading*, 1, makes a similar point in referring to the 'slightly evangelistic flavour' of many textbooks.

[83] Gunn and Fewell, *Narrative*, 8, 11.

[84] Barton, *Reading*, 5.

[85] Alter and Kermode, 'General Introduction', 2 (my italics).

Finally, as Levenson notes, historical criticism fully endorsed the classical liberal political ideal, which expects scholars 'to eliminate or minimize their communal loyalties' as this would ensure that 'the wars of religion would be no more'.[86] The roots of this concept, which resulted in the privatization of religion, Levenson traces back to the aftermath of the Thirty Years' War and, more specifically, to the influence of writers such as Hobbes, Spinoza and Richard Simon.[87] Yet this liberal ideal too has come under attack by those who, like Wright, stress that Christianity is 'public truth' and that it 'offers a story of the whole world'.[88] As Wright notes, 'stories come into conflict with each other' because 'they claim to make sense of the whole of reality. Even the relativist, who believes that everybody's point of view on everything is equally valid even though apparently incompatible, is obedient to an underlying story about reality which comes into explicit conflict with most other stories '.[89]

While this is not the place to develop a strategy for countering the as yet undiminished urge to keep religion privatized, let me point out that, in my estimate, rhetorical-critical theory has much to offer in this respect.[90] After all, as Lentricchia has noted, the point of criticism is not only to interpret texts but, in so doing, to change our society.[91]

Reviewing Historical-Critical Methodology and Theory

In the light of these objections to the historical-critical paradigm, the methodological procedures it involves and the results it has produced, it just will not do simply to 'get on with it'. Yet this is precisely what the majority of scholars seem to be doing, and what some have even argued for.

Thus, while there are now a significant number of scholars who would be dismissive of works like Schart's on the genesis of the XII, one is surprised to find just how much acceptance there still is for this kind of approach. In a recent review, Nogalski has made it clear that he regards Schart's 'arguments of literary relationships between texts [as] quite convincing'.[92] Indeed, he judges Schart's

---

[86] Levenson, *Hebrew Bible*, 118.

[87] Ibid., 117.

[88] Wright, *New Testament*, 41f.

[89] Ibid., 41.

[90] See e.g., Compier, *Rhetorical Theology*, for an argument for a rhetorical hermeneutic and theology, a defining feature of which is the concept of persuasion.

[91] Lentricchia, *Criticism*, 10.

[92] Nogalski, review of Schart, *Entstehung*, 505. Nogalski does, however, stress that some of the formal criteria and broad thematic correspondences utilized by Schart 'would seem to require more consideration'.

methodology to be 'philosophically sound', and applauds him for having 'contributed a carefully considered treatment which places the idea of a redactional unity of the XII upon more solid footing, and provides reasoned theories which deserve careful evaluation in the ongoing discussion of the XII'.[93]

These judgements are rather surprising given the severe limitations of Schart's study. To start with, I don't think that one can simply take the redactional theories advocated by Wolff and Jeremias as one's starting point, as Schart has done. Already in the seventies, Wolff's analysis of the book's redactional layers had been questioned by Rudolph[94] whose commentary was, however, largely ignored until it was 'rediscovered' by Paul who made extensive use of it in his Hermeneia volume.[95] And while Wolff's commentary has remained very influential (especially in Germany), the late eighties and early nineties saw the appearance of a number of commentaries that were highly critical of the redaction-critical route taken by Wolff and his followers. In addition to Paul's work, mention should be made of Hayes's commentary as well as the Anchor Bible contribution by Andersen and Freedman.[96] It is therefore just not good enough for Schart to 'defend' his decision to follow Wolff and Jeremias by pointing out that this places him within the mainstream of literary-critical scholarship.[97] While this may still be true, Schart's assertion has a somewhat hollow ring to it at a time when those operating within 'the mainstream' are under heavy attack from all corners.

Secondly, without intending to go into all the details at this point, let me emphasize that I disagree with Nogalski's judgement about Schart's arguments concerning the literary relationships between texts, as I do not find them convincing. One of Schart's pet terms is the phrase 'significant connections', which, if present, would point to literary dependencies. However, in not a few cases, I was unpersuaded by what Schart considers to be 'significant connections'. As already said, this is not the place to go into details.[98] But, in my estimate, redaction critics urgently need to reassess their methodological approach with the aim of developing some criteria for what does amount to 'significant connections' that point to literary dependencies and what does not.[99]

---

[93] Ibid. For a review that is much more critical of Schart's work, cf. Sweeney, 'Recent European Studies'.

[94] Rudolph, *Joel*.

[95] Paul, *Amos*, passim.

[96] Hayes, *Amos*; Andersen and Freedman, *Amos*.

[97] Schart, *Entstehung*, 50 n. 1.

[98] Möller, review of Schart, *Entstehung*, for further comments.

[99] Schultz, *Search*, for an assessment of various attempts of establishing verbal parallels in the prophets. Given the largely negative character of the remarks made above, I should stress that redaction criticism has made an important contribution to biblical studies in regarding the redactors not as adulterators of the material but as creative authors in their own right.

Thirdly, although Schart has a brief discussion of recent synchronic readings of the XII, in his own redaction-critical analysis he does not begin to do justice to the literary-critical insights associated with the 'literary turn' in biblical studies.[100] Consider, for instance, his treatment of the poetry-prose 'problem' characteristic of so many prophetic passages. According to Schart, passages such as Amos 2:10–12 that mix the two modes or that are difficult to classify are immediately 'suspect'. That is to say, they stand a good chance of being classified as insertions.[101]

Schart is completely undeterred by the insistence of Kugel, Berlin, Alter and others[102] that it is not always possible, especially in the prophetic literature, to make a clear-cut distinction between the two modes of poetry and prose.[103] Alter, for instance, notes that 'we . . . tend to think of prose and poetry as distinct, even opposed, categories. For the ancient Hebrews, these were not strict oppositions, and sometimes they could be intertwined in baffling ways.'[104] If this is so, and a glance at the texts suggests that it is, then one needs to exercise great caution in utilizing supposed inconsistencies in the employment of poetry and prose as a criterion for determining redactional operations.

However, some may perhaps think that, in discussing the flaws of a work like Schart's, I am on a wild-goose chase. Has not Old Testament scholarship in general moved on to a more mature treatment of the texts? Have we not learned from the 'literary turn' in biblical studies? Well, I am not so sure. As Barton has pointed out, 'source analysis [is] still flourishing all over the world despite the supposed paradigm-shift away from it'.[105] This in itself would not be a problem if at least we could be sure that what we are seeing today is a new kind of source analysis that has learned from the failures of the past and the criticisms in the present.[106]

That aside, I want to come back at this point to Seitz's suggestion that, recognizing the limitations of historical criticism, we need to restrict the size of its playpen by allowing the approach no more than a preparatory role. Even

---

[100] Cf. Sweeney, 'Recent European Studies', for a similar judgement.

[101] Schart, *Entstehung*, 60f.

[102] Kugel, *Idea*; Berlin, *Dynamics*; Alter, *Art of Biblical Poetry*.

[103] Petersen and Richards, *Interpreting*, 13f., rightly speak of a 'poetry-prose continuum'.

[104] Alter, 'Introduction', 15.

[105] Barton, 'Historical Criticism', 7; cf. also Long, 'Historiography', 152, who notes that 'the continued influence of the historical-critical method should not be underestimated'.

[106] Of course, as Barton, Sternberg and others have pointed out, this applies both ways. If we believe in the importance of both, source-oriented *and* discourse-oriented analysis, then exegetes from both ends of the spectrum need to enter into dialogue and learn from each other.

though this is a laudable attempt to bring Old Testament interpretation back on track, one fears that it will do little more than alleviate the problems caused by an inappropriate approach. Moreover, I am not convinced that to define the task of historical criticism as one of 'spotting repugnance', as Seitz has suggested,[107] is a wise move. Given this definition, would one not have to conclude that, for instance, Rudolph's commentary on Amos failed, in historical-critical terms, by 'removing' some of the 'repugnance' identified by Wolff?

Even more importantly, however, in the light of what we have said above, I wonder whether we can still be sure that the historical-critical methods are not wrong, as Childs and Seitz have argued. This is not to decree that they are, but to suggest that we need to re-evaluate them very carefully by subjecting them to painstaking analysis of their literary-critical assumptions and philosophical underpinnings. Rendtorff, in whose estimate the discipline of Old Testament studies is in a crisis, expects, quite realistically, that some will not recognize the symptoms of this crisis, but 'will expect that solutions to the problems can be found through an even more rigorous and even more precise application of the old methods'.[108] This, Rendtorff thinks, will only benefit the discipline, which is, of course, not to be denied. Rigour and precision are always welcome. Yet before we call for improved application, I believe we ought to have another look at the methods themselves. This has been stressed also by Dobbs-Allsopp who claims that

> if historical criticism is to continue to thrive and contribute to the critical discourse in biblical studies, it must show a willingness to submit itself continually to *rigorous theoretical scrutiny*, and, if need be, to cast aside aspects of its theory and practice which are no longer compelling.[109]

Finally, I believe we should be prepared at least to consider the possibility that not a few of our treasured theories – or should I say, assured results? – concerning the genesis of the Old Testament books, the development of Israelite religion and other aspects of Old Testament study might be seriously flawed. Indeed, if there is anything in the criticisms mentioned earlier, this is precisely what is to be expected, although it is difficult to be sure to what extent it will be so. Hall has made a similar point with reference to the new literary-critical insights, stressing that we must not only consider in what way they can enrich biblical exegesis in the present and in the future but also how far their previous absence has undermined the methods, and conclusions, of earlier scholarly generations.[110] Taking into account also the philosophical problems mentioned

---

[107] Seitz, *Word*, 99; see above.
[108] Rendtorff, 'Isaiah 6', 180.
[109] Dobbs-Allsopp, 'Rethinking', 271 (my italics).
[110] Hall, *Seven Pillories*, 110.

earlier, one wonders to what extent, for instance, a canonical approach that builds upon historical-critical achievements can help us in our attempt to work towards the renewal of biblical interpretation.

Considering the Future of Historical Criticism

Having just pointed to several issues that need to be dealt with if we are to come to terms with the legacy of historical criticism, let me end by developing briefly two aspects that appear to me to be of particular importance in this context. First, I want to make a plea for an historical approach. Beset with difficulties the historical-critical enterprise may be, but these notwithstanding I agree with those who urge us not to scrap it altogether. Perhaps the most important contribution of historical-critical scholarship to biblical interpretation has been to make us aware of the historical and cultural location of the texts. Given this undeniable achievement, it would be misguided to go back to the ahistorical readings characteristic of the so-called 'pre-critical' era. However, we would be just as mistaken, in my opinion, in embracing postmodern theories of interpretation that advocate an equally ahistorical approach. Secondly, at a time when we are increasingly aware that 'there is no such thing as an innocent [i.e. objective] reading',[111] I want to raise the issue of a Christian approach. And by that I mean one that does not only spring into action once the interpreter has fulfilled his historical-critical duties, as suggested by Seitz, but one that informs the interpretive process throughout.

A plea for an historical approach

With objective interpretation having been branded an illusion, proponents of postmodern strategies of reading now argue that the reader must be given pride of place in the interpretive process. If objectivity is not within our reach, then we, as readers, might as well take over and use the text as a playing field in which we can romp to our heart's desire. Against this line of approach, I want to reaffirm the importance of historical inquiry on the basis of the pragmatic, ethical and salvific considerations advanced by Dobbs-Allsopp in his article on 'Rethinking Historical Criticism'.[112]

First, 'pragmatically, the radical historicist's denial of history . . . fails to account for the historically real'. That is to say, although 'we must always talk about and describe things from some perspective and using some language, it

---

[111] Althusser, '*Capital*', 14.

[112] Dobbs-Allsopp, 'Rethinking', 263.

does not follow that everything then is perspective and description'.[113] Indeed, as Sternberg notes, 'the antihistorical argument never goes all the way . . . Nobody, to the best of my knowledge, has proposed that we each invent our own biblical Hebrew'.[114] Hirsch has made a similar point, arguing that 'if we believe from experience that linguistic communication through texts past or present has *ever* occurred, then the dogma of radical historicity is rendered improbable'.[115]

Thus, because texts have a reality independent of the reader, we need to wrestle with their otherness. What that means has been illuminated by Hart in his contribution to the present volume. Defining the task of the historian as 'one of imaginative construction', Hart notes that, in her quest to understand a text from the past, the historian needs to try to become a 'surrogate member' of a past community.[116] This is because, as Levenson has pointed out, 'the Bible [as indeed any other text] can never be altogether disengaged from the culture of its authors'.[117]

Any interpretation that disregards the cultural location of the text is in great danger of resulting in 'misinterpretation'. Eco helpfully illustrates this with reference to Wordsworth's poem 'I wandered lonely as a cloud', which contains the line 'a poet cannot but be gay'. As Eco notes, to understand what Wordsworth is saying in this phrase, it is crucially important that we be familiar with the meaning the term 'gay' had in Wordsworth's day and age lest we produce a reading that has 'misinterpretation' written all over it.[118]

Dobbs-Allsopp's second reason for advocating a historical approach is ethical. He notes that 'any program for literary study which would make a claim on our critical attention must have the capacity to respect the other built into it'.[119] Thiselton in this context invokes the New Testament concept of *agapē*, calling for a 'creative regard for the Other, . . . a love prompted by will, not by prior "like-mindedness"' and for 'respect for the otherness of the Other as Other'.[120] This, I believe, is an important point to make, especially in today's climate when interpretation is increasingly seen as an exercise of power.

Finally, a historical approach is commendable also because of what Dobbs-Allsopp has called its salvific benefits, noting that knowledge of the past can

---

[113] Ibid., 264, 265.

[114] Sternberg, *Poetics*, 10.

[115] Hirsch, *Validity*, 257.

[116] Cf. also Sternberg, *Poetics*, 10, who stresses that although we will never be able 'to become people of the past, it does not follow that we cannot approximate to this state by imagination and learning . . . still less that we must not or do not make the effort'.

[117] Levenson, *Hebrew Bible*, 123.

[118] Eco, 'Author', 68.

[119] Dobbs-Allsopp, 'Rethinking', 268.

[120] Thiselton, *Interpreting God*, 42, 51, 109.

enable us to criticize present ideologies.[121] C.S. Lewis, who was an ardent defender of an approach to interpretation that takes the historical location of the text seriously, makes the same point by stressing that the study of the past can 'liberate us from the present, from the idols of our own market-place'.[122] In addition to the corrective potential of historical study, attention should be drawn also to the transformational capacity of all good literature. Lewis elaborates on this in *An Experiment in Criticism*, noting that literature can grant us 'experiences other than our own'.[123] He goes on to say that whoever 'is contented to be only himself . . . is in prison. My own eyes are not enough for me, I will see through those of others . . . Literary experience heals the wound, without undermining the privilege, of individuality . . . In reading great literature I become a thousand men and yet remain myself.'[124]

However, true transformation is possible only if we are willing to 'appreciate the letter of [for instance] the biblical text in all its foreignness and complexity' desiring 'to hear something other than our own voices'.[125] Otherwise, if we as readers take over, as it were, eager to use the text for our own purposes, then there is a real danger that all we will see in even the greatest of texts is 'only the reflection of our own silly faces', as again Lewis once put it in a discussion of allegorical interpretation.[126] This, surely, must be something that we need to – and would want to – avoid.

Historical criticism and Christian Scripture

This then takes us to our final point, namely, the unhappy marriage of historical criticism and Christian Scripture. Let me begin this section by referring once more to Levenson, who is adamant that 'historical criticism should not be abandoned'. What he thinks must be abandoned, however, are 'its totalistic claims'.[127] That is to say, according to Levenson, there must be room also for traditional religious approaches that do not accept historical-critical presuppositions. Krentz, on the other hand, arguing for a somewhat different 'solution', urges us to 'seek to use historical criticism in the service of the Gospel'.[128]

---

[121]   Dobbs-Allsopp, 'Rethinking', 269f.

[122]   Lewis, *'Descriptione'*, 12. However, we should note that Lewis actually goes on to say that the study of the past can liberate us from the past as well, which has also been pointed out by Dobbs-Allsopp, 'Rethinking', 269.

[123]   Lewis, *Experiment*, 139.

[124]   Ibid., 140, 141.

[125]   Seitz, *Word*, 99.

[126]   Lewis, *Reflections*, 102.

[127]   Levenson, *Hebrew Bible*, 123.

[128]   Krentz, *Historical-critical Method*, 61.

But how can that be done? Or perhaps more to the point, is it realistic to expect that an approach that works with an immanentist concept of history can be employed in the service of the gospel? Is not at the heart of the gospel a message that transcends the principles of analogy and correlation?[129] As Long has noted, 'the very center of Old Testament historiography – the notion that God is the Lord of history – is denied a priori by the fundamental assumptions of the historical method as typically practiced'.[130]

By the same token, one also wonders whether it is any more realistic to assume that a historical-critical approach governed by secular and sometimes even distinctly anti-Christian notions[131] can assist us in our quest to read the Old Testament as part of Christian Scripture.[132] This, however, is precisely what, for instance, proponents of the canonical approach seem to be hoping. Being less optimistic in that respect, I believe that Levenson has hit the nail on the head in noting that

> most Christians involved in the historical criticism of the Hebrew Bible today . . .
> seem to have ceased to want their work to be considered distinctively Christian . . .
> They are Christians everywhere except in the classroom and at the writing table,
> where they are simply honest historians striving for an unbiased view of the past.[133]

However, as the 'unbiased view' of the historical-critical approach has turned out to be a chimaera, it has become necessary to reassess the underlying presuppositions of critical biblical scholarship. Especially those wishing to read the biblical texts as Christian Scripture – which is an endeavour that in itself already implies a specific bias – need to reconsider whether, and to what extent, the historical-critical approach as traditionally practised can contribute to that venture. Secondly, in the light of Dobbs-Allsopp's criteria for historical inquiry it also needs to be asked how far historical-critical scholarship has actually done justice to its objects of investigation. In particular, one wonders whether

---

[129] Levenson, *Hebrew Bible*, 123, is well aware of these problems, as is apparent in his claim that 'historical criticism is necessary (*though not necessarily in accordance with Troeltsch's principles*)' (my italics).

[130] Long, 'Historiography', 155.

[131] Note, e.g., Sundberg's point that scholars in the Troeltschian tradition read the Bible *etsi deus non daretur* (as if there were no God). Or note Spinoza's claim, made in his *Tractatus theologico-politicus*, that 'the rule for interpretation should be nothing but the natural light of reason which is common to all – not any supernatural light nor any external authority' (quoted in Plantinga, 'Scripture Scholarship', 250).

[132] See Bartholomew, *Reading*, 88f., who has pointed out that 'throughout Krentz's account of the historical critical method there is a tension between reading Scripture as Scripture and the handling of it by historical criticism as another ancient text'.

[133] Levenson, *Hebrew Bible*, 29.

historical critics have always respected the *otherness* of the texts in question, including the philosophical concepts that inform these texts.[134]

To conclude, the renewal of historical criticism requires a reconceptualization of the approach that engages constructively with the philosophical, literary-critical, theological and socio-religious criticisms sketched above. However, at a time when we are increasingly aware of the social location of the investigating scholar and the important – and undeniable – role played by his or her presuppositions, it may also mean that scholars who wish to hear the biblical texts as Christian Scripture can begin to become 'honest *Christian* historians striving for a constructive and ethical dialogue with the past', to modify Levenson's phraseology slightly. As we have seen above, it is important that this dialogue be an ethical one, i.e. that the historian – whether Christian or not – respect the otherness of the other and be prepared to allow the texts to challenge his or her own *Weltanschauung*.

I therefore concur with Collins that 'the inevitability of presuppositions should not be taken as an invitation to excel in bias'.[135] However, in Collins's view 'to excel in bias' seems to be tantamount to being 'open to transcendence'.[136] He fails to see that those who exclude transcendental causes could just as well be accused of 'excelling in bias', for, as has been pointed out by Plantinga, what we are dealing with are simply 'different philosophical/theological positions that dictate different ways of pursuing Scripture scholarship'.[137] Given these positions, my contention is that scholars committed to reading the Bible as Scripture need to consider whether it is possible to renew biblical interpretation without, at the same time, renewing historical criticism. More specifically, what is required is a type of historical criticism that allows for a perspective such as has been advocated by LaCocque and Ricoeur who note that the biblical

---

[134] See in this context LaCocque and Ricoeur, *Thinking Biblically*, xv, who point out that in theological discourse 'philosophical speculation is . . . inextricably intermingled with what deserves to be called "biblical thought"'. They go on to venture the 'working hypothesis . . . that there are modes of thought other than those based on Greek, Cartesian, Kantian, Hegelian, etc. philosophy' and that the biblical texts 'are forms of discourse that give rise to philosophical thinking' (ibid., xvi).

[135] Collins, 'Critical Biblical Theology', 7, quoting Stendahl. Stendahl had put it thus: 'the relativity of human objectivity does not give us an excuse to excel in bias, not even when we state our bias in an introductory chapter' ('Biblical Theology', 22).

[136] In Collins's essay the above quote is preceded by the remark that 'some biblical theologians [Collins refers to Stuhlmacher at this point] suggest that we should refashion the presuppositions of scholarly method and replace the "hermeneutic of suspicion" with a "hermeneutic of consent" that would be "open to transcendence"' (Biblical Theology', 7).

[137] Plantinga, 'Scripture Scholarship', 267.

text *teaches* – this is what the word *torah* means. And the community *receives* instruction. Even when this relation surpasses that between authority and obedience to become one of love, the difference in altitude between the word that teaches with authority and the one that responds with acknowledgment cannot be abolished. In this regard, faith is nothing other than the confession of this asymmetry between the word of the teacher and that of the disciple . . .'[138]

Bibliography

Alter, R., *The Art of Biblical Narrative* (New York: Basic Books, 1981)

—, *The Art of Biblical Poetry* (New York: Basic Books, 1985)

—, 'Introduction to the Old Testament' in idem and F. Kermode (eds.), *The Literary Guide to the Bible* (London: Fontana Press, 1989), 11–35

Alter, R., and F. Kermode, 'General Introduction' in idem (eds.), *The Literary Guide to the Bible* (London: Fontana Press, 1989), 1–8

Althusser, L., 'From *Capital* to Marx's Philosophy', in idem and E. Balibar, *Reading Capital*, tr. Ben Brewster (New York: Pantheon Books, 1970), 11–39

Andersen, F.I., and D. N. Freedman, *Amos: A New Translation with Introduction and Commentary* (AB, 24A; New York: Doubleday, 1989)

Bartholomew, C.G., *Reading Ecclesiastes: Old Testament Exegesis and Hermeneutical Theory*, (AnBib, 139; Rome: Editrice Pontificio Istituto Biblico, 1998)

Barton, J., 'Historical Criticism and Literary Interpretation: Is There Any Common Ground?' in S.E. Porter, P. Joyce and D.E. Orton (eds.), *Crossing the Boundaries: Essays in Biblical Interpretation in Honour of Michael D. Goulder* (BIS, 8; Leiden: E.J. Brill, 1994), 3–15

—, *Reading the Old Testament: Method in Biblical Study* (London: Darton, Longman & Todd, 1996²)

---

[138] LaCocque and Ricoeur, *Thinking Biblically*, xvii. However, Collins, 'Critical Biblical Theology', 8, has sought to defend the pursuit of a Troeltschian type of historical criticism because 'it has provided a framework within which scholars of different prejudices and commitments have been able to debate in a constructive manner' (cf. also 15). But, as Levenson and Plantinga have pointed out, this is a delusion. Plantinga, 'Scripture Scholarship', 268, for instance, has rightly noted that Collins's principles 'would be accepted by only a tiny minority of contemporary Christians'. Levenson, too, is sceptical as to whether historical criticism has actually facilitated a constructive debate, remarking that Collins "has not explained how the Troeltschian historicism that he endorses can provide a context for dialogue with anyone who does not accept its presuppositions' (*Hebrew Bible*, 120). Indeed, Levenson goes on to point out that 'were we historical critics to be classed as a religious body, we should have to be judged a most minuscule sect indeed – and one with a pronounced difficulty relating to groups that do not accept our beliefs' (ibid.).

Berlin, A., *The Dynamics of Biblical Parallelism* (Bloomington: Indiana University Press, 1985)

Childs, B.S., *Biblical Theology in Crisis* (Philadelphia: Westminster Press, 1970)

—, *The Book of Exodus: A Critical, Theological Commentary* (OTL; Louisville: Westminster Press, 1974)

—, *Introduction to the Old Testament as Scripture* (Philadelphia: Fortress Press, 1979)

—, *Old Testament Theology in a Canonical Context* (Philadelphia: Fortress Press, 1986)

Clines, D.J.A., 'Story and Poem: The Old Testament as Literature and as Scripture', *Int* 34 (1980), 115–127

Collins, J.J., 'Is a Critical Biblical Theology Possible?' in W.H. Propp, B. Halpern and D.N. Freedman (eds.), *The Hebrew Bible and Its Interpreters* (Winona Lake, IN.: Eisenbrauns, 1990), 1–17

Compier, D.H., *What Is Rhetorical Theology? Textual Practice and Public Discourse* (Harrisburg: Trinity Press International, 1999)

Dobbs-Allsopp, F.W., 'Rethinking Historical Criticism', *BibInt* 7 (1999), 235–271

Eagleton, T., *Literary Theory: An Introduction* (Oxford: Basil Blackwell, 1996[2])

Eco, U., 'Between Author and Text' in idem, R. Rorty, J. Culler and C. Brooke-Rose, *Interpretation and Overinterpretation*, ed. Stefan Collini (Cambridge: Cambridge University Press, 1992), 67–88

—, *Six Walks in the Fictional Woods*, The Charles Eliot Norton Lectures 1993 (Cambridge, MA: Harvard University Press, 1995)

Gadamer, H.-G., *Truth and Method*, rev. tr. J. Weinsheimer and D.G. Marshall (London: Sheed & Ward, 1989[2])

Gowan, D.E., 'The Book of Amos: Introduction, Commentary, and Reflections' in L.E. Keck, et al. (eds.), *The New Interpreter's Bible* (Nashville: Abingdon Press, 1996), 7:337–431

Gunn, D.M., and D.N. Fewell, *Narrative in the Hebrew Bible* (OBS; Oxford: Oxford University Press, 1993)

Hall, D.R., *The Seven Pillories of Wisdom* (Macon: Mercer University Press, 1990)

Harvey, V.A., *The Historian and the Believer: The Morality of Historical Knowledge and Christian Belief* (New York: Macmillan, 1966)

Hayes, J.H., *Amos – The Eighth-Century Prophet: His Times and His Preaching* (Nashville: Abingdon Press, 1988)

Hirsch, E.D., Jr., *Validity in Interpretation* (New Haven: Yale University Press, 1967)

Jeremias, J., *The Book of Amos: A Commentary*, tr. D.W. Stott (OTL; Louisville: Westminster / John Knox Press, 1998)

Krentz, E., *The Historical-critical Method* (London: SPCK, 1975)

Kugel, J.L., *The Idea of Biblical Poetry: Parallelism and its History* (New Haven: Yale University Press, 1981)

LaCocque, A., and P. Ricoeur, *Thinking Biblically: Exegetical and Hermeneutical Studies*, tr. D. Pellauer (Chicago: University of Chicago Press, 1998)

Lentricchia, F., *Criticism and Social Change* (Chicago: University of Chicago Press, 1983)

Levenson, J.D., *The Hebrew Bible, the Old Testament, and Historical Criticism: Jews and Christians in Biblical Studies* (Louisville: Westminster / John Knox Press, 1993)

Lewis, C.S., 'De descriptione temporum' in idem, *Selected Literary Essays*, ed. W. Hooper (Cambridge: Cambridge University Press, 1969), 1–14

—, *Reflections on the Psalms* (London: Fount, repr. 1977)

—, *An Experiment in Criticism* (Cambridge: Cambridge University Press, repr. 1992)

Lohfink, N., 'Gab es eine deuteronomistische Bewegung?', in W. Gross (ed.), *Jeremia und die 'deuteronomistische Bewegung'* (BBB, 98; Weinheim: Beltz Athenäum, 1995), 313–382

Long, V.P., 'Historiography of the Old Testament', in D.W. Baker and B.T. Arnold (eds.), *The Face of the Old Testament: A Survey of Contemporary Approaches* (Grand Rapids: Baker Book House, 1999), 145–175

McIntyre, J., 'Historical Criticism in a "History-Centred Value System"' in S.E. Balentine and J. Barton (eds.), *Language, Theology and the Bible: Essays in Honour of James Barr* (Oxford: Clarendon Press, 1994), 370–384

Möller, K., 'Rehabilitation eines Propheten: Die Botschaft des Amos aus rhetorischer Perspektive unter besonderer Berücksichtigung von Am. 9,7–15', *EuroJT* 6 (1997), 41–55

—, 'Presenting a Prophet in Debate: An Investigation of the Literary Structure and the Rhetoric of Persuasion of the Book of Amos' (unpub. PhD thesis, Cheltenham and Gloucester College of Higher Education, Cheltenham, 1999)

—, Review of Aaron Schart, *Die Entstehung des Zwölfprophetenbuchs*, *Jahrbuch für evangelikale Theologie* 13 (1999), 105–108.

Nogalski, J.D., review of Aaron Schart, *Die Entstehung des Zwölfprophetenbuchs*, *TLZ* 124 (1999), 503–505.

Paul, S.M., *Amos: A Commentary on the Book of Amos*, Hermeneia (Minneapolis: Fortress Press, 1991)

Perdue, L.G., *The Collapse of History: Reconstructing Old Testament Theology* (OBT; Minneapolis: Fortress Press, 1994)

Perlitt, L., *Vatke und Wellhausen: Geschichtsphilosophische Voraussetzungen und historiographische Motive für die Darstellung der Religion und Geschichte Israels durch Wilhelm Vatke und Julius Wellhausen* (BZAW, 94; Berlin: Alfred Töpelmann, 1965)

Petersen, D.L., and K.H. Richards, *Interpreting Hebrew Poetry* (Minneapolis: Fortress Press, 1992)

Plantinga, A., 'Two (or More) Kinds of Scripture Scholarship', *Modern Theology* 14 (1998), 243–278

Polzin, R., ' "The Ancestress of Israel in Danger" in Danger', *Semeia* 3 (1975), 81–97

Rendtorff, R., 'Isaiah 6 in the Framework of the Composition of the Book' in idem, *Canon and Theology*, tr. and ed. M. Kohl (Edinburgh: T. & T. Clark, 1994), 170–180

Rudolph, W., *Joel, Amos, Obadja, Jona* (KAT, 13.2; Gütersloh: Gerd Mohn, 1971)

Schart, A., *Die Entstehung des Zwölfprophetenbuchs: Neubearbeitungen von Amos im Rahmen schriftenübergreifender Redaktionsprozesse* (BZAW, 260; Berlin: W. de Gruyter, 1998)

Schultz, R.L., *The Search for Quotation: Verbal Parallels in the Prophets* (JSOTSup, 180; Sheffield: Sheffield Academic Press, 1999)

Seeberg, R., *Die Kirche Deutschlands im neunzehnten Jahrhundert: Eine Einführung in die religiösen, theologischen und kirchlichen Fragen der Gegenwart* (Leipzig: Deichert, 1903)

Seitz, C.R., *Word without End: The Old Testament as Abiding Theological Witness* (Grand Rapids: Eerdmans, 1998)

Stendahl, K., 'Biblical Theology: A Program' in idem, *Meanings: The Bible as Document and as Guide* (Philadelphia: Fortress Press, 1984), 11–44

Sternberg, M., *The Poetics of Biblical Narrative: Ideological Literature and the Drama of Reading* (Bloomington: Indiana University Press, 1987)

Strauss, L., *Natural Right and History* (Chicago: University of Chicago Press, 1953)

Sweeney, M.A., 'Three Recent European Studies on the Composition of the Book of the Twelve: Review Essay', *Review of Biblical Literature* [http:www.bookreviews.org] (1999)

Thiselton, A.C., *Interpreting God and the Postmodern Self: On Meaning, Manipulation and Promise* (Edinburgh: T. & T. Clark, 1995)

Troeltsch, E., 'Über historische und dogmatische Methode in der Theologie: Bemerkungen zu dem Aufsatze "Über die Absolutheit des Christentums" von Niebergall' (1898), in idem, *Gesammelte Schriften*. II. *Zur religiösen Lage, Religionsphilosophie und Ethik* (Tübingen: J.C.B. Mohr [Paul Siebeck], 1922[2]), 729–753

Watson, F., *Text, Church and World: Biblical Interpretation in Theological Perspective* (Grand Rapids: Eerdmans, 1994)

Wolff, H.W., *Joel and Amos: A Commentary on the Books of the Prophets Joel and Amos*, tr. W. Janzen, et al. (Hermeneia; Philadelphia: Fortress Press, 1977)

Wright, N.T., *The New Testament and the People of God* (Minneapolis: Fortress Press, 1992)

10

Critical but Real: Reflecting on N.T. Wright's *Tools for the Task*

Thorsten Moritz

In 1992 Tom Wright published volume one of what many – myself included – regard as one of the most important projects in New Testament studies for a long time. The project title is *Christian Origins and the Question of God*. Its particular significance derives not least from the fact that Wright demonstrates a remarkable degree of epistemological and hermeneutical sophistication.[1] His aim is to contribute to a resolution of the crisis in biblical hermeneutics by providing a critical-realist account[2] of early Christianity. He intends to do so by facing up to the postmodern challenges to traditional biblical scholarship without, however, falling into the trap of simplistically searching for 'objective' or 'timeless' truths.[3] Instead he proposes a 'hermeneutic of love'[4] based on an epistemology of

---

[1] For a philosopher who gives Wright high marks on methodological sophistication see Martin, *Elusive*, 134–139.

[2] Debates about the appropriateness of human language for describing the entities to which this language refers are not peculiar to the theological or the philosophical academy. One finds similar conversations in the natural sciences (cf. Boyd, 'Current', 41–82).

[3] Again, similar extremes (such as those of postmodern 'no meta-narrative' relativism on the one hand and a fundamentalist objectivism on the other) can be found in virtually all sciences (cf. Avis, *God*, 144f. and especially van Huyssteen, *Realism*, 7–15). Avis is a little more optimistic and suggests that it might be difficult to find 'paid-up naïve realists in the scientific community' (145).

[4] Wright, *People*, 64 (cf. Stuhlmacher's similar phrase 'Hermeneutik des Einverständnisses').

critical realism.[5] In terms of a *renewal* of biblical interpretation it is imperative to examine Wright's discussion of methodology in New Testament
interpretation.

Volume one is entitled *The New Testament and the People of God* (1992)[6] and
will be the focus of this chapter.[7] It has three main sections, the second and third
of which discuss first-century Judaism and the narrative world of early Christianity. These two sections are lucid, witty, immensely erudite and academically inspiring. But it is the first main section – entitled *Tools for the Task* –
which is crucial for our purposes. I once asked a research student to read this
section carefully and to come back the following week so that we could discuss
it. He rang me a couple of days later and confirmed that he found it lucid, witty
and immensely erudite; but was it really necessary? He concluded that perhaps
he was not the 'theological type' after all and is now married and works for a
major insurance company.

But to take the student's initial question seriously, how necessary are the
kinds of considerations which fill the first 114 pages of *The New Testament and
the People of God*? Having reached the end of those pages many a New Testament scholar is tempted to think 'let's move on to the real work'. And yet it is
those pages that set the scene for the entire project. Wright does his best to instil
in his readers a strong sense of the hermeneutical responsibility inherent in
theological interpretation,[8] and he does so by appealing to 'critical realism'.
Having pointed out above that critical realism is a well-established category in a
variety of sciences, it is equally clear that it is used in diverging ways by different

---

[5] See Avis's discussion of 'qualified realism' in his *God*, 149–151, where he refers to a
number of scholars who employ a variety of terminology to express essentially the same
kind of hermeneutical awareness (Barker, Bowker and Soskice use the term 'critical
realism'; Tillich coined the phrase 'symbolic realism' and Berdyaev reversed the
phrase: 'realist symbolism'. Peacocke speaks of 'qualified realism' and Newton-Smith
of 'temperate rationalism'. All of them insist that there are things 'out there' that can be
theorised about usefully, but at the same time that the theories or descriptions themselves are constructions of the mind that must not be mistaken for reality itself (e.g.
Barbour, *Models*, 36f.). One should also add Torrance, *Reality*, passim, who discusses
realism in theology in some detail.

[6] I reviewed volume 2 (*Jesus and the Victory of God*) extensively in *EuroJT* 6.2 (1997),
179–183.

[7] It is a matter of surprise to me that the recent volume, *Jesus and the Restoration of Israel*
(ed. C. Newman) pays so little attention to Wright's treatment of methodological
issues in his first volume. The exception is McGrath's contribution 'Reality, Symbol
and History' which consists of theological reflections on Wright's portrayal of Jesus but
which has a brief section on critical realism (162–168). Also Evans, 'Naturalism', in the
same volume, though Wright disagrees with much of Evans's assessment ('Dialogue').

[8] Importantly and rightly he rejects any artificial separation of history from theology.

academic constituencies. Wright himself uses it pretty much in the sense suggested by Ben Meyer in his *Critical Realism and the New Testament* (1989).[9] They both share the concern to find and apply to the New Testament an epistemology which avoids the abyss of naïve realism and positivism on the one hand and relativistic pragmatism and phenomenalism on the other (so-to-speak the optimistic and pessimistic versions of the Enlightenment epistemological legacy).[10] The critical realist is conscious of the subjectivity of all human existence, but insists on differentiating between authentic and inauthentic subjectivity on the grounds of recognizing the reality and basic accessibility of 'the things out there'. Wright's development of this (as should become clear throughout this chapter) runs along the following line: because critical realism succeeds better than alternative approaches in accounting for the storied nature of our universe, it presents us with the best opportunity to renew our understanding of history, literature and theology. It is the argument of this chapter that critical realism (as developed by B.F. Meyer and N.T. Wright) offers a promising starting point for renewing biblical interpretation.

Context

Attempts to articulate one's awareness of the complexities involved in the interpretation of history are not new in theology, even less in the philosophy of religion. What is fairly new within New Testament scholarship is the strong desire to locate 'the entire phenomenon of text-reading within an account of the storied and relational nature of human consciousness'.[11] Wright's endeavour depends largely on two premises. In order of priority they are (1) the storied nature of all human knowledge (i.e. stories form the fundamental matrix of worldview), and consequently (2) the desirability and essential possibility of uncovering human intentionality in texts and events.[12] As far as the latter (intentionality) is concerned there is a recognition that authorial intention is not by definition identical with textual meaning (the text may contain echoes, evocations and the like which were not in the author's mind). By the same token, authorial intention may not be embodied successfully in the text. And no matter how hard the author intends a certain illocution (let alone perlocution), intention by itself cannot guarantee the embodiment of the

---

[9] The term became *en vogue* in theology in the mid-eighties as the following major studies show: McFague, *Metaphorical Theology*; Peacocke, *Intimations of Reality*; van Huyssteen, *The Realism of the Text*; and Soskice, *Metaphor and Religious Language*.

[10] Wright, *People*, 34.

[11] Ibid., 61.

[12] Ibid., 54–64.

intended meaning in the utterance or text. Meyer had already lamented that a Hirschian hermeneutic[13] – understood in a reductionist and empiricist fashion – leads to a mistreatment of the text as an index of the author's intellectual processes. This effectively is to commit what Wimsatt and Beardsley famously called the 'intentional fallacy'.[14] Beardsley, of course, then went on to promulgate the virtues of 'semantic autonomy' which, he argued, occurs the very moment when mental processes are committed to writing. Somewhat dubiously he bases this on Hirsch's own observation that occasionally authors are made aware of and agree with meanings in their own earlier texts which at the time had not occurred to them at all.[15]

Why mention the Beardsley/Hirsch debate at this point? It seems to me that given Wright's authorially centered and intentionalist language (there is talk of 'entering the author's mind',[16] of the need to locate reading 'within an account of the storied and relational nature of human consciousness',[17] the meaning of history lying 'in the intentionalities of the characters concerned',[18] the necessity to find out what humans in the past 'thought they were doing, wanted to do, or were trying to do'[19] and of historical meaning deriving from the interplay of human intentionality, etc.[20]), the question of the relationship between his appropriation and development of Meyer's critical-realist approach[21] and Hirsch's defence of the author is worth exploring. It is true that the latter became something of a black sheep in the literary critical family not long after the publication of *Validity in Interpretation* (1967). At a time when even Gadamer's 'two horizons' approach almost looks conservative (in the sense that he ascribes at least *some* determinative significance to the text) this is not surprising. Had Hirsch published a decade or two earlier he probably would have got away with it. As it stands, even his friendly critics feel compelled to cover their

---

[13] The reference is of course to E.D. Hirsch's *Validity in Interpretation*.

[14] Wimsatt and Beardsley, 'Fallacy', 1–13.

[15] Beardsley, 'Meaning', 169–181. For a rejoinder see Meyer, *Critical*, 39f. It stands to reason that to confront an author with a variety of interpretations of his or her work is hardly conclusive evidence of semantic autonomy, unless the question of validity in textual interpretation is excluded from the start.

[16] Wright, *People*, 61f.

[17] Ibid., 61.

[18] Ibid., 95.

[19] Ibid., 109.

[20] Ibid., *People*, 91 (cf. 56–58 and 62–64).

[21] Meyer, to be sure, derives much of his inspiration from Lonergan's *Method in Theology* and *Insight*, but also from Collingwood, *Idea of History*. Wright was able to draw on Meyer's work from 1989 after the completion of his first draft of *People* (32). Meyer's monograph *The Aims of Jesus* was published in 1979.

tracks by pointing out that many would today regard Hirsch as an old-fashioned positivist whose *jeu d'esprit* offers a recommendation dressed up as a heu-
ristic argument[22] and whose meaning and significance distinction betrays a
Cartesian dualism between subjectivity and objectivity.[23] Anthony Thiselton's
strategy is to point out the inadequacy of Hirsch's pre-Wittgensteinian hermeneutic in a post-Gadamerian world[24] and to effectively conclude that it is best
not to devote much further discussion to 'Hirsch's own over-simplified arguments'.[25] This piece of advice was apparently not lost on Wright who – despite,
I suspect, certain sympathies for Hirsch – omits any reference to him altogether. And yet the question needs asking: how far has the Meyer/Wright
defence of critical realism progressed from Hirsch's somewhat dated
phenomenology?

At first glance, Wright appears to use the same kind of language for which
Hirsch has been taken to task for the last thirty years. But he does not actually
mention, let alone appeal to Hirsch or any of his closer allies.[26] Instead he repeatedly and quite rightly assures his readers that he has no wish to fall either
into the positivistic trap or indeed the phenomenalistic one. Wright does acknowledge his considerable debt to Meyer.[27] If, therefore, we ask Meyer
about his relationship to Hirschian phenomenology, we find him quite forthcoming. He confirms his significant sympathies with Hirsch, though not
without noting some deficiencies. He argues that Hirsch's case would have
been stronger had he not committed the identity fallacy (i.e. to regard
authorial meaning and valid textual meaning as identical[28]) or indeed the

---

[22] E.g. Juhl, *Interpretation*, 12.

[23] Vanhoozer, *Meaning*, 84, points to Kuhn's philosophy of science according to which
'scientific knowledge is not a copying of reality but a construction of it' and concludes
that, in the light of this particular objection, it is 'not so much Hirsch's definition of
meaning that needs redoing . . . so much as his outdated conception of scientific
knowledge'. In other words, Hirsch errs when he thinks that meaning can somehow
be appropriated objectively. Non-realists would add that Hirsch also errs when he
thinks that the subjective act of consciousness and the object of consciousness can be
separated as if they existed independently from each other.

[24] A phrase which Hirsch himself would be loath to accept – cf. his excursus (*Validity*,
245–264) where he refutes some of Gadamer's central presuppositions. Thiselton's
phrase 'post-Gadamerian' presumably refers primarily to (a) Gadamer's insistence on
the inevitable and even desirable fusion of the two horizons of text and reader, and (b)
his strong attention to the role of the reader's *Vorurteil* in interpretation.

[25] Thiselton, *Horizons*, 13.

[26] Such as Juhl.

[27] Wright, *People*, 61.

[28] A view defended not only by Hirsch but also by Knapp and Michaels, 'Theory', 20.

ontological fallacy of equating meaning with a mental phenomenon.[29] Once this is rectified – and Meyer suggests better ways of rectifying it than Beardsley had done[30] – Hirsch's case, according to Meyer, becomes quite persuasive.[31] So what is attractive about Hirsch's case and what are the weaknesses?

A major aspect of Hirsch's understanding of intention is his indebtedness to the early Husserl's phenomenology which distinguishes between the mental *act* of consciousness and the *phenomenon* or *object* which results from this act. The latter has no meaning apart from the former. Consequently, Hirsch, in his pursuit of authorial intention, does not 'differentiate consistently between the intention of the author . . . extrinsic to the text . . . and the intention of the author . . . expressed by the text'.[32] He assumes that by engaging the object of the author's experience the interpreter effectively gains access to the author's intention without having to enter his psyche in a romanticist fashion. Since it is not possible to be conscious without being conscious of *something*, the term 'intention' denotes the relationship between mental consciousness and the something at which this consciousness aims, that is, the message or meaning. Words only mean something if that meaning is someone's conscious meaning – or, in speech-act terminology, where someone does something with words.[33] In themselves words are incidental.[34] 'There is no such thing as the sense of the text.'[35]

Hirsch does not deny a multiplicity of *possible* meanings of any text, but he insists that authors who change their minds about their own intended meanings in earlier texts do not actually change those earlier meanings – they

---

[29] Meyer, *Critical*, 40.

[30] Ibid., 36–41.

[31] However, one might ask Meyer whether his notion of textual meaning is not in effect an authorial meaning (of sorts) of the actual readership (a point accepted quite freely by Hirsch himself, *Aims*, 8).

[32] Ibid. 36; though Osborne, *Spiral*, 394, seems to think, by implication, that Hirsch *does* want to separate authors from texts. But that is only true on the conceptual level, not on the level of authoritative interpretation (cf. Hirsch, *Validity*, 8f.).

[33] Similarly Vanhoozer, *Meaning*, 233f.

[34] Hirsch, *Validity*, 4. In the light of this claim I am not sure whether Thiselton's criticism that Hirsch espouses 'a largely *semantic* notion of meaning' (his italics) is altogether fair (*Horizons*, 13).

[35] Wolterstorff, *Discourse*, 172; cf. Vanhoozer, *Meaning*, 82. One might compare this, for instance, with Sternberg's insistence that 'our only concern is with "embodied" or "objectified" intention' (*Poetics*, 9). Sternberg examines this with reference to the category of 'story'. We shall see that for Wright the notion of story leads to critical realism in all three areas of literature, history and theology. He argues for a hermeneutic that integrates all three areas.

simply use those words effectively to create new meaning.[36] The very act of changing one's mind is an admission that there is something to be changed, namely earlier authorially intended meaning. What marks out Hirsch's contribution is not a denial that a text might mean all sorts of things, but that out of that multiplicity of meanings the one that matters from the point of view of validity in interpretation is that intended by the author at the time of composition. Anything else would be to give way to semantic autonomy. (On a rainy day Hirsch would famously apply the phrase 'cognitive atheism' to his non-realist adversaries, especially Derrida – whether Hirsch was ever tempted to apply this phrase to the late Husserl is less clear.)

Critical Realism

I asked the question about the relationship between Wright's critical realism and his 'hermeneutic of love'[37] on the one side and the old-fashioned Hirschian hermeneutics of innocence on the other.[38] If it is true that the latter can no longer be maintained on Hirsch's terms,[39] how does Wright's own project of recovering the intentionality of the biblical actors and authors compare? How can understanding of human intentionality[40] – in this case that of ancient authors – occur in the context of interpreting texts? How different is his view of intentionality really from Hirsch's? Does he espouse a more refined understanding, perhaps along the lines of Searle[41] who puts less stress on the 'mental act' of intentionality and more on the personal and institutional backgrounds and behavioural networks of speech-acts?[42] There is little doubt that underlying Wright's hermeneutic is a more refined ontology of meaning[43] than that

---

[36] *Validity*, 9. This differs markedly from Derrida's iterability concept where the repeatability of a text is not contingent on authorial intention (cf. Vanhoozer, *Meaning*, 78).

[37] Wright, *People*, 64.

[38] That is the assumption that consciousness is somehow self-transparent on a surface level. The counter view is one of a hermeneutic of suspicion (the view that a text is not capable of making its author's consciousness transparent).

[39] Vanhoozer, *Meaning*, 84f.

[40] Vanhoozer, ibid., 221, evoked a similar phrase ('understanding texts is ultimately a matter of interpreting human action') building on Ricoeur's suggestion that 'meaningful action is like a text' in that both need to be interpreted. But unlike Ricoeur Vanhoozer interprets action along the lines of a refined speech-act model.

[41] Searle, *Intentionality*, 160–179.

[42] Searle, *Construction*. See Thiselton, *Horizons*, 297–300, for a discussion of Searle's refinement of Austin's view of illocutionary acts.

[43] One which, incidentally, is not dissimilar to Vanhoozer's (*Meaning*, 299ff.), which was published later.

reflected in Hirsch's *Validity in Interpretation*.[44] But I suggest that the main differences between Wright's critical realism and the hermeneutics of innocence operate not primarily on the level of semantics or meaning or indeed intentionality, but in the area of narrative epistemology, particularly the role played by narratives[45] in the formation and subversion of worldview. Having said that, one needs to examine Wright's packaging of critical realism as a *distinct* alternative to previous approaches to the interpretation of early Christianity. It seems to me that despite numerous assurances that his endeavour is in no sense either positivistic or phenomenalistic (or indeed romanticist), any hermeneutic as strongly cognitional and historically oriented as his will find it difficult to avoid hints of historical positivism. Despite tremendous sympathies for Wright's appropriation of critical realism, I have to ask how realistic it is to present it as a novel *via media* which gets the interpreter from A to B unscathed, despite the 'snakes in the grass'.

Critical realism is for Wright a way of acknowledging that the thing to be known is other than the knower (realism), but that knowledge occurs only along the spiralling path of dialogue (i.e. hypothesis – verification/falsification) between knower and the thing to be known.[46] There is something to be known, but the act of knowing or understanding is subjective. Knowledge is subject to one's location, community and especially to the grid of one's worldview. Worldview depends on location and community. In short: it is contingent on one's narrative world. This is why Wright focuses sharply on the role of stories, both in the lives of the interpreters, as well as in the historical world of the texts' genesis. Knowledge occurs when people find things that fit the grid of their worldview. The telling of stories in the Bible has among its chief aims the subversion of the hearers' and readers' worldviews.

So far this seems straightforward and lucid. Except, of course, that some of this sounds phenomenalistic and some of it positivistic. This is hardly surprising. For the phenomenalist too argues that knowledge is subjective and the positivist agrees with the critical realist about the separate reality of the object 'out there'. Some resemblance between critical realism and phenomenalism and with a chastened positivism cannot in the final analysis be avoided. Critical realism is precisely about combining the strengths of a variety of approaches. What puzzles me is Wright's claim that critical realism, by insisting (rightly) that all knowledge is mediated, is entirely unrelated to a revived 'form of positivism, albeit in a chastened mood'.[47] What might such a 'chastened positivism'

---

[44] Although, to be fair to Hirsch, he provided a more refined account in his *The Aims of Interpretation* (1976).

[45] This will be our main focus in the second half of this chapter.

[46] Wright, *People*, 35, 45.

[47] Ibid., 37.

– from which Wright distances himself – look like? It would be represented, he
suggests, by the claim that when all the right 'allowances have been made, there
simply are some things which can still be said, on the basis of empirical sense-
data, about the world external to the observer(s)'. But if Wright is correct that
such a scenario is not possible even in principle or at any level, what is the point
of insisting, as he does quite rightly, that the realist 'acknowledges the reality of
the thing known'?[48] How is it, to use his words, that 'We all know that the hare
does in fact overtake the tortoise'?[49] How much daylight is there between the
realist and the positivist? And at the other end of the spectrum, if knowledge
occurs within the grid of worldview – and I agree that it does – does this not
vindicate the phenomenalist *to a degree*? Yes, Wright's critical realism goes
beyond historical positivism by recognizing that knowledge is a 'worldviewish'
category, not an objectivist one. And yes, he stops well short of the
phenomenalist's inevitable privatization of knowledge by locating interpretation within the 'larger story'. In that sense critical realism is a sensible *via media* –
but I am not so convinced that it is quite as discrete or novel an approach as
Wright implies. Wright the historian (and therefore interpreter) is still very
much interested in what happened, why it happened and what was intended to
happen.[50] What really matters is not the novelty character of critical realism as a
hermeneutical theory, but the way Wright uses 'story' and 'stories' as categories which help to control the interpretation of the history of early Christianity.[51]

My understanding of Wright's interpretative model as reflecting a moderate
hermeneutical syncretism is not unlike his own verdict concerning C.S.
Lewis's debates with exponents of romanticist readings (such as E. Tillyard).[52]

---

[48] Ibid., 35.

[49] Ibid., *People*, 42.

[50] For relevant passages see notes 17–21 above.

[51] Wright is astute enough to anticipate the charge of subjectivism or phenomenalism.
He responds by discussing verification of knowledge claims and by concluding that it is
impossible to construct a good working hypothesis on the basis of sense-data alone
(*People*, 37). Granted – as Wright demonstrates quite masterfully – one needs the larger
dimensions of worldview and stories within which to locate sense data. But that, it
seems to me, is a response to the positivist, not the phenomenalist. Wright's emphasis
on the fundamental and subversive nature of stories is exemplary, and his application of
those insights to the biblical texts and extra-biblical ancient Jewish texts is outstand-
ingly refreshing. But how radically different from a chastened hermeneutic of innocence is his basic epistemology (chastened in the sense of recognizing that the
phenomenalist has a point too)? Any answer to that question needs to await examination of his use of 'stories' as a hermeneutical category (see below).

[52] Ibid., 55f.

Wright detects an element of right on all sides. No, we can*not* work out what an author had for breakfast that morning, but yes, it is *in principle* desirable to get to know the author's intention. Incidentally, when Wright expresses concern that Lewis's aversion against saying too much about authors might be pushed too far, so that not only the *desirability* but even the *possibility* of knowing the author's intention is rejected,[53] one wonders whether he got the order wrong, though this is not clear. Does he mean(!) that the danger of pushing the Lewis line too far is that not only the (pragmatics of the) *possibility* but even the (principle of the) *desirability* of knowing the author's intention is rejected?[54] Be that as it may, perhaps one should not penetrate too far into the mind of the author. Back to the Lewis-Tillyard debate. Wright implies that there is right on both sides. Agreed. And that, I think, is true of the positivist-phenomenalist divide as well. The thrust of the question should not be 'How can we put as much daylight as possible between critical realism on the one side and positivism and phenomenalism on the other?' but rather, 'How can we ensure that the strengths of both positions (and there are some!) are integrated in a controllable fashion?'[55] And here Wright has far more to offer than recourse to the good old hypothesis/verification model. Specifically, he puts a premium on the role of what he calls 'larger stories', that is, those frameworks in people's lives that accommodate not only the hypotheses which need to be verified, but the very stuff which gives meaning to worldviews. Hypothesis and verification remain, but they operate on a different level, namely that of the controlling stories.[56]

How can we integrate historical and sociological research with the interpretation of ancient texts without seeking to do what the positivist also seeks to do, albeit under different preconceptions? Granted that it would be naïve to suggest that the process of acquiring knowledge moves in a straight line from the observation of sense-data to interpretation – without *Vorurteil*, to use Gadamer's phrase – it would be equally naïve to deny that the sense data play an important role at the beginning of historical inquiry[57] or that we could somehow find an alternative point of entry into the hermeneutical process which would bypass the sense data. What we can do is to reflect critically on the

---

[53] Ibid., 56.

[54] This way of putting it would absolutize the poem more than just to say that it may not be possible to recover the original intention.

[55] For the issue of controlling narratives see Wolterstorff, *Divine*, ch. 1, who uses the expression 'control beliefs'.

[56] Crossan, *Birth*, 97, laments that Wright's hypothesis and verification theory bypasses some major historical conclusions from the past, while presupposing some of them in practice (such as the view that the synoptic gospels are to be preferred to John as sources of information about the historical Jesus).

[57] As understood by Meyer in his earlier monograph *The Aims of Jesus*, 87f.

components effective in the two horizons. Wright reminds us that one of these major components is that of 'storied knowledge'. Whether we term this process of reflection 'critically realist' or whether we refer to it as a 'hermeneutical spiral' may seem immaterial. Most would agree with Wright – including Hirsch – that the process involves hypothesis and verification. My own preference would be to retain the expression 'critical realism' in distinction to and alongside 'hermeneutical spiral' to indicate precisely the component of storied knowledge. But what does 'storied knowledge' mean and what are the dynamics operative within it?

I currently know of no better guide in the world of New Testament scholarship for epistemological reflections than Wright with his insistence that knowledge occurs when the interpreter's hypothetical stories fit best with the stories already in place.[58] But in describing his own epistemological and hermeneutical stance he ends up using plenty of language which sounds noticeably similar to that used by Hirsch. This is not altogether surprising for he finds himself operating somewhere in the triangle of positivism, romanticism and phenomenalism. While he would clearly want to reject any identification with any of these 'isms', this is easier said than done for someone who rightly argues for a 'both-and' hermeneutic (i.e. to do justice to both pairings, reader-text and author-text)[59]. Before examining in more detail his approach to storied knowledge, I propose to summarize briefly my assessment of Wright's proposal so far.

In some areas Wright's approach is fairly traditional:

(1) He puts a high premium on historical accuracy.[60] For instance, his interpretation of the parables depends greatly on his reconstruction of their original historical setting. This is not a criticism, but the simple observation that a major ingredient of his interpretative endeavour is not at all dissimilar to the motivation behind various traditional critical approaches.

(2) The checks and balances he proposes for critical realism amount, at least initially, to the age-old hypothesis and verification framework. He knows himself (and says so) that this is hardly new.[61] What is new within New Testament studies is his articulate insistence that the verification of hypotheses must operate within a framework of recognizing the storied nature of knowledge. This we need to explore further.

(3) Wright stresses that the old subjective-objective dualism misses the point. But when applying this to the question of meaning and significance

---

[58] Wright, *People*, 45.
[59] Ibid., 62, 66.
[60] Ibid., 66f.
[61] Ibid., 37, 42, 98, 103.

(which he refers to as *continuing meaning*; or in Vanhoozer's terms, *intended* and *extended* meaning), he continues to insist on differentiating between different levels of appropriateness.[62] I agree that this is necessary[63] but can't see how it differs greatly from Hirsch who adopts a mediating stance in the debate between Heideggerians and Husserlians about the suitability of various metaphors for describing conscious acts (Husserl: 'bracketing'; Heidegger: 'circle'[64]). Yes, Hirsch does insist with Husserl that the content of consciousness can be *conceptually* differentiated or bracketed within the communicative act,[65] but he is equally clear that one 'cannot have a meaning without having its necessarily correlative effect or value'.[66] This is compatible with Wright's critical realism (and with Vanhoozer's understanding of communicative speech acts for that matter), and neither Hirsch nor Wright nor Vanhoozer seem particularly revolutionary at this point.

In the light of Wright's emphasis on intentionality[67] and his use of telescope and microscope imagery[68] one might be forgiven for suspecting a degree of old-fashioned positivism. But that would, as we shall see, be rather precipitate. So in what way has Wright advanced the hermeneutical discussion? So far two points have emerged which alone make reading *The New Testament and the People of God* compulsory for biblical scholars: (1) Wright's clear understanding of the ideological role of narratives (especially in the formation and subversion of worldviews) and his ability, based on that, to ask the interpretative questions that really matter theologically. (2) His consistent application of his critical-realist framework to his study of first-century Judaism and the stories formulated during that time (including, of course, the gospels).

Above I hinted at Wright's anticipation of the criticism that his understanding of knowledge as occurring only within the grid of worldview sounds subjectivist or phenomenalist. He responds by pointing to the spiral of hypothesis and verification and by insisting that there can be no empiricist arguments, only the 'one about puddings and eating'.[69] Of course, there is another saying about cakes and eating. And that raises the question whether Wright is having his and eating it. What support does he provide for the contention that his version of hermeneutical realism is more refined than the hermeneutics of innocence, yet without falling into the trap of phenomenalism? What are the

---

[62] Ibid., 67 (cf. 44), 91f.
[63] For reasons given by Vanhoozer in *Meaning*, 228ff., 259ff.
[64] Hirsch, *Aims*, 2–13.
[65] Ibid., 4f.
[66] Ibid., 8.
[67] Wright, *People*, 55–58, 62–64, 109–11, 118.
[68] Ibid., 62.
[69] Ibid., 45.

controls? And how does the interpreter get from A to B despite the 'snakes in the grass'?

How to Do Things with Stories

It would at best be unfortunate – more likely criminal! – to discuss Wright's appropriation of critical realism without looking in some detail at his examination of story and stories as epistemological categories. For Wright (and for others before him; one thinks of Frei, Sternberg, Alter and others) story and stories are major vehicles of worldviews – they even play a determining role in the formation of the latter. They are not the stuff of decoration and adornment, if anything they are at the very centre of the stuff of life itself. The reason why Wright insists that we need a critical-realist epistemology is that our universe itself is storied.

To talk of critical realism without talking about stories would be little more than to acknowledge that the so-called hermeneutical circle is in fact a hermeneutical spiral. That in itself is hardly earth shattering news, not even in the field of New Testament studies. What the *Tools for the Task* section in *The New Testament and the People of God* offers goes beyond advertising new terminology for a widely agreed concept. However, I do not see the retrieval of the principle of critical realism as such as Wright's most significant contribution. That seems to me to be his exploration of the precise linkage between 'the thing out there' (realism) to be communicated via texts and the (critical) act of reading the text which advances the discussion most. The main link, to use Wright's phrase, is that of 'storied knowledge'.[70] We cannot interpret properly unless we understand that there is no such thing as propositional truth if by that we mean something other than storied knowledge. Unless, therefore, reading is located within an appreciation of the significance of the stories behind the author (real or implied), *and* the text (including its history of effect), *and* the audience (again real or implied) *and* the one doing the reading/interpreting, the text read is likely to be misconstrued, to use Wright's metaphors,[71] as a mirror, a kaleidoscope, a telescope or a microscope, rather than as a complex instrument of subversion, confirmation, challenge, confrontation, intentionality – in short: ideology.[72] It may be true that the endeavour to keep the various interpretative horizons together is not peculiarly critically realist.

---

[70] Ibid., 38ff.

[71] Ibid., 62, 90, 94.

[72] I am not using the term 'ideology' here in the somewhat pejorative postmodernist sense of 'any form of restrictive faith'. On critical realism as an antidote to postmodernist construals of ideology see Meyer, *Reality*, 141–43.

So what is? It is partly the insistence that to understand the ideological nature of texts and interpretation means to allow notions of the empirical and the intentional and the rational to enter the process of making interpretative decisions,[73] but also and importantly the insistence that, as in the case of all human knowledge, interpretation is storied and relational.[74] It is this realization that enables Wright to articulate his epistemology within the triangular web of story, knowledge and worldview. For Wright, knowledge is about assessing the degree of fit between hypothesis and those stories already in place.[75] Not unlike Wolterstorff ('control beliefs') and perhaps Milbank ('metanarrative realism'),[76] it is here that he anchors the control needed to avoid hopeless subjectivism.

There are of course numerous ways to cut the hermeneutical cake. Some have (mis)used texts as cameras into the author's mind, others saw the ideal text as a true reflection of the realities or events conveyed. And there are those for whom texts are little more than an invitation to readers to reflect on their own mental activities or the structures of human existence. A critical-realist epistemology is always going to resist these approaches by centring around an account of intentionality which avoids the flight from understanding[77] without falling into positivism or indeed romanticism.[78] We shall have to look at the question of intentionality below, but not before asking how Wright puts the categories of story and stories to use in his articulation of critical realism.

If stories provide the most powerful ways of mediating worldview, it follows that they operate at a fundamental level of human existence. They cannot therefore be translated into 'propositional truth' without reducing the complex but powerful triangle of story, knowledge and worldview to something with far less public relevance or meaningfulness or indeed transformative power. But the critical-realist case for taking seriously the storied nature of

---

[73] On the question of the role of empirical data in the retrieval of knowledge Wright chooses his words more carefully than Meyer. While the former never tires of reminding his readers that working one's way up from empirical data, in however chastened a fashion, is essentially positivistic (*People*, 37, 82), the latter is less coy when it comes to highlighting the importance of empirical data (*Reality*, 142f.). But both agree that the myth of 'sense-knowing' being like ocular vision is just that, a myth.

[74] Wright, *People*, 44f.

[75] Ibid., 62.

[76] Wolterstorff, *Divine*, ch. 1; Milbank, *Theology*, ch. 12.

[77] Meyer, *Reality*, 115.

[78] This is the focus of many of Lonergan's writings. For an appreciative account of the latter see Meyer, *Reality*, ad loc. Meyer complains that 'For two hundred years exegetes have tried to read the New Testament through idealist, then romantic, then positivist, then existentialist, and all along through common-sense naïve-realist lenses, and failed even more conspicuously' (70f.).

knowledge and interpretation rests equally strongly on the perceived need for a *degree* of objectification[79] or control. How efficient is a story-focused critical realism à la Wright at avoiding positivistic pitfalls without going soft on control? It is clearly not enough to keep distancing oneself from sense-data-centred approaches – including what Wright likes to call 'chastened positivism' – unless one is prepared to show at what (other) level human knowledge operates. That other level cannot be intentionality as such (although it may play a part), as many a positivist would make that same appeal. But it could be (and in my view is) the level of worldview, that is the level within which intentionality can only make sense. The location of stories on the map(s) of worldviews – or better: the way stories mediate, challenge, confront, reshape, etc. those worldviews – is what determines meaning. It follows that all parties involved in the operation of worldviews have a role to play in interpretation. Put differently: critical realism as an attempt to articulate the triangle of worldview, stories and knowledge seeks to secure the determinedness of meaning by taking seriously the interplay of worldviews between the communicative partners in interpretation (both real and implied) while at the same time giving each of those partners their proper role. It is the fit between interpretative hypothesis and the worldviews embodied in the text, which matters crucially in forming judgements about correctness or lack of it in interpretation. This shifts the focus in interpretation from atomistic exegesis to larger narrative concerns without sacrificing the keen desire to distinguish between appropriate and inappropriate interpretations.

In regard to Wright's particular exposition and defence of critical realism a number of questions must be raised, some with a view to assessing the usefulness of his approach, others with a view to isolating the actual scholarly advances offered by Wright. One advance is undoubtedly that the discussion has moved on from the early days of speech-act theory ('how to do things with words'[80]) to 'how to do things with stories'. It is the correlation between text and what is 'out there' that is at stake in speech-act theories – the same is true of Wright's appropriation of critical realism, albeit on the levels of narratives and worldviews, not utterances and illocutions, though the two pairs are closely related. It would be fruitful to consider in some detail the similarities in approach between speech-act theory and critical realism.[81] There seem to me to be clear structural parallels between, say, Searle's exposition of the

---

[79] This reflects the understanding that meaning refers to an objective reality, however difficult it may be in the circumstances to determine correct meaning.

[80] This is the title of Austin's publication of his 1955 Harvard lectures.

[81] To my knowledge the classic exponents of speech-act theory in biblical studies and theology (such as Thiselton and Wolterstorff) have not yet interacted extensively with the kind of critical realism espoused by B.F. Meyer and N.T. Wright.

hypothesis that language is a rule-governed form of behaviour[82] and Wright's insistence that texts can only communicate effectively within the storied contexts of the various partners engaged in the communicative process. However, any detailed examination of the similarities in their approaches will have to wait for another day.[83]

Wicked Wolves and Wicked Tenants

What, then, makes a story a story and how are stories best analysed? Wright makes recourse to Greimas's actantial analysis, but over against structuralist approaches he combines this with a strong emphasis on the historical. It seems clear therefore, as Blomberg rightly remarks,[84] that Wright has no interest in Greimas's determinist philosophical stance. Blomberg wonders why Wright uses Greimas at all and concludes that he must have regarded these visualizations as helpful for illustrating the various Jewish storylines which Wright detects in Judaism, and especially the story or stories of Jesus. I suspect that there is more to it. If critical realism is about seeing text as the link between the reality out there and the stories and worldviews of the various agents in communication, it must find ways of providing control without falling into positivism. It seems to me – although Wright does not actually say so – that the Greimasian analysis of stories provides him with a measure of control by insisting that there is a formal dimension to stories. He illustrates this with reference to Little Red Riding-Hood and, by analogy, with reference to the parable of the Wicked Tenants. Presently I am not convinced that Wright's use of Greimas actually adds significant insights to his (or others') understanding of either text. Actantial analysis may be a good way of illustrating the interpreter's construal of storyline, but does it actually open up new interpretative dimensions? Wright thinks so and points to the observation that the parable of the Wicked Tenants illustrates the controversy in early Christian circles (between observant and non-observant Jews) about 'different tellings of the story of Israel's god, his people, and the world'.[85] But this observation seems to be based more on the interpreter's appreciation of the knowledge-story-worldview triangle in general than actantial analysis in particular.

The degree of benefit to be derived from applying Greimas's analysis to the Jesus stories (and those of Second Temple Judaism in general for that matter) is

---

[82] Searle, *Speech*, 16.
[83] For a preliminary exploration along similar lines (with particular reference to Sternberg) see Wolterstorff, *Discourse*, 235–252.
[84] Blomberg, *Stuff*, 30.
[85] Wright, *People*, 76.

debatable. But more significant for our purposes is one of Wright's little asides. For the sake of argument he reduces the story of Little Red Riding-Hood to the following: 'Little Red Riding-Hood was sent by her mother to take some food to her grandmother; she did so and they were all happy.'[86] This, Wright comments in the light of actantial analysis, would hardly qualify as a story, for it has no plot. Similarly, the sentence 'Little Red Riding-Hood took some food to her grandmother, but a wolf ate them both' does not qualify as story (for Wright). It is difficult to imagine why that should be so, if not because the sheer brevity of these versions makes them unavailable for Greimasian actantial analysis. As Barton maintains,[87] a different ending to the Little Red Riding-Hood story (such as the woodcutter freeing the wolf and marrying Little Red Riding-Hood) would change the entire worldview of the story. But surely, not to have such a resolution does not make the story less of a story simply because Greimas's actantial analysis demands a final denouement. There is value in applying actantial analysis to the stories in the sense that this forces the reader to slow down and to avoid jumping to quick conclusions, but I am not persuaded that it actually helps us a great deal with understanding the nature of stories. On that front, Wright's analysis of what I called the triangle (knowledge, story, worldview) is more compelling and even indispensable, for it is there that critical realism most persuasively carves out for itself a credible niche between 'chastened positivism' and phenomenalism.

Intentions, Intentions . . .

In the introduction to this contribution I noted that Wright puts considerable stress on the issue of authorial intention. So where are the differences to, say, the likes of E.D. Hirsch who regard authorial intention as nothing less than the main criterion for securing determinate meaning? For Wright, the issue is not primarily the status of authorial intention as such, but the wider issues surrounding the role of intentionality in human interaction and historical awareness. I therefore noted under the heading above, 'How to Do Things with Stories', that alongside the category of stories it is the issue of intentionality which seems to me to be one of the most crucial components of Wright's critical realism.[88] Before Wright it was primarily Meyer, at least within biblical studies, who focused on intentionality (and decision-making as the peak of human intentionality) as the key to historical understanding and who

---

[86] Ibid., 71.

[87] Barton, *Reading*, 116.

[88] If one had to add a third category that marks out Wright's appropriation of critical realism it would have to be his pursuit of historical and socio-political plausibility. On

developed this specifically with reference to Jesus' perspective and purpose.[89] When contemplating intentionality, Meyer does not subscribe to the naïve-realist construal of intentionality where the subject 'simply' knows an object, passively, infallibly and objectively. Meyer calls this the 'cognitional myth', a myth which tends to have as its corollary the view that consciousness is a subdivision of intentionality insofar as it denotes the subject's presentation of itself to itself as object. Rather, as Lonergan and Meyer insist, intentionality is the motivation behind or the locus of the human orientation towards knowing truth ('truth' here being understood as meaning that 'consciously corresponds to its object').[90] Intentionality is existentially human. Applied to the interpretation of texts this means that the intended sense can be located intrinsically in the text itself and that intentionality becomes once more the primary focus of interpretation. There is authentic subjectivity and there is inauthentic subjectivity. And the differentiation between the two hinges precisely on the interpreter's awareness of and attention to historical intentionality. It would, for instance, be naïve to propose an interpretation of the gospels which ignored their (and the interpreter's!) faith stance. Likewise, it would be inherently implausible to insist on isolationist interpretations of some of the (seemingly) vague kingdom parables of Jesus rather than to fit them within Jesus' wider intentionality. Both Meyer and Wright repeatedly – and to my mind rightly – lament the fact that points such as these need to be established all over again. And both have consistently devoted their energy to doing precisely that.

In the light of this general background, what role does authorial intention play within Wright's hermeneutic? The answer has to be a resounding 'I'm not quite sure.' It should certainly not be excluded;[91] in fact, it should be

---

his historical method – especially as compared with that of Troeltsch – Evans, *Naturalism*, 180–205, though whether Evans's attempt to show a significant proximity between Wright and Troeltsch (as far as historical method is concerned) is justified is at least debatable. See, for instance, Wright's discussion of 'miracles' on 92f. which suggests grave differences between his critically realist epistemology and Troeltsch's naturalism. I suspect Evans took his lead from a little side comment by Wright regarding certain similarities between Troeltsch's analogy principle and the suggestion that one might derive present 'meaning' from ancient intentionalities (*People*, 95 n. 30). See also Martin, *Elusive*, 134–141, who offers a quite different assessment of Wright's (for Martin essentially non-naturalistic) stance.

[89] Meyer, *Aims*, 175.

[90] The same argument could be applied *mutatis mutandis* not only to reality claims, but to aesthetic and ethical considerations (Meyer, *Reality*, 60). Wright, *People*, 94f., also regards intentionality at its most basic level as representing nothing less than the 'meaning' of history.

[91] Wright, *People*, 39, 56.

defended.[92] It can't be replaced by structuralist formalism,[93] (a) because the two stand in each other's way, and (b) because history itself is not just about what happened, but about how what happened relates to the intentionalities of the characters involved.[94] In principle it is possible to know an author's 'basic' intention,[95] just as it is possible to know what Caesar intended when crossing the Rubicon or King David when he chose Jerusalem.[96] But given the often-stressed significance of human intentionality for studying the meaning of history in general,[97] one wonders what the role of authorial intention is on the level of textual interpretation. Is (1) authorial intention just one factor of many in the distinction between appropriate and inappropriate interpretations? And (2) are there levels of meaning which transcend authorial intention? Wright's answer to the first question is 'yes': we need a theory of reading, which does justice to the particularity, as well as the otherness of the reader and the text, but also of the text and the author.[98] His answer to the second question is also 'yes'. He accepts the presence of *sensus plenior* in the New Testament (such as when Caiaphas speaks a word of the Lord without intending to) and regards it as an example of such a transcendent meaning.[99] The same could in principle be claimed for examples of allegory:[100] 'we have to make allowance for a *je ne sais quoi* which lies beyond what the author explicitly had in mind at the time'.[101] So once more, what precisely is the role of authorial intention in Wright's herme-neutic, especially if one refuses with Wright to restrict meaning to authorial intention?[102]

On a general level, Wright offers an extended discussion of aims, intentions and motivations in people's lives. Aims are about a person's fundamental direction in life. Intention is the specific application of the aim in particular (in principle repeatable) situations, that is, one's strategy.[103] Motivation is one's sense of appropriateness regarding one's specific action on one particular occasion. History is about all of the above plus the worldviews within which or *vis-à-vis* these dimensions operate. Terminologically this is helpful because it demarcates this type of approach to history from romanticizing and psychologizing

---

[92] Ibid., 58f.

[93] Ibid., 57.

[94] Ibid., 109, 111–113.

[95] Ibid., 56, 58, 118.

[96] Ibid., 95, 111.

[97] See for instance ibid., 93.

[98] Ibid., 62.

[99] Ibid., 58.

[100] Ibid., 57.

[101] Ibid., 58.

[102] Ibid., 62 n. 37, 66.

[103] This might be a more helpful term here than 'intention'.

exegesis. One would have wished for a similar clarification with reference to authorial intention. How is one to understand phrases like 'author's basic intention' and 'author's meaning'?[104] Does it refer to the author's aims on the level of story/stories? Or his rhetorical strategy? Or her motivation? Perhaps it is not justified to transfer these classifications from human intentionality to textual interpretation. Having said that, is it not Wright's aim – or even intention? – to hold together human intentionality as the stuff of historical meaning on the one hand and textual meaning on the other hand?

Wright's almost casual use of the expressions 'author's meaning' and 'author's intention' as virtual synonyms,[105] which stands in stark contrast to his careful classification of aims, intentions and motivations elsewhere,[106] signals an apparent disinterest in examining authorial intention at any level other than that of the fundamental stories of people's lives as well as the worldviews embodied in or challenged by the text/s to be interpreted. Similarly, there is a relative silence when it comes to 'meaning'. It is in principle determinable;[107] this implies the need to distinguish between more appropriate and less appropriate meanings in interpretation.[108] Meaning functions on different levels, the deepest of which is that of stories and worldviews. At the other end there is the basic level of meaning conceived as the intentionalities of the characters involved.[109] Here Wright appears to use 'meaning' in the sense of (as others would say) 'significance'. Where on the literary-critical map that stretches from Knapp and Michaels (meaning is authorial intention)[110] via speech–act theory (meaning is about illocutions achieved within language conventions)[111] to Ricoeur (the semantic autonomy of the text)[112] and Derrida (deconstruction) does Wright locate himself with reference to authorial intention?[113]

It goes without saying that a critical-realist epistemology needs to avoid construing meaning in either positivistic or phenomenalistic terms.[114] But what does it mean to avoid these extremes? It means in the first instance to debunk

---

[104] Ibid., 57f.

[105] Ibid., 56–58 (perhaps one could add 'author's mind' here as well, 59.

[106] Ibid., 110ff.

[107] Ibid., 62.

[108] Ibid., 66f., 91f.

[109] Ibid., 66, 95.

[110] Knapp and Michaels, 'Against Theory'.

[111] Searle, *Speech*.

[112] Ricoeur, *Interpretation*, 29.

[113] See Vanhoozer, *Meaning*, 241ff., for discussions of the notion of authorial intention since Hirsch.

[114] Wright, *People*, 66, 117. Needless to say, for Wright this rules out any association with Knapp and Michaels at one end of the spectrum, or Derrida at the other, but it is less clear where he would position himself nearer the centre of the map.

the cognitional myth that puts data perception prior to the grasping of larger realities.[115] More specifically it means to avoid any pretense to objectivity. That's fair enough. But it seems quite a challenge to avoid both pitfalls purely by being aware of one's viewpoints and by reading against the canvas of the 'larger stories'.[116] Yes, a critical-realist reading will want to be true to itself and the public world. And yes, readers will ideally be willing to be challenged and subverted at the level of stories and worldviews. And yes, the critical-realist reader will hopefully be equipped with a sound historical awareness. But could the 'ideal critical realist' not still be accused of actually being a chastened positivist? What is it about Wright's historically focused critical realism that marks it out as non-positivistic? The distinguishing feature is surely not Wright's strong historical interest as such, but his pursuit of historical research within an intentionality framework, a framework which consists primarily of the triangle discussed above: knowledge-story-worldview.

It seems to me that it will not do to accuse the positivist of seeking to interpret texts with one eye on their particular historical contexts while (quite rightly) doing precisely the same thing oneself. The 'chastened positivist' knows as well as Wright that the interpreter's historical accuracy is a prerequisite for getting at intentionalities (whether those of the real or implied author or those of the characters involved in the story). When Wright describes the positivistic parables critic as one who focuses on the historical context of the parable, that would also be an accurate description of some of his own work on the parables in *Jesus and the Victory of God*. Does the positivist, on one level at least, not seek to do precisely that which Wright himself calls for, that is, accurate historical reconstruction?[117] Even what Wright says about the dependence of any continuing meaning of parables on their being read historically sensitively[118] does not sound essentially different from Hirsch's old meaning-significance distinction. My conclusion is once more that the real difference between critical realism à la Wright and chastened positivism lies in Wright's much-needed attention to the overarching categories of story and worldview. It is here that his historically focused approach[119] demarcates itself from chastened positivism most substantially.[120]

---

[115] Ibid., 43.

[116] Ibid., 66f.

[117] Ibid., 66–69.

[118] Ibid., 67.

[119] Because Wright pursues his historical reconstructions from the top down (i.e. by making a larger hypothesis the grid through which the appropriateness or inappropriateness of interpretations ought to be judged) rather than starting with the normal critical tools, the term 'historicist' would not be appropriate here.

[120] To be sure, as the previous footnote implies, Wright's 'story approach' has major ramifications in the area of applied methodology.

The Proof of the Pudding . . .

The word 'pudding' may not feature in the 'Selected Topics' index of *The New Testament and the People of God*, but it appears fairly regularly in the main text.[121] It is shorthand for hypothesis and verification as key aspects of historical method.[122] It is about trying out and adjusting explanatory stories until the following are achieved: inclusion of relevant data, inner coherence or simplicity, and usefulness of the explanatory story to throw light on other related areas. Because there usually is no one fixed point against which hypotheses can be tested, a balance has to be found between inclusion of data and simplicity. None of this is new, as Wright himself acknowledges,[123] though his critique of some forms of tradition-historical criticism which try to achieve this balance by postulating early Christian 'schools', movements and communities is well taken.

This process of hypothesis and verification is sometimes called the 'hermeneutical spiral'.[124] Wright too speaks of a 'spiral of knowledge': all knowledge is derived from this epistemological spiral.[125] Every time one goes around the spiral the lenses of the telescope have altered, but every time there are still lenses. In his discussion of spirals and telescopes one finds Wright fighting on two fronts once again. Yes, critical realism does not abandon knowledge of the extra-linguistic world or the fact that there are facts; but no, critical realism does not yield to a positivist construal of access to the data. Yes, critical realists employ a strongly historical approach; but no, they are not historicists. Yes, snooker may seem to some like an inferior form of billiards; but no, to insist that it is not does not make me a positivist. And so on. In this fashion Wright's argument snakes its way through the epistemological jungle. The result is a credible plea for thorough historical work, which never loses sight of the larger and smaller stories involved. Whether it is possible to claim for such an approach that it puts as much daylight as Wright claims between itself and chastened positivism on the one hand and forms of phenomenalism on the other hand may be another matter.

So What's New?

It is clear where and how Wright locates himself on the epistemological map. The careful process of how he arrives at this location is significant for New

---

[121] See for instance 45, 57, 70.
[122] Ibid., 98–109.
[123] Ibid., 45, 103.
[124] Osborne, *Spiral*.
[125] Wright, *People*, 86, 109.

Testament study. Equally significant and impressive are the results of applying his epistemology to the question of Jesus and the (synoptic) gospels.[126] If the proof of the pudding is in the eating, this one seems pretty good. But to what extent does Wright's appropriation of critical realism advance New Testament scholarship? The answer, I think, is 'quite considerably'. There are two areas where it has become important to recover lost ground and to establish firmer foundations than have been laid before. One is the recovery of solid historical research as a non-negotiable dimension in gospel research. The other is to give notions of human intentionality their proper place within such research.

A number of open questions remain: how *should* the interpreter handle allegories and instances of *sensus plenior*? And if authorial intention is as important as he says, how does that relate to his (justified) claim that a text is an entity on its own? One detects a certain vagueness in Wright's argument here. It is not enough, though correct, to point out that certain 'potential meanings' are more appropriate than others,[127] or even to make such 'present meanings' contingent on the degree of correspondence between present and ancient intentionalities.[128] The general place accorded by Wright to human intentionality is to be welcomed from the perspective of a renewal of biblical interpretation – but the specifics of how human intentionality relates to matters of validity in textual interpretation need further exploration. It is true that Wright is concerned not only with a critical-realist view of reading, but also a critical-realist philosophy of history as well as a critical-realist view of theology. But the question remains: what precisely is the role of authorial intention in textual interpretation?

On a related matter, if 'significance' is not something that is artificially added on to events, actions, writings or speech (a view which would be indefensible and which to my knowledge those who make the case for maintaining a meaning-significance distinction have not held in the first place[129]), the question still remains: how *does* one move from intentionalities and worldviews and storylines to 'present meaning'? This is not an area which *The New Testament and the People of God* addresses in any detail, unless, of course, if worldview and story have now taken the place 'significance' held in earlier discussions. Have they? It seems to me that this – that is, the issue of stories and worldviews – is where the most significant advances have been made. And it is here that Wright's work is most significant from the perspective of a renewal of biblical interpretation, for neither positivism nor phenomenalism takes the story dimension of knowledge and interpretation seriously.

---

[126] Wright, *Jesus*.

[127] Wright, *People*, 67

[128] Ibid., 95

[129] I am here thinking of traditional exponents (such as Hirsch) of this distinction.

Wright's attention to the hermeneutical foundations of New Testament theology gives new impetus to the quest for such renewal. Most significant is Wright's emphasis on storied knowledge and the implications of this for the methodologies involved in interpreting narratives such as the gospels. This is so not least because it enables the interpreter once more to attempt to offer homogenous interpretations of these narratives, rather than to get lost in atomistic methodologies. It is difficult to see how any attempt to renew biblical interpretation could bypass Wright's proposals. Following the publication of *The New Testament and the People of God* it should no longer be possible to ask questions about meaning and significance without doing so against the backcloth of the larger stories involved at author, text and reader level. I think one can't be so sure that this necessarily involves a nearly comprehensive debunking of much of redaction criticism and form criticism.[130] Perhaps we need a both-and hermeneutic here as well. But these critical methodologies, and others for that matter, undoubtedly need to be subservient to the story dimension highlighted so effectively in *The New Testament and the People of God*. Wright's second volume, *Jesus and the Victory of God*, has already shown how much more fruitful his approach proves on the levels of both interpretation and relevance compared with older less sophisticated approaches, such as that of Hirsch. Critical realism as espoused and developed by Wright is not in principle incompatible with a Hirschian phenomenology, but it avoids some of the positivistic pitfalls of the latter and consequently succeeds in moving significantly beyond it in terms of interpretative yield. Equally importantly, by developing critical realism as a way of exploring the linkage between history, literature and theology, Wright succeeds in laying the foundations for a closer relationship between biblical studies and theology.

Bibliography

Austin, J., *How to Do Things with Words* (Cambridge, MA.: Harvard University Press, 1975)

Avis, P., *God and the Creative Imagination: Metaphor, Symbol and Myth in Religion and Theology* (London and New York: Routledge, 1999)

Barbour, I., *Myths, Models and Paradigms: A Comparative Study in Science and Religion* (New York: Harper & Row, 1974)

Barton, J., *Reading the Old Testament: Method in Biblical Study* (London: Darton, Longman & Todd, 1984)

---

[130] As implied in *People*, 52f., 87, 105. It is worth remembering that historical reconstruction, which is so important for Wright, lies at the heart of these methodologies. One can understand Crossan when, in reviewing Wright's method, he insists that one should not by-pass the methodologies and results of tradition-criticism without good reason (*Birth*, 96f., 100).

Beardsley, M.C., 'Textual Meaning and Authorial Meaning', *Genre* 1 (1968), 169–181

Blomberg, C., 'The Wright Stuff' in C. Newman (ed.), *Jesus and the Restoration of Israel* (Downers Grove: InterVarsity Press, 1999), 20–39

Boyd, R., 'The Current Status of Scientific Realism' in J. Leplin (ed.), *Scientific Realism* (Berkeley: University of California Press, 1984), 41–82

Collingwood, R.G., *The Idea of History* (Oxford: Oxford University Press, 1946)

Crossan, J.D., *The Birth of Christianity* (New York: HarperCollins, 1998)

Evans, C.S., 'Methodological Naturalism in Historical Biblical Scholarship' in C. Newman (ed.), *Jesus and the Restoration of Israel* (Downers Grove: InterVarsity Press, 1999), 180–205

Hirsch, E.D., *Validity in Interpretation* (New Haven: Yale University Press, 1967)

van Huyssteen, W. *The Realism of the Text: A Perspective on Biblical Authority* (Pretoria: University of South Africa, 1987)

—, *The Aims of Interpretation* (Chicago: University of Chicago Press, 1976)

Juhl, P.D., *Interpretation: An Essay in the Philosophy of Literary Criticism* (Princeton: Princeton University Press, 1980)

Knapp, S., and W.B. Michaels, 'Against Theory' in W.J.T. Mitchell (ed.), *Against Theory: Literary Criticism and the New Pragmatism* (Chicago: University of Chicago Press, 1985), 11–30

Lonergan, B., Insight: A Study of Human Understanding (London: Longmans, Green & Co., 1958)

Martin, R., *The Elusive Messiah: A Philosophical Overview of the Quest for the Historical Jesus* (Boulder: Westview, 1999)

McFague, S., *Metaphorical Theology: Models of God in Religious Language* (London: SCM Press, 1983)

Meyer, B.F., *The Aims of Jesus* (London: SCM Press, 1979)

—, *Critical Realism and the New Testament* (Allison Park: Pickwick, 1989)

—, *Reality and Illusion in New Testament Scholarship* (Collegeville: Liturgical Press, 1994)

Milbank, J., *Theology and Social Theory: Beyond Secular Reason* (Oxford: Basil Blackwell, 1990)

Newman, C.E., (ed.), *Jesus and the Restoration of Israel: A Critical Assessment of N.T. Wright's Jesus and the Victory of God* (Downers Grove: InterVarsity Press; Carlisle: Paternoster Press, 1999)

Osborne, G.R., *The Hermeneutical Spiral* (Downers Grove: InterVarsity Press, 1991)

Peacocke, A., *Intimations of Reality: Critical Realism in Science and Religion* (Notre Dame: University of Notre Dame Press, 1984)

Ricoeur, P., *Interpretation Theory: Discourse and the Surplus of Meaning* (Fort Worth: Texas Christian University Press, 1976)

Searle, J.R., *Speech Acts* (Cambridge: Cambridge University Press, 1969)

—, *Intentionality: An Essay in the Philosophy of the Mind* (Cambridge: Cambridge University Press, 1983)

—, *The Construction of Social Reality* (London: Penguin Books, 1995)

Soskice, J.M., *Metaphor and Religious Language* (Oxford: Clarendon Press, 1985)

Sternberg, M., *The Poetics of Biblical Narrative: Ideological Literature and the Drama of Reading* (Bloomington: Indiana University Press, 1985)

Thiselton, A.C., *New Horizons in Hermeneutics* (London: HarperCollins, 1992)

Torrance, T., *Reality and Scientific Theology: Theology and Science at the Frontiers of Knowledge* (Edinburgh: Scottish Academic Press, 1985)

Vanhoozer, K., *Is There a Meaning in This Text?* (Grand Rapids: Zondervan, 1998)

Wimsatt, W.K., and M.C. Beardsley, 'The Intentional Fallacy' in D. Newton-deMolina (ed.), *On Literary Intention* (Edinburgh: Edinburgh University Press, 1976), 1–13

Wolterstorff, N., *Divine Discourse: Philosophical Reflections on the Claim That God Speaks* (Cambridge: Cambridge University Press, 1995)

Wright, N.T., *The New Testament and the People of God* (London: SPCK, 1992)

—, *Jesus and the Victory of God* (Minneapolis: Fortress Press, 1996)

—, 'In Grateful Dialogue' in C. Newman (ed.), *Jesus and the Restoration of Israel* (Downers Grove: InterVarsity Press, 1999), 244–277

11

'In the Arms of the Angels': Biblical Interpretation, Christology and the Philosophy of History

Colin J.D. Greene

From the 17th century onwards, the comprehensive paradigm 'History' was developed in Europe, as a way of interpreting human beings and nature, God and the world. In this paradigm time ceased to be conceived of in terms of the cycle of the recurring seasons; it was now thought of as the line of human goals and purposes.[1]

Setting the Scene

We are seeking a profound and thoroughgoing renewal of contemporary biblical interpretation because there would appear to be a crisis of confidence in the community of biblical scholarship. That crisis, as has been noted in other chapters in this volume, is part of a wider socio-political, cultural, economic and intellectual crisis which inevitably occurs when a civilization is in the midst of a vast cultural transition.[2] How we describe and refer to this transition is of course a matter of much debate. Whether or not the great 'scientific and technological project'[3] called modernity has genuinely collapsed, or whether it is simply temporarily undergoing a change of emphasis and direction whereby our intrusive technological manipulation of nature has given way to an equally intrusive economic exploitation of the global market, is an important ingredient to that

---

[1] Moltmann, *The Way of Jesus Christ*, 227.
[2] Bartholomew, 'Uncharted Waters: Philosophy, Theology and the Crisis in Biblical Interpretation', ch. 1 in this volume.
[3] Moltmann, *The Way of Jesus Christ*, 63f.

wider discussion, which does, of course alert us to the parameters of the continuing modernity versus postmodernity debate.[4]

What we can be sure about, however, is that the renewal we seek that will initiate a new, courageous and engaging reopening of the book in the context of our contemporary cultural hinterland, cannot be left to the community of biblical scholarship alone, but must instead become a shared interdisciplinary endeavour. Overindulgent specialization has been one of the recurring features and diversionary tactics of modernity, which has both isolated biblical scholarship from other contributory disciplines and rendered such scholarship largely blind to its own philosophical and cultural presuppositions.[5]

In this chapter I wish to contribute to that interdisciplinary process from the perspective of what has come to be known as the philosophy of history. To begin with, and in true postmodern fashion, I will recount a story. It is, I believe, a fascinating and compelling story of the genesis and development of modern critical, historical biblical scholarship. That story is narrated from other vantage points and perspectives elsewhere in this volume. I shall concentrate to a large extent on the personalities and disputes which led to the unravelling of what I consider to be one of the central and fundamental aspects of the overall plot, namely, what became known as the 'Jesus of history' versus 'Christ of faith' debate. My reasons for doing so emerge from a strongly held conviction appropriate to one whose main discipline is that of systematic theology, which is that one essential criterion for evaluating the success or otherwise of critical historical scholarship should be the ability of such scholarship to create a sound foundation for Christology. When this is achieved then the person of Jesus Christ is rediscovered not just in the pages of scripture but also amidst the pluralism and fragmentation of contemporary culture. Furthermore, in the course of performing this particular task it will become clear that it matters a lot which philosophy of history one eventually decides to embrace and therefore, precisely because of this fact, the artificial distinctions between biblical scholarship, systematic theology and philosophy have a tendency quite simply to break down. Similarly, whether the story I recount can be afforded the status of history, or whether it is purely a cultural construct, we will only adjudicate upon at the end of our particular version of the story.

Secondly, I shall contend that the interpretative framework for that story is, and always has been, particular philosophies and conceptions of history,

---

[4] Habermas, 'Modernity versus Postmodernity', *New German Critique* 22 (1981).

[5] In that sense we should take note of Sternberg's comment that biblical study is not a discipline per se but is located at the intersection of the humanities. Consequently, 'the progress it so badly needs is conditional either on all-round expertise, not given to humans or on a truly common pursuit of knowledge' (Sternberg, *The Poetics of the Biblical Narrative: Ideological Literature and the Drama of Reading*, 21–22).

philosophies which since the Enlightenment have been deeply intertwined, some would say contaminated, by the myth, or dogma, of human progress.

Finally, we will endeavour to make the philosophical presuppositions concerning the nature of history which continually infiltrate the main aspects of the story explicit by examining and evaluating the cultural and socio-political factors that dominate both the construction and consumption of contemporary historiography. In the process we will take due note of the interesting contention that as far as the cultural history of the west is concerned, there are now three contenders for the throne of what is often loosely termed a philosophy of history and they are, realist or empiricist, idealist, and now, of course, postmodern. Only the latter claims to have disabused itself of any pretensions to accurately describe or portray past events, circumstances or historical connections as they originally happened, or were so understood, and this includes any association with the myth of historical progress.

Introduction

It is a commonplace to note that one of the distinguishing characteristics of the Enlightenment was the way people understood and experienced history. Moltmann, in the quote above, refers to the fact that there had been previous notable changes in the conception of history. As a means to introducing our overall theme we will look briefly at these changing conceptions of the philosophy of history. Both the ancient and oriental worldviews were dominated by a cyclical view of history analogous to the cycles of the seasons in nature. This largely pessimistic view of history regarded the rise and fall of civilizations and nations as a cycle of growth and decline from which nothing new was to be expected or gained. During the Patristic period, particularly due to the influence of Tertullian, Eusebius, Athanasius and Augustine, this notion of history was replaced by the Judeo-Christian conception of history as basically a straight line running from creation to the eschaton with the Christ event understood as the crucial mid-point of salvation history.[6] This more optimistic idea of history incorporates into the picture the notion of divine superintendence (the doctrine of providence), as well as the eschatological fulfilment of the historical process in the future kingdom of God.[7]

The Enlightenment school of history preserved the Christian schema of linear succession but removed the theological infrastructure. In other words

---

[6] See Pelikan, *Jesus Through the Centuries*, 21–34.

[7] It is surely interesting and apposite that Kierkegaard in *The Concept of Anxiety* noted that real history emerged from the narrative of the Old and New Testaments and consequently was diametrically at odds with the Greek dualism of time and eternity.

God as the controlling agent in history was replaced with the notion of human progress. This is admirably expressed in the words of one of the chief representatives of this deist notion of history, A.N. de Condorcet: 'emancipated from his shackles, released from the empire of fate and from the enemies of progress, advancing with a firm and sure step along the path of truth, virtue and happiness'.[8] In the eighteenth century another concept of history began to take root, particularly in Germany. The historicist school of thought developed out of romanticism and the influence of Hegel's philosophical rewriting of the history of civilization. Historicism abandoned the idea of history as a progressive development with a beginning and an end. Instead, history was understood as the story of the growth of distinctive societies and cultures. The historian's task was to understand and enter into such cultures different from his own through the technique of empathy. The main exponents of this view of history were Johann Gottfried Von Herder (1744–1803) and Leopold Von Ranke (1795–1886).[9]

The Secularization of History

It is of course an entirely legitimate question to ask how this secular notion of history arose. As we would expect, there were theological, political and cultural antecedents to the Enlightenment concept of history which centred around the interpretation and understanding of the Bible, which, in turn, contributed greatly to the genesis of modernity. It is here where the first chapter in the story begins with the emergence of a new historical-critical approach to the Bible which sat very uneasily alongside the old doctrine of the inspiration or perspicuity of scripture.

The beginnings of an inchoate understanding of the nature of history can be found in the Reformers' radical engagement with the scriptures and the advancement of the doctrine of *sola scriptura*. Luther's distinction between law and gospel gave precedence to a thoroughgoing Christocentric interpretation of scripture. The law referred to the moral ordering of society ordained by a righteous God to stem the flow of human sin and wrongdoing. The gospel was the divine antidote to sin and lawlessness, that 'happy exchange' whereby our sin and trespass was expunged by the cross of Christ. The primacy of the gospel of grace allowed Luther to dispense with the medieval system of exegesis based upon allegorization and attend instead to the literal sense and historical context of the text. In so doing he also refused to allow the liberating voice of scripture to be silenced or circumscribed by the magisterium of the Roman Catholic church. In both respects

---

[8] De Condorcet, *Sketch of a Historical Picture of the Progress of the Human Mind*, 201.
[9] See Bebbington, *Patterns in History: A Christian Perspective on Historical Thought.*

Luther's attitude toward scripture was indicative of his willingness to recognise, at least to an extent, the essential historicity of existence. All humanity, all institutions are affected by the hurly-burly of events. This acknowledgement of history led Luther to refuse to identify the church as instituted by Christ with the church of the papacy.[10]

This emerging sense of the historicity of the text was silenced by later Protestant orthodoxy, which, unfortunately retreated into a scholastic view of scripture as a repository of doctrine and proof texts, replacing the authority of the Pope with that of the Bible.

The secularization of history received renewed impetus from the political processes of emancipation set in motion by the deleterious effects of the Wars of Religion. Here one figure predominates: Baruch Spinoza (1632–77). Spinoza, a native Jew of Holland and a victim of anti-Semitism, had just reason for wanting to curb the excesses of religious enthusiasm which had convulsed Europe and traumatized so many of her citizens. In his *Theological-Political Treatise* we discover the beginnings of a defence of liberal democracy which develops via a thoroughly modern and ultimately rationalist hermeneutic of suspicion in regard to the Bible. There were four basic ingredients to his new method of exegesis.

First of all, the various books of the Bible, like all other books, must be 'explained in relation to the mundane causes, historical conditions, and cultural presuppositions of the times in which they were written'.[11] Here Spinoza anticipates one of the revered tenets of modern, historical biblical criticism which permits the opening up a gap between the horizon of the contemporary interpreter and the original historical context of the biblical writings. Furthermore, Spinoza interprets the past anachronistically as a reality fundamentally different from a contemporary viewpoint. Thus, the biblical perspective of attributing everything to the activity of God does not cohere with a modern understanding of reality as controlled by the dictates of reason.

Secondly, Spinoza opts for a secular as opposed to a literal understanding of the biblical texts. Divine agency is replaced by human advocacy and so the Bible is unshackled from its bonds to ecclesiastical control and treated like any other document of literary merit. The Bible may be inspirational and divine in origin but it is subject to the same canons of rationality as any other form of literature.

---

[10] Harrisville and Sundberg, *The Bible in Modern Culture*, 16. I know of no finer treatment of the history of modern biblical criticism than that presented by Harrisville and Sundberg. Cf. also Brueggemann, *Theology of the Old Testament*, 1–4; O'Neill, *The Bible's Authority: A Portrait Gallery of Thinkers From Lessing to Bultmann*.

[11] Ibid. 44.

Thirdly, the truth of scripture is that which is accessible to reason and is manifest in its correspondence to what is regarded as normal moral sensibilities. The Bible teaches true virtue and wisdom, but it is virtue accessible to the rational mind and its corollary the natural moral conscience.

Finally, the proper interpretation of scripture is the domain of the intellectual elite. The masses swayed by religious fervour and prejudice must be held in check by the scientific and historical study of the Bible undertaken by the intelligentsia. Taking all four principles together it is clear why Strauss upheld Spinoza rather than Reimarus as the father of modern historical biblical criticism.

> The motivation for historical criticism of the Bible is clear. It is a primary means to free society from the destructive force of religious passion. That is to say, the purpose of this new exegesis is not proclamatory or dogmatic, but political. The content of the Bible is investigated with an eye firmly fixed on its social effect. By undercutting religious passion, Spinoza encourages doubt. From doubt, Spinoza believes there will spring the social good of tolerance.[12]

Similar cultural and political factors came to the fore with the development of English deism and its preference for a natural religion wholly accessible to and explicable in terms of reason. This is nowhere better illustrated than in John Tolland's *Christianity not Mysterious* (1696), although, to a certain extent the scene had already been set by John Locke's *The Reasonableness of Christianity* (1695). Tolland deploys Lockean epistemological principles to draw a decisive parallel between the progressive knowledge of finite realities and the concepts and doctrines of the gospel, understood in a largely ethical and moralistic sense. Both are open to rational investigation because reason is the only basis for certitude and truth. In a manner which is entirely reminiscent of Locke's clear and distinct ideas derived from sense experience, divine revelation is reduced to a means of imparting information which complies with our moral sensibilities.[13] Accordingly, deist exegesis operates with the same fundamental hermeneutical principle as that of Spinoza, namely, that the same rules of interpretation apply to the Bible as do for any other, secular literature. Once this is recognized then the apostolic message is reducible to 'Piety towards God and the Peace of Mankind',[14] both of which can become the basis for a new political settlement. This, of course, is exegesis in the humanist and Puritan tradition, whereby the gospel is purloined as that which entirely complies with the canons of scientific rationality. In order to achieve this, however, Tolland makes a distinction between

---

[12] Ibid., 45.

[13] In this regard see Reventlow, *The Authority of the Bible and the Rise of the Modern World*, 294–308.

[14] Ibid., 299.

the pure unsullied ethics of the gospel and the degenerative superstition, legalism and clericalism of the post-apostolic period. So history emerges in the distinction between the gospel of moral rectitude and the doctrinal mystification of later Christianity. Here Tolland, almost unwittingly, anticipates Harnack's equally positivistic conclusion that Christology represents the Hellinization of the original gospel of Jesus, and at the same time he exhibits a fundamental feature of liberal Protestant exegesis, namely, 'that Roman Catholic Christianity was a false development of primitive Christian faith that distorted the clarity of the gospel'.[15]

The Dogma of Human Progress

A further crucial factor in the development of an essentially secular philosophy of history was the Enlightenment's deep and abiding fascination with the myth of progress. The modern world, in contrast to the medieval world, is one dominated by the notion of human progress and self-advancement. Two hundred years later it is easy to see how this new-found confidence in human progress was but a secularized alternative to the doctrine of providence. There were obviously contributory reasons for such a paradigm shift in public awareness. Britain's industrial revolution became the pattern for similar social developments in Europe and beyond.

> The growth of European power provided, as it were, the material support for the assumption that the new outlook on the world was founded on a firm base which both provided security and offered emancipation from the dogma of tradition.[16]

As is often the case in history one dogma was simply replaced by another, however significant advances in science, technology, medicine and public health helped to fuel the belief in the notion of human progress. Ably incorporated into the philosophical empiricism of Hume[17] and the political theory of Adam Smith[18] gradually history itself began to be understood as the inevitable forward march of human achievement and civilization. In England the dogma of progress later became associated with what Herbert Butterfield called the 'Whig interpretation of history', the tendency to interpret the past in terms of the progressive ideas of the present.[19] The same ideas were vigorously pursued

---

[15] Harrisville and Sundberg, *The Bible in Modern Culture*, 52.

[16] Giddens, *The Consequences of Modernity*, 48.

[17] Hume, *Enquiries concerning the Human Understanding and concerning the Principle of Morals* (1748).

[18] Smith, 'Inquiry into the Nature and Causes of the Wealth of the Nations'.

[19] Butterfield, *Christianity and History*.

on the continent by such thinkers as the Marquis de Concorcet,[20] Henri de Saint Simon[21] and Auguste Comte.[22]

The latter particularly was interesting because Comte combined an epistemological positivism with an evolutionary view of social dynamics. Thus, we have the theological age when early civilizations attributed all natural causation to the direct intervention of God; next came the metaphysical age with a corresponding search for natural causes; now, of course, humankind had reached the scientific age when all knowledge was based on observation, deduction and the discovery of scientific laws. Comte's views easily coalesced with the social Darwinism of the nineteenth century which developed directly out of Darwin's theory of evolution. In that sense, the moral and social advancement of humanity was viewed as analogous to the progress of evolutionary development taking place at the biological and natural level. The evolutionary paradigm continued to gain ascendancy in the natural sciences and cosmology, however the idea of the upward progress of humanity continued to be associated with the new science of historical research and investigation. Not surprisingly modern critical, historical biblical scholarship could not remain immune from such developments in the wider field of historiography. The modern paradigm of history is one which no theologian could afford to ignore and in that sense, as we have already indicated, there is a particular story to be told which clearly shows how much the new science of historical investigation was dominated by a progressive and positivistic philosophy of history.

Jürgen Moltmann believes that the dominance of the paradigm of history has been injurious to the task of finding an appropriate Christology for the postmodern situation of today. He does recognize, however, that the development of this paradigm contributed to the success of the human project, *scientific and technological society*, because it enabled human beings to detach themselves from the world of nature and view themselves as masters of their own destiny and fate. Similarly, it produced the modern science of history with its reliance upon historical-critical skills of investigation and interpretation. Our consciousness of time as a dynamic historical process was broken up into the sequence of past, present and future, and the awareness of temporal distance from past events, traditions and cultures, became one of the significant new features of our own worldview. In similar fashion, Raimundo Panikkar views the Christian preoccupation with history with notable equivocation, precisely

---

[20] De Condorcet, *Sketch of a Historical Picture of the Progress of the Human Mind* (1795).

[21] De Saint Simon, 'On the Reorganisation of European Society' (1814).

[22] Comte, 'Positive Philosophy' (a series of Paris lectures, 1830–42). Comte was the founder of the philosophy of positivism which spawned the development in analytic philosophy known as 'logical positivism'.

because it easily became aligned with the secular notion of linear progress and so contributed to the rise of western imperialism with the consequent destruction of other, native cultures.[23]

In both respects the Enlightenment forced upon every succeeding generation the liberal ideal of reverence before history. Clearly during the eighteenth and nineteenth centuries this was optimistically conceived in terms of the forward march of civilization and progress, however two world wars and the human slaughter of numerous other conflicts has tarnished this ideal in the twentieth century, some would say almost beyond repair. The relationship between the Christian faith and the new paradigm of history has shown the same ability to swing from naïve fraternity to open warfare, to the present situation of an uneasy truce. Or to change the metaphor:

> Even when the methods of historical inquiry have been accepted by Protestant theologians, the marriage of theology and criticism has not been a tranquil one. No sooner has a measure of domestic bliss seemed assured than a new disturbing characteristic of one of the mates has emerged and a reappraisal of the relationship has taken place.[24]

Not surprisingly, it was the rationalist, progressive and anti-supernatural view of history, a product of Enlightenment deism, which first struck a discordant note in the relationship between the Christian faith and history. On the basis of these premises, it seemed that any liaison between the modern paradigm of history, biblical interpretation and Christology, was doomed to failure. It is at this point that the second chapter in the rise of historical-critical investigation of the Bible commences. Not only does the plot thicken but all the main protagonists in the debate are now clearly identified and delineated.

'The Ugly Broad Ditch'

The difficulty was summarized, some would say immortalized, in the words of Gotthold Ephraim Lessing (1729–81):

> If no historical truth can be demonstrated, then nothing can be demonstrated by means of historical truths. That is: accidental truths of history can never become the proof of necessary truths of reason . . . That, then is the ugly broad ditch which I cannot get across, however often and however earnestly I tried to make the leap[25]

---

[23] Panikkar, *The Trinity and the Religious Experience of Man: Icon-Person-Mystery*.

[24] Harvey, *The Historian and the Believer*, 8.

[25] Lessing, *Theological Writings*, 53–55.

Religious faith, according to the canons of critical reason must rest upon so-called necessary truths, that are true for all time and cannot therefore depend upon the contingencies and vagaries of historical probability. In that sense

> Lessing has brought us to the place where the nature and value of historical inquiry is judged in terms of its relation to the interpreter's present horizons. Lessing urges the limitations of historical inquiry not because history cannot speak to these horizons, but because it cannot provide the kind of truth which rationally compels assent.[26]

Understandably, for many in the seventeenth and eighteenth centuries the weakness of history as a means of acquiring knowledge seemed only too evident when compared with the natural sciences. History could only deal with contingencies and probabilities. So when it comes to remarkable events such as the miracle of the resurrection, upon which much of the Christian faith is founded, how are we to ascertain what actually took place? How reliable is the evidence, given that the gospel accounts appear to flatly contradict each other? David Hume contended that any evidence that relied on eyewitness accounts was inevitably flawed.[27] More to the point, how does the historian accurately gain access to the past? How does he or she interpret events and what role does the historian's judgement play in making sense of past events? The historian does not simply record brute facts but interacts with the evidence, some of which may already have been subject to interpretation and disputation.

> The historian's craft is therefore as much an art as a science. He is seldom dealing with material that can furnish him with a clear Yes or No to his questions. It is always a matter of probability, and in the assessment of this kind of probability personal factors, such as intuition, or having the feel of the period enter in. Given the same evidence and the same method, one man will be better than another at reconstructing the past.[28]

Clearly, even knowledge of the recent past is the subject of much contentious argument because we are dealing with human agents whose motives and reasons for taking a particular course of action are often far from clear. How do we gain access to what people thought about themselves and their world and, more particularly, how then are we to assess the claim that one particular individual is the unique revelation of the eternal God? These and many other issues surfaced when Lessing published, between 1774 and 1778 and under a pseudonym, the famous *Wolfenbuttel Fragments*, originally written by Hermann

---

[26] Thiselton, *The Two Horizons*, 65.
[27] Hume, *Essays on Miracles* (1748).
[28] Nicholls, *The Pelican Guide to Modern Theology*, vol. 1, 56.

Samuel Reimarus (1694–1768), erstwhile Professor of Oriental languages at Hamburg. Of the seven fragments of Reimarus's *Apology*, published by Lessing, the two which caused most controversy were 'On the Resurrection Narratives' (1777) and 'On the Intentions of Jesus and His Disciples' (1778).

Reimarus continually hovered unsuccessfully between a public acceptance of the tenets of Protestant orthodoxy and the private imbibing of the new rationalist religion of deism. Consequently, he was the first exponent of the Enlightenment to postulate a radical dichotomy between the Jesus of history and the Christ of faith. Wielding the reductionist canons of critical reason he dispensed both with miracles as legendary additions to the biblical text and with any notion of historical revelation as being incompatible with the necessary and universal character of truth. More importantly, he argued that Jesus was an apocalyptic visionary teacher who mistakenly believed himself to be the promised Messiah who would free the Jews from foreign occupation. Jesus never intended to invent a new religion; indeed his message was pure Jewish eschatological and political expectation, namely, that the earthly realization of the kingdom of God was imminent and that it would involve the defeat of Israel's Roman oppressors.

He claimed that the disciples invented the story of the resurrection to conceal the real truth and concocted the theory of the atonement as a way of giving saving significance to Jesus' death.

> The real Jesus of history has thus been concealed by the apostolic church, which has substituted a fictitious Christ of faith, the redeemer of humanity from sin, in the place of a thoroughly human figure, whose failure to live up to his followers' expectations led to their preferring a glorious invention to a failed reality.[29]

Reimarus' radical scepticism gained few admirers at the time; however, as others have noted, his trenchant rationalist criticism of the gospel tradition unearthed all the main dilemmas of modern biblical criticism.[30] He was the first biblical critic to take serious note of the eschatological context of Jesus' message, even if he wrongly interpreted this solely in terms of the Davidic political expectation of the Messiah. In so doing he raised the central issue of Jesus' relationship to his native Judaism and the even more thorny issue of Jesus' relationship to the early Christian communities. His distinction between the self-understanding of Jesus and that of the early church was based on the conviction that the delay of the parousia caused a real problem for the apostles and the early church, which necessitated a radical reappraisal of the Jesus tradition. In all respects Reimarus initiated the first serious attempt to erect a bridge across Lessing's ontological and epistemological ditch.

---

[29] McGrath, *The Making of Modern German Christology*, 35.

[30] In this regard see Harrisville and Sundberg, *The Bible in Modern Culture*, 62–63.

The Bridge under Construction

It is clear that the early practitioners of historical criticism overvalued the epistemological scope of the new science. The aim was to get at the facts, uncover what really happened, and separate fact from fiction. As Van Harvey points out, underlying this endeavour was 'an almost Promethean will to truth'.[31] In that sense, almost all of the early contributors to the new science – the three wise men, Wellhausen, de Wette and Wrede included – unwittingly fell victim to a form of historical positivism.[32] Not surprisingly, this new endeavour was greeted with hostility by many, particularly in England, because the supposition, advocated by both Spinoza and Lessing, that the Bible could be investigated like any other collection of ancient literature, appeared to conflict with the belief in its supernatural inspiration. For others, the issues were couched in a way which typified the ethos of the Enlightenment, namely, freedom of enquiry versus dogma, and critical investigation versus superstition and obscurantism. 'Some of the earlier nineteenth-century reconstructions of the life of Jesus, such as those of Strauss and Bauer, were motivated as much by hatred of the dogmatic picture of Jesus as by love of their subject.'[33]

In this respect the battle lines between the church's public profession of Jesus as the Christ and the scholars' increasing private uncertainty and scepticism were already being drawn up.

For the latter the tools of the trade were the so-called lower and higher criticism, the application of which began to yield surprising results. In Old Testament studies the Wellhausen (1844–1918) thesis gained ascendancy. Moses was not the author of the Pentateuch as had been previously believed; rather, what in fact we discover through historical-critical analysis, is the development of Israelite religion from early primitive to ethical monotheism to 'degenerate legalism', described euphemistically as J, E, D and P.[34] In New Testament studies Wrede's radical repristination of Reimarus's scepticism rapidly became

---

[31] Harvey, *The Historian and the Believer*, 4.

[32] Cf. Rogerson, *Old Testament Criticism in the Nineteenth Century: England and Germany*; also Brueggemann, *Theology of the Old Testament*, 1–61; and Wright, *Jesus and the Victory of God*, 1–25. In regard to de Wette, Howard in *Religion and the Rise of Historicism: W.M.L. de Wette, Jacob Burckhardt, and the Theological Origins of Nineteenth-Century Historical Consciousness* notes, 'In christological matters, de Wette remained fully committed to the underlying Kantianism of Fries' categories, which forbade rapprochment between *Wissen, Ahnung*, and *Glaube*. Yet de Wette's ambiguous phraseology attests to the difficulty he had as a biblical critic wrestling with the Christ-history problem. For this reason, the category of "mystery" became almost a necessary refuge' (88).

[33] Nicholls, *The Pelican Guide to Modern Theology*, vol. 1, 53.

[34] Cf. Brueggemann, *Theology of the Old Testament*, 12–13.

the new orthodoxy.[35] The gospels were not straightforward eyewitness accounts, nor were they conceivable as biographical accounts of Jesus' life; rather, we actually know very little about Jesus except what the early church allows us to glimpse between the layers of fiction and fabrication. So began the refinement and development of historical-critical techniques which dissected and scrutinized the biblical documents in an attempt to lay bare the historical sources, origins, literary forms and early redactions that gave rise to the early church's confession of Jesus as the Christ.

The nineteenth-century quest for the historical Jesus, as initiated by Schleiermacher and undertaken by various representatives of German Protestantism, was a consequence of this progressive and positivistic view of history. In the process the prevailing philosophy or philosophies of history and religion underwent some notable changes! The deist rationalist preference for natural religion rapidly gave way to the Kantian moralist equivalent which often combined with the Hegelian idealist alternative and so ironically the new science of biblical criticism could not escape the philosophical undercarriage which continually propelled it in diverse directions. Nowhere was this more apparent than in the controversy that surrounded the publication of David Friedrich Strauss's *Life of Jesus* in 1834. Strauss (1808–74) subjected the New Testament to the rigours of historical-critical analysis in an attempt to separate fact from fiction, reality from legend and myth. His basic conclusion was that the New Testament was written by people who shared a non-scientific, mythical worldview typical of more primitive cultures. In such societies events and circumstances were attributed to the agency of supernatural beings. Strauss interpreted myth (*mythos*) in a Hegelian sense as a primitive stage in the self-realization of spirit (*geist*) in the course of history. He detected the evidence of myth in most of the traditions surrounding the birth, life, ministry and death of Jesus. He argued that the supernatural expectations surrounding the Old Testament belief in the Messiah, namely, that he would heal the sick, raise the dead, perform miracles and, like Elijah and Enoch, ascend into heaven, were simple transposed onto the historical Jesus by the New Testament writers themselves. While some of these interpretations may have a basis in the actual history of Jesus, that in itself is of no theological import. At the end of his book Strauss resorted to a Hegelian interpretation of Jesus as the realization of the Absolute in the realm of history. According to Albert Schweitzer (1875–1965), 'Scarcely ever has a book let loose such a storm of controversy; and scarcely ever has a controversy been so barren of immediate result. The fertilizing rain brought up a crop of toadstools.'[36]

---

[35] Wrede, *The Messianic Secret*.
[36] Schweitzer, *The Quest for the Historical Jesus*, 96.

Strauss's work did, however, stimulate others to continue the quest for the original Jesus. Much of this research was influenced by studies in the synoptic problem. It was accepted that Mark was the first gospel which had been used in either written or oral form by Matthew and Luke and that the fourth gospel could not be regarded as a legitimate source for the history of Jesus. The Hegelian influence in biblical studies continued unabated and formed the philosophical background to the brilliant scholarship of Ferdinand Christian Baur (1792–1860). Baur at times is hardly aware of how much he has systematically imbibed the high-octane vapours of the Hegelian religion of the Absolute, which, correspondingly, requires that we see in all historical particulars the self-realization of the Universal Spirit. So, for instance, while critical of the negative strain of historical criticism present in Strauss's work, nevertheless, he exhibits the same rationalist tendency to exclude miracle, eschatology and dogma from the proper scientific study of the biblical texts. Although Baur attributed a genuine Messianic consciousness to the historical Jesus, expressed particularly through his interiorization of the Mosaic law, he, like Wrede, tended to interpret the genesis of Christianity in terms of the disputes and controversies that beset the early Christian church. In that sense it was Baur, rather than Strauss, who bequeathed the greatest debt to subsequent New Testament scholarship. For instance, in true positivist fashion he denied that the resurrection could ever be the object of empirical investigation, a strategy repeated again and again by his successors. Similarly, it was Baur who broke with the Reformation understanding that it was the doctrine of justification that formed the heart of Pauline theology. Consonant with his insistence on finding objective grounds for faith, rather than subjective dispositions, he located the centre of Paul's thought in the overpowering reality of the cross of Christ:

> A death which ran so directly counter to all the facts and presuppositions of the Jewish national consciousness . . . must have a scope far transcending the particularism of Judaism. There can be no doubt that this was the thought in which the apostle first discerned the truth of Christianity.[37]

Furthermore, it was Baur who became convinced that early Christianity was racked by a bitter controversy between Jewish particularism and Gentile universalism, epitomized by the dispute between Peter and Paul; and that early Christianity largely borrowed its forms of government, organization and initiation from contemporary Judaism. Finally, Baur saw in the Johannine corpus the fiercest antipathy to Judaism which in the gospel resolved around the designation of Jesus as the enfleshed Logos. Consequently, he came to the

---

[37] Baur, *Die Tübinger Schule*, quoted in Harrisville and Sundberg, *The Bible in Modern Culture*, 117.

conclusion that the idealized picture of Jesus as the incarnate Logos should be rejected in favour of a Jesus made accessible by historical analysis. The Hegelian idealist presuppositions of Baur, however, would never have allowed him to draw the inevitable empiricist conclusions from this analysis as did Wilhelm Bousset (1865–1920), namely, that on the basis of such research all that remained was to construct a 'life-like portrait which, with a few bold strokes, should bring out clearly the originality, the force, the personality of Jesus'.[38] Rather, those who were motivated and inspired by idealist presuppositions possessed an altogether more ambitious exegetical intent:

> Namely, one finds among idealists an inclination to interpret the identity of Jesus Christ by locating his significance, not in the transcendence of human consciousness, but in the notion that an individual known as Jesus Christ somehow became an indispensable, exemplary expression of all human consciousness, one who embodied the experience of human nature and instigated a cultural process to inspire and improve humanity – beginning with the European peoples.[39]

Clearly here we encounter the dogma of historical and cultural progress in one of its most trenchant forms.

There were two major presuppositions that controlled the corporate endeavours of those who tried valiantly to traverse Lessing's ditch. Both were exemplified in the theology of the two main representatives of liberal Protestantism.

The first presupposition was that endorsed by Albrecht Ritschl (1822–89). While Ritschl resembled Schleiermacher in espousing a soteriological approach to Christology, he clearly differed from him in replacing the latter's reliance upon the religion of feeling with a more ethical approach. In that sense, as Robert Jenson notes, 'liberal theologians derived their analysis of human existence and the location therein of religion from Immanuel Kant: religion was understood as the interior presupposition of moral action and religious doctrines as "value judgements"'.[40] And it was precisely at this point that Ritschl most fiercely disagreed with Baur, his close friend and former teacher. Consequently, access to Christ is not to be found in mystical union but through the concrete and largely ethical experience of redemption and reconciliation mediated to us through the Christian community of faith. The founder of this community was the historical Jesus; so it is essential that the gospel tradition concerning Jesus himself could be established as trustworthy. The way to do that, and here is the nub of the issue, was to gain access through historical investigation to the actual religious convictions of Jesus himself. These Ritschl

---

[38] Quoted by Harvey, *The Historian and the Believer*, 11.
[39] Howard, *Religion and the Rise of Historicism*, 92.
[40] Quoted in Ford, *The Modern Theologians*, vol. 1, 30.

interpreted in a distinctly Kantian sense as the ethical ideal of the kingdom of God and the universal fraternity of humanity.

The second presupposition was found in the influential work of Adolf von Harnack (1851–1930) on the history of Christian dogma. Harnack concluded that the early church's Christological dogmas represent the Hellenization of the original gospel message. That original gospel was the person of Jesus: 'Jesus does not belong to the gospel as one of its elements, but was the personal real-ization and power of the gospel, and we still perceive him as such.'[41] What Harnack actually perceived, however, was 'a deJudaized Jesus with a social programme'.[42] Not surprisingly then, the person of the historical Jesus becomes accessible to us when we divest him of the metaphysical accretions imposed on him by the dogmaticians of the early church. Then we discover a Jesus who is the personal realization of the fatherly love of God towards humanity. In that sense:

> Harnack constructs a model of theology in which one identifies the basis of religion in the message of the gospel, then teaching this to people by relating it to the highest achievements of culture and society. Implicit in this model is the conviction, first, that education is the task of the theologian, and second, that society and culture have reached such a stage of development that one can speak of their goodness, truth and beauty in the same way that one speaks of the Christian religion. For Harnack it is axiomatic that historical research and critical reflection reveal that such a relationship between religion and culture is not only possible, but also what God actually wants, as expressed in Jesus' life and message.[43]

Clearly, in all of this we find the virtual domestication of the Christian faith, the elimination of all that is odd, controversial, angular and inimical to a progres-sive idea of religion and culture, which is exactly the nature of the dispute which was to break out subsequently between Harnack and Karl Barth.[44] Simi-larly, we find the nineteenth-century obsession with the teachings of Jesus in order to characterize him as a teacher of religion of a decidedly post-Kantian ethical variety.

The Bridge Collapses

This whole edifice of historical-critical investigation, based as it was on these positivist premises, was to collapse under the combined assault of three notable

---

[41] Harnack, *What is Christianity?*, 145.

[42] Wright, *Jesus and the Victory of God*, 58.

[43] Jones, *Critical Theology*, 15.

[44] For an informative, interesting and relevant review of this dispute see Jones, *Critical Theology*, 11–37.

theologians of this era. For two of them, the assault was embodied in the publication of a particular book.

The first attack was the publication in 1896 of Martin Kähler's seminal study, *The So-called Historical Jesus and the Historic, Biblical Christ*. In that work Kähler (1835–1912) demonstrated that the historical sources do not yield the kind of information about Jesus that both Ritschl and his predecessors had assumed:

> The Jesus of the 'Life of Jesus' is merely a modern variety of the products of human creative art, no better than the infamous dogmatic Christ of Byzantine Christology; they are both equally far removed from the true Christ. Historicism is at this point just as arbitrary, just as humanly haughty, just as pert, and as 'faithlessly gnostic' as the dogmatism which in its own day was also modern.[45]

Kähler asserted that the gospels pay scant attention to the life of Jesus or his own inner religious life; rather the real Christ is the preached Christ. The gospels were written from faith to faith, they are kerygmatic documents that contain the faith convictions of their writers. The attempt to circumvent the Christ of faith in some misguided search for the historical Jesus was doomed to failure, because the real intent of the gospel writers was to witness to the crucified and risen Lord.

The second point of attack was the publication of Albert Schweitzer's study of the 'life of Jesus movement', *The Quest for the Historical Jesus*, in 1906. In this book Schweitzer accepted that the nineteenth-century quest of the historical Jesus had 'loosed the bands by which he had been riveted for centuries to the stony rocks of ecclesiastical doctrine, and rejoiced to see life and movement coming into the figure once more'.[46] At the same time he also exposed the inadequacy and inner tensions of the attempt to isolate the historical Jesus from the interpretative context of the early church. In words later immortalized by the Roman Catholic modernist George Tyrrell (1861–1909), those who had undertaken the quest for the historical Jesus had merely caught a glimpse of their own reflection at the bottom of the hermeneutical well. Schweitzer, building on the work of the New Testament scholar Johannes Weiss (1863–1914), also recovered the essential eschatological context of Jesus' teaching and self-understanding. This similarly served to discredit the idealized Jesus of liberal Protestantism, portraying Jesus instead as essentially a disillusioned apocalyptic, a strange enigmatic and wholly otherworldly figure, who threw himself upon the wheel of history in a vain attempt to force God's hand. The wheel, however, eventually turned and crushed him, leaving him the victim of an ambiguous religious fate.

---

[45] Kähler, *The So-called Historical Jesus and the Historic, Biblical Christ*, 43.

[46] Schweitzer, *The Quest for the Historical Jesus*, 397.

Schweitzer's suspicion that the historical Jesus may in fact be irretrievable and that those who attempt this particular task inevitably end up with a Jesus of their own making has remained a central concern of modern Christology. William Hamilton, for instance, in a recent book concludes that the modern search for a political Jesus is just as elusive. It always remains a pointless and fruitless exercise because 'There is no Jesus as he really was. What we find, wherever we look, is always fiction, and usually ideology.'[47]

The combined assault of these two theologians effectively demolished the bridge Protestantism had endeavoured to construct across Lessing's ditch. It became clear that consecutive theologians had been labouring under a mistaken ideal of historical objectivity and failing to take into account the presuppositions, indeed the dogmas, that the historian brings to their study. In that sense as Hans-Georg Gadamer perceptively noted, the Enlightenment continually exhibited 'a prejudice against prejudice'.[48] Not surprisingly, therefore, as the writers of a recent symposium demonstrate, the authority and validity of the Enlightenment legacy of historical-critical exegesis of the scriptures is still an issue which divides the contemporary church.

> Biblical critics frequently claim that their use of the historical-critical method is free of confessional assumptions and theological motivations, that their approach enjoys the status of objective historical science. Upon close scrutiny, however, it is possible to show that historical critics approach the texts with their own set of prior commitments, sometimes hiddenly linked to ideologies alien or hostile to the faith of the Christian church.[49]

The third attack on the progressive positivists' already beleaguered positions came from Ernst Troeltsch (1865–1920). Troeltsch's contribution to the debate has proved the most difficult to refute. H.G. Drescher, for instance, noted that Troeltsch recognized 'like no other theologian of his time, the upsetting and urgent features of the relation between faith and history'.[50] As a representative of the history of religions school, which embraced the historicist view of history, he sought to demonstrate how all religious ideas must be understood within their original historical *Sitz im Leben* (situation in life). In order to achieve this, the historian must use the three principles of historical enquiry:

(1) *Criticism*. All judgements about the past cannot be claimed as either true or false but are mere probabilities always liable to revision and refutation.

---

[47] Hamilton, *A Quest for the Post-Historical Jesus*.
[48] Gadamer, *Truth and Method*, 241–245.
[49] Braaten and Jenson, *Reclaiming the Bible for the Church*, xi.
[50] Quoted in Coakley, *Christ Without Absolutes*, 191.

(2) *Analogy*. We are able to make such probable judgements only if we pre-suppose that our own experience of events is not radically dissimilar to the experience of people in the past.[51]

(3) *Correlation*. All historical events are interdependent and interrelated, so every event must be understood in terms of its historical antecedents and consequences.

Troeltsch believed that these principles were incompatible with Christian faith, because they necessarily excluded from the field of historical enquiry any event, such as the resurrection, that could only be understood as a unique act of God. He himself embraced a form of historical relativism which tended to view Christianity as the point of convergence of all other religions. Whether Christianity could be viewed as absolute or not required a criterion of judgement which was not yet available to the historian.[52]

The heyday of progressive liberalism took place between the end of the Napoleonic wars and the outbreak of the First World War (1814–1914). The development of European culture and expansionism coupled with the intellectual freedom of enquiry epitomized by the German university system, permitted the three ideals of Enlightenment scholarship to appear almost unassailable. The triumph of reason, the realization of political autonomy and the obvious sense of progressive historical, intellectual and economic development saturated the mores of liberal bourgeois society. It was this cultural and intellectual climate which allowed historical-critical scholarship to flourish; however, cracks were already appearing in the edifice.

> During the nineteenth century, the apologetic effort of liberal theology had been directed toward the identification of Jesus with modern culture as the prototype of universal religious experience. As God entered the heart of Jesus, so he enters our hearts, directing us to the just life. The kingdom of God was understood to be the key biblical symbol for this experience. In the latter decades of the century, historical scholarship began to cut the nerve of this apologetic by locating Jesus firmly in the context of apocalyptic expectation.[53]

In this sense one of the dilemmas of historical scholarship isolated by Reimarus, namely the relationship of the historical Jesus to first-century Palestinian Judaism, was beginning to be conceived in a decidedly Schweitzerian fashion.

---

[51] The principle of analogy was for Troeltsch the direct opposite of Spinoza's principle of anachronism. Spinoza, in fact, postulated a radical dichotomy rather than a similarity between the experience of ancient peoples and that of his contemporaries.

[52] Troeltsch, *The Absoluteness of Christianity*.

[53] Harrisville and Sundberg, *The Bible in Modern Culture*, 204–205.

The second fundamental issue for Christology – the relationship of the historical Jesus to the Christ of faith of the early Christian community–was to prove an even more illusive issue upon which there is still no scholarly consensus.

With the outbreak of the First World War and the bloody ferment that ensued, the progressive development of European civilization gave way to hell on earth. The resilient doctrine of progress was temporarily buried in the trenches and human slaughter of a war fought with the new weapons of technological advancement. The sad irony of a war conducted between the irresolvable tension of old strategies and new weapons was not lost on journalists, political commentators and historians. The young theologians who lived through the carnage and heartache were subsequently to turn their own considerable intellectual armoury against the bridge liberal historical scholarship had valiantly endeavoured to construct across Lessing's ditch, and ultimately many of them were to abandon it altogether.

The Bridge Abandoned

The legacy of Troeltsch, however, was never expunged from the theological agenda, even in the midst of the extreme theological reaction to liberal Protestantism that took place with the advent of the new theology of crisis, spearheaded by Karl Barth (1886–1968).

'A half-century ago Barth and Bultmann hailed the collapse of the quest of the historical Jesus. The one positive gain of the quest, in their view, had been to demonstrate its own sterility for the life of faith.'[54]

Dialectical theology as it became known, returned to the radical existentialism of Søren Kierkegaard (1813–55), which was inherently sceptical of any attempt to ground the divinity of Christ upon historical investigation of his life and ministry. Kierkegaard, in a manner reminiscent of Lessing, had asked the question 'How can something of a historical nature be decisive for an eternal happiness?'[55] His own solution to the problem of Lessing's historical ditch was to attempt to cross it by means of an existential leap of faith. Barth and his colleagues, Friedrich Gogarten (1887–1967) and Rudolf Bultmann (1884–1976), on the other hand, railed against the three ideals of liberalism – history, ethics and religion – in the name of God, the wholly transcendent Other, separated from us by an 'infinite qualitative distinction' which no historical bridge could traverse:

---

[54] Meyer, *The Aims of Jesus*, 107.
[55] Kierkegaard, *Concluding Unscientific Postscript*.

> If I have any system, it is restricted to bearing in mind, as much as possible, what Kierkegaard called the 'infinite qualitative distinction' between time and eternity, in its negative and positive aspects. 'God is in heaven, and you are on earth.' For me, the relation of this God and this person, the relation of this person and this God, is, in a nutshell, the theme of the Bible and the totality of philosophy.[56]

Barth is attributed with the honour of recovering normative biblical exegesis in the face of the positivist and reductionist tendencies of liberal historical scholarship. He subjected the rationalist canons of modernity to his own fearsome epistemological critique which involved the re-establishment of the autonomy of theology as essentially a discipline which operates within its own fiduciary framework, namely, 'faith seeking understanding'.

> Since Barth exposed objective scholarship as theory-laden, it does not follow that his theological premise would be granted any privilege. It does, however, make inescapable the recognition that there is no innocent or neutral scholarship, but that all theological and interpretative scholarship is in one way or another fiduciary. Barth's sustained polemic against religion is that *all such practice of meaning that eventuated in liberalism must be critiqued, not because it is neutral, but because it flies in the face of the subject it purports to study* – namely, the work and presence of the Holy God who cannot be grasped in such conventional and autonomous categories.[57]

Barth later went on to construct the Christological metaphysics of the *Church Dogmatics* which involved a return to the Logos Christology of Athanasius and the Alexandrian tradition. However, both the architectonic structure and scope of the *Dogmatics* continued to demonstrate the fecundity and versatility of his newly liberated biblical theology. Bultmann, on the other hand, with the help of the two Martins, messrs Kähler and Heidegger, continued to maintain a radical scepticism towards history as a reliable foundation for personal faith in Christ, preferring instead a Christology based on the existential encounter between the believer and Christ in the preached kerygma.

> The salvation-occurrence is nowhere present except in the proclaiming, accosting, demanding, and promising word of preaching. A merely 'reminiscent' historical account referring to what happened in the past cannot make the salvation-occurrence visible. It means that the salvation-occurrence continues to take place in the proclamation of the word.[58]

A radical scepticism towards the search for the historical Jesus can stem from theological motives. In Bultmann's case it was an application of the

---

[56] Barth, *The Epistle to the Romans*, Introduction.
[57] Brueggemann, *Theology of the Old Testament*, 18.
[58] Bultmann, *Theology of the New Testament*, 302.

Reformation doctrine of justification by grace through faith without recourse to reason, historical science or dogma. Similarly, his own commitment to form-critical analysis was based on the conviction that there was no material continuity between the synoptic tradition and the kerygma of the early Christian communities; rather, the only connection was the mere historicity of the Christ event about which, he claimed, we can know virtually nothing. Bultmann's own answer to what we might possibly ascertain from the biblical material about the historical Jesus left no doubt that this was not a figure on which to stake one's life!

> With a bit of caution we can say the following . . . Characteristic of him are exorcisms, the breech of the Sabbath commandment, the abandonment of ritual purification, polemic against Jewish legalism, fellowship with outcasts such as publicans and harlots, sympathy for women and children: it can also be seen that Jesus was not an ascetic like John the Baptist . . . but gladly ate and drank a glass of wine. Perhaps we may add that he called disciples and assembled about himself a small company of followers . . . We can only say of his preaching that he doubtless appeared in the consciousness of being commissioned by God to preach the eschatological message of the breaking-in of the Kingdom of God . . . We may thus ascribe to him a prophetic consciousness . . . The greatest embarrassment to the attempt to reconstruct a portrait of Jesus is the fact that we cannot know how Jesus understood his . . . death . . . What is certain is merely that he was crucified by the Romans, and thus suffered the death of a political criminal . . . It took place because his activity was misconstrued as political activity. In that case it could have been – historically speaking – a meaningless fate. We cannot tell whether or how Jesus found meaning in it. We may not veil from ourselves the possibility that he suffered a collapse.[59]

What then of the early Christian kerygma with its obvious high Christological affirmations? Here we encounter the Bultmannian category of myth, that is, statements that objectivize the divine reality and activity and therefore already witness to a process of Hellenization. All such statements must be demythologized and now, enter left, a new philosophy of history, translated into Heideggerian existentialist categories, in order that the saving significance of the kerygma may be heard and understood in the context of the modern world.[60] Here we encounter, yet again, what inevitably takes place when Christology is reduced to soteriology or philosophical existentialism, namely, that critical reduction of scale whereby the only significant Jesus is the Jesus *pro nobis*, that is, the one who meets us in our existential need and despair. Once this route is taken, history, indeed any wider appreciation of the significance of society, culture and nature, is dissolved into anthropology.

---

[59] Bultmann, 'The Primitive Christian Kerygma and the Historical Jesus', 22–24.
[60] Schnackenburg, 'Christology and Myth', 336–355.

Clearly, Bultmann's critics could discern the Achilles heel of his system. If the living Word who meets us in the preached kerygma is loosed entirely from the Word made flesh, have we not undercut the doctrine of the incarnation at source and left ourselves with a mere historical lacuna, a Christ idea about a suffering and justifying Saviour who could just as easily have been the invention of the apostle Paul?[61] Bultmann's disciples were deeply vexed by the dilemma. Ernst Käsemann (b. 1906), Gunther Bornkamm (1905–90), and Ernst Fuchs (1903–83) differed in their respective approaches to the problem, but they were all agreed that if faith in the preached Christ were allowed to float free from any anchorage in the synoptic tradition then Christology must pay the ultimate price. Might it be the case that in some sense, as yet not clearly determined, the story and history of Jesus is subsumed within the kerygma of the early church and therefore a new quest for the historical Jesus should and could begin?

What then of the ubiquitous dogma of progress which had been conspicuous by its absence during the bloody inferno of two world wars? Not surprisingly, with the new-found optimism and prosperity of the post-war period it found its way back into the mental furniture of ordinary people, historians and – dare we assume? – biblical scholars.

> These embers, however, were fanned into a stronger flame by the material prosperity that western nations enjoyed in the quarter century following the Second World War. Progress seemed a fruit of the planned economy. Despite the more recent waning of the popular mood of optimism, it would probably be true to say that elements of the idea of progress remain widely diffused – though less widely diffused in the world of scholarship than in the mind of the man in the street.[62]

The myth of progress now emerged from the turpitude and dying embers of nineteenth-century bourgeois European civilization in two quite distinct ideological forms, Marxism and capitalism. Both fixed their gaze on the future through the lens of historical determinism and both sought to revisit history through the mechanisms of their own prejudices and presuppositions. Incorporated into their respective systems was the same well-worn secular notion of the inevitability of human progress, although this time given a decidedly economic twist. It is surely not without significance that in this cultural context a new quest for the historical Jesus should once again take root.

---

[61] This formed the basis of Joachim Jeremias's (1900–1979) objections to the Bultmannian position. See Jeremias, *The Problem of the Historical Jesus*.
[62] Bebbington, *Patterns in History*, 89.

The Bridge Revisited

It was Ernst Käsemann (b. 1906), who inaugurated the new quest with a lecture specifically on this issue delivered in October 1953.

The old quest for the historical Jesus had been based on the presupposition of a radical discontinuity between the Christ of faith and the historical Jesus. That discontinuity Käsemann accepts as real but not absolute; rather, he suggests that the kernel of the kerygma about Jesus is already there in embryonic form in the ministry of Jesus himself. Already in 1952 he had claimed:

> Only if Jesus' proclamation decisively coincides with the proclamation about Jesus is it understandable, reasonable, and necessary that the Christian kerygma in the New Testament conceals the message of Jesus; only then is the resurrected Jesus the historical Jesus. From this perspective we are required precisely as historians, to enquire behind Easter . . .[63]

Käsemann's approach reflects what Tom Wright has discerned as the preference among New Testament scholars since Schweitzer for the silhouette and icon rather than the concrete historical reality of the man Jesus.[64] We peer through a glass darkly, this time the New Testament kerygma, for any reflection or image of the wandering Rabbi from Nazareth, hoping that by some stroke of luck we might happen upon that hidden continuity between the earthly Jesus and the exalted Lord. Käsemann found that link in the interconnecting substratum of primitive apocalyptic. Apocalyptic, however it is understood, links Jesus' message about the present and coming kingdom of God and the early church's proclamation concerning a risen and exalted Saviour. Contra Bultmann, Käsemann insisted that the Pauline doctrine of justification was informed by this eschatological tension between the already and the not yet and therefore could not be reduced to a mere existentialist anthropology. With the delay of the parousia, however, it was inevitable that the legitimization of the leadership of the early Christian communities would become a real issue. In that sense apocalyptic was displaced, largely neutralized and eventually removed from the later development of the Christian faith into what Käsemann, like Baur, designated as 'early catholicism'. Käsemann's antipathy towards this development stemmed as much from his conviction that the apolitical, bourgeois, twentieth-century equivalent was his own Württemberg Church tradition. The necessary corrective to such parochialism Käsemann locates in the Pauline proclamation of the cross of Christ. Here we discover Christian existence lived in obedience to the continuity between the mission of Jesus to seek and save the lost and the Pauline conviction that through the

---

[63] Quoted in Pannenberg, *Jesus – God and Man*, 56.
[64] Wright, *Jesus and the Victory of God*, 1–27.

cross God was reconciling the whole cosmos to himself. The cross and resurrection of Christ therefore become the non-negotiable *sine qua non* of the
Christian faith:

> What for me may under no circumstance go overboard is this one single thing: the
> message of the justification of the godless . . . Our God is not chiefly concerned with
> strengthening, bettering or preserving of the pious and the victory of religiosity in
> the world, but with freeing people and the earth from the demonic power of god-
> lessness.[65]

In his dispute with his old master, Käsemann had virtually singlehandedly set
the agenda for the important and considerable theological endeavours that
were to ensue from his labours. Apocalyptic now became the way to advance a
full-blown theology of history which, in a radically inclusive manner,
endeavoured to lay the ghost of Lessing to rest, the contours of which were
sketched out by Wolfhart Pannenberg (b.1928) in his essay *Redemptive Event
and History* (1959). Similarly, an equally inclusive theology of the cross
advanced the cause of a new political theology whereby the righteousness of
God is revealed in the justification of the godless and the godforsaken, an
agenda which eventuated in a book which took the theological world by
storm, Jürgen Moltmann's *The Crucified God* (1973).

The Bridge Reinstated

> History is the most comprehensive horizon of Christian theology. All theological
> questions and answers have meaning only within the framework of the history
> which God has with humanity, and through humanity with the whole creation, di-
> rected towards a future which is hidden to the world but which has already been re-
> vealed in Jesus Christ.[66]

This concise statement outlined the parameters of Pannenberg's theology of
history, and signalled his return to the idealist tradition which views history as
essentially the self-manifestation of the Absolute. Pannenberg, probably the
greatest systematic theologian of the modern era, has consistently advocated
the need to forge a new theology of history and, in that sense, he anticipates a
lot of the present discussion about the need to develop a new theological biblical hermeneutic.[67] It is instructive to outline the main components in this

---

[65] Käsemann, *Widerstand im Zeichen des Nazareners*, 29f., quoted in Harrisville and
Sundberg, *The Bible in Modern Culture*, 249.
[66] Pannenberg, 'Redemptive Event and History', 15.
[67] Cf. Watson, *Text and Truth*; Vanhoozer, *Is There a Meaning in This Text?*

agenda because at this stage in the story we find a theologian who embraces a particular philosophy of history where Christological issues are no longer merely tangential to the plot but utterly central and crucial to how we understand both the nature of history and religion, and here the third chapter in our narrative begins.

(1) History is the arena of God's self-revelation and interaction with the world. God is revealed indirectly through the reflex of his action in the public field of human history. There can be no separation between salvation history and ordinary history. History is a seamless robe which defies such arbitrary distinctions.[68]

(2) History is an interrelated nexus of events which only receives its unity, and therefore its ultimate meaning and significance, from the perspective of its end. This notion of universal history was akin to that developed by Hegel and later espoused by Wilhelm Dilthey. Pannenberg differs from Hegel, however, in his affirmation of the eschatological dimensions of the biblical view of history, and in his refusal to subordinate the biblical material to a speculative philosophy of history. In this respect, his own version of an interdisciplinary approach builds on the work of biblical scholars such as Gerhard von Rad, Ernst Käsemann and his former colleagues Rolf Rendtorff (b. 1927) and Ulrich Wilckens (b. 1928), in seeking to demonstrate the importance of the apocalyptic and eschatological framework of meaning for a new theology of history:

> Revelation is no longer understood in terms of a supernatural disclosure or of a peculiarly religious experience and religious subjectivity, but in terms of the comprehensive whole of reality, which, however, is not simply given, but is a temporal process of a history that is not yet completed, but open to a future, which is anticipated in the teaching and personal history of Jesus.[69]

Consequently, history is eschatologically determined which corresponds to the biblical perspective that creation is an historical process moving towards its consummation in the coming kingdom of God.

As history is also the story of God's self-revelation, indeed, his trinitarian self-realization, it follows that his complete self-unveiling will only take place at the end of history as well.[70]

---

[68] Cf. also Braaten, *New Directions in Theology Today.*, vol.2: *History and Heremeneutics.*

[69] Pannenberg, *Revelation as History*, preface to the American edition, ix.

[70] While the trinitarian schema of Pannenberg's theology of history was anticipated to a certain extent in *Revelation as History*, it was only fully worked out in the first volume of his *Systematic Theology* where he constructed his own highly original trinitarian doctrine of God.

The end of history and therefore also the definitive self-revelation of God, has occurred proleptically in Christ's resurrection from the dead. This is so because this event can only be properly understood within the context of apocalyptic Judaism, as a foreshadowing of the general resurrection from the dead that was expected at the end of history.

This ontology of history can be summarized by the statement 'existence anticipates essence.' Everything exists in anticipation of its fullness of being and meaning which is as yet hidden in the undisclosed future of God.

> Since the emergence of historical consciousness, the unity of all reality is conceivable only as a history. The unity of truth is still possible only as a historical process, and can be known only from the end of the process . . . The unity of truth is possible only if it includes the contingency of events and the openness of the future.[71]

The exegetical and dogmatic bases to this theology of history were laid out in a book which provoked a storm of controversy and criticism, *Revelation as History*, published in 1961. The book represented the interdisciplinary work of a group of scholars who became known as 'the Pannenberg circle'. Their corporate endeavours were designed both to construct a more comprehensive category of revelation from the basis of biblical apocalyptic, and to find an alternative to what they regarded as the limitations of the ahistorical Word of God theologies of both Barth and Bultmann. In so doing they fully embraced a particular philosophy of history which had deep affinities with the Hegelian idealist tradition.

Christological Considerations

The Christological implications of this theology of history were fully developed by Pannenberg in his *Grundzüge der Christologie* (*Jesus – God and Man,*) (1964/8) and later in the second volume of the *Systematics* (1994). Again we will lay them out in point form:

(1) The Christological affirmation of Jesus' unity with God must be firmly anchored in Jesus' proclamation of the coming kingdom of God and the resurrection. The historicity of both must be cogently demonstrated and maintained. This constitutes Pannenberg's endorsement of the new quest for the historical Jesus, namely, that the message *of* Jesus and the message *about* Jesus are linked by the eschatological horizon of the coming kingdom of God.

(2) Jesus' proclamation of the nearness of the kingdom of God implied a claim to unique authority, in that Jesus in his own person was the mediator of

---

[71] Pannenberg, 'What is Truth', 27.

the future rule of God. That claim to authority was ambiguous and brought Jesus into conflict with the religious establishment which led to his execution.

(3) Jesus' message looked to a future confirmation which the early church discerned in the resurrection. As noted already, the resurrection is an apocalyptic concept which refers to the general resurrection from the dead awaiting the end of history. To claim that this has proleptically taken place in the destiny of one man is to make two fundamental Christological affirmations:

    (a) The resurrection was a divine confirmation or validation of Jesus as the personal realization of the saving rule of God.

    (b) The resurrection consequently becomes the basis for affirming Jesus' personal unity with God.

(4) The resurrection is a real event in history. Consequently its historicity must be maintained against all attempts to dissolve it into the religious subjectivity of those who supposedly witnessed the event. This point has been well expressed by Dale Allison: 'Belief in the resurrection of Jesus is not likely to be explained away by the sociological fact that faith can, despite everything, declare the fulfilment of its hopes. The mystery of the resurrection is not dissolved so easily.'[72]

Consequently, Pannenberg stands by the validity of the resurrection appearances and the tradition of the empty tomb, both of which, he claims, are open to historical investigation.

This, of course, immediately brought Pannenberg into conflict with Troeltsch's three canons of historical research. His basic point is that these three criteria represent an unwarranted anthropological constriction or secularization of the field of historical enquiry. Take, for instance, the principle of analogy or the belief in the homogeneity of all events. This is only so from the standpoint of the human observer whose perspective is always a limited one. Why, if the possibility of a unique event is not ruled out in the natural sciences, should it be disqualified from the probabilities of history? Pannenberg asserts that if you come to the biblical texts with the prior presupposition that the dead do not rise, then this is to approach history with an already predetermined worldview. Why not let the evidence speak for itself on the basis of a worldview that is always open to the contingencies and novelties of history itself?

> As long as historiography does not begin dogmatically with a narrow concept of reality according to which 'dead men do not rise', it is not clear why historiography should not in principle be able to speak of Jesus' resurrection as the explanation that is best established of such events as the disciples' experiences of the appearances and the discovery of the empty tomb.[73]

---

[72] Allison, *The End of the Age has Come*, 168.
[73] Pannenberg, *Jesus – God and Man*, 109.

(5) On the basis that the resurrection was actually the breaking in of the future kingdom of God, then this event has unique ontological significance:

(a) First of all, it links Jesus ontologically to the future of God's rule and therefore with the deity of God.

(b) Secondly, it shows that the resurrection also has retroactive ontological power, taking up Jesus' pre-Easter life and ministry as that which was also linked with the being of God. From the perspective of the resurrection, then, we can move backwards to the incarnation and view this as a valid summary statement concerning Jesus' pre-existent unity with God.

(6) The way to approach the contentious issue of Jesus' unity with God, that is, his divinity, is not through his relationship to the pre-existent Logos but indirectly through Jesus' relationship to the Father. Jesus is one with the Father whose kingdom he proclaimed because he differentiates himself from him, and this self-differentiation forms the basis of their unity. Jesus perceives his vocation as a giving of himself away to the mission of the Father. As he gives up himself, or differentiates himself from the Father, so he makes room within his own life and ministry for the will and rule of the Father, mediated to him through the Spirit, and that constitutes his divinity.

Pannenberg asserts that this is the only way to avoid the logical difficulties of Chalceldonian Christology. The central problem that faced both Alexandrian and Antiochene Christology was how to conceive of the unity of the Logos and the man Jesus through the incarnation. This led to all the difficulties of whether the Logos was the personalizing element in the incarnation, or whether the Logos united with the man Jesus of Nazareth. Reformation Christology sought to circumvent the two-nature impasse through the concept of the *communicatio idiomatum* (each nature communicates its attributes to the other), and later eighteenth- and nineteenth-century Christology explored the possibilities implicit in the notion of *kenosis*. Pannenberg's answer is to say that Jesus' unity with the Logos can only be approached indirectly through Jesus' primary relationship to the Father.

(7) Finally, Jesus' claim to equality with God was interpreted as blasphemous and led to his crucifixion. The separation from the Father experienced on the cross was the ultimate expression of Jesus' self-differentiation from the Father in his act of total obedience and self-surrender. 'This obedience led him into the situation of extreme separation from God and his immortality, into the dereliction of the cross. The remoteness from God on the cross was the climax of his self-distinction from the Father.'[74]

---

[74] Pannenberg, *Systematic Theology*, vol. 2, 375.

In the light of the resurrection Jesus is confirmed in his mission and vocation to be the son of God. His awareness of his own finitude, and therefore the need to differentiate himself from the Father, is seen as the paradigm of the relationship of the finite to the infinite. By any standards the theological integration of Pannenberg's Christology is impressive. He demonstrates how historical-critical biblical interpretation, systematic-theological analysis and philosophical perspicuity can rescue the Christian religion from its reduction to morality as was the case in Kant, or a speculative philosophy of history as pertained to Hegel. In the process, however, he constructs a particular theology of history which remains deeply indebted to both a critical-realist and idealist perspective. So is he or is he not in the arms of the angels? Let us now begin the process of adjudication to which we referred in our scene-setting exercise.

Assessment

Few modern theologians have had the temerity to object to the dominance of the modern paradigm of history in every area of theological concern. The issue of the historicity of past events and their accessibility to us today, particularly the foundational events surrounding the person, ministry, mission, and the cross and resurrection of Jesus, have dominated the Christological horizon. The metaphysical background to Christology, the question of Jesus' divinity and his relation to the God he represents, has taken second place to the concern to retrieve the historical Jesus as the primary focus of Christological concern.[75] Thus John Macquarrie, in his attempt to delineate what is essential for a viable modern Christology, begins his apologia with the historical question:

> We have seen that anyone who would think or write about Christology today must face the considerable disarray that has arisen over the historical question. What do we know with reasonable certainty about the historical figure Jesus of Nazareth? And how much do we need to know in order to evaluate the claims that have been made for him?[76]

Macquarrie endeavours to plot his own cautious route through this particular debate, but not once does he raise any doubts about the validity or otherwise of this modern obsession with history.

---

[75] There were obviously exceptions to this general trend, for instance Barth, Tillich and, to a certain extent, Rahner. The difference between all of these and, for instance, Pannenberg and Moltmann is that the latter only arrive at metaphysical concerns when they have endeavoured to settle the historical and hermeneutical issues that necessarily pertain in any modern discussion of Christology.
[76] Macquarrie, *Jesus Christ in Modern Thought*, 348.

We have concentrated our attention on Wolfhart Pannenberg because he has consistently advocated that there is no form of human knowledge other than that which is embedded within the traditions and events which history seeks both to preserve and interpret. He also refuses to be unnerved by the so-called distinction between Christology from below and above, opting against one in favour of the other. Rather, he endeavours to show how both imply the other and how it is possible to build a Christology which takes this relationship seriously.[77] It is certainly possible to level criticisms at Pannenberg's impressive endeavours, one of the most serious of which being whether or not he has correctly understood the nature of apocalyptic.[78] However, that immediately brings us to the nub of the issue, which is, given the fact that there is no objective, value-neutral or non-ideological history, has anyone yet correctly understood the precise nature of apocalyptic expectation or is this inevitably an historical construct? We could equally well have taken the biblical interpretation and christological reflections of Edward Schillebeeckx and Hans Küng as examples of two Roman Catholic theologians who agree with the fundamental premise that our access to the real Jesus is via the route of critical-historical investigation, and yet, precisely because of the secular and positivistic historical stance they adopt are forced to make other moves to guarantee the divinity of the Saviour.[79] To a large extent, philosophy as the traditional partner in dialogue with theology has given way to history, and particularly hermeneutics, as the new focus of attention. It is only now at this late stage in the evolution of the modern 'scientific and technological project' that dissenting voices are

---

[77] It is certainly true that in the first edition of *Grundzuge der Christologie* Pannenberg appeared to be advocating a Christology from below. In the postscript to the fifth German edition, however, he sought not only to acknowledge this deficiency but also began to raise doubts concerning the validity and logic of the distinction as an elucidation of the Christological issues: 'It seems to me that the limitations of the present book lie in other places. These are connected with the limitation within the history of tradition approach "from below", which is carried through here by treating the reality of God as a *presupposition* of Christology. This point has not really become thematic in the discussion so far. There is, to be sure, a section about the doctrine of the Trinity in my book. But the statements of this section are almost limited to the deity of Jesus in distinction from Father and Spirit. As a consequence, God's action in Jesus' history is certainly not bypassed, but still it does not become thematic as God's action' (404–405).

[78] So, for instance, Tom Wright contends, 'One of the things for which Schweitzer has become most famous is now increasingly questioned: "apocalyptic" was for him, and for the ninety years since he wrote, almost synonymous with the end of the space-time universe, but it is now clear that this is a bizarre literalistic reading of what the first century knew to be thoroughly metaphorical' (*Jesus and the Victory of God*, 81).

[79] Cf. Küng, *On Being a Christian,* 119–163 and Schillebeeckx, *Jesus and Experiment in Christology*.

being heard which seek to subvert the continued ascendancy of the paradigm of history.

These voices come from the advocates of postmodernity who are suspicious of the claim that history can, or ever did, represent, or indeed, interrogate reality. The demise of the grand narrative which sought to explain everything within the terms of some universal frame of reference, has cast a shadow over the all-encompassing tendencies of history and has now been replaced by the postmodern condition of 'incredulity toward metanarratives'. So, for instance, Jean-François Lyotard has argued in a recent article that any overarching theory of universal history is really a form of cultural imperialism. It is the way one dominant culture supplants and overcomes the legitimacy of another in the vain search for universal meaning.[80] Within the confines of postmodern theory, universality has given way to particularity and the recognition of the importance of cultural contexts as critical evidence of the sociological and political conditioning of all our knowledge, both of the past and the present. 'Claims to objectivity, neutrality or empirical truth are subverted by showing the problematic status of 'facts', the need of the historian always to impose some plot and order are taken as facts, and the inevitable bias towards particular cultures, groups, and political interests.'[81]

Even within contemporary theology there are those who are suspicious of the claim that history mirrors reality. Rather, it is claimed that history merely portrays ideological self-interest and the inevitable bias of one cultural aspiration over and against another.[82]

As we have noted already, one theologian to voice similar concerns has been Jürgen Moltmann. He asserts that the ascendancy of the modern paradigm of history has aided and abetted the ruthless subjugation of nature by technology. By making ourselves the sole subjects of history, we have severed the connection between ourselves and the history of the natural world. It is only the ecological crisis which has alerted us to this fact and so also revealed the considerable limitations of the modern investment in our own historical destiny: 'The more human beings put themselves above nature the less they know who they really are. The modern crisis of identity and humanity are an inescapable result of the self-isolation of human beings from nature.'[83] Moltmann advocates a theology of mutual interdependence, or *perichoresis*, where the history of nature and human beings are put on an equal footing within a new covenantal relationship.

---

[80] Lyotard, *Missive on Universal History*, 43–64.
[81] Ford, *The Modern Theologians*, vol. 2, 292.
[82] See, for instance, Taylor, 'Terminal Faith'.
[83] Moltmann, *The Way of Jesus Christ*, 271.

Other critical voices have come from within the circle of feminist thought. Here the concern has been over the identification of history quite literally with *his* story, to the virtual exclusion of *her* story. The modern paradigm of history has been exposed as a particular version of the 'androcentric fallacy'. It is only in recent years with the rise of feminist critical analysis that we have taken due note of the fact that the history of the modern world has indeed been the history of the dominance of the masculine psyche:

> Many generalisations could be made about the history of the Western mind, but to-day perhaps the most immediately obvious is that it has been from start to finish an overwhelmingly masculine phenomenon: Socrates, Plato, Aristotle, Paul, Augustine, Aquinas, Luther, Copernicus, Galileo, Bacon, Descartes, Newton, Locke, Hume, Kant, Darwin, Marx, Nietzsche, Freud . . . The Western intellectual tradition has been produced and canonised almost entirely by men, and informed mainly by male perspectives.[84]

What, then, of the modern economic conception of history as that which has been driven largely by the engine of two competing ideologies, namely, capitalism versus communism? The origins of this dispute go back to Hegel and Marx and both ideologies espouse a developmental, progressive notion of historical evolution:

> For both of these thinkers, there was a coherent development of human societies from simple tribal ones based on slavery and subsistence agriculture, through various theocracies, monarchies, and feudal aristocracies, up through modern liberal democracy and technologically driven capitalism. This evolutionary process was neither random nor unintelligible, even if it was possible to question whether man was happier or better off as a result of historical 'progress'.[85]

It is also the case that both thinkers, operating within the parameters of these premises, posited a possible end to universal history when humanity's most basic and fundamental socio-political needs and aspirations were realized in a universal form of human society. For Hegel this was the democratic nation-state and for Marx it was egalitarian communism. According to Francis Fukuyama, a modern interpreter of their respective theses, it is Hegel who has won the day. Despite the deep pessimism about the possibility of historical progress which has accompanied the continuing atrocities of this century of 'mass death', and despite the intellectual bombardment of the notion of progress by contemporary philosophers and historians, what we have actually witnessed in recent history is the near total collapse of both military-authoritarian

---

[84] Tarnas, *The Passion of the Western Mind*, 441.
[85] Fukuyama, *The End of History and the Last Man*, xii.

rightist regimes and their leftist counterpart, totalitarian communism. Fukuyama argues that the Hegelian notion of the end of history has been realized in the victory of liberal democracy over its ideological and economic counterpart. Obviously, in some sense history continues: patterns of succession and development, the conflict of competing ideologies, the rise of religious fundamentalism and political nationalism are all part of the historical and cultural fabric of contemporary life. However, it could seem that in the spread of liberal democracy throughout the world we have arrived at an inherently stable form of society that protects, nourishes and satisfies our basic socio-political needs. According to Fukuyama this is based on the realization of two prior underlying prerequisites. The first is the development of modern natural science and technology, which in turn has led to the realization of the capitalist ideal of continued economic expansion bolstered by the rise of the global economy:

> All countries undergoing economic modernisation must increasingly resemble one another: they must unify nationally on the basis of a centralised state, urbanise, replace traditional forms of social organisation like tribe, sect, and family with economically rational ones based on function and efficiency, and provide for the universal education of their citizens. Such societies have become increasingly linked with one another through global markets and the spread of a universal consumer culture. Moreover, the logic of modern natural science would seem to dictate a universal evolution in the direction of capitalism. The experiences of the Soviet Union, China, and other socialist countries indicate that while highly centralised economies are sufficient to reach the level of industrialisation represented by Europe in the 1950s, they are woefully inadequate in creating what have been termed complex 'post-industrial' economies in which information and technological innovation play a much larger role.[86]

Fukuyama does concede that there is no necessary inner connection between advanced economic industrialization and liberal democracy. While economic expansion and development may have led inexorably to the victory of capitalism over communism, the logic of modern natural science is insufficient to account for this fact. Returning to Hegel and this time, Nietzsche, Fukuyama asserts that the second crucial determinant is the desire for recognition or self-esteem which creates the basis for equality and the mutual recognition of human and civil rights, which, in turn is central to the development of modern liberal democracy:

> Recognition is the central problem of politics because it is the origin of tyranny, imperialism, and the desire to dominate. But while it has a dark side, it cannot be

---

[86] Ibid., xiv–xv.

simply abolished from political life, because it is simultaneously the psychological ground for political virtues like courage, public-spiritedness, and justice. All political communities must make use of the desire for recognition, while at the same time protecting themselves from its destructive effects. If contemporary constitutional government has indeed found a formula whereby all are recognised in a way that nonetheless avoids the emergence of tyranny, then it would indeed have a special claim to stability and longevity among the regimes that emerged on earth.[87]

Clearly, Fukuyama's thesis can be contested and he himself argues for a more robust form of social democracy than has hitherto been exhibited in international affairs. However, what is common to the nature versus history, men versus women, and capitalism versus communism interpretations of history is the postmodern ambivalence about power relations. Nietzsche and Foucault's conviction that all human knowledge, value judgements and the rise of historical consciousness is ideologically controlled, driven by the will to power, has become firmly situated in the postmodern psyche and indeed in the contemporary evaluation of the nature of history.[88] Before we assess the integrity or otherwise of this claim it would seem apposite to inquire first of all into the nature and practice of contemporary historiography.

The Making of History

Here we need to ask, again from the postmodern perspective on performance, not what the historian presumes his or her task might be, but how they actually practise or perform their task: how does the historian go about making or constructing history? Clearly this involves the interconnectivity of a number of crucial factors.

First of all, historians bring themselves to the task: their own values, prejudices, self-evaluation, academic position, ideological interests, and personal preferences.

Secondly, they bring with them their epistemological presuppositions and preferences, be they Marxist, empiricist, feminist, positivist, idealist, progressive, liberationist, postmodernist, etc., or a range of these possibilities. Clearly, we are referring here to the educational, political, cultural and economic situatedness of the historical interpreter.

Thirdly, they bring with them their research skills or lack of them, the use of various techniques or methods of enquiry and the application of certain consensus-driven 'tools of the trade'. Here theory and practice mutually inform

---

[87] Ibid., xxi–xxii.
[88] In this regard see Nietzsche, *The Will to Power*, and Foucault, *Power/Knowledge*.

one another. It matters a lot whether we think of history as a universal inter-connected nexus of events or just one damn thing after another. Similarly, how do we evaluate the importance of cause and effect, or the notion of the funda-mental homogeneity of all events, or the psychological mechanism of empathy, or the interpretation of history by use of analogous or anachronistic criteria?

Fourthly, the historian works with, interprets, deconstructs and evaluates both primary and secondary material, although this does not imply a value judgement in regard to the importance of one in relation to another. The histo-rian may have a preference for original artefacts and primary sources, or he or she may attribute equal value to biographical and therefore already interpreted accounts of such information and data.

Fifthly, the historian is required to write up their research and so evolve their own, or borrow some other interpretative framework. Once again, therefore, epistemological, ideological, methodological and personal factors clearly come into play.

Finally, there is the consumption of such constructed histories by other aca-demics, or the scholarly community, or, indeed, the populace at large. Now, of course, we are indebted to the literary critics who remind us that no two read-ings need be literally the same. There is always the *différence* between one inter-pretative horizon and another. There is always the potential to misunderstand, misapply, wrongly judge or misconstrue, or indeed, to deconstruct the text as it is read in a new context. And, of course, there is also still some sense of scholarly consensus, or the testing and refining of historical hypotheses among a com-munity of interested and committed historians.

In terms of the common coinage of all six factors, it is difficult to ignore nowadays the prominence of the word 'ideological'. How we learn to read history depends on how we interpret those who construct history and they, by and large, are the product of the dominant cultural ideology which has pro-duced such history in the first place. George Steiner expresses the nature of the problem we face:

> Croce's dictum 'all history is contemporary history' points directly to the onto-logical paradox of the past tense. Historians are increasingly aware that the conventions of narrative and implicit reality with which they work are philosoph-ically vulnerable. The dilemma exists on at least two levels. The first is semantic. The bulk of the historian's material consists of utterances made in and about the past. Given the perpetual process of linguistic change not only in vocabulary and syntax but in meaning, how is he to interpret, to translate his sources . . . Reading a historical document, collating the modes of narrative in previous written his-tory, interpreting speech-acts performed in the distant or nearer past, he finds himself becoming more and more of the translator in the technical sense . . . And

the meaning thus arrived at must be the 'true one'. By what metamorphic magic is the historian to proceed?[89]

In terms of the dominant cultural ideologies that have controlled the construction of history in western civilization there are three variations on a single theme, namely, realist or empiricist, idealist, with a new contender recently appearing on the scene, namely, postmodern. The single theme that unites all three is the conviction that the truth is basically 'out there' in some form or another waiting to be discovered. It is either 'out there' empirically in the real world to which we can gain genuine epistemic access provided we use the right 'tools' of investigation; or it is 'out there' in someone's mind be that the mind of God or the problem of 'other minds' and therefore must be disclosed to us; or it is 'out there' in somewhat disconnected and interrupted form waiting to be deconstructed or reconstructed by ourselves. In that sense, as Whitehead once remarked, the history of western philosophy is still basically a series of footnotes to Plato. The fundamental question remains: what is the nature of truth and how is the truth mediated to us and in what form is it discovered or appropriated by us? Is truth mediated to us through the eternal forms, or through the self-disclosure of the eternal God in and through the unfolding events of history, or through the universal application of reason to the traditions, discourses, narratives and still resonating evidences of the past, or through the acceptance that truth is largely our own ideological construction?

In the empiricist tradition history is correspondingly the way we gain access through the application of critical reason to the various forms of knowledge we have about the past. In the idealist tradition history is the way we gain entry to the divine mind or the mind of others through the critical application of empathy. The material we investigate may be largely the same, that is artefacts, documents, archaeological data, census information, maps, etc. However, for the realist-empiricist, that information does and can inform us about the world of the past, and for the idealist, it informs us about what other minds thought about themselves and the world of the past. In both traditions certain cultural factors dominate the interpretation of the past. History is organized along a value scale which, by and large with a few critical reservations, has been positivistic, programmatic, progressive and liberal. There are still apparently such things as ascertainable facts, granted that they arrive replete with ready-made interpretations which it is the historian's task to assess, evaluate and interpret – usually by venturing a particular hypothesis or interpretative framework which tries to make sense of the available information in as parsimonious and convincing a way as possible. In order to achieve this, historians must accept the inevitability of progressive development because they work within a

---

[89] Steiner, *After Babel*, 134–136.

developing tradition of scholarship and enquiry and, usually, it is also granted that they should avoid prejudicing the evidence through bias or wanton misrepresentation.

For the postmodernist there is no such thing as the past – we are in fact cut off from the past by an ontological gap, a version of Lessing's ditch – so there is only the way we construct the past and we do so inevitably through our own ideological and epistemological preferences. In terms of this latter perspective and

> in these arguably postist days – post liberal, post western, post-heavy industrial, post Marxist – the old centres barely hold, and the old metanarratives no longer resonate with actuality and promise, coming to look incredible from late twentieth-century sceptical perspectives ('Fancy anybody ever believing in that'). Possibly no social formation we know of has so systematically eradicated intrinsic value from its culture so much as liberal market capitalism, not through choice, but through the 'cultural logic of late-capital'. Accordingly, as George Steiner has noted, 'it is this collapse, more or less complete, more or less conscious, of those hierarchical, definitional value gradients (and can there be value without hierarchy?) which is now the major fact of our intellectual and social circumstances'.[90]

The postmodernist, consequently, readily accepts that there is really a smorgasbord of historical perspectives because 'from Nietzsche to Freud to Saussure to Wittgenstein to Althusser to Foucault to Derrida'[91] we have ransacked our various disciplines and found them all variously devoid of foundations. It is surely interesting that in terms of the political processes of intellectual discourse, it is liberalism that has again won the day.

From the perspective of postmodern discourse, the integral relationship between the modern dogma of progress and the development of modern historical-critical study of the Bible, witnesses precisely to the reality of ideological construction. There is obviously no historical Jesus nor indeed a Christ of faith, nor any historical evidence for a clear delineation of the relationship between them, there is only Bultmann's, Schweitzer's, Käsemann's, Pannenberg's or Wright's constructed histories of the narratives, stories and loose causal identities which form our perception of the past. The only way to avoid this conclusion is to accept on the basis of some sort of philosophy of universal history that it is possible to arrive at a theology of history where both the unity and the end of history are centrally related to christological convictions and this, of course, is precisely what Pannenberg, again with the help of the idealist tradition, has endeavoured to achieve. The choice in modern biblical scholarship appears to range fairly evenly across the critical-realist, idealist and

---

[90] Jenkins, *Rethinking History*, 63.
[91] Ibid., 64.

postmodern alternatives. Should we be surprised that theology must own its debt to a philosophy of history? The failure to do so leads to the same postivistic, progressive and liberal pursuit which has recently eventuated in yet another attempt to build a modern flyover across Lessing's ditch.[92] What is now called the new 'New Quest' or the 'Third Quest' to unearth the historical Jesus seems destined to dress up an old scarecrow in modern designer label clothes. In the process all the old fallacies, fables and fictions of modern biblical scholarship are simply revisited or repositioned in a schema that cannot relinquish or indeed recognise the positivistic myth of progress.

> The renewed New Quest works . . . with an overall picture of Christian origins that ought now to be abandoned. It is the Bultmannian picture, with variations: a de-Judaized Jesus preaching a demythologised, 'vertical' eschatology; a crucifixion with no early theological interpretation; a 'resurrection' consisting of the coming to faith, sometime later, of a particular group of Christians; an early sapiential/gnostic group, retelling the master's aphorisms but uninterested in his life story; a Paul who invented a Hellenistic Christ-cult; a synoptic tradition in which rolling aphorisms, as they slowed down, gathered the moss of narrative structure about themselves, and gradually congealed into gospels in which the initial force of Jesus' challenge was muted or lost altogether within a fictitious pseudo-historical framework. This modern picture, in fact, is the real fiction.[93]

The above carries merit, however, if it is *not* based on the presupposition that a faculty called good historical judgement is somehow immune to ideological control or influence. Such a position is in our view equally a fiction and the continual infiltration of historical science by the myth or dogma of human progress demonstrates the point. Laws of history, or ideological shifts in the construction of history are easy to discern because we create them, and of course, in the end we destroy them when they no longer support the reigning plausibility structure by which we measure our place in the order of things.

> 'Was not "the law of progress" so much in evidence thanks to powers sufficiently skilful, resourceful and unscrupulous or callous to make the "progressive" live and spread and the "backward" shrink and die? Was it not the case that laws of history and progress came to rule thought when such powers came to rule the world? And is it not the case that, short of the return of such powers, the modern certainty of progress and, more generally, of historical direction, are unlikely to rise from the postmodern ashes?'[94]

---

[92] For an intriguing survey see Wright, *Jesus and the Victory of God*, 28–78. For an equally interesting account of similar developments in the field of Old Testament studies see Provan, 'Ideologies, Literary and Critical: Reflections on Recent Writing on the History of Israel'.

[93] Wright, *Jesus and the Victory of God*, 79–80.

[94] Bauman, 'Postmodernity and its Discontents', 200.

Bibliography

Allison, D., *The End of the Age has Come: An Early Interpretation of the Passion and Resurrection of Jesus* (Edinburgh: T. & T. Clark, 1987)

Barth, K., *The Epistle to the Romans*, tr. E. Hoskyns (Oxford: Oxford University Press, 1968⁶)

Bartholomew, C.G., *Opening the Book for a New Millennium* (Carlisle: Paternoster: Grand Rapids: Zondervan, 2000)

Bartsch, H.-W. (ed.), *Kerygma and Myth: A Theological Debate*, tr. R.H. Fuller (London: SPCK, 1953)

Baumar, Z., *Postmodernity and its Discontents* (Cambridge: Polity Press, 1997)

Bebbington, D., (ed.) *Patterns in History: A Christian Perspective on Historical Thought* (Leicester: Inter-Varsity Press, 1979)

Braaten, C.E., *New Directions in Theology Today*, vol. 2: *History and Hermeneutics* (London: Lutterworth, 1968)

Braaten, C.E., and R.A. Harrisville (eds.), *The Historical Jesus and the Kerygmatic Christ* (Nashville: Abingdon Press, 1964)

Braaten, C.E., and R.W. Jenson, *Reclaiming the Bible for the Church* (Grand Rapids: Eerdmans, 1995)

Brueggemann, W., *Theology of the Old Testament* (Minneapolis: Augsberg Press, 1997)

Bultmann, R., *Theology of the New Testament*, vol. 1 (London: SCM Press, 1952)

—, 'The Primitive Christian Kerygma and the Historical Jesus' in C.E. Braaten and R.A. Harrisville (eds.), *The Historical Jesus and the Kerygmatic Christ* (Nashville: Abingdon Press, 1964)

Butterfield, H., *Christianity and History* (London: Fontana Books, 1949)

Coakley, S., *Christ Without Absolutes* (Oxford: Clarendon Press, 1988)

Comte, A. 'Positive Philosophy', in D. Bebbington (ed.), *Patterns in History: A Christian Perspective on Historical Thought* (Leicester: Inter-Varsity Press, 1979)

Condorcet, A.-N. de, *Sketch of a Historical Picture of the Progress of the Human Mind*, tr. J. Barraclough ([1795] London: n.p., 1955)

Ford, D., *The Modern Theologians*, vol. 1 (2 vols; Oxford: Basil Blackwell, 1989²)

Foucault, M., *Power/Knowledge* (New York: Pantheon Books, 1980)

Fukuyama, F., *The End of History and the Last Man* (New York: Free Press, 1992)

Gadamer, H.-G., *Truth and Method* (London: Sheed & Ward, 1975)

Giddens, A., *The Consequences of Modernity* (Cambridge: Polity Press, 1990)

Habermas, J., *Lectures on the Philosophical Discourses of Modernity* (Cambridge, MA.: MIT Press, 1987)

Hamilton, W., *A Quest for the Post-Historical Jesus* (London: SCM Press, 1993)

Harnack, S. von, *What Is Christianity?* (London: Thomas Bailey, 1904)

Harrisville, R.A., and W. Sundberg, *The Bible in Modern Culture* (Grand Rapids: Eerdmans, 1995)

Harvey, V.A., *The Historian and the Believer* (London: SCM Press, 1967)

Heelas, P. (ed.), *Religion, Modernity and Postmodernity* (Oxford: Basil Blackwell, 1998)

Howard, T.A., *Religion and the Rise of Historicism: W.M.L. de Wette, Jacob Burckhardt, and the Theological Origins of Nineteenth-Century Consciousness* (Cambridge: Cambridge University Press, 2000)

Hume, D., *Enquiries concerning the Human Understanding and concerning the Principle of Morals*, ed. L.A. Selby-Bigge (Oxford: Oxford University Press, 1955)

—, 'Essay on Miracles' in idem, *Dialogues Concerning Natural Religion*, ed. N. Kemp Smith (London: n.p., 1947²)

Jenkins, K., *Rethinking History* (London and New York: Routledge, 1991)

Jeremias, J., *The Problem of the Historical Jesus*, tr. N. Perrin (Philadelphia: Fortress Press, 1964)

Jones, G., *Critical Theology* (Oxford: Polity Press, 1995)

Kähler, M., *The So-called Historical Jesus and the Historic, Biblical Christ*, tr. C. Braaten (Philadelphia: Fortress Press, 1984)

Kierkegaard, S., *Concluding Unscientific Postscript* (Princeton: Princeton University Press, 1968)

—, *The Concept of Anxiety*, tr. R. Thomte (Princeton Princeton University Press, 1980)

Küng, H., *On Being a Christian*, tr. E. Quinn (London: Collins, 1977)

Lessing, G.E., *Theological Writings*, ed. H. Chadwick (Stanford: Stanford University Press, 1957)

Lyotard, J.-F., 'Missive on Universal History' in idem *Correspondance 1982–85* (Paris: Galilee, 1986)

Macquarrie, J., *Jesus Christ in Modern Thought* (London: SCM Press, 1990)

McGrath, A., *The Making of Modern German Christology 1750–1990* (Grand Rapids: Zondervan, 1994)

Meyer, B.F., *The Aims of Jesus* (London: SCM Press, 1979)

Moltmann, J., *The Way of Jesus Christ* (London, SCM Press, 1990)

Nicholls, W., *The Pelican Guide to Modern Theology*, vol. 1 (Harmondsworth: Penguin Books, 1969)

Nietzsche, F., *The Will to Power* (New York: Random House, 1967)

O'Neill, J.C., *The Bible's Authority: A Portrait Gallery of Thinkers From Lessing to Bultmann* (Edinburgh: T. & T. Clark, 1991)

Pannenberg, W., *Grundzüge der Christologie* (Gütersloh: Gerd Mohn, 1964)

—, *Jesus – God and Man* (London: SCM Press, 1968)

—, (ed.), *Revelation as History* (London: Sheed & Ward, 1969)

—, 'Redemptive Event and History' in idem *Basic Questions in Theology*, vol. 1 (London: SCM Press, 1970)

—, 'What is Truth' in idem *Basic Questions in Theology*, vol. 2 (London: SCM Press, 1971)

—, *Systematic Theology*, vol. 1, tr. G.W. Bromiley (Edinburgh: T. & T. Clark, 1991)

—, *Systematic Theology*, vol. 2, tr. G.W. Bromiley (Edinburgh: T. & T. Clark, 1994)

Pannikkar, R., *The Trinity and the Religious Experience of Man: Icon-Person Mystery* (London and New York: n.p., 1973)

Pelikan, J., *Jesus Through the Centuries* (Newhaven: Yale University Press, 1985)

Provan, I., 'Ideologies, Literary and Critical, Reflections on Recent Writing on the History of Israel', *JBL* 114.4 (1995), 585–606

Reventlow, H.G., *The Authority of the Bible and the Rise of the Modern World* (London: SCM Press, 1984)

Rogerson, J.W., *Old Testament Criticism in the Nineteenth Century: England and Germany* (London: SPCK, 1984)

Saint Simon, H. de, 'On the Reorganisation of European Society' (1814) in D. Bebbington (ed.) *Patterns in History: A Christian Perspective on Historical Thought* (Leicester: Inter-Varsity Press, 1979)

Schillebeeckx, E., *Jesus and Experiment in Christology* (Glasgow: William Collins & Sons, 1979)

Schnackenburg, R., 'Christology and Myth' in H.-W. Bartsch (ed.), *Kerygma and Myth: A theological Debate* (London: SPCK, 1953)

Schweitzer, A., *The Quest of the Historical Jesus: A Critical Study of its Progress from Reimarus to Wrede* ([1906] London: A. & C. Black, 1954)

Smith, A., 'Inquiry into the Nature and Causes of the Wealth of the Nations' in D. Bebbington, (ed.), *Patterns in History: A Christian Perspective on Historical Thought* (Leicester: Inter-Varsity Press, 1979)

Steiner, G., *After Babel* (Oxford: Oxford University Press, 1975)

Sternberg, M., *The Poetics of the Biblical Narrative: Ideological Literature and the Drama of Reading* (Bloomington: Indiana University Press, 1985)

Tarnas, R., *The Passion of the Western Mind* (New York: Ballantine Books, 1991)

Taylor, M.C., 'Terminal Faith' in P. Heelas (ed.), *Religion, Modernity and Postmodernity* (Oxford: Basil Blackwell, 1998)

Thiselton, A.C., *The Two Horizons* (Carlisle: Paternoster, 1980)

—, *New Horizons in Hermeneutics* (London: HarperCollins, 1992)

Troeltsch, E., *The Absoluteness of Christianity* (London: SCM Press, 1972)

Vanhoozer, K.J., *Is There Meaning in This Text?* (Grand Rapids: Zondervan, 1990)

Watson, F., *Text and Truth* (Edinburgh: T. & T. Clark, 1997)

Wrede, W., *The Messianic Secret* (London and Cambridge: James Clark, 1971)

Wright, N.T., *Jesus and the Victory of God* (London: SPCK, 1996)

12

An Experiment in Biblical Criticism: Aesthetic Encounter in Reading and Preaching Scripture

Stephen I. Wright

Introduction

In his book *An Experiment in Criticism* C.S. Lewis proposed that the basis of literary criticism, instead of being a judgement about books, should be a judgement about types of reading. Judgement about books would then follow as the corollary. That is, he suggested, the quality of literature is gauged by the extent to which it bears reading and rereading with a profound and rapt attentiveness. To a reader approaching a work in this spirit

> the first reading of some literary work is often . . . an experience so momentous that only experiences of love, religion or bereavement can furnish a standard of comparison. Their whole consciousness is changed. They have become what they were not before.[1]

This is what Lewis called 'literary reading', and he contrasted it with reading which is a mere vehicle for easy thrills or egoistic fantasizing ('castle-building', to use his term[2]). This article will seek to show how Lewis's 'experiment', and especially his description of 'literary' reading, may offer us new possibilities for our thinking about reading the Bible,[3] and thus for the renewal of biblical hermeneutics.

---

[1] Lewis, *Experiment*, 3.
[2] Ibid., 51f.
[3] For a treatment of the experiential dimension of Bible reading drawing on perspectives from Augustine to Jung see ch. 1, 'Biblical Empirics', in Brown, *Text and Psyche*, 31–57.

The term 'literary' in biblical studies today tends to be associated with various kinds of non-realist philosophies of language, a mistrust of the capacity of texts to mediate truth, and an undervaluation of the human dimensions of writing and reading.[4] This scenario does have some positive aspects;[5] and my purpose is not to suggest that a simplistic return to the days before such associations is either possible or desirable. But it is evidence of unfortunate amnesia when even a description of the 'literary paradigm' of biblical reading in *The New Interpreter's Bible*, a leading current biblical reference tool, mainly assumes that the word 'literary' *must* now carry this kind of philosophical baggage.[6] For instance, the article sets the 'literary paradigm' over against the 'historical paradigm' by asserting that in the former 'the text is viewed ahistorically or atemporally'.[7] The result of such an association of ideas is that biblical scholars may overlook the relevance for their own discipline of a kind of literary criticism with a much longer pedigree than current fashions, a criticism of which Lewis was a distinguished Christian representative. Rooted in the Romantic period, this is a literary criticism permeated with aesthetic sensibility, which celebrates the human response to the other which takes place in literary reading. It is an approach to literature which is still alive and well in secular faculties.[8] Moreover, in applying it to Scripture, we may ground it not in the sceptical Romantic position (exemplified by P.B. Shelley and Matthew Arnold) which *substituted* an aesthetic-literary valuation of Scripture for a religious one, but in the continental Romantic idea that an aesthetic-literary appreciation could *enrich* a religious one. The latter stance derives from the Romantics' conception that truth could be disclosed equally validly through aesthetic as through scientific means, a conception which in turn owed much to Kant's suggestion that the aesthetic sensibility might provide the link between the realms of pure reason and that which could be known to our senses.[9]

---

[4] See for instance the vision of the future for biblical literary studies at the conclusion of Moore, *Literary Criticism*. On postmodern conceptions of the literary see the essay by Craig Bartholomew in this volume. For a critique by a secular literary scholar of one such conception, that which speaks of 'the death of the author', see Burke, *Death and Return*.

[5] See Jasper's generally positive description of the current biblical-literary scene in *Bible and Literature*, 56–60. See below, n.73, on the affinity between the approach to the gospels of Stephen Moore, cited by Jasper as representative of postmodern literary criticism of Scripture, and that of the 'new homiletic', which I assess positively.

[6] Holladay, 'Contemporary Methods', 136–147.

[7] Ibid., 139. The subsection is called, oddly, 'meaning as aesthetics': aesthetic sensibility seems definitely absent from the 'literary paradigm' as Holladay describes it.

[8] See, e.g., Fuller and Waugh (eds.), *Arts and Sciences*.

[9] See Jasper and Prickett (eds.), *Bible and Literature*, 7ff.

Lewis was reacting to the foolish haste with which critics within the aesthetic-literary tradition tended to exalt or condemn authors.[10] Such judgements, he suggested, merely reflected the fashionable taste of the moment. However, if one inquired as to the way that a particular author was *read*, one might come to a much surer sense of the quality of their work. Literature which consistently yielded up treasures to a variety of readers all reading in a 'literary' way would have its worth thus revealed; while literature which seemed to be 'enjoyable' only by means of 'unliterary' reading would likewise be seen in its true colours:

> For the accepted valuation of literary works varies with every change of fashion, but the distinction between attentive and inattentive, obedient and wilful, disinterested and egoistic, modes of reading is permanent.[11]

At first sight this line of thought may seem only tangentially relevant to Scripture. The issue for biblical scholarship today is not mainly how to decide between different literary *evaluations* – between the claims of those who might assert the 'superiority' of Luke to Matthew, for instance, on grounds of style or skill of composition. A generation ago, perhaps, the admonitions of Lewis about the folly of setting up firm canons of taste might have hit a target among biblical scholars who argued, for instance, for the intrinsic superiority of one literary form to another and built models of historical development on such judgements.[12] But on a more fundamental level than this, Lewis's book may imply a theological challenge. *Ought we to let the way the Bible responds to good reading dictate what we say about its nature and status, rather than let preconceived views of its nature and status dictate what 'good reading' of it entails?*

Lewis himself did not write at length about 'literary criticism' of Scripture, though he criticized the sceptical position of those who substituted an aesthetic valuation of it for a religious one, suspecting 'that those who read the Bible as literature do not read the Bible'.[13] By this I think he meant precisely that the serious Bible readers he encountered were those who valued Scripture *not* just for the beauty of its poetry and prose (in the Authorized Version, of course!) but for its content.[14] It is exactly the emphasis on receptiveness to content as

---

[10] Lewis, *Experiment*, 105–112.

[11] Ibid., 106.

[12] See the debate about the parables, and valuations of 'allegory'. For a rebuttal of the older assertions of the intrinsic literary superiority of Jesus' parables to those of the rabbis see Young, *Jesus*.

[13] Lewis, 'The Literary Impact of the Authorised Version', 46, cited in Jasper and Prickett (eds.), *Bible and Literature*, 8.

[14] Cf. George Steiner's criticism of *The Literary Guide to the Bible* ('Review') that it failed, in this sense, to be literary enough: it concentrated on human techniques to the exclusion of asking about the nature and ultimate origins of the Bible's extraordinary evocations.

well as to form which marks his *Experiment*, and which leads me to suspect that he would have been very amenable to its application to Scripture.[15]

There is a sense in which this article (like Lewis's proposal) is not strictly about *hermeneutics* at all. As I shall show, there is a difference between interpreting a text (carrying the inevitable suggestion of translating it into something else) and dwelling in a text, encountering the reality which it mediates. It is that encounter with which I am concerned. However, this chapter asserts its place in a volume about the renewal of hermeneutics by way of reminding the discipline of hermeneutics that, necessary as it is to a Christian understanding and proclaiming of biblical truth, it should recognize its own limits. As Friedrich Schelling intuited, '*encountering* the strange, the alien, the unfamiliar, the different, in short the Other, is a pre-condition for interpreting and understanding persons and selfhood'.[16] 'Hermeneutics' – like dogmatics in Barth's thinking – serves the reading and preaching of Scripture, but does not fully describe or circumscribe these activities, whose goal is not to interpret a text but to meet and praise God. To reach that goal, we need not only the discipline of hermeneutics but also, I suggest, the kind of 'literary reading' which Lewis articulates.[17]

The Humble Reader

Lewis's proposal, if applied to our theory and practice of Bible reading, would first mean shifting attention from inherent qualities of the text to the quality of our reading of it. Our first object of 'criticism' would not be the Bible, but the reader.

The attractiveness of this proposal as a way of thinking Christianly about reading, and especially reading the Bible, should be evident. The suggestion that it is the reader who is under judgement, not the text, answers well to a Christian awareness of fallibility, classically expressed in such texts as 1 Corinthians 4:5, *we* are not to act as judges, for the Lord will judge all. Lewis writes: 'We must begin by laying aside as completely as we can all our own preconceptions, interests, and associations.'[18] He echoes important Christian themes as he

---

[15] Lewis also wrote that he dreaded 'an over-emphasis on the poetical element' in the words of Jesus, as obscuring his human qualities, including 'the homely, peasant shrewdness' (Lewis, 'Christianity and Literature', 4). Receiving the texts as they are counters the tendency to idealize the speaker. Cf. also Christensen, *Lewis on Scripture*, 77–80.

[16] Cited in Thiselton, *Interpreting*, 50 (my emphasis).

[17] This chapter therefore runs in parallel with Trevor Hart's, which deals with the importance of the imagination in hermeneutics itself.

[18] Lewis, *Experiment*, 18.

uses the language of surrender, of self-emptying and self-opening, and of the enlargement of consciousness:

> The primary impulse of each is to maintain and aggrandize himself. The secondary impulse is to go out of the self, to correct its provincialism and heal its loneliness. In love, in virtue, in the pursuit of knowledge, and in the reception of the arts, we are doing this. Obviously this process can be described either as an enlargement or as a temporary annihilation of the self. But that is an old paradox; 'he that loseth his life shall save it'.[19]

This emphasis on the reader's attitude may be interestingly contrasted with the contemporary approach, also reader-centred, advocated by David Clines.[20] Clines asserts quite aggressively the *authority* of the reader.[21] For Clines, the reader is the ultimate arbiter, the champion who resists all attempts at control (overt or covert, actual or suspected) by the social or institutional forces imposing their interpretations. This advocacy of readerly authority is accompanied by an urge to subject the Bible to critical scrutiny – a criticism more far-reaching than has yet been practised in the academy, largely deferential as it has been to ecclesiastical interests.[22]

Lewis, by contrast, advocates not the authority of the reader, but his submission to the text. 'The first demand any work of art makes upon us is surrender.'[23] It is not a question of asserting the individual's prerogative to decide on the meaning of the text. To the contrary, it is a question of the individual's yearning to open herself as fully as possible to the text and the realities which it reveals. The *critical* gaze, for Clines, is directed to the text: what historical factors are conditioning it? What moral or cultural stances does it disclose?[24] For Lewis, it is directed to the reader: how open *am I* to everything to which this text introduces me? Clines' model of reading is built around conflict, suspicion, assertiveness, control. Lewis's is built around relationship, trust, submission and surrender. It is not hard to see in Clines the insistence that 'critical reason', so central to the Enlightenment,[25] should be applied unbridled and without reserve throughout the sphere of biblical studies; but also the more recent ancestry of his position in Nietzsche and the assertion of the individual's will to power.[26] Lewis, on the other hand, finds a more natural precursor in the central

---

19 Ibid., 138.
20 Clines, *Bible*.
21 Ibid., 15–18.
22 Ibid., 25–28.
23 Lewis, *Experiment*, 19.
24 Clines, *Bible*, 20ff.
25 Cf. Tillich, *Perspectives*, 31f.
26 On this concept see Tillich, *Perspectives*, 197–207.

Romantic awareness of aesthetic sensibility as a bond between the personal and the universal, and thus as a vital mediating force in human culture.[27]

But if indeed we turn our critical attention to *ourselves* as readers, is *the Bible* then unjustifiably exempted from the kind of criticism which Clines urges? If we open ourselves to the text as Lewis suggests, if we dwell upon it with wonder and let it enlarge and transform our consciousness – and if 'we' are not only ordinary Bible readers, but also the scholarly community even as it pursues its academic calling – does that not let the Bible off the hook? Do its possible moral ambiguities, or social conditioning by oppressive forces, go unchallenged?

We shall return to this question in the section '*Logos* and *Poïema*' below. For the moment, we note that to read as Lewis recommends is not necessarily to exclude the making of critical judgements about the standpoint of the text. It does not foreclose the issue whether, for instance, a text might originally have reinforced male domination or élite oppression, or might in some circumstances do so today. It merely insists that the making of such judgements is not the *purpose of literary reading*, which is simply a generous self-opening to the perspective of the other.[28]

Using and Receiving

Lewis draws a distinction between 'using' and 'receiving' works of art: 'the many *use* art, and the few *receive* it'.[29] '"Using" is inferior to "reception" because art, if used rather than received, merely facilitates, brightens, relieves or palliates our life, and does not add to it.'[30] With respect to this distinction Lewis makes an important clarification about literature as distinct from other art forms. Since literature consists of words, and words always point beyond themselves, there is always a sense in which *reading* does involve 'using'. The question, says Lewis, is whether the reader wants to 'use' the 'content', that to which the words point, for some ulterior end, or simply to 'receive' it, to 'rest in it'.[31] In other language, he is locating the literary experience in a simultaneous encounter with the signified and the signifier. The literary experience is a state of aesthetic contemplation in which both words and that to which they point are perceived and received in a moment pregnant with significant possibility. It is an experience which enlarges us.

---

[27] Cf. Schiller, 'Aesthetic Education', 27.10.

[28] Cf. the resistance to the reduction of aesthetics to ideology mounted by Bell, 'Metaphysics'; Bloom, *Canon*, 17f.

[29] Lewis, *Experiment*, 19.

[30] Ibid., 88.

[31] Ibid., 89.

How may this apply to reading the Bible? We may leave aside the question whether the Bible is 'art', for this is precisely the kind of prejudgement the 'experiment' challenges. Prima facie, there would seem to be a strong case for regarding the Bible as richly responsive to 'literary' reading, but that is just what we do not need to decide. Our question, rather, is about the theological appropriateness of the distinction between 'using' and 'receiving'.

The first point to be made is that 'receiving' holds in nice balance the elements of personal encounter, and enlargement by that which is beyond us. Pietistic Bible reading by the 'ordinary Christian reader' has been strong on personal encounter, but the scholarly world since the Enlightenment has been suspicious of the readings of the unschooled as lacking a grounding in the objective historical features of the text. It was easy to dismiss the 'insights' of such pietism as reflections of the reader's own psyches or predilections.[32] There was an acute sense of an unbridgeable gulf – Lessing's famous 'ugly ditch' – between uncertain historical truths and the convictions of faith. But Kant cautiously discerned a possible bridge across it in his *Critique of Judgement*: the aesthetic sense might be able to unite the world knowable only to the senses and the 'moral imperative' which was Kant's distillation of the meaning of faith.[33]

This was the hint on which the Romantics seized.[34] The Romantic insight and longing was that aesthetic (including literary) experience might heal the breach, offering a genuine encounter with the other – even the numinous or divine. But biblical scholarship seems to have been reluctant to accept aesthetic-literary experience (as the Romantics conceived it) as an ingredient of faith and medicine for its own wound, that which may bind together the individual in his or her receptiveness and the reality on to which the Bible opens.[35]

To speak of 'reception' of a work of literature is to point to its affecting power, but also, simultaneously, to the claims of its otherness. A reader who merely 'uses' the text to develop his own doctrine, or reinduce a previous spiritual experience, or soothe his nerves, or support a previously held opinion, or confirm him in some psychological or emotional imbalance – the sorts of activity which have given pietism a bad name – is *not* 'receiving' it. Devoted Bible readers might do well to reflect whether they are simply 'using' Scripture merely to 'facilitate, brighten, relieve or palliate' their life, rather than to add to

---

[32] An example of such mistrust is to be found in Jülicher, *Gleichnisreden*, vol. 1, 48, where he castigates the early interpreters of Jesus' parables for their claims to 'keen insight' (*Scharfsinn*). In fact, Enlightenment rationalism and pietism have a deep affinity through the concept of the inner light: see Tillich, *Perspectives*, 19–23.

[33] See Cooper (ed.), *Aesthetics*, 123; Tillich, *Perspectives*, 82f.

[34] On this see Jasper and Prickett (eds.), *Bible and Literature*, 8, 29.

[35] On the neglect of the aesthetic-literary apprehension of reality in biblical studies see Craig Bartholomew's citation of Rogerson, *de Wette*, 27 (n. 23 in ch. 1 of this volume).

it. But the alternative to 'using' the text like this is not to give up on the idea of personal encounter altogether, but to let it be the kind of self-emptying, truly receptive encounter which Lewis describes.

The second point is that the theologian is challenged about the extent to which she, just like the unschooled pietist, is 'using' the text rather than 'receiving' it. When the development of a theology on the basis of the text becomes the sole *goal* of our Bible reading, there is no receptive encounter. Indeed, the very activity of 'interpretation' may have the same effect. Hermeneutics is no less necessary than theology. But to 'interpret' is always to have one's sights on something beyond the text, to get through it to a meaning or an application or a world or an intention, after which – effectively – the text may be left behind.

This is *not* to imply that the text of Scripture should be regarded as ultimately having no reference to anything beyond itself. We should note carefully the clarification Lewis draws concerning the 'use' of words to point beyond themselves. He is very clear about the reality of literary referentiality, contrasting literature here with music:

> there can never be . . . a purely literary appreciation of literature . . . The first note of a symphony demands attention to nothing but itself. The first word of the *Iliad* directs our minds to anger; something we are acquainted with outside the poem and outside literature altogether.[36]

The receptive reader will be the one fully alive to the *reality of which the text speaks*, but who grasps in the same moment the textual signing of that reality, and holds the two together in fertile contemplation. Lewis himself draws the religious analogy for the activity of 'resting' in the reality signified by the work: 'it may be compared (upward) with religious contemplation or (downward) with a game'.[37] Perhaps it is out of suspicion that literary reading has to be merely game-like that professional Bible readers have often eschewed it;[38] comparing it to religious contemplation may shed a different light on things.

Thirdly, the scholar or ordinary reader with an historical training and interest should receive nothing but encouragement from Lewis. Such a person may perhaps be surprised to discover that the kind of literary critic whom he found most helpful was 'Dryasdust':

---

[36] Lewis, *Experiment*, 27f.

[37] Ibid., 89.

[38] Cf. Jasper in Jasper and Prickett, *Bible and Literature*, 52, commenting on the attitude of biblical scholarship for at least two centuries: ' "literary readings" have always been accused of flippancy, and the insights of art and literature generally neglected, mainly because of the weighty claims of historicism'.

> Obviously I have owed, and must continue to owe, far more to editors, textual crit-
> ics, commentators, and lexicographers than to anyone else. Find out what the au-
> thor actually wrote and what the hard words meant and what the allusions were to,
> and you have done far more for me than a hundred new interpretations or assess-
> ments could ever do.[39]

Lewis strongly attacked the assumptions of *historicism*,[40] but *history* was for him a
sine qua non of literary study. It was precisely the historian's work on the texts
which made it possible for the contemporary reader to receive them, enter into
them, appreciate them, be enlarged by them. Contrary to Holladay's description of the 'literary paradigm' of reading Scripture as ahistorical, noted above,[41]
Lewis's 'literary reading' immerses itself in the pastness of ancient literature.
Here again Lewis is heir to the Romantics, this time in their valuation of the
past.[42] Holladay seems surprisingly unaware of any kind of literary criticism
other than the new criticism and its successors. He rightly says that literary
critics are not interested in questions of historical causality per se,[43] but this
would have seemed to Lewis an astonishingly banal point to make: as if the
labours of Dryasdust could ever have been conceived as an end in themselves!
The historian's technical work is simply a necessary preliminary to full aesthetic
reception, appreciation of the text for what it is.[44]

David Cooper offers an enlightening parallel from environmental aesthetics. He asks why it is from an aesthetic point of view, as well as an ecological
one, that, for instance, an ancient forest should be preserved. He points out that
if aesthetics were merely a matter of receiving pleasurable sensations, there
would be no *aesthetic* reason why such a forest should not be cut down and
replaced by replanted trees from elsewhere (or even artificial replicas) which
give the same pleasure of sight and smell. But, as he says, there is more to it than
that, for

> as we know from our experience of *art*, receiving pleasurable sensations is not all, or
> even much, of what aesthetic appreciation consists in. It is because there is much

---

[39] Lewis, *Experiment*, 121.

[40] See his essay of that title, in the course of which he makes an explicit comparison
between the historian and the literary critic, as contrasted with the scientist (111f.).

[41] Holladay, 'Contemporary Methods', 139.

[42] Cf. Tillich, *Perspectives*, 83f.

[43] 'Rather than seeing a text as the product of historical causes, those who work within
the literary paradigm tend to view a text as a finished product' (Holladay, 'Contemporary Methods', 138).

[44] Holladay in fact exemplifies a tendency among biblical scholars to bring 'literary
criticism' under the umbrella of 'hermeneutics', thus hiding from view the concern of
the literary critic with reading as moment of encounter.

more to it than that which is the reason, of course, why we find unacceptable the substitution for an original painting of even the best forgery. The forgery, when we know it is one, cannot evoke a relationship to its times, a place within a tradition of art, which the original can. No more could the substitute forest be invested with a sense of age and of a relationship to the people and animals who have lived in it, in the way the original forest is. Such evocations and investments shape our aesthetic responses to things, be they forests or paintings.

More generally, aesthetic appreciation is a rich and complex stance we adopt to-wards both artifacts and natural things. It is, for example, to approach things with a readiness to respond to intimations and evocations. To reduce that richness and complexity to a readiness to experience pleasurable sensations is to parody and belit-tle the aesthetic sensibility.[45]

Aesthetic response, in other words, binds perceiving subject and perceived object in a fecund and subtle relationship which enhances both the subjectivity of the former and the objectivity of the latter.[46]

Popular evangelical spirituality finds it hard to hold together in Bible reading these elements of personal encounter and enlargement by the historical 'other'. Again, we may trace this malaise to the tendency to subsume 'reading' under 'interpretation'. An anxiety about the acceptable boundaries of interpre-tation, countered by overemphasis on the criterion of 'original meaning', coexists with an anxiety about the Bible remaining a merely external docu-ment without impact on the heart, countered by appeal to pietist individual-ism. Gordon Fee and Douglas Stuart exemplify this double anxiety in their book *How to Read the Bible for All its Worth*. On the one hand, the object of interpretation is rigidly limited: 'a *text cannot mean what it never meant*'.[47] On the other, readers are exhorted to do their own work on the text before consulting any of the commentaries: 'one does not *begin* by consulting the experts'.[48] But what is the point of delaying to consult the experts if one's own discoveries are destined to be disallowed because one does not know enough Hebrew, Greek or ancient history to discern the 'original' meaning? It may be necessary for a manual of *interpretation* to set out various stages in the interpretative process. But for the business of *reading* (the announced subject of Fee and Stuart's book!)

---

[45] Cooper, 'Keeping an Eye', 11.
[46] Cf. this description of Austin Farrer's concept of scriptural reading: 'the imagination draws together the ancient and sacred literature of the Scriptures, their tradition of theological reading and the response of the contemporary reader to the structure of the text, in a single moment of vision and inspiration' (Jasper and Prickett, *Bible and Litera-ture*, 54). Cf. Lewis, *Experiment*, 140f.
[47] Fee and Stuart, *How to Read*, 26.
[48] Ibid., 21.

a more unified conception of the activity is required. If we want to write of an order of procedure, Lewis the 'literary reader' would in fact send us to 'Dryasdust' the commentator *first*! He reverses thus a popular stereotype of 'literary' Bible reading as irredeemably sunk in subjectivism. Knowing the historical details, we can be open to receive. Aesthetic sensibility, embracing textual otherness and personal response in the same moment, refuses the artificial restriction of 'meaning' to a putative 'original' location, but still celebrates the historical particularity of the text; knows the call of the text upon the individual heart but lives happily with the text as a publicly accessible, shared, external document.

As a postscript to these remarks on Lewis's distinction between 'using' and 'receiving' as they may be applied to Scripture, it is interesting to note his chapter 'On Myth'.[49] Here he points out that while in the case of literature in general it is a mark of 'unliterary' reading to give minimal attention to the words and concentrate on the pleasure, emotion or self-indulgent fantasy they are being 'used' to generate, in the case of myth this readiness to discard the words is a mark of a genuine love of the myth: the story itself is what matters. Myth is 'extra-literary',[50] so it is inappropriate to give it the same *kind* of attention as literature in general:

> The pleasure of myth depends hardly at all on such usual narrative attractions as suspense or surprise. Even at a first hearing it is felt to be inevitable. And the first hearing is chiefly valuable in introducing us to a permanent object of contemplation – more like a thing than a narration – which works upon us by its peculiar flavour or quality, rather as a smell or a chord does.[51]

Should we not recognize that there may be parts of the Bible story which are of so much greater moment than the words in which they are clothed that we miss the point if we concentrate on the details of the text rather than the story itself? Lewis's account of myth may help us (paradoxically, it might seem) to recover a sense of the *reality* beyond the words of many of the great stories of Scripture: creation, exodus, exile, passion, resurrection, the visions of Revelation. Many parts of these stories may indeed be amenable to 'literary reading', a continual dwelling upon the words *with* the realities, and indeed require it if they are to go on yielding up their riches to us. We might well try to locate passages on a spectrum between those in which the precise words are vital and those in which the story itself is all. But as we seek to make the Bible an 'open book' for a generation to whom 'books' in general, and therefore any idea of 'literary reading', remain closed, Lewis – the great literary critic himself! – surprisingly

---

[49] Lewis, *Experiment*, 40–49.
[50] Ibid., 43.
[51] Ibid.

draws our attention to the latter as well as the former end of this spectrum, to see that some of the greatest narratives possess in themselves a power which makes the words in which they are told quite secondary. Without in any way passing a judgement about historicity (and Lewis himself was severe on biblical scholars who did not recognize the Gospels as essentially historical reportage[52]), to invoke the category of 'myth' may subvert a bibliolatry which concentrates on *littera* not *spiritus*.[53]

Logos and *Poiéma*

Lewis's 'literary reader' comes to the text as not only *logos* (something said) but also *poīēma* (something made).[54] It therefore speaks and addresses him, pointing to realities with words, informing, commanding, promising; but is also itself an object of contemplation which draws him into new experience.

Lewis affirms that '[o]ur experience of the work as Poiema is unquestionably a keen pleasure',[55] but that this is a very exalted kind of enjoyment that really ought not to be described by the same term as lower forms of 'pleasure' at all. To enter into the literary work as *poīēma*

> is less like looking at a vase than like 'doing exercises' under an expert's direction or taking part in a choric dance invented by a good choreographer. There are many ingredients in our pleasure. The exercise of our faculties is in itself a pleasure. Successful obedience to what seems worth obeying and is not quite easily obeyed is a pleasure.[56]

He goes on to state:

> The experience could not thus affect us – could not give *this* pleasure – unless it were good for us; not good as a means to some end beyond the Poiema, the dance, or the exercises, but good for us here and now.[57]

Poīēma and *logos* have a symbiotic relationship. Unless we approach the work as *poīēma*, we have no chance of 'receiving' it at all, and yet 'the imaginations,

---

[52] Lewis, 'Modern Theology', 154–157.

[53] On Lewis's understanding of myth (including his view of the incarnation as 'myth become fact') see Christensen, *Lewis on Scripture*, 57–77. On myth and Scripture cf. also Barr, *Bible*, 55–59.

[54] Lewis, *Experiment*, 132.

[55] Ibid.

[56] Ibid., 134.

[57] Ibid.

emotions, and thoughts out of which the Poiema builds its harmony are aroused in us by, and directed towards, the Logos and would have no existence without it'.[58]

> We visualize Lear in the storm, we share his rage, we regard his whole story with pity and terror. What we thus react to is something, in itself, non-literary and non-verbal.[59]

Furthermore, it is important to locate the goodness of the literary experience neither solely in its character as *poïema* – 'for it is out of our various interests in the Logos that the Poiema is made'[60] – nor solely in its character as *logos* – for 'we need not believe or approve the Logos'.[61] It is located, rather, in the 'enlargement of our being',[62] our admission 'to experiences other than our own'.[63] Since the *logos* comes to us in the framework of *poïema*, literature is not reducible to the communication of facts; it invites us into experience. 'We want to see with other eyes, to imagine with other imaginations, to feel with other hearts, as well as with our own.'[64]

In what sense, then, might we read the Bible in such a way, as not only *logos* but also *poïema*? At this point many a theological instinct probably backs away from transferring Lewis's thinking to Scripture. The objections might be summarized as reluctance to see the Bible as *poïema* at all, and reluctance to admit that the *logos* it bears may speak simply of others' experiences, real or imagined, rather than of ultimate truth.

That we should approach the Bible as (potentially) a work of literary art, a *poïema* from which we seek the kind of pleasure to be found in other literary encounters, seems at first sight to underestimate the seriousness of what is at stake in coming to this book. In fact, however, as we have seen, our concern (and Lewis's) is precisely *not* with prejudging the status of the text before us, but rather with giving it the benefit of the doubt, opening ourselves to the *possibility* of its bearing the character of a *poïema*. And prior to being a 'work of literary art' a *poïema* is simply a thing made. A little reflection will show that we regularly and necessarily in fact approach the Bible not simply as *logos* which addresses us, but as an object of contemplation or, in Lewis's metaphor, a 'dance' through which we are guided.

---

58 Ibid., 136.
59 Ibid.
60 Ibid., 137.
61 Ibid., 136.
62 Ibid., 137.
63 Ibid., 139.
64 Ibid., 137.

This happens on at least three levels. First, the level of individual books (and sections within them). Consider Job. As we listen to the speeches of Job and his friends, as we enter into their perspectives and, at the opening and close, the perspective of God, we are not only allowing ourselves to be informed or commanded. The words do not come *straightforwardly* as *logos*. They invite, and provoke, consideration as *poïema*. We are led into a rather sophisticated procedure – the 'dance' metaphor is apt – in which we go first down one path, then another; we wonder about the significance of the opening heavenly scene for the story and its resolution, we feel Job's anguish and his friends' helplessness, we recognize and are drawn into the all-too-familiar postures of standardized 'wisdom' and angry despair. We seek to make sense of the whole through consideration of the parts. Put at its simplest, we find ourselves in active contemplation of what this book *is*, of its configuration and the implications of that. To think of it purely as *logos*, to describe the process of reading Job as just 'listening to what the text says', is to flatten the process of reading from three dimensions to two. And it is, of course, to miss the point that the book itself invites us to see many of the *logoi* in Job as inadequate or simply wrong. Analogous things could be said of reading any biblical book. Whether or not they conform to anything we might describe as 'literary art', de facto we are concerned with them as *poïemata*, things which have been fashioned. 'We' here includes not only or mainly an avant-garde of literary-minded biblical critics, but scholars of all types and thoughtful individual Bible readers. As soon as the historian or the ordinary reader observes herself thinking 'this is a collection of prophecies' or 'this is an expression of Johannine Christianity' she has caught herself in the act of treating a biblical book as *poïema*.

The second level on which we almost instinctively treat Scripture as *poïema* is in our reading of its first part as 'the Old Testament'. Many passages of the Old Testament, for instance in the prophets and the psalms, do indeed seem to address the Christian with a remarkable directness. Many an invitation to praise, faith, hope or repentance seems to come to us as pure *logos*. But Christians have always known that they would be falling short in their use of the Old Testament if they failed to go beyond listening to its words as *logos*. We know that we need to ask what this collection of thirty-nine books *is* for the church; and as soon as we do that, we treat the collection as *poïema*. What *is* the law for us? What *are* the imprecatory psalms? Various models have been proposed for describing the nature of the Old Testament in relation to the New. Elements of validity may be found in all of them: there are senses in which the Old Testament relates to the New as foil, as balancing pointer to Christ from before, as typological foreshadowing, as main volume to appendix, as overture to main movement in salvation history.[65] But openness to the text as *poïema* implies that

---

[65] Cf. Barton, *Invitation*, 39–44.

we should not come with any preconceived notion as to what it is. The literary experience generally – and the experience of Christians in wrestling with the Old Testament – is precisely one of *asking the question* 'What is it?'. The question always begs to be answered, and yet we resist answering it too quickly and neatly, or the being of the text will be obscured beneath our formulations, and we are in danger of closing ourselves to the very nature about which we are so earnestly asking.

The third level of concern with Scripture as *poēma* inevitably follows. This is our concern with the Bible as a whole. People would not turn to Scripture, and Christians would certainly not return to it with such extraordinary regularity, were not a recognition of its *being* something for church and world, and an eagerness to find out 'what', an almost instinctive dimension of our relation to it. This recognition is crucial to our actual use of it. We shall go badly astray if, having discerned the unique nature of Scripture, we then use it as if it were pure *logos*, addressing us directly in unmediated fashion, and forget that it is also *poēma*. Again, it is in the Bible's provocation of fertile reflection on its nature that we find the Christian experience of reading it to be an authentically literary one, which ought to be named and celebrated as such. How do we describe the Bible? As founding story, charter of salvation, God's lively oracles in print, myth of origin and end, historical witness? As with the Old Testament, we may recognize truth in all such descriptions, yet be unwilling to adopt any one as dominant and therefore reductive.

The answers to the question 'What is the Bible?' will be as varied as the personal stances of the questioners. To seek to grasp to any degree what the Bible (like any cultural object) *is* means to reach for the ultimately ineffable; certainly to reach beyond what can be stated in a form to which, in principle, all humanity might agree. To ask what such a text *is* brings into view not only the play of all the world upon it, but the play of the text upon the world – not only its contemporary world, but all subsequent history which it has influenced, including, not least, me as I read. To go on asking, to stay with the moment of contemplation, is the medium of aesthetic knowing. And yet the experience of reading it with others can be a profoundly uniting one; the aesthetic sensibility need by no means be solipsistic.

We turn now to consider the Bible as *logos*, and to face the objection that surely, in the case of Scripture and unlike literature generally, it *does* matter that the *logos* be something to which we can give both cognitive and moral assent. Are we not invited by Scripture into a world of *truth* whose moral demands upon us are absolute? We are (surely) doing more than enlarging our experience by entering into that of others: we are encountering on a profound level God as he is and the world as it is.

In response to this, we note first that it is no part of Lewis's case that what is really true and good *may not* be met with in literary reading, or that 'literary reading' is satisfied only with pure fictiveness, fantasy or amorality in a text. It is simply that the literary pleasure is not dependent upon the cognitive and ethical elements. The possibility is not excluded that when we read Scripture in a literary way we may encounter truth and goodness.

Yet even if Scripture is the locus of such an encounter, it is not a necessary corollary that every human *logos* within it should be true or moral. Lewis's description of literary reading – in which the ultimate sway of *logos* is held in check by the character of the work as *poïēma* – offers us a helpful way of holding in balance reverence for the text and a necessary critical stance towards the claims of its *logoi*. Precisely because we treat Scripture as *poïēma*, we do not need to accept every human claim it contains as trustworthy, every humanly imagined world it portrays as desirable, every commandment as unsullied by ideological interest, every hero of Israel as heroic for us. The realities which Scripture reveals to us, and its words of command and promise, are complex and manifold. Here are realities of human community, of human sin; exhortations and warnings moulded by various cultural settings; insights both brilliant and flawed; stories rooted in a history profoundly shaped by human minds as well as shaping them; wonderful dreams; and not least, the reality of the activity and being of God. The alert reader cannot but approach such a book with readiness to muse over, test, critique the *logos* which it offers him. The kind of criticism advocated by Clines can and should be practised on the Bible; but not in his spirit of autonomous, domineering readership. It is nothing other than the literary reader's humble openness to the Bible as *poïēma*, that same attitude which refuses to allow its character as *logos* to be all, which saves such criticism of its *logos* from destructiveness. With all its complexities and ambiguities, the Bible remains a work to be endlessly pondered and contemplated. Humanly, its *logos* may be flawed, but its character as *poïēma* assures us that this is not the whole story.

But what of the word of God? Can a flawed human *logos* be or become a flawless divine one? Philosophically, Nicholas Wolterstorff has (to my mind) satisfactorily demonstrated the naturalness with which the speech of one person (such as one of the biblical authors) may 'become' the speech of another (such as God).[66] In literary criticism, it is a commonplace to recognize that different 'voices' may be heard in a text: straightforward *logos* is refracted by its location in *poïēma*. We may 'hear' the voice of the author herself, or the voice of a character in her drama or literary work; perhaps also the voice of tradition or the voice of another writer. *Pace* atheistically-based deconstruction, which (unsurprisingly) 'gags the speaking God'[67] in radical mistrust of the mediating ability of texts, there is no reason why we should not 'hear the voice' of God

---

[66] Wolterstorff, *Divine Discourse*.

[67] Cf. Ovey, 'Deconstruction'.

through and between the fallible human 'voices' which speak through the text. After all, historical scholars have, for two centuries or more now, detected a composite of human 'voices' in various parts of Scripture (different Pentateuchal strands, different sources and traditions in the gospels, and so on). But more importantly, not only may the divine *logos* address us through human *logoi*; the divine *creativity* may also be embodied in this human *poïēma*. To discern God not only as speaker in the Bible, but as maker of the Bible, is to lift the literary experience of wonder and enlargement which Lewis describes on to a new plane altogether.

It might be objected that this still does not do justice to the Bible as 'special revelation'. For is not the trace of God upon all human creativity, and therefore upon all literary *poïēmata* of whatever kind? If the human *logoi* of Scripture may be (in principle) as fallible as those of any other book, have we betrayed the distinctiveness of Scripture altogether? Not at all. Scripture is its own best advocate. Lewis's 'literary reading' consists precisely of a willingness to be open to whatever riches the book before us may yield to patient self-surrender. To invite people to come to Scripture simply as literature, without preconceptions about its status, is to open it up to the world beyond the church.[68] To come to Scripture with the expectation that it is both *logos* and *poïēma*, in the configuration pinpointed by Lewis as the guarantor of literary experience, is not to renege on its uniqueness. On the contrary, it may be the only way by which its true uniqueness may be personally discovered.

Encounter through Preaching

Lewis wrote that '[i]f literary scholarship and criticism are regarded as activities ancillary to literature, then their sole function is to multiply, prolong and safeguard experiences of good reading'.[69] One might be tempted to draw an analogy between the function Lewis here assigns to literary critics, and that of the Christian preacher. But to ensure 'good reading' of the Bible by individuals is too limited an aim for preaching: valuable in itself, it would not encompass the dynamic and corporate dimensions of responsiveness to the word of God by the people of God. And Lewis's account of 'literary reading' may itself seem to us, notwithstanding its advantages, too individualized and book-focused to be a fitting model for the opening of the Bible to church and world today.

I wish to suggest, however, that in *the act of preaching itself* – understood as the public opening-up of Scripture among a body of people, by whatever means –

---

[68] See Barr, *Bible*, 59–61.
[69] Lewis, *Experiment*, 104.

something analogous to Lewis's literary experience does and should take place. We may work this out through a brief review of the features of 'literary reading' already noted. In keeping with Lewis's emphasis on the reader, our focus will be first on the *hearers* of preaching – and not as mere passive receptacles, but as active participants.

Like the receptive reader, opening herself to whatever the text has to offer, the receptive listener to preaching will adopt a position of humility before what she hears, not stand in judgement over it. Only so can there be real encounter between the hearer and the realities which the text, through the medium of the preacher, opens up. Otherwise the listener turns into a mere detached critic. As with 'literary reading', it is a question of the listener giving the sermon the benefit of the doubt; it *may* not always yield much to such attentiveness, but without such self-opening it *cannot* give the hearer anything of real worth.

The listener who wishes to benefit from preaching will be a 'receiver' rather than a 'user'. The one who listens simply to have prejudice reinforced or feelings soothed – not to mention other motives such as the ranking of various preachers whose offerings one has 'tasted' – will not find preaching to be a place of encounter. For the duration of the sermon, the attentive listener 'rests' in the words of the sermon. Like the attentive reader who holds together in contemplation both the realities signified by the words and the words themselves, he receives that to which the words bear witness as well as meditating on the way the words themselves are ordered.

The receptive listener will approach the sermon as both *logos* and *poiēma*. She will be alert to what it says – its declarations, commands, testimonies, promises, questions. But she will recognize that this *logos* comes in the form of a *poiēma*, fashioned by a human mind. As in the case of reading the Bible, it is the character of the sermon as *poiēma* which enables the fallibility of its *logoi* to be recognized without the loss of respect. Furthermore, it is the (good) sermon's character as *poiēma* which makes the (receptive) hearer a genuine participant in the sermon – in Lewis's phrase, one who takes part 'in a choric dance invented by a good choreographer'.[70] We enter into the various movements of the sermon which the preacher has devised, and it is through that participation that we start to see with other eyes: that the *logos* becomes no longer an external word, but a window onto truth.

What would be the corollaries of such a view of preaching in our conception of the relationship between Scripture, sermon and preacher?

First, the preacher is seen not only as *interpreter of Scripture* but as *agent of encounter with the 'other' which Scripture mediates*. It is her task not only to speak of what Scripture 'meant' or 'means', and then 'translate' it into a contemporary

---

[70] Ibid., 134.

setting.[71] 'Interpretation' belongs essentially to the substructure of a sermon. It does not capture what it is to let Scripture be opened up to human encounter. But is 'agent of encounter' too high a role for the preacher? Is she not then the equivalent of a pre-Reformation mediator-priest? This objection would carry weight if the task of preaching is thought of too strictly as the preserve of the few. But important contemporary thinking stresses, from various angles, the ministry of the word as a ministry of the whole people of God. The early Christian communities and 'dissenting' Christian fellowships at different periods of history can provide models for us here.[72] Even if the regular preaching of a church is carried out by only one or two people, they can be people engaged in an ongoing 'sacred conversation' with a Christian community concerned as a whole with discerning the word of God.[73] Nor should the observation of decreasing levels of literacy (general and biblical) cause us to revert to a pre-Reformation model of strictly controlled access to the Scriptures. We do not need to connive with retrograde cultural trends such as the decline in reading. We should be aiming at *more* than an individual and book-based encounter with God's story, but we need not be content with less. We should surely hold on to Tyndale's vision of all sorts and conditions of people being able to read and understand the word of God – a vision that will enable such a 'sacred conversation' to happen. And is it sheer inertia which prevents churches exploring more dramatic models of preaching in which a variety of voices are heard?

One could argue, I think, that it is precisely when the preacher is seen *only as an interpreter* that the danger of her being exalted into a position of authoritative mediator arises. Of course the trained minister will function as an authority in the sense that she is specifically equipped to understand the languages, contexts, theology and so on of the Bible. In this sense she may be analogous to Lewis's 'Dryasdust' critic who can provide all the detailed historical information necessary for 'literary reading' (though – as many a homiletician will say – such 'dryasdust' information will normally be subterranean rather than obvious in a sermon!). But when the definitive role of the preacher is seen as being the one who tells the congregation 'what it really means' or 'what it means for us today', she becomes the one who cracks the code and holds the key, the one who fundamentally disables the people of God from receiving the word of God. When, however, she (together with others in the church) lets the words of Scripture and the realities to which they point be received in moments of fertile *encounter*, that surely is when the word is at work.

---

[71] For a critique of the 'bridge' paradigm of preaching, in which the preacher's task is to relate the supposed preachable 'content' of a section of Scripture to a contemporary situation see Farley, 'New Paradigm', 165. I am grateful to Peter Barber for alerting me to this article.

[72] See Murray, 'Interactive Preaching'.

[73] See Schlafer, *Surviving the Sermon*, 57f.; Rose, *Sharing the Word*.

Secondly, then, to view the event of preaching as a place of encounter analogous to that which takes place in 'literary reading' is to *let Scripture have its true
authority*. The emphasis, in other words, is on leading people out of themselves
and the prison of their own perspectives to the great 'other' which the Bible
mediates. As we have seen, 'literary reading' delights in the historical particularity, even strangeness of the text. It responds to the text in a mode which
binds it to the present not through some strategy that appears by sleight-of-
hand to eliminate the distance between past and present, but through a conscious *measuring* of the distance, stressing a sense of human continuity across it.
Analogously, preaching would give us a sense of the text in its otherness: not an
alienating otherness, but an interesting and inviting one. This otherness is the
corollary of the revelation of God in a particular historical period.

The sense that preaching must lead us all out of ourselves into the otherness
of the biblical world and the revelation of God may shed new light on the idea
that the appropriate way to 'interpret' Scripture is to 'perform' it.[74] In thinking
about preaching in particular, it has become a commonplace to assert the
performative nature of the sermon as a speech-act, and that one must therefore
attend to the form of the biblical text as carefully as to its content.[75] It is no good
to preach a parable as though it were a doctrinal exposition, a psalm of praise as
though it were a moral exhortation, and so on. The concept is that an effective
sermon will not simply explain and apply the biblical text, but somehow actually reproduce its original impact. So far, so good. But there is a tendency for
'performance' preaching to want to go further: the stress – perhaps inseparable
from the very notion of 'performance' – is on the present impact of the text
rather than the unique contingencies of its original setting. It is as if the preacher
tends to arrogate to *himself* the role of Scripture and in doing so pushes Scripture out of view.

An example of how this relegation of Scripture may happen in 'perfor-
mance preaching' appears in a powerful sermon of Trevor Williams entitled
'The Parable of the Broadcaster', cited with approval by John Goldingay.[76]
Taking his cue from Jesus' parable of the sower, Williams tells the story of

---

[74] See Barton, *Invitation*, ch. 8, and literature cited there.

[75] The stream of American thinking which has come to be known as the 'new homiletic' stresses this point. See especially Craddock, *Authority* and *Preaching*; Lowry, *Plot
and Parable*; Long, *Preaching*; Graves, *Sermon*. Note also the affinity of this approach
with the poststructuralist criticism of Stephen D. Moore: 'Rather than take a
jackhammer to the concrete, parabolic language of the Gospels, replacing graphic
images with abstract categories, I prefer to respond to a pictographic text
pictographically, to a narrative text narratively, producing a critical text that is a
postmodern analogue of the premodern text that it purports to read' (*Mark and Luke*,
xviii, cited in Jasper and Prickett, *Bible and Literature*, 59).

[76] Goldingay, *Models*, 84–86.

Patrick Murphy, a car fitter who subjects himself to a constant flow of information throughout the day, mostly from the radio. He survives this barrage by mentally switching off so that he hears only what he wants to hear. The occasional good intentions sparked off by something he hears get buried in the onward flow of chatter. This account of Murphy's daily life is followed by this conclusion:

> My name is Patrick Murphy and so is yours. None of us listen to most of what we hear. And if we do listen, we won't allow it to change us very much. We can't afford to. So how much that God wants to say to us never gets through?
>
> If you have ears to hear, then hear.[77]

This undoubtedly effective talk reproduces well, we may think, the *impact* of Jesus' parable. But it raises questions about the relationship of the sermon to the text. Has not the message been made so 'present' as to push out of view the historical character of the text? We gain no sense of Jesus as speaker of the parable, of the parable in the context of his ministry, of the many echoes of the Old Testament which it contains, of the particular place and authority of the parable as part of Christian Scripture, of the ways that it has been interpreted through history. Recalling Lewis's categories, we might say that the sermon as *poiēma* has been fashioned purely out of the parable as *logos*, not out of the parable as *poi ēma*. We have been sharply addressed by what the text says, but we have not been allowed to stop and see what it is.

Now one could argue that this does not matter. If the important thing is the impact of scriptural truth upon a congregation, why dwell upon difficult, unclear, subtle features of the text in its historical and theological contingency? Is that not the business of the lecture-room rather than the pulpit? Is not the force of the message in danger of being dissipated through attention to such details? But there is no need to compel ourselves to choose between these alternatives. Preaching as medium of encounter with God through Scripture can surely aim to encompass and communicate a sense *both* of the impact of what the text says *and* of response to what it is. Indeed, the advocates of 'performance' can be encouraged by the thought that (in Lewis's terms) taking seriously what the *text* 'is' (*poiēma*) is not a matter of detached observation, but of careful participation. Further, to preserve a sense of the text's historical strangeness in preaching can be seen as an important safeguard against the preacher taking on too authoritative a mediating role, a guarantee of maintaining the true openness of the Book.

The third corollary of relating the event of preaching to what happens in 'literary reading', however, is that *full encouragement is given to the creativity of both*

---

[77] Ibid., 86.

preacher and hearers. A high view of the authority of Scripture, expressed in advocacy of 'exposition',[78] has tended to go with a low view of the place of the human players in preaching. The preacher's task has been seen simply as repeating the message of Scripture in his own words. Karl Barth wrote that 'preaching should be an explanation of Scripture; the preacher does not have to speak "on" but "from" (*ex*), drawing from the Scriptures whatever he says. He does not have to invent but rather to repeat something.'[79] More recently, J.I. Packer put it thus:

> *the Bible is doing the talking.* The preacher is treating himself as a mouthpiece for the biblical Word of God, and that Word is coming through. He has resisted the temptation to stand in front of his text, as it were, speaking for it as if it could not speak for itself, and putting himself between it and the congregation; instead, he is making it his business to focus everyone's attention on the text, to stand behind it rather than in front of it, to become its servant, and to let it deliver its message through him.[80]

A laudable desire to 'let Scripture speak' can, however, be deceptive if we think that this can happen almost without human aid.[81] Human creativity is present in some measure even in the most self-effacing of preachers. My point here is that if we acknowledge, celebrate and nurture this creativity we will actually facilitate, rather than hinder, the possibility that preaching can be a place of encounter with God through Scripture. Here the 'new homiletic' emphasis on letting the various forms within Scripture be the starting point for the aims and structures of our sermons, which has dominated much homiletic thinking since the publication of Fred Craddock's *As One Without Authority* in 1971, seems to me crucially important. For what this approach requires is precisely a much *deeper* engagement with the text than is suggested by the phraseology of 'repetition' and 'explanation'. The preacher is called on not merely to expound its 'meaning', but to enter into its rhetorical dynamics, feel its emotional power, and *then* to give of her own imaginative resources in letting that dynamism generate a sermon that will be a means of encounter with God through the text. In short, the preacher will first take part herself in the 'choric dance' of the text as *poïēma*, and then lead others into it through the *poïēma* which she is inspired to make as a result. And in *both* these stages there is that self-emptying of imaginative empathy and effort, Lewis's '[s]uccessful obedience to what

---

[78] For an exposé of the variety of ways that preachers have sought to define 'exposition', together with an attempt to re-establish the usefulness of the term, see Bryson, *Expository Preaching.*

[79] Barth, *Prayer and Preaching*, 69.

[80] Packer, 'Authority', 206.

[81] For a fuller account of how such thinkers have sought to evade the inevitable question of the preacher's person, see Resner, *Preacher and Cross*, 58–65.

seems worth obeying and is not quite easily obeyed',[82] which should assure the doubters who advocate simple self-effacing 'exposition' that this kind of creative preaching is truly faithful to God, to Scripture, to the hearers, and to the task of proclamation. The challenge for the preacher, I suggest, is to let the *logos-in-poïema* of the text find its counterpart and reach the hearers through the *logos-in-poïema* of the sermon.

But there is also a challenge for the hearers: it is their creativity as well, which is encouraged here. This mode of preaching as unashamed *poïema* poses questions, invites active involvement in its flow. Hearers are to give themselves in participation in the sermon's *poïema* so that its *logos* may not only be heard *but experienced*.

Centrally, such preaching constantly (if implicitly) reminds the hearers that *they have work to do* in discerning the truth of God in the sermon. The very fact that the sermon comes as human *poïema* should guard against any naïve assumption that the preacher's words can be swallowed whole as if they were 'purely scriptural' or indeed divine. Both 'performance' and 'exposition' are in danger of appearing to eliminate this distance between the preacher's words and those of God. 'Performance' preaching may err by taking the *logos* of the text, its central thrust, and turning it into a *poïema*, carrying the implied message: here is the unadulterated truth of God, to be experienced now. But, as we have seen, it may fail to treat the *text* as *poïema*, obscuring what it is, and dangerously making the preacher-as-performer act the part of God or a scriptural author. 'Expository' preaching on the other hand may err by taking the *poïema*, the text as it is, and turning it into simple *logos*, carrying the implied message: here is the Scriptural text, and this is what it says and means. But it may fail to treat the *sermon* as *poïema*, thus not helping the hearers to experience the truth of God, and dangerously, once again, making the preacher-as-expositor wear the seductive mask of authoritative interpreter of God's *logos* – rather than letting her be seen in her obvious, fallible, self-giving creativity.

Of course, if the sermon is faithful, its *logos* will be a window on to the reality of Scripture and the God to whom it bears witness. But it is crucial that the hearers grasp the nature of the sermon as *poïema*, or their encounter with God through preaching will be overdependent on the preacher and will not allow for the proper exercise of their own faculties. This accords with the insight that preaching is a sacramental act.[83] Its significance is found not only in what the preacher says, but in *the fact that* a word is thus spoken in the name of God. Every sermon is a sign and pledge of God's communicative nature, his desire to reveal himself to and enter into relationship with his creatures. In the

---

[82] Lewis, *Experiment*, 134.

[83] On this see Coggan, *New Day*. Cf. also, on the sacramentalism of the romantic tradition (in which Lewis stands), Phillips, 'Romantic Tradition'.

listener, therefore, there is a (usually instinctive) movement in thought from 'What is the preacher *saying*?' to 'What *is* this sermon for me today?' What the sermon is will always transcend what it says. Just as the receptive reader of Scripture reflects on the being as well as the speaking of the text, and in that reflection may find it to be 'the word of God', not theoretically but experientially, so the receptive listener to preaching hears the word of God by not only attending to the preacher's claims and admonitions but also asking how in the mystery of providence these words may *be* the word of God for her.[84] If the preacher is aware of the sacramental dimension of what he is doing, he will recognize that mystery. God's address to an individual through the preacher's words may differ significantly from what the preacher intended to communicate or achieve, in the same way that his address to us through Scripture, as we meditate on what Scripture is for us, may differ significantly from what the scriptural author intended.[85] And we note that in neither case does this invalidate or render pointless either the intention of the preacher/author, or enquiry after it.

The need to balance 'exposition' and 'performance' in preaching relates, broadly, to the twin literary fallacies exposed by Wimsatt and Beardsley in their famous essays.[86] Both fallacies promote a criticism which ultimately draws attention away from the text itself by reducing it to its causes (the intentional fallacy) or its effects (the affective fallacy).[87] Expository preaching, as often practised, is in danger of underplaying the affective power of Scripture through concentration upon a limiting 'original meaning'.[88] Performative preaching is in danger of underplaying the historical location of the text through concentration upon its powerful effect. Lewis's understanding of 'literary reading' points to a preaching which avoids both dangers.

What metaphor may we use for the activity of preaching which avoids the possibly unhelpful associations of 'performance' and 'exposition'? Perhaps 'exhibition' opens up possibilities. A modern museum seeks to do far more than lay out artefacts in glass cases or arrange pictures on walls. Through its geographical layout, in words and pictures, in sounds, moving images and even smells, through posing questions and offering plentiful opportunities to interact by touching and feeling, it tells a story which aims to make sense of its

---

[84] The mistake of identifying the efficacy of the sermon too closely with the preacher's own words is dubbed by Resner 'homiletical donatism' (*Preacher and Cross*, passim).

[85] Cf. Browne, *Ministry*, 29: 'Poets and preachers cannot predict or control the response that people make to their utterances; to make a poem or a sermon is to give it a life of its own.'

[86] 'Intentional Fallacy' and 'Affective Fallacy'.

[87] Wimsatt and Beardsley, 'Affective Fallacy', 345.

[88] For a statement of this danger, confident that preaching can remain 'expository' and avoid it, see Clements, 'Expository Preaching', 4.

exhibits and locate them with reference to the present. Similarly, we need in preaching both to display Scripture in its historical strangeness and creatively to reproduce the power of its testimony; in doing so we shall tell an implicit story which respects both Scripture and hearers yet joins them together. 'Performance' preaching has a tendency to eliminate the distance between text and hearers. 'Exposition' first tends to heighten it, then attempts to bridge or remove it, but often sounds contrived and artificial as it does so. 'Exhibition' involves a proper measuring of the distance between text and hearers, bridging the gap yet locating both in their appropriate contexts.

Reading, Preaching and Doxology

David Jasper and Stephen Prickett write of the close connection of the concept of the 'spiritual' in world religions with *writing*. Christianity with its Scriptures is no exception: 'the spiritual status of the Bible is, as it always has been, inescapably bound up with its material textuality'.[89] The implication of taking 'literary reading' as a model for reading and preaching Scripture is that our *goal* is not to decode or interpret, but to encounter, contemplate and worship. This model offers to help the scholarly discipline of biblical hermeneutics recover its spiritual context.

For a Christian, aesthetic contemplation is not only a matter of pondering the beauty of a thing. It consists in perceiving, meditating on and adoring *the glory of God* revealed in the created object.[90] I suggest that it is important for the doxological goal of our reading and preaching that we think of *Scripture* as creature of God (*poiēma*), not just as word of God (*logos*). To identify it simply as word of God, *agent* of creation, risks appearing to make it into an attribute of deity. To recognize it as creature of God is to be drawn into contemplation of the God whom it reveals. If this seems to put it on a level with other works of literature, we should recall that Lewis's emphasis on the attitude of the reader does not at all presuppose that all works of 'literature' will be of a similar ilk; it simply allows each to exercise its unique power upon us. To see the Bible as a creation (divine and human) is to hint at a degree of divine inspiration in other works of literature also, without in any way undermining the Bible's uniqueness. To consider it as literature which will repay the same kind of self-opening attention as other great works is not to belittle it, but to open it up to readers beyond the ranks of those who already believe. The transition from literary encounter to worship will be a natural one which cannot be imposed from outside.

---

[89] Jasper and Prickett, *Bible and Literature*, 2.

[90] For statements of this point from a variety of angles, rooted in Patristic and medieval traditions, see Milbank, et al. (eds.), *Radical Orthodoxy*.

If our chief end is to know God, and enjoy him forever, it is fitting that the texts through which he reveals himself should be enjoyed as well as studied and obeyed.[91] Whether one encounters them in private reading or in some kind of preaching event, the self-surrendering participation of 'literary reading' seems an indispensable condition of the enjoyment of both texts and their Creator.

Bibliography

Barr, J., *The Bible in the Modern World* (London: SCM Press, 1973)

Barth, K., *Prayer and Preaching*, tr. B.E. Hooke (London: SCM Press, 1964)

Barton, S.C., *Invitation to the Bible* (London: SPCK, 1997)

Bell, M., 'The Metaphysics of Modernism: Aesthetic Myth and the Myth of the Aesthetic' in D. Fuller and P. Waugh (eds.), *The Arts and Sciences of Criticism* (Oxford: Oxford University Press, 1999), 238–256

Bloom, H., *The Western Canon: The Books and School of the Ages* (London: Papermac, 1995)

Brown, S., *Text and Psyche: Experiencing Scripture Today* (New York: Continuum, 1998)

Browne, R.E.C., *The Ministry of the Word* (London: SCM Press, 1958)

Bryson, H., *Expository Preaching: The Art of Preaching through a Book of the Bible* (Nashville: Broadman & Holman, 1995)

Burke, S., *The Death and Return of the Author: Criticism and Subjectivity in Barthes, Foucault and Derrida* (Edinburgh: Edinburgh University Press, 1992)

Christensen, M.J., *C.S. Lewis on Scripture* (London: Hodder & Stoughton, 1980)

Clements, R., 'Expository Preaching in a Postmodern World', *Cambridge Papers* 7.3 (September 1998)

Clines, D.J.A., *The Bible and the Modern World* (Sheffield: Sheffield Academic Press, 1997)

Coggan, D., *A New Day for Preaching: The Sacrament of the Word* (London: SPCK, 1996)

Cooper, D., 'Keeping an Eye on Nature', *Durham First* 9 (spring 1999), 10–11

Cooper, D. (ed.), *Aesthetics: The Classic Readings* (Oxford: Basil Blackwell, 1997)

Craddock, F.B., *As One Without Authority* (Nashville: Abingdon Press, 1971)

—, *Preaching* (Nashville: Abingdon Press, 1985)

Farley, E., 'Toward a New Paradigm for Preaching', in idem and T.G. Long (eds.), *Preaching as a Theological Task: World, Gospel, Scripture* (Louisville: Westminster / John Knox Press, 1996), 165–175

---

[91] On literary form and image in Scripture as gateways to encounter with the mystery of God, cf. Jasper, *Literature and Religion*, 82. Lewis's description of 'literary reading' enables a much closer relationship between such reading and worship than is permitted by Barr's, *Bible*, 65f.

Fee, G.D., and D. Stuart, *How to Read the Bible for All its Worth* (Bletchley: Scripture Union, 1993²)

Fuller, D., and P. Waugh (eds.), *The Arts and Sciences of Criticism* (Oxford: Oxford University Press, 1999)

Goldingay, J., *Models for Interpretation of Scripture* (Grand Rapids: Eerdmans: Carlisle: Paternoster, 1995)

Graves, M., *The Sermon as Symphony: Preaching the Literary Forms of the New Testament* (Valley Forge, PA.: Judson Press, 1997)

Holladay, C.R., 'Contemporary Methods of Reading the Bible' in *The New Interpreter's Bible* (Nashville: Abingdon Press, 1994), 125–149

Jasper, D., *The Study of Literature and Religion* (Basingstoke: Macmillan, 1992²)

Jasper, D., and S. Prickett (eds.), *The Bible and Literature: A Reader* (Oxford: Basil Blackwell, 1999)

Jülicher, A., *Die Gleichnisreden Jesu*, 2 vols. (Freiburg: J.C.B. Mohr [Paul Siebeck], 1899²)

Lewis, C.S., *An Experiment in Criticism* (Cambridge: Cambridge University Press, 1961)

—, 'The Literary Impact of the Authorised Version' in *They Asked for a Paper* (London: Geoffrey Bles, 1962), 26–50

—, 'Christianity and Literature' in *Christian Reflections*, ed. W. Hooper (London: Geoffrey Bles, 1967), 1–11

—, 'Historicism' in *Christian Reflections*, ed. W. Hooper (London: Geoffrey Bles, 1967), 100–113

—, 'Modern Theology and Biblical Criticism' in *Christian Reflections*, ed. W. Hooper (London: Geoffrey Bles, 1967), 152–166

Long, T.G., *Preaching and the Literary Forms of the Bible* (Philadelphia: Fortress Press, 1989)

Lowry, E.L., *The Homiletical Plot: The Sermon as Narrative Art Form* (Atlanta: John Knox Press, 1980)

—, *How to Preach a Parable: Designs for Narrative Sermons* (Nashville: Abingdon Press, 1989)

Milbank, J., C. Pickstock and G. Ward (eds.), *Radical Orthodoxy* (London: Routledge, 1999)

Moore, S.D., *Literary Criticism and the Gospels: The Theoretical Challenge* (New Haven: Yale University Press, 1989)

—, *Mark and Luke in Poststructuralist Perspectives* (New Haven: Yale University Press, 1992)

Murray, S., 'Interactive Preaching', *Evangel* 17.2 (summer 1999), 53–57

Ovey, M., 'Deconstruction: Gagging the Speaking God?', *Cambridge Papers* 2.4 (December 1993)

Packer, J.I., 'Authority in Preaching' in M. Eden and D.F. Wells (eds.), *The Gospel in the Modern World* (Leicester: Inter-Varsity Press, 1991), 198–212

Phillips, P., 'The Romantic Tradition and the Sacrament of the Present Moment: Wordsworth and Tillich' in D. Brown and A. Loades (eds.), *Christ: The Sacramental Word* (London: SPCK, 1996), 202–214

Resner, A., Jr, *Preacher and Cross: Person and Message in Theology and Rhetoric* (Grand Rapids: Eerdmans, 1999)

Rogerson, J.W., *W.M.L. de Wette, Founder of Modern Biblical Criticism: An Intellectual Biography* (Sheffield: Sheffield Academic Press, 1992)

Rose, L.A., *Sharing the Word: Preaching in the Roundtable Church* (Louisville: Westminster / John Knox Press, 1997)

Schiller, F., 'On the Aesthetic Education of Man' (tr. E. Wilkinson and L. Willoughby) in D. Cooper (ed.), *Aesthetics: The Classic Readings*, (Oxford: Basil Blackwell, 1997), 123–136

Schlafer, D.J., *Surviving the Sermon: A Guide to Preaching for Those Who Have to Listen* (Cambridge, MA.: Cowley, 1992)

Steiner, G., 'Review of R. Alter and F. Kermode (eds.), *The Literary Guide to the Bible*', *The New Yorker* (11 January 1988), 94–98

Thiselton, A.C., *Interpreting God and the Postmodern Self: On Meaning, Manipulation and Promise* (Edinburgh: T. & T. Clark, 1995)

Tillich, P., *Perspectives on 19th and 20th Century Protestant Theology* (London: SCM Press, 1967)

Wimsatt, W.K., and M.C. Beardsley, 'The Affective Fallacy' (1949) in D. Lodge (ed.), *20th Century Literary Criticism: A Reader* (London: Longman, 1972), 345–358

—, 'The Intentional Fallacy' (1946) in D. Lodge (ed.), *20th Century Literary Criticism: A Reader* (London: Longman, 1972), 334–345

Wolterstorff, N., *Divine Discourse: Philosophical Reflections on the Claim that God Speaks* (Cambridge: Cambridge University Press, 1995)

Young, B.H., *Jesus and His Jewish Parables: Rediscovering the Roots of Jesus' Teaching* (Mahwah, NJ.: Paulist Press, 1989)

13

A Missional Approach to Renewed Interpretation

Harry Daniel Beeby

To seek 'renewal' assumes first an existing condition that is unsatisfactory and then a judgement on and estimate of the nature of the condition. What then is wrong with present interpretation? We need to find the breaks before we try to fix them.

I believe that biblical understanding, investigation, reading and usage are in crisis; that the questions and the problems that face us are almost beyond numbering but that among all the approaches to be made there is one, rarely considered, which is so important that renewal will fail if it continues to be neglected. The approach is of those who read in the Bible the account of the *missio Dei* and who believe that it provides a trajectory essential to full hermeneutical renewal.

If we are in a crisis and a missional reading is part of the medicine, what lies at the root of the crisis?

Which Crisis?

Consideration of 'the crisis in biblical interpretation' quickly produces the realization that use of the singular is an error. We face a plurality of crises and these fall into quite different categories according to their roots and origins. Is the problem the deficiencies of the historical-critical approach or the pressures of modernity and postmodernity? Was Constantine the culprit when he married the public realm to the gospel, or was it British deism, or Humboldt when he reorganized the modern university, or Schleiermacher when he 'invented' modern theology, or do we blame Descartes, Spinoza and Kant? Is the problem to be found in historical events and persons, in philosophy or in the dichotomy of faith and reason? And these are not all the possible avenues of approach. There are many others and perhaps all have, in various ways, contributed to the present critical situation.

A plural problem requires a plural answer but it does not require the assumption that all contributions are equally responsible. What it does require is an attempt to determine and mark importance where it exists and to seek for problematic areas within the mass which most others might neglect. I first wish to concentrate on two areas, not obviously similar but which, in different ways, will lead to an understanding of the Bible as the record of the *missio Dei* and therefore, both in analysis and conclusion, will dwell on the apostolate; on election for sending and on redeeming testimony. The vocabulary will be missional, the concepts missiological and well nourished by missionary act and missionary demand.

The choice of the two areas and the dominant theme is not a statement of exclusion. It may imply priority but if so it is a priority which will be incomplete without dialogue and salvific friction.

The Bible's Inbuilt Tension: The One and the Many

Stephen Prickett reminds us that

> our word 'Bible' is derived, via the French *bible*, from the late Latin *biblia* a feminine singular noun meaning simply 'the (single) book'. In earlier Latin, however, *biblia* was not taken to be the feminine singular, but the neuter plural form, which, following the Greek *ta biblia*, meant 'the (individual) books' . . . Right from the start, however accidentally, our sense of what the Bible is has contained a tension between singularity and plurality, between unity and diversity. The Bible was 'the book of books': an ambiguous phrase implying that it was a collection of works somehow contributing to a mysterious unity greater than the sum of its parts, and, at the same time, the pre-eminent and superlative book . . .[1]

This brief philological history provides us with one means to analyse the crisis and also gives us a clue to its resolution. The Bible exists in tension. It is both singular and plural, it is one and it is many. It is human and divine. There is a cultural context and an ecclesiastical context. There is that which responds to the intellectual and conceptual but also that which responds to the religious and theological, both to 'reason' and to faith; to the historical questions and the acknowledgement of transcendence. For most of the church's history this has been accepted and the mysterious transcendent unity has had priority and

---

[1] Prickett and Barnes, *Bible*, 1, 2.

provided most of the reason for preserving the human plurality. The Bible has reflected its Lord who is human and divine. It has shared a nature similar to the church, his body which is one, holy, catholic and apostolic but also divided, tainted, sectarian and apostate. But somewhere along the way the biblical nature, the many in the one, came apart, or, more precisely, the unity was lost. If I were writing a book some chapters here could be devoted to what caused the loss but in a brief chapter brief statements will have to suffice if the argument, even in outline, is to be given any semblance of completeness.

A lost unity prompts us to ask questions about the nature of the loss and who are the losers. Has it been liberals, biblical scholars with their constant acts of academic separation and suspicion of unity? I believe that the loss is endemic and that most of Protestantism and much of the Catholic Church has opted for fragmentation. I use the word advisedly to distinguish the resulting splinters from parts because existing parts assume an existing whole which has almost entirely disappeared. The extremes of Protestantism, in very different ways but under the same pressures, have been largely deprived of a unified sacred scripture. Academics and 'evangelicals' have both turned the parts of a sacred scriptural whole into items in a library of religious literature.

In biblical scholarship, scripture (partly for its own sake) was removed from its home in the church and committed to institutions with other beliefs that denied its essential unity. It ceased to be interpreted within the faith of the church. No longer an 'it' but a 'them', it could not continue to be an authoritative metanarrative read as a Christ-centred, Christ-witnessing, unified narrative conforming to a trinitarian rule of faith. Reduced to a type of religious literature, to being scripture books in a library of world scriptures, the Bible was no longer the Book of Books, a divine word to the world, true for believer and unbeliever alike. It was left detached and privatized, unable to address the public realm because its authority was not inherent within itself but dependent on the choice and conviction of the individual reader. Its truth was not its own and absolute but truth on loan at the discretion of the autonomous lender.

Scripture's essential nature disappeared with the loss of tension and, with it, went authority, unified narrative and missionary rights. Institutions which with their assumed 'objectivity' and freedom from harmful prejudice had proved to be orphanages that robbed their charge of its essence with hidden dogmas and a prejudice against the right prejudice. The Bible awaits the beadle who will return the scriptures to the church.

The Bible and Culture: Rectifying Relationships

The second area which provides pointers to helpful analysis of the crisis and their partial resolution is that where the Bible meets the world, where the word of God encounters the works of man; the quicksands of gospel and culture. From the beginning God's people have lived closely with the surrounding cultures. Genesis chapters 1 and 6 show strong Akkadian influence. Abraham left Ur for Canaan and went to Egypt. Moses was an Egyptian 'prince' but then a rebel. Elijah and Hosea fought the local idols. Jesus and the disciples lived with the three environments of Rome, Greece and Judaic Judaism. The gospel has never been isolated from cultural influence, influencing and being influenced, and such relationships have been and are ubiquitous and complex beyond description. At times it has been bitter conflict – a cross and thorns, at times God's people depended on neighbours for life and food as when Israel turned to Egypt; at times the meeting appeared as a dialogue or controversy between God the creator and God the redeemer. Much of our present biblical crisis is attributable to great shifts in the interface between church and world, between gospel and culture.

After the first three centuries when Christians were aliens in a persecuting world, the fourth century saw the great reversal when the crown of thorns became identified with imperial power, as opposition turned to partnership and Christendom was born. Now, in the west, we live amidst the ruins of Christendom but live confused by its continuing illusory existence; believing but not believing and little aware that we often mistake darkness for light and retreat for progress. For centuries we saw the world through the eyes of the Bible, colleges and hospitals were named after saints and theology was the queen of the sciences. We now live after the second great reversal as we see the Bible critically through the eyes of the reigning culture. Christians commute between two worlds. Brief spells are spent with the ultimate truths of resurrection and Trinity but lives are lived in a 'real world' where these are meaningless embarrassments. In this world we have found a place for the sixty-six biblical books on crowded shelves with the histories and with literature but resurrection, Trinity, and scriptural mystery have no place and can have no place except in a world where they are the beginning and the end and explain and remake all inbetween. Perhaps our age is the first when the culture was not shaped by a confessed faith but by unconfessed assumptions and it is in this age that we struggle to interpret what we have called 'the word of God'.

In the first area examined we discovered that the natural tension within the Bible had been lost and with it the essential unity which gives us scriptural cohesion and authority and, with them the important Christian view of universal history from creation to new creation. In the second area we have referred to a related loss caused by cultural pressures which have grown mainly since the seventeenth and eighteenth centuries. Under these pressures the west, and wherever its power extends, struggles with a descripturized Bible. With rare exceptions the churches and their Bibles live and falter with fragmentation, canons within a canon, a privatized church, blindness to idolatry within the culture, a limiting historicism, the excessive significance of personal experience, neglect of the Old Testament, a weakened ecclesiology, a loss of biblical unity and a failure to realize that we speak of a scripture we no longer possess. Much of the church has opted for a personal belief within a privatized church. The gospel has largely ceased to be public truth and the word 'Scripture' has become a kind of lip-service to a lost past. The Book of Books which reads us and our culture has become reduced to an anthology of honoured religious writings read through the lenses and fashions of cultural change.

Scripture Unique and Singular: A Missional Move

In my first section I made missionary promises which so far I have not kept. It was not oversight; mission is indeed on the horizon but it required as a preface a glance at the offending crises and a survey of the mission field. The crises I have suggested involve a vanishing scripture, a descripturized Bible; the pagan prospect is heathen in new ways that cry out for new, untried mission and missionary interpretations.

The thesis is that the Bible read as scripture centres on the *missio Dei*. It is the record of the word and works of the loving, revealing God who created in love and redeems in love. It is a universal history brought about by the *dabar* of the Triune God. It is a missionary record that tells of a sending God who sent the Spirit to bring order from the *tohu wa bohu*, who sent forth Noah safe on the water to see a rainbow of promise, who sent out Abraham full of promise and blessing to the nations, who formed Israel to be a light to the nations, who sent his Son, the true Israel and his Spirit to bring into being the church, the new Israel, to witness as the body of Christ to the new creation, born with the resurrection, and to the coming Jerusalem large enough for all tribes and tongues and peoples to enter in. The movement from creation to new creation is a missionary movement, an electing. God electing to send witnesses to tell the good news of the saving God to all mankind and all creation. Read within the faith of the church can this then be further substantiated?

First, the Christian canon was reordered by moving the latter prophets of the Hebrew Bible from the centre to the end of the Christian Old Testament. This served to bring them physically nearer to the birth of the Christ they were now reinterpreted as foretelling. The move reinforced the conviction almost everywhere present in Jesus' own teachings and in those of the New Testament writers, that the whole canon was centred on Christ, that it should be Christologically interpreted, and in having arisen out of the work of the missionary God, was ergo the *vade mecum* of the missionary church commissioned and sent (according to Vatican II) to serve as the *lumen gentium*. In a small book *Canon and Mission*, I have argued for the interdependence of canon and mission. That is that the canon read as scripture is a missionary document and that Christian mission in its completeness requires the whole canon. Also I have claimed that if that argument is valid then a missionary hermeneutic should be given a high place in scholarly interpretation. Such an argument, among many other issues, raises the question as to whether canon and canonization occurred as necessities in the process of a missionary need being met. J.A. Sanders[2] and others who have written on canon criticism provide material for a positive answer. In what follows I shall be drawing on my book.

The canon of the Torah appears in the period of exile when the exiles ask Ezekiel how they are to live. Without land, without temple, without sacrifice and priestly ministration who were they? Were they still Israel and if so what kind of Israel were they in an unclean land? What was their way of life and their way of worship? Was there continuity with the past and was there hope for coming generations? All the great human questions were present: life, identity, lifestyle, survival and continuity. Is God still our God giving us life or are we dry bones in a graveyard?

Israel had come into being through covenant that rested on a story. She was the creature of that story, living by it and living out of it; but the old, old story of Jahweh and his love seemed to have lost its power. Was the story still true and was it still applicable or should it be hung with harps on the willows? Sanders sees such questions always lying behind the need for a canon: life, identity, lifestyle, continuity and hope. The questions are addressed to the truth and authenticity of the story that has lain behind their life, identity, lifestyle, continuity and hope in previous generations. To such questions the canonical process responds with two major aspects – stability and flexibility. The stability element ensures continuity with the past. There must be faithfulness to the primal story and this faithfulness provides stability and security in the present and promises it in the future. This stability which the community longs for is paired with extreme adaptability that at times can even be ambiguous about whether the story is the exodus story or the David story. The adaptability and flexibility are essential to meet the challenges of new situations and changing circumstances.

The greatest exercise of the force of adaptability is evident in the way the Hebrew scriptures are appropriated by the writers of the New Testament and the early church. The Hebrew scriptures were the scriptures of Jesus Christ and the apostles. They were authoritative, and appeal was made to them at every turn for validation of the religious upheaval that was taking place. Everything was grounded in their truth. The 'historical' truth of what was happening depended on the 'historical' truth of Israel's Bible but this, paradoxically, resulted in the virtual reduction of the historical significance of the Hebrew

---

[2] Sanders, *Sacred Story*.

scriptures as they are turned into an unintended prologue to the New Testament. Having become part of the Christian scripture, the historical context of the Hebrew scriptures becomes secondary. Beginning with our Lord himself, they are now seen as prophecy and preparation for the coming of Jesus. Old Israel's function, it is now assumed, was to prepare for the true Israel, the church. The old exodus, with its old interpretation of political freedom, becomes a threat because the new liberation, the new exodus, has come in Christ.

The Jews, who did not recognize what was happening and did not greet the Messiah, could no longer understand this scripture – a veil covered their faces. The Hebrew scriptures that were instrumental in creating the New Testament had to die to the church as they were turned into the Old Testament. The Hebrew scriptures were historically prior but the New Testament is logically and theologically prior because it is the new which fashions the old. Jesus poignantly says that the Jews searched the scriptures for life. They were asking the old canon the right questions but were not getting the right answers because the adaptability of the canon-creating process had overtaken them. The scriptures still hold the key to life and identity, lifestyle, continuity and hope, but only if they were now seen to be the Old Testament, which took its place alongside the New Testament in the greater whole, the church's canon.

Does this thumbnail sketch of a fraction of the canonical process have anything to say that is relevant to our main question of scripture and mission? Are they so closely related that it is difficult to think of them apart? Is it possible in any sense to say that the canon exists for mission and that the *missio Dei*, the *missio Christi* and the *missio ecclesiae* are in great part the explanation for the existence of the canon? Dare we advance a step further as we query whether Christian mission can effectively exist without the canon and also whether we can effectively understand the canon unless we are constantly aware of its missionary roots, its growth in mission and its missionary imperative? Is mission hidden beneath the non-missionary language of the canonizing process?

Some of the Answers

Does the above glance at the canonizing process which gave us holy scripture reveal some, if not all, of the essentials of mission? The human quest is a series of questions: who am I and how do I live? Where am I and why am I? How do my present and past relate, and what is my future? With whom do I journey and how do I journey? Such questions are part of the human side of mission. Christianity affirms that the Christian scripture contains the divine response to these questions. Part of that response is to judge the questions and to reform them in the light of the answer in Christ.

The canon and its contents come to us as the answer to such seeking. It witnesses to the whole truth of God. It carries the whole story that is necessary for all humankind at all times. It carries the variety that is necessary to meet all eventualities in all ages. Therefore it comes in paradox and tension, in ambiguity and ambivalence, in contrast and contradiction. It provides an ethos, an identity, an understanding in a problematic world, order in a disorderly world. Somehow the ambiguity of the canon provides the certainty that all people need. In its ambiguity it is our bulwark in an ambiguous world; its apparent unreality and irrelevance to the so-called real world witness to the true reality that judges and redeems. It bears the story that gives life and provides survival and continuity. It judges the novel and the changing and enables us to reject or redeem what existence presents to us. It does this by a proclamation that is both complex and simple, stable and adaptable, certain and flexible, and that has Christ at its centre. Is this mission? And if so is mission of the essence of the Christian canon? I believe it is.

The Completed Canon as Missional

So much for the canonizing process, what of the finished product? Does it read as a missionary narrative that arises out of mission, promotes mission and requires a prominent place to be given to a missional hermeneutic? I offer a few token examples of such reading which are, perhaps, more obvious to literary critics than to biblical scholars.

(1) The canon moves from creation to new creation, from the heavens and the earth to the new heavens and the new earth, from a rural Eden to an urban Eden. This movement of renewal, restoration and redemption is through a sent Spirit, a sent nation, a sent Son and a sent community.

(2) The ubiquitous descent-ascent pattern that belongs to the whole Bible, the pattern that Northrop Frye[3] has taught us to call the 'U' pattern, is found not only in the whole but in almost every part. Supremely it is present in the *kenosis* hymn of Philippians 2:5–11. This paradigm permeating the whole is the central tale of the sent Son's risen witness to the sent nation, the sent apostles, the sent church and the lost world: the mission pattern.

(3) The canon is about distorted relationships – God and creation, God and humankind, person with person, humanity and creation, the person and the self – and their total restoration in Christ. Christ is the reconciler witnessed to by the reconciled and reconciling community: the missionary church.

---

[3] Frye, *Code.*

(4) The canon is ordered so that all before Christ focuses on him and all after him radiates from him. But how will they hear without a preacher? There has to be the narrative and the storyteller, the testimony and the acted word – there has to be mission.

(5) The clear message of the canon is a monotheizing message, but it appears in a sea of polytheism and idolatry, both within and without the chosen people. The whole debate is present; it is a parliament in which the elect constantly face the opposition; all the dialogues and the trialogues are represented. The one God is witnessed to as creator and redeemer in the midst of all that makes belief in God unlikely and which threatens His believers. It is unwelcome testimony in a resisting environment – 'He came to His own and His own received Him not,' but the darkness, not comprehending him, did not overwhelm. The light shone. This means that the very presentation of Father, Son and Holy Spirit is a missionary presentation. Trinitarian monotheism in the canon comes to us as a missionary resistance movement. It is a counter-culture within the Bible itself. The canon is given to the church in a fallen world in an apostolic missionary form but with the assurance that the light shines in the darkness with a brightness independent of our comprehension.

Recovering Scripture: A New Mission

In analysing the present crisis in biblical interpretation I spoke first of a lost tension and a disappearing scripture and secondly of a brilliant culture which descripturizes the Bible. Having spent some time viewing the Bible as a missionary canon the question inevitably rises as to how some reality can be given to such an understanding. How is the scriptural value restored and a retreating scripture recovered? How does the church of today say 'Scripture' with all that a missionary canon implies? 'Scripture' with this significance can only be said under two quite different sets of circumstances. The first was the period we roughly refer to as Christendom, which lasted from the fourth century for about a thousand years. During that period the worldview of Europe was largely the worldview of scripture. In one way at least, this was disastrous because missionary demand was largely obscured: Europe was converted. You do not evangelize a region where citizenship and Christian belief are identified. The disaster however, was balanced by the fact that the Bible was scripture. The tension held firm because government, society and culture united to provide the necessary plausibility structure. The word of God reigned but its missionary meaning was stilled. The Bible was scripture and few dared or wished to demur.

We now live in a cultural situation which is almost exactly the opposite. Increasingly the church becomes aware of the surrounding paganism and idolatry and of plausibility structures which support almost anything but scriptural revelation. The cry increasingly is for mission but it remains little more than a cry because we have lost the missionary canon that makes mission possible. We are intending missionaries but have no missiology for the west because we have let slip our hold on scripture. How then do we in our time meaningfully say 'Scripture' and how do we recover it for church, academy and culture?

The answer, of course, is mission. An unrelenting missionary stance, novel, untried and widespread. First a three-pronged mission:

(1) *Mission to our own minds*. We are all intellectual atheists with commuting minds. In church we confess God as creator and redeemer and the Trinity as the ultimate 'fact'. In school and college we study creation but call it nature and ignore the God who made it. We study history and ignore its Lord whom we adore in church. The Bible and church's ground of all being has no significant place on the educational curriculum. The modern and the postmodern mind is the first mission field.

(2) *Mission to the church*. Parts of the church are partly apostate. We must ask if we are true to our creeds. We fear certainty and must ask whether our dogma-resistance is a camouflage for the hidden dogmas and lurking creeds of our idolatrous culture. Is liberalism a cover for concealed illiberality and is uncertainty founded on the destructive certainty that there is no certainty?

Can we learn to preach from the scriptures and not about the Bible? To preach to enable us all to live in the world but to claim it for Christ? To demonstrate that scripture is public truth and not just private preference? Can we be apostolic like the apostles, confessed aliens and eccentrics to the culture for the culture's sake, that it may be redeemed?

(3) *Mission to the culture*. One day the kingdoms of this world will become the kingdom of Christ. This is the church's mission because it is *missio Dei*. If we are to recover scripture the mission of recovery must go hand in hand with mission to culture and mission to culture demands the certainty and authority which we only possess from God through his word in scripture.

Other Missions

The three-pronged mission is to predictable targets, but 'an unrelenting missionary stance' arising from a restored missionary canon would result in a vast range of missions both novel and strange. I mention but two.

If, as I have suggested, part of the present crisis is the loss of tension between the 'human' Bible and the divine scriptures and, if academic biblical studies are governed by a great variety of pre-understandings but rarely include among them the faith of the church, then can we do something to rectify this?

Modernity favoured pluralism in allowing us the variety of assumptions loosely attached to the dominant one of historical criticism, but it was a limited pluralism that generally excluded the traditional faith of the church. Postmodernism has opened the door in such a way that it would be difficult to preclude parallel courses in biblical faculties. My proposal is that alongside the existing courses which among the manifold presuppositions might include everything from the atheistic to the feminist, there could be courses taught within the confessed faith of the church. The tension created could be beneficial to both types of course and it would be one way of restoring the natural but lost tension between the two natures implied in the original *biblia*.

The second 'mission' is still novel but has been tried. Based upon Lesslie Newbigin's biblical convictions and his plan for mission to western culture there was in 1992 a large consultation organized by *The Gospel and Our Culture* movement with the title The Gospel as Public Truth. The aim was 'to test the thesis that the Christian gospel provides a positive critique of contemporary western culture, a sound historic basis for its unity and coherence and the only sure ground of hope for public life in our society and our time'. Four hundred Christian specialists drawn from the disciplines of epistemology, history, science, the arts, education, healing, economics and the media met for a week and argued, prayed, laughed and learned. More than the thesis was tested. As well as tested patience and belief there was a great strain placed upon our understanding of the Bible towards the end of the second millennium which has brought its authority almost to breaking point. Certainty seemed to lie more in the disciplines than in the testing gospel. But it was a start, and from that small beginning there has been growth and some fruits.

One fruit has been a deepening awareness of the crises that exist in biblical interpretation and some acknowledgement that one way to begin to resolve them is not only to recover the Bible's missionary message for pulpit and classroom, but to be immersed equally in the missiological and missional, and also the awesome task of mission in post-Christendom. Missiology is largely a historical science but it has visible, if not strong, links with theology. The practice of mission obviously has connections with a limited range of biblical texts but rarely with what is recognizable as the missionary canon. Notoriously, biblical studies, on the whole, proceed comfortably without even a nodding acquaintance with mission or missiology.

Early in this chapter I promised a vocabulary of 'mission', 'missional' and 'missiological'. These all belong together – the praxis, the adjectival, the science – and the latter should be prescriptive of the praxis and not merely historical. I hope that this chapter contributes a little to such a contention, but far more do I hope that such a vocabulary begins to find a permanent place in biblical studies.

Interpreting a Missionary Canon: An Exegetical Note

Lay Christians who read the Bible usually use it selectively; it is difficult not to be subjective and selective as we pick and choose to find textual support for decisions. Scholars tend to analyse the Bible and then to deal with isolated pericopes. So we all dissect. How then do we approach scripture as a unified missional whole? Two clues; one is missional.

First, we need complete honesty as neither the unity nor the mission is immediately apparent. The Bible presents no consistent ethic or ideology; its consistency is its witness to the mystery of God Almighty and the mysterious *missio Dei*, and mystery is hard to handle. The Bible is like Hansard; a series of debates within a literary parliament that has sworn allegiance to one sovereign lord but welcomes opponents and suffers traitors. It is rare that the Bible gives one clear answer to a question. If it did the history of the church would have been more peaceful and the sects, schisms and denominations fewer. Orthodox, Catholic, Protestant and a thousand splinters all, with some legitimacy, can appeal to one or other of the biblical voices.

This biblical parliament includes wisdom books which differ greatly from the prophets. Within wisdom Job does not agree with Proverbs, and Ecclesiastes is out of tune with almost everybody. The prophets include Jeremiah and Isaiah who concur on much but differ considerably. God both supports kingship and oppresses it, law struggles with gospel, and particularism and universalism stand side by side. Differing accounts of creation differ in almost everything except the essential 'God created' and, at the heart of all this argument is a love wherein the Son of God accuses His Father of desertion. This is the raw material of interpretation. No wonder that some deny to it any unity. But it has a unity: a unity in tension, a harmony of conflicting forces that can speak to all sorts and conditions of humanity, in all sorts and conditions of human joy and anguish. At times we must hear one voice more than others. In affluence we must hear the vocation to poverty, in strength we must be conscious of the power of weakness; severity must temper goodness and law nourish grace lest it become cheap.

Now, as the reader is asking what this has to do with mission, I come to the second clue, and this is missional. Having accepted the controversy and tension in the Bible, and having seen that the conflict is varied, let us ask if some, if not all, is related to mission and if so can we examine the relationship for signs of anything that aids our argument? I believe that much of the conflict is the result of the canon being a missionary canon.

Mission rarely occurs without conflict. It involves testimony of that which is potentially the cause of change; at its most typical it is designed to proclaim the truly holy to the false and pseudo-sacreds and this is a recipe for conflict. Warfare is not intended as the prior aim but it is unavoidable. *Metanoia*, unless it is sought, is not welcome. It is a road that is hard and narrow and can be very bloody. It is overshadowed by a cross. The word for witness is the word for martyr and the perceptive music-hall picture of the missionary has him in a stewing pot. The missionary word of witness brings judgement first and then redemption; almost without exception the missionary word is a word of conflict.

The Old Testament has been termed a hymn to upheaval and the New Testament is no less so. Jesus faced the apostles and the world about Him with the question, 'Whom say ye that I am?' This question and all the related ones demanded an answer and the answer compelled interpretation. The interpretation brought division among the hearers and with the division controversy and conflict as some believed and some opposed. Conversation can be gentle and peaceful. Mission more often than not is accompanied with struggle, friction and conflict. Jesus was trouble. The Prince of Peace came 'not to bring peace but a sword'. The whole Bible, like its Lord, demands interpretation and decision; these judge and invite, and some of us accept and some reject. The scripture is trouble and most of the trouble is missionary trouble.

This missionary paradigm is seen, perhaps at its clearest in Acts 19–20 and in the epistle to the Ephesians. For more than two years Paul proclaims the kingdom of God in Christ to a community devoted to the goddess Diana. There is no account of direct attack but the result is uproar and tumult as every aspect of society is put in hazard. Ephesians gives us a glimpse of the early outcome of the upheaval, especially in chapters 1 and 2, and looks beyond when everything in heaven and earth will be brought into a unity in Christ (Eph. 1:10).

As an aid to biblical exegesis and missionary interpretation I wish to regard the scriptural canon as being formed and understood around three different but related forms of missionary friction:

(1) Some time ago in an unpublished doctoral thesis, *Myth and Mission*, I argued that scripture could be seen as resulting from the encounter of the word of God with the cultures of the surrounding nations. The evidence of such transformed borrowing begins in the early chapters of Genesis where Akkadian myths are appropriated largely to oppose their mythology and its associates. This process, I suggested, continues in later books with some Western Semitic myths found in Ugaritic tablets. Restricted by thesis limitation to certain myths, I also suggested that the transformed material I examined was but a fragment of what could be found throughout the total canon. 'Borrowed' language opened wide the gates to this activity and we still give thanks for and still struggle with the borrowed *logos* in John. With temerity I further maintained that these manifold transformed borrowings were a form of cultural encounter which was a form of mission.

(2) The second friction is the one I have referred to above, and that is the internal friction and controversy which is found everywhere in the canon. This friction with external cultures, which is part and parcel of the formation of the canon, is followed by the friction which exists within the complete scripture and this again is a missionary friction. Hosea, for example, in his diatribe against the disastrous inroads made into Israel's religion by Canaanite idolatry uses elements of the latter as weapons in his awesome purifying mission. The Canaanite agricultural system which was fuelled with fertility rituals and imitative magic is appropriated by Hosea and transferred to the force of the covenant relationship with Jahweh (Hos. 2:21–23). In his horrified response to idolatrous beliefs in sexuality within the godhead his whole teaching centres round the fact that Jahweh has a wife – Israel. This is one example of a ubiquitous feature in both testaments.

(3) The third friction is wherever the words, images and presuppositions of scripture meet the words, images and presuppositions of the world's cultures: the cultures which are our cradles and whose values and traditions are reflected in all we do and all we are. How does the friction function?

Contemporary images and values provide models and paradigms for almost all our decisions and actions. A career consists of getting your feet onto a ladder that leads to affluence and security. Success is measured in financial terms, the exercise of power and the possession of goods commensurate with having 'arrived'. We are walking containers of the myths and models of our day. The third friction (perhaps 'explosion' would be more appropriate) occurs when these words come into collision with the images, models and presuppositions of scripture. The priority of economics, the sanctity of politics, racial prejudice, class superiority, nationalism, the absolutizing of equality, increasing GNPs, etc., need to be attacked and vanquished by the dominant images and values of scripture: trust, worship, sacrifice, generosity, faith, hope, love and obedience. The cross and resurrection model must fight our securities based on force, power and money; biblical 'hierarchies' must modify our belief in equality which is so often concealed envy; the values of an advertising culture must be undermined by apostolic honesty and passion for truth.

These three frictions are not the whole of mission but their acceptance greatly aids our understanding of what it is. Acceptance confirms that the Bible is a missionary scripture in its entirety; it confirms that there is an essential place in the Bible for conflict and controversy – a missional place, and that a satisfactory hermeneutics must give a permanent place to mission, the missional and missiology.

Exclusive, Prominent or Prior? Questions and Comment

The church has known Platonic and Aristotelian hermeneutics, allegorical, existential, anthropological and evolutionary hermeneutics. This century has seen national-socialist, Marxist and apartheid hermeneutics. There are pietistic and moralistic hermeneutics. The dominant form of interpretation for almost two centuries has been controlled by the historical-critical ascendancy with its various progeny of atomism, geneticism, positivism, literary analysis, literary criticism and the canonization of the diachronic method. Missionaries and evangelists have used the Bible with a missionary understanding but missionary hermeneutics seem to have little if any place in the publications of biblical scholars. This I find disturbing. Am I barking up a wrong tree or even a non-existent one? I will proceed with the assumption that it is a real tree and a sequoia at that – which I see so clearly – but that there are questions and need for comment.

First, the missionary hermeneutic I am pleading for is not exclusive. Such a dogma would be unwarranted reductionism. A canon which has emerged via every kind of dialogue – dialogue within God (Hos. 11), God with Israel, God with the nations, God in creation, God in redemption, God with humankind, the person with the self, etc. – allows for a variety of starting points. The question is not one of exclusion but of priority.

Second, a missionary hermeneutic should have high priority because it pre-supposes a canonical hermeneutic that gives full range to the inner dialectics of scripture and recognizes that the missionary demands were not the sole demands in the process of canon formation. The canon is also a response to ethical, liturgical, social and political demands but these are secondary in the relation to the all-embracing needs and demands of the church's mission.

Third, I believe that some form of missionary hermeneutic should have the highest priority and this for several reasons:

(1) A missionary canonical hermeneutic is one that emerges from within scripture and is not external to it, and furthermore it not only takes place within a holistic reading of the scriptures but, seen as a triple missionary friction from creation to the new creation, its own form accords with the holistic form of a missionary canon.

(2) Good grounds can be given for according to a missionary hermeneutic a normative function. It can function as a positive norm by affirming all that supports the belief that the *verbum Dei* truly expresses the *missio Dei*, It can also function in a negative way by critiquing hermeneutics that are external rather than internal, that have little or no place for the *missio Dei* or that are controlled by ideologies or concepts that are unsympathetic to the main thrust of scriptural meaning or even inimical to it. Some classrooms may have legitimate

places for atheistic or Hindu approaches to the Bible but scripture within the church's faith can find no such place.

(3) Finally, a missionary hermeneutic combines the conceptual with action. It provides a place for the missionary and missional as well as the missiological. It does not end in thought but moves to decision and action. It is not governed by the world's understanding of the world's need but meets that need as it is seen and interpreted in the light of the gospel. It is not satisfied with anything less than the most significant, demanding, sacrificial, all-embracing praxis, but it does not begin in praxis or with any praxis-dominated ideology. It attempts to be faithful to the creative and redemptive word of the missionary Trinity who promises his disciples into mission: 'You will be my witnesses.'

Bibliography

Beeby, H.D., *Canon and Mission* (Harrisburg: Trinity Press International, 1999)

Bosch, D.J., *Transforming Mission: Paradigm Shifts in Theology of Mission* (Maryknoll: Orbis Books, 1991)

Childs, B.S., *Introduction to the Old Testament as Scripture* (London: SCM Press, 1979)

—, *Biblical Theology of the Old and New Testaments* (London: SCM Press, 1992)

Frei, H.W., *The Eclipse of Biblical Narrative: A Study in Eighteenth and Nineteenth Century Hermeneutics* (New Haven: Yale University Press, 1974)

Frye, N., *The Great Code: The Bible and Literature* (London: Routledge & Kegan Paul, 1982)

Newbigin, L., *Foolishness to the Greeks: The Gospel and Western Culture* (Geneva: WCC, 1986)

—, *The Gospel in a Pluralist Society* (London: SPCK, 1989)

Prickett, S., and R. Barnes, *The Bible* (Landmarks of World Literature; Cambridge: Cambridge University Press, 1991)

Sanders, J.A., *From Sacred Story to Sacred Text: Canon as Paradigm* (Philadelphia: Fortress Press, 1987)

14

Deconstructing the Tower of Babel: Ontotheology and the Postmodern Bible

Brian D. Ingraffia

'Come, let us build ourselves a city, with a tower that reaches to the heavens, so that we may make a name for ourselves and not be scattered over the face of the whole earth.' But YHWH came down to see the city and the tower that the men were building. YHWH said, 'If as one people speaking the same language they have begun to do this, then nothing they plan to do will be impossible for them. Come, let us go down and confuse their language so they will not understand each other.' So YHWH scattered them from there over all the earth, and they stopped building the city. That is why it was called Babel – because there YHWH confused the language of the whole world.

—Genesis 11:4–9

The church preaches, I believe, and the Old Testament describes, a God Who acts, Who *comes to us*, in Revelation and Redemption . . . The God we care about . . . is the living God, Who moves toward us out of His will and love, and Who laughs at all the towers of Babel we build to Him.

—John Updike, *Roger's Version*, 22

The writers of *The Postmodern Bible*, the collective project published by Yale in 1995, begin by describing the crisis we must pass through in order to renew biblical interpretation, that is, 'the crisis of legitimation confronting biblical criticism today – whose reading counts? how are different readings adjudicated?'[1] They assert that this crisis 'is a direct consequence of the intensification of those very aspects of critical self-consciousness that were prominent in the birth of modern scientific study of the Bible (Frei, 1–16) . . . Both the

---

[1] *The Postmodern Bible*, 13.

postmodern and the modern share common cause in reaction to the grip of an uncritical premodern tradition.'[2] I agree that both modernism and postmodernism react against 'premodern tradition,' especially any orthodox Christian tradition, but I reject their overly simplistic valorization of (post)modern self-consciousness as 'critical' and denigration of premodern tradition as 'uncritical.'[3] I will argue instead that postmodern theory relies uncritically upon the modern ontotheological tradition it deconstructs in its rejection of biblical theology.

In *Postmodern Theory and Biblical Theology*, I argue that we must distinguish between biblical theology and ontotheology in order to renew biblical interpretation. The term ontotheology originates, as far as I know, in the work of Kant, who described what is commonly called the ontological argument for the existence of God as ontotheological. In his *Critique of Pure Reason*, Kant makes his first, and in my mind most important, distinction between *theologia rationalis*, a theology based 'upon reason alone,' and *theologia revelata*, a theology based 'upon revelation.' Kant goes on to divide rational theology into two kinds, transcendental and natural, explaining that 'The person who believes in a transcendental theology alone, is termed a *Deist*; he who acknowledges the possibility of a *natural* theology also, a *Theist*.' According to Kant, transcendental theology aims to prove the existence of a Supreme Being either based upon general experience, which leads to *Cosmotheology*, or based upon 'mere conceptions,' which Kant terms *Ontotheology*.[4]

The god of ontotheology is the god of Descartes who is exposed as a projection by Feuerbach. Feuerbach writes that

> God as God, that is, as a being not finite, not human, not materially conditioned, not phenomenal, is *only an object of thought* . . . Thus the understanding is the *ens realissimum*, the most real being of the old ontotheology. 'Fundamentally,' says onto-theology, 'we cannot conceive God otherwise than by attributing to him without limit all the real qualities which we find in ourselves.'[5]

While Feuerbach seeks to celebrate this god in his religion of humanity, Marx, Nietzsche, and Freud expose this god as a self-serving illusion. Consequently, Merold Westphal argues that 'we need to see Marx, Nietzsche, and Freud,

---

[2] Ibid.

[3] Thiselton, in *New Horizons*, asserts that premodern hermeneutics of faith 'does not imply that pre-modern thinkers did not raise critical questions; but that the basic frame of reference within which doubt or questions were expressed remained a fundamentally theological one which, informed by Christology and the creeds, was perceived to deserve at least provisional trust,' 143.

[4] Kant, *Critique of Pure Reason*, 367.

[5] Feuerbach, *The Essence of Christianity*, 38 (my emphasis).

along with Luther and Barth, as expressing a Promethean protest against . . . *the piety that reduces God to a means or instrument for achieving our own human purposes with professedly divine power and sanction*'.[6] This is the reason Barth can assert that the atheistic negation of God applies only to 'a deity that demonstrates its existence by having a place in a world-view of human construction.'[7] Thus I call for us to continue to separate the God of the Bible from the god of the philosophers, to separate the God revealed in the Bible from the god constructed in ontotheology.

Heidegger and Derrida take up the term ontotheology to describe that which needs to be deconstructed in the history of metaphysics. In his seminal essay 'The Onto-theological Constitution of Metaphysics' Heidegger describes the forgetting of the ontological difference, the difference between Being and beings, in the history of metaphysics that occurs as a result of the equation of God and Being as the ground and cause of beings.

> When metaphysics thinks of beings with respect to the ground that is common to all beings as such, then it is logic as onto-logic. When metaphysics thinks beings as such as a whole, that is, with respect to the highest being which accounts for everything, then it is logic as theo-logic.[8]

The origins of Heidegger's destruction of ontotheology can be found in Christian theology, especially the opposition in the writings of Paul, Luther, Pascal and Kierkegaard to the use of philosophy to prove the existence of God. But unlike these theological thinkers, Heidegger seeks to free philosophy from subordination to theology, rather than seeking to free theology from its subordination to an alien philosophy.[9]

Although he locates the origins of ontotheology in the forgetting of writing, in the forgetting of *différence* in logocentrism, rather than in the forgetting of the ontological difference, Derrida follows Heidegger in his rejection of the theological character of metaphysics. Derrida seeks to overcome ontotheology through a deconstruction of 'all the theological and metaphysical impediments that have limited'[10] the development of a grammatology.

---

[6] Westphal, *Suspicion and Faith*, 6 (his emphasis).
[7] Barth, *Christian Life*, 128.
[8] Heidegger, *Identity and Difference*, 71.
[9] It is here that my analysis of ontotheology differs from Westphal's in his 'Overcoming Onto-theology.' Westphal takes Heidegger at his word when he asserts that he is only opposing ontotheology, not Christian faith. I try to expose the anti-Christian motivations of Heidegger's fundamental ontology in the section on Heidegger in my *Postmodern Theory and Biblical Theology*.
[10] Derrida, *Of Grammatology*, 4.

In their deconstruction of western metaphysics, Heidegger and Derrida depend upon the modern description and devaluation of Christianity in the works of the modern masters of suspicion. The modern and the postmodern are aligned in their misreading of and opposition to Christianity.

In my own analysis of the western tradition, I use the term 'ontotheology' to describe the synthesis of Greco-Roman philosophy (onto-logy) and Judeo-Christian revelation (theo-logy) that forms the basis of western metaphysics, as well as in a broader sense to name any idolatry which worships a god of human construction. The critique of ontotheology begins in the Christian tradition, as Westphal describes for us: 'Theology becomes onto-theology when Jerusalem sells its soul to Athens by buying in on the latter's project. Within Christian history, the critique of onto-theology belongs to a tradition of dehellenizing repristination.'[11] In order to free biblical theology from ontotheology, to divorce Jerusalem from its marriage with Athens in Christian tradition, I look to the Judeo-Christian Scriptures.[12] The God revealed in the Bible is a God who comes to us, who comes 'down' to us, just as Yahweh 'came down' to see the Babylonian city and tower. God in the New Testament 'comes down' in the incarnation, in the *kenosis* of Christ, and the Holy Spirit is also described as descending upon Christ at his baptism and upon his disciples at Pentecost.

In contrast, the god of the philosophers is a god created in our own image, the god of ontotheology. In my final, Barthian formulation, ontotheology is the attempt of humanity to reason, imagine, or earn our way 'up' to God. As John Updike writes, paraphrasing Barth's central theological assertion: 'The god who stood at the end of some human way would not be God.'[13] In Updike's novel, *Roger's Version*, Roger Lambert, an aging ex-minister who now works at a liberal divinity school attached to a New England university, tells Dale Kohler, a young graduate student seeking to prove the existence of God with a computer, that 'You're trying to make God stand at the end of some human path . . . You're building a Tower of Babel.'[14] Westphal argues that the theological origins of the critique of ontotheology should encourage us to identify 'the demand for a critique of onto-theology as arising from a theology that recognizes its own onto-theological tendencies and sees these as temptations to be resisted.'[15]

---

[11] Westphal, 'Overcoming Onto-theology,' 157.

[12] In referring to the Bible as the Judeo-Christian Scriptures, I don't mean to emphasize the appropriation of the Hebrew Bible as the Old Testament; rather, I want to stress that the New Testament needs to be read in the context of the Hebraic Scriptures.

[13] Updike, *Roger's Version*, 42.

[14] Ibid., 187.

[15] Westphal, 'Overcoming Onto-theology,' 159.

From the Modern to the Postmodern Babel

In the modern period western culture began to rebuild towers of Babel in the name of humankind alone. In *Gravity's Rainbow*, Thomas Pynchon represents the secularization that occurs in modern western culture in his description of 'the Hospital of St. Veronica of the True Image for Colonic and Respiratory Diseases.' While maintaining a reference to the Christian conception of charity, this hospital can only hope to postpone not over-come death. In a parody of the biblical narrative of the Tower of Babel, Pynchon describes the hospital as a

> Victorian paraphrase of what once, long ago, resulted in Gothic cathedrals – but which, in its own time, arose not from any need to climb through the fashioning of suitable confusions toward any apical God, but more in a derangement of aim, a doubt as to God's actual locus (or, in some, as to its very existence), out of a cruel network of sensuous moments that could not be transcended and so bent the inten-tions of the builders not on any zenith, but back to fright, to simple escape, in what-ever direction . . .'[16]

Pynchon mocks Gothic cathedrals as towers of Babel which express hu-manity's need to climb or ascend toward the heavens, toward an apical God, that is, towards the highest point or summit. According to Pynchon, Christians reached toward this God of the heavens 'through the fashioning of suitable *confusions*' (my emphasis), that is, through the building of Bab-els. After the doubt which leads to the loss of belief in God, the modern, secular builders of Babel are still unable to reach the heavens. With im-proved technology but without a clear aim, the builders cannot transcend the Babylon of London. But it is not God who scatters the people in this postmodern parable. Rather it is we who scatter ourselves, driven not by God but by fear of our own cruelty, by fear of those who would seek to impose their language upon us and force us to build their tower of Babel, those with the power to descend, godlike from the sky, to destroy towers and cities in a single blast.

In our postmodern period, we have begun to celebrate our exile into the confusion of Babel. In a collection of essays on Genesis by contempo-rary writers, David Shapiro even asserts that 'secularists, modernists, and Spinozists like myself . . . customarily pray in the direction of the Tower of Babel.'[17]

---

[16] Pynchon, *Gravity's Rainbow*, 46.

[17] Shapiro, 'The Story,' 63.

From the Modern to the Postmodern Bible

But before continuing my study of postmodern prayers toward Babel, I first want to survey the contemporary landscape to analyze the transition from the modern to the postmodern Bible. Anthony Thiselton characterizes premodern hermeneutics as based on trust, modern hermeneutics as guided by doubt, and postmodern hermeneutics as dominated by suspicion.[18] Both the moderns and the postmoderns criticize the supposedly uncritical trust that premodern Christians had in the Bible as the word of God. The historical–critical method developed during the Enlightenment used modern rationalism and empiricism to raise doubts about the origins and meaning of Scripture.

Descartes, in pursuing his method of doubting everything possible to arrive at the certainty of first principles, uses philosophy to question premodern theology. Descartes inaugurates modern ontotheology in the introduction to his *Meditations on First Philosophy* by writing that 'I have always thought that two questions – that of God and that of the soul – are chief among those that ought to be demonstrated by the aid of philosophy rather than theology.'[19] Rather than looking to God's revelation toward us, Descartes seeks to reason his way up to God. Instead of allowing God to come and question him, Descartes questions the existence of God. Although he doesn't deny that God exists in the end, he uses the certitude he has in the existence of his autonomous ego to guarantee the existence of God. He believes that he can reach God by building upon classical foundationalism.

Spinoza uses Enlightenment rationalism to develop a modern biblical hermeneutics. He 'determined to examine the Bible afresh in a careful, impartial, and unfettered spirit, making no assumptions concerning it.'[20] Here is a powerful example of how the postmodern critique of the modern makes room for a return to theological hermeneutics.[21] Postmodern theory has taught us, correctly I think, that there is no such thing as a presuppositionless interpretation. A person's presuppositions or beliefs shape the way he or she interprets a text. Premodern Christian hermeneutics, supposedly 'precritical,' knew that one's faith or perspective on the world determined how one interpreted the biblical text.

---

[18] Thiselton, *New Horizons*, 143.

[19] Descartes, *Meditations*, 1.

[20] Spinoza, 'Tractatus,' 8.

[21] This return to a theological hermeneutic does not necessarily mean the establishment of a biblical fundamentalism, as R.P. Carroll argues in his critique of the neo-fundamentalist elements in postmodern culture ('Poststructuralist Approaches,' 51). For a sophisticated formulation of a renewed theological hermeneutics in biblical interpretation which avoids biblicism, see especially F. Watson, *Text*.

Spinoza is a seminal force in the creation of the modern Bible which reduces Scripture to a collection of myths, myths which according to Spinoza are useful only to teach morality to the uneducated masses.[22] Spinoza asserts that 'Revelation has obedience for its sole object, and therefore, in purpose no less than in foundation and method, stands entirely aloof from ordinary knowledge; each has its separate province, neither can be called the handmaid of the other.'[23] Like Heidegger after him, Spinoza seeks to free philosophy from its subordination as a handmaid to theology, the queen of the sciences in the medieval period.

Although he claims to be protecting Scripture as well as philosophy, Spinoza seeks to replace the God of the Bible with the god of ontotheology. According to Spinoza's 'presuppositionless' hermeneutics, 'The Israelites knew scarcely anything of God, although He was revealed to them.'[24] Using the historical-critical method, which assumes that Enlightenment rationalism and empiricism has correctly and comprehensively understood the world, Spinoza explains that precritical readings of the Bible are based upon the scientific ignorance of the Jews: 'if the Jews were at a loss to understand any phenomenon, or were ignorant of its cause, they referred it to God.'[25] Popkin explains how Spinoza 'totally secularized the Bible as a historical document.'[26] Spinoza inaugurates the historical-critical method that has dominated biblical scholarship for much of the past three centuries:[27]

> Thus having excluded any supernatural or divine element in the Biblical text, Spinoza's contextualism took on a radically different form than those before and after him who used similar materials to elucidate what they took to be a divinely inspired text. For Spinoza the meaning of what was related in Scripture was to be found, and exhausted, in elucidating the linguistic formulation, the historical context, and the personality of the Biblical author.[28]

Spinoza's hermeneutics are by no means without presuppositions. He begins and ends his work with the belief that reason 'is mistress . . . of the whole realm of truth.'[29]

---

[22] Spinoza, 'Tractatus,' 15.

[23] Ibid., 10.

[24] Ibid., 38.

[25] Ibid., 21.

[26] Popkin, 'Spinoza and Bible Scholarship,' 403.

[27] Cf. Frei, *The Eclipse*, 42. 'Spinoza's brilliant and prophetic 'Tractatus Theologico-Politicus' (1670) sets forth most of the important principles of an interpretation at once rationalistic and historical-critical which were to be developed over the course of the eighteenth century.'

[28] Ibid., 399.

[29] Ibid., 198.

Locke, born the same year as Spinoza, uses Enlightenment empiricism to question biblical revelation. He makes a distinction between original and traditional revelation. Original revelation is given directly by God who imprints his message upon the senses of the prophet, but when the prophet communicates this message to others, it becomes secondhand or traditional revelation. Consequently we have to use reason to determine if traditional revelation is based upon a genuine experience of an original revelation from God. For Locke, as it is for Spinoza, '*Reason* must be our last Judge and Guide in every Thing.'[30] While Locke himself determined that it was reasonable to trust the Scriptures as the word of God, Enlightenment reason will be used in deism and higher criticism of the Bible to raise doubts about the hermeneutics of faith practiced by premodern Christians.

After modern philosophy deems the Bible to be mythology, the distinction in premodern Christianity between sacred Scripture and human literature is brought into doubt. In the view of the Romantics, the Bible becomes a great work of literature. Prophets have always been poets and poets have always been prophets, but Shelley insists that prophecy is an attribute of poetry rather than poetry being an attribute of prophecy.[31] Literature takes over the role formerly played by religion. This marks the difference between philosophical modernity and literary modernism. Though both are based upon a secularization of Christian theology, 'Reading literature as scripture makes a late appearance because, unlike nature and history, which could be read as texts written by God, literature is humanly produced.'[32] In the Victorian period, Matthew Arnold declaims like an Old Testament prophet that 'There is not a creed which is not shaken, not an accredited dogma which is not shown to be questionable, not a received tradition which does not threaten to dissolve.' Therefore, 'The future of poetry is immense, because in poetry . . . our race, as time goes on, will find an ever surer and surer stay.'[33] In his confidence that the historical-critical method has destroyed the power of traditional, theological interpretations of the Bible, Arnold looks to literature to provide the values formerly provided by Christian readings of the Bible.

In the later Romantics and in literary modernism, literature becomes locked in a battle with religion as poets seek to usurp the role of the priests of culture from the church. Therefore, it is only late in the modern period that the Bible begins to be studied as literature. It is this view which has only recently begun to replace the dominance of historical-critical hermeneutics in academic study of the Bible. Robert Alter and Frank Kermode's work *The Literary Guide*

---

[30] Locke, *An Essay*, 704.
[31] Shelley, 'A Defense of Poetry.'
[32] Kort, *Take, Read*, 59.
[33] Arnold, 'Study of Poetry,' 603.

to the Bible criticizes the historical-critical method because it 'diverted attention from biblical narrative, poetry, and prophecy as *literature*, treating them instead as more or less distorted historical records.'[34] Alter and Kermode concede that we shouldn't ignore historical research, 'when they are relevant to their more literary purposes. Nor should it be supposed that we are careless of the religious character of the material under discussion simply because our aims are not theological.'[35] But their final goal is to combine historical and literary readings of the Bible to develop 'a revision of past readings, a *modern Bible.*'[36] In his earlier work on the gospels, Frank Kermode calls for literary readings of the Bible by 'secular critics' who don't have any 'doctrinal adhesion . . . unless it is that doctrinal adhesions are bad things.'[37] Thus the Bible as literature movement promotes itself as an alternative to theological as well as historical-critical readings of Scripture. In the chapter on the book of Genesis written for this modern Bible, J.P. Fokkelman begins his essay by noting that Genesis can be hard to understand for at least two reasons:

> The difficulties have not been diminished by two centuries of the so-called Higher Criticism, a historical-critical approach – an 'excavative scholarship,' as it has been called – that subjects the text to serious reduction. Philologists and historians are apt to regard the text as a source for something beyond itself because their proper interest or attention is directed to contextual realities. And theologians tend to read the text as message, and to that end separate form from content without realizing that in doing so they violate the literary integrity of the text.[38]

Thus Genesis is hard to understand for us moderns because of the distortions of theological and historical-critical readings. In developing a literary reading of Genesis, Fokkelman reads it as a story written by 'the creative writer responsible for the final version of the text.'[39]

In Robert Alter's 1981 work, *The Art of Biblical Narrative*, he also contrasts literary readings of the Bible with historical-critical and theological approaches, arguing that the view of the Bible as sacred history has been used to discourage literary readings of the Bible:

> The Hebrew Bible is generally perceived, with considerable justice, as sacred history, and both terms of that status have often been invoked to argue against the applicability to the Bible of the methods of literary analysis. If the text is sacred, if it was

---

[34] Alter and Kermode, *The Literary Guide*, 3.
[35] Ibid., 2.
[36] Ibid., 4 (my emphasis).
[37] Kermode, *The Genesis*, viii.
[38] Fokkelman, 'Genesis,' 36.
[39] Ibid.

grasped by the audiences for whom it was made as a revelation of God's will, perhaps of His literal words, how can one hope to explain it through categories developed for the understanding of such a fundamentally secular, individual, and aesthetic enterprise as that of later Western literature? And if the text is history . . . is it not presumptuous to analyze these narratives in the terms we customarily apply to prose fiction, a mode of writing we understand to be the arbitrary invention of the writer . . . ?[40]

While I believe Alter is closer to the truth when he reads the earliest Genesis narratives not as 'myth, legend, and folklore,' as the historical-critical method does, but rather as 'artfully conceived fiction,' I nevertheless believe that, in the end, it is a confusion of categories to read the Bible simply as 'a fiction made to resemble the uncertainties of life in history.'[41] The genre of the Bible as 'holy Scripture' must be taken into account.[42] T.S. Eliot was right when he asserted that those who read the Bible as literature 'are merely admiring it as a monument over the grave of Christianity.'[43]

This is not to say that an emphasis upon the literary qualities of the biblical texts has not had some positive consequences in the academic study of the Bible. Alter clearly articulates how a literary approach to the Bible benefits by using the techniques of close reading developed in the new criticism:

What role does literary art play in the shaping of biblical narrative? A crucial one, I shall argue, finely modulated from moment to moment, determining in most cases the minute choice of words and reported details, the pace of narration, the small movement of dialogue, and a whole network of ramified interconnections in the text.[44]

This application of the new critical practice of 'close reading' played an important role in reopening the biblical texts for modern culture. And just as the new critics emphasized the need to read a work of literature as a unity, so did Alter and others read the Bible as a unified text, like premodern Christians and unlike the theologians who used the historical-critical method to tear the Bible to shreds. Thus *The Literary Guide to the Bible* announces that 'the interpretation of the texts as they actually exist has been revalidated.'[45] Nicholas Wolterstorff describes how the dominance of the historical-critical method is 'now threatened by persistent questioning of some of its assumptions and by the emergence of various modes of Scripture interpretation which, each for its own

---

[40] Alter, *The Art*, 23.
[41] Ibid., 27.
[42] See Watson, *Text*, 227.
[43] Eliot, 'Religion and Literature,' 344.
[44] Alter, *The Art*, 3.
[45] Alter and Kermode, *The Literary Guide*, 4.

reasons, attends to the text itself rather than to that which lies behind the text. They converge around the text.'[46] Just as historical background is used by the new critics, despite their emphasis upon the text itself, so historical-critical hermeneutics can be used to help in the interpretation of the text of the Bible as we have it, as it has been canonized by the believing communities of Judaism and Christianity. Wolterstorff reminds us that 'it was part of the traditional practice of Christians to regard the Bible as *one book*,'[47] and literary readings of the Bible tend to follow this practice. In addition, literary readings of the Bible, despite their modernist, secular bias, have restored our sense of the power of the biblical texts. As Shapiro writes, 'So then, at least, we acknowledge the power of the stories.'[48]

While not doubted, the power of the biblical stories comes under extreme suspicion in postmodern biblical studies. *The Postmodern Bible* sees all interpretation as a 'power play,'[49] and the goal of the writers is 'to call reigning structures of power and meaning into question' by 'opening up biblical scholarship to literary and cultural critical theory.'[50] Regina Schwartz in her critique of the monotheism of the Bible acknowledges that 'We secularists have barely begun to acknowledge the biblical influence, confidently, and I think mistakenly, believing that a sharp division has been achieved between the premodern sacred worldview and the modern secular one.'[51] But with postmodern suspicion, Schwartz emphasizes the negative effects that the Bible has had upon western culture:[52]

> through the dissemination of the Bible in Western culture, its narratives have become the foundation of a prevailing understanding of ethnic, religious, and national identity as defined negatively, over against others . . . it has been the biblical narra-

---

[46] Wolterstorff, *Divine Discourse*, 16.

[47] Ibid., 204

[48] Shapiro, 'The Story,' 64.

[49] *The Postmodern Bible*, 3.

[50] Ibid., 4.

[51] Schwartz, *The Curse*, 6.

[52] I don't want to be unfair to Regina Schwartz's work on the Bible. She does write in the passage I cite that the influence of the Bible has also been for good as well as for ill. In addition, she concedes that 'It could be otherwise. In addition to Cain's legacy of violent identity formation against the Other, the Bible has much to teach us about how difficult it is to designate the foreigner and how permeable the boundaries of any people are' (9). But it is undeniable that Schwartz has emphasized what she calls 'the dark side of monotheism.' However Schwartz has said she is currently working on 'the bright side of monotheism,' that is, its emphasis upon charity. She has even written that 'it is the cultural appropriations, the acts of interpretation . . . and not necessarily the narratives themselves, that turn the Bible into a weapon' ('Teaching a Sacred Text,' 192).

tives, for better and for worse, that have wielded so much influence, even more than the classics, with the result that the Bible could be deployed against whatever 'Canaanites' people wanted to loathe, conquer, or exile.[53]

There's no doubt that this critique of the uses of Christian theology in western culture is valid. But I want to question with Kevin Vanhoozer whether it is 'the interpretation or the text which is oppressive?'[54] For the most part, postmodern interpretations of Scripture have been based upon suspicion of the text as well as its interpretations.

The Postmodern Bible, like earlier literary approaches, criticizes the historical-critical method because it 'brackets out the contemporary milieu [of the reader] and excludes any examination of the ongoing formative effects of the Bible.'[55] Ricoeur also criticizes the historical-critical method for ignoring the subsequent effect of the Bible on later readers and communities, as well as the subsequent effect of later readers on the Bible, or as he calls it, the 'trajectory' of the biblical text. In *Thinking Biblically*, Ricoeur and André LaCocque seek to combine the historical-critical method with insights taken from contemporary hermeneutical theory. They 'integrate into the method of historical-criticism one of the most interesting recent developments in biblical studies, which we may call attending to the *Wirkungsgeschichte* or even the *Nachgeschichte* of sacred texts,'[56] or what has been translated in Gadamer's *Truth and Method* as the effective history of the text. But while Ricoeur seeks to expand the historical-critical method, *The Postmodern Bible* sets itself in opposition to the modern 'scientific method' valorized in the Enlightenment, especially its desire for certainty.

The Postmodern Bible also sets itself in opposition to the earlier, more modernist readings of the Bible as literature. The writers note that Alter and Kermode's modernist Bible specifically excludes ideological critical theories such as Marxism, feminism, and deconstruction. In contrast, *The Postmodern Bible* asserts that 'there is no innocent reading of the Bible, no reading that is not already ideological.'[57] While I basically agree with this critique of supposedly objective, presuppositionless interpretations of the Bible, I find the word ideology here too tainted with postmodern suspicion. While he agrees that there are no interpretations without presuppositions, pre-understandings both conscious and unconscious, Werner Jeanrond, in his work *Theological Hermeneutics,* articulates the negative connotations associated with ideological interpretation:

---

[53] Schwartz, *The Curse*, x.
[54] Vanhoozer, 'The Spirit,' 151.
[55] *The Postmodern Bible*, 1.
[56] Ricoeur and LaCocque, *Thinking Biblically*, xi.
[57] *The Postmodern Bible*, 4.

Do we allow our pre-understanding to be challenged in the act of reading or do we impose it uncritically and violently on the text . . . ideological interpreters defend their particular 'readings' at all cost and remain hostile to all calls for a change of attitude, perspective or world-view.[58]

Consequently I prefer to refer to the role of 'beliefs' (rather than ideology) in interpretation, both the beliefs of the reader and the beliefs of the writer. Wolterstorff, in his study of *Divine Discourse*, argues that 'interpreters cannot operate without beliefs about the discourser; specifically, beliefs as to the relative probability of the discourser intending and not intending to say one thing and another.'[59] To help illustrate the role of belief in the interpretation of the Bible, I will compare and contrast premodern and postmodern interpretations of the Tower of Babel narrative in Genesis.

Bible or Babel

I will begin with an exegesis of the biblical narrative, an exegesis based upon what Thiselton calls 'believing reading,' which he defines as follows:

It is not that believers understand some new propositional content unknown to unbelievers or enquirers; it is that they . . . perceive themselves as *recipients or addressees* of directed acts of commitment, or of promise. They perceive the utterances in question as carrying with them illocutionary and extra-linguistic *consequences*.[60]

This kind of theological reading of Scripture seeks to supplement Scripture with the Holy Spirit, rather than with human reason. Vanhoozer, in ways similar to Thiselton and Wolterstorff, translates Calvin's description of the role of the Holy Spirit in the theological reading of Scripture into the language of speech-act theory. 'The Spirit convicts us that the Bible contains God's illocutions and enables us to respond to them as we ought.'[61] I call this type of exegesis a *spiritual* reading of Scripture, thereby emphasizing the need for the Holy Spirit and the practice of the spiritual life described in the Bible, in order to help us avoid violently imposing our own views upon the text or our own views of the text upon others.

Following the lead of canonical criticism of the Bible, I will emphasize the context within which the Babel narrative appears in the Bible. I will rely upon two commentaries, John H. Sailhamer's exegesis of Genesis in *The Expositor's*

[58] Jeanrond, *Theological Hermeneutics*, 6.
[59] Wolterstorff, *Divine Discourse*, 196.
[60] Thiselton, *New Horizons*, 598.
[61] Vanhoozer, 'The Spirit,' 156.

Bible Commentary and Gerhard von Rad's influential work on Old Testament theology. While I would categorize both readings as ultimately theological, Sailhamer makes use of literary analysis and von Rad uses the findings of historical-critical readings of Genesis to help them in their interpretation of the theology of the Old Testament.

Sailhamer reads the narrative of Genesis as a unified text and therefore emphasizes the placement of the Babel narrative within the story of humanity's creation and fall and God's plan for the redemption of the nations through the election of Israel.

> Although by itself the story of the building of Babylon makes good enough sense as the story of man's plans thwarted in God's judgment, its real significance lies in its tie to the themes developed in the surrounding narratives. The focus of the author since the beginning chapters of the Book of Genesis has been both on God's plan to bless mankind by providing him with that which is 'good' and on man's failure to trust God and enjoy the 'good' God had provided. The characteristic mark of man's failure up to this point in the book has been his attempt to grasp the 'good' on his own rather than trust God to provide it for him.[62]

Sailhamer further notes that the narrative of the creation and fall of humanity uses the direction 'eastward' to symbolize humanity's movement away from God. First Adam and Eve are sent east out of the garden for disobeying God. When Cain is punished for murdering his brother, he goes to live 'east of Eden,' and the narrative of the Tower of Babel emphasizes that Babylon was founded as 'men moved eastward' (Gen. 11:2).

> In light of such intentional uses of the notion of 'eastward' within the Genesis narratives, we can see that here too the author intentionally draws the story of the founding of Babylon into the larger scheme at work throughout the book . . . In the Genesis narrative, when man goes 'east,' he leaves the land of blessing . . .[63]

Von Rad also emphasizes the context of the Babel narrative, noting that it marks the end of primeval history and the beginning of saving history in Genesis. 'The story of the Tower of Babel is therefore to be regarded as the end of the road upon which Israel [and according to the text, humanity as a whole] stepped out with the Fall.'[64] LaCocque, in his exegesis of Genesis, notes the structural parallels which run through Genesis: 'Genesis 3 describes the break in the relationship between man and woman; chapter 4 between brothers; chapter 9:20–27 within the family, chapter 11:1–9 among peoples.'[65]

---

[62] Sailhamer, 'Genesis,' 105.
[63] Ibid., 104.
[64] Von Rad, *Old Testament Theology*, 163.
[65] LaCocque and Ricoeur, *Thinking Biblically*, 7.

Sailhamer continues his literary analysis by developing a close reading of the specific language used by the author of Genesis, arguing that 'the author has left the reader with definite, though subtle, indications of the story's meaning. The clues lie in the repetition of key words within the story.' Sailhamer develops a close reading of the narrative in order to answer the central question raised in interpretations of the story, that is the question concerning 'why God judged the builders of the city.'[66] And it is in answering this question that premodern and subsequent believing readers differ most substantially from postmodern interpreters.

Because believing readers have put their trust in the God revealed in the Bible, they believe that Yahweh had a good reason for punishing the builders of the Tower of Babel. The writer of the biblical narrative asserts that the Babylonians are building a city 'with a tower that reaches to the heavens, so that we may make a name for ourselves and not be scattered over the face of the whole earth' (Gen. 11:4). The Babylonians desire to achieve fame and glory. One's name in the Hebrew Bible refers to one's reputation. The builders are motivated by pride. Even the religious component of their motivation, the desire to reach the heavens, results from their rebellious pride.

Like Adam and Eve in the Garden of Eden, the Babylonians desire to be 'like gods.' And just as God intervenes in the Garden of Eden to prevent Adam and Eve from eating the fruit of the tree of life, so does he here intervene to prevent the success of the Babylonian project. While the Babylonians build the tower so that they will 'not be scattered,' Yahweh punishes them by making them unable to communicate and 'scattering them over the face of the earth.' According to Sailhamer's believing reading, 'God, who saw that their plans would succeed, moved to rescue them from those very plans and return them to the land and the blessing that awaited there.'[67] Wouldn't God's punishment be a blessing to those forced by a despotic power to build a tower for the glory of the ruling powers? But even if God didn't prevent humanity from eating from the tree of life and from constructing their tower up to the heavens as a way of 'rescuing' humanity, even if they are simply punishments, believing readers like Augustine have always interpreted the confusion of human languages to be the result of a '*merited* punishment'.[68]

In contrast, postmodern interpreters of the Babel narrative have blamed Yahweh rather than humanity, finding God to be ethically culpable. While David Shapiro's reading, largely as a result of the influence of rabbinic teaching, continues to see the confusion of languages as a genuine punishment, he does doubt God's motives. 'Perhaps even the supernal Draughtsman is silently

---

[66] Sailhamer, 'Genesis,' 104.

[67] Ibid., 105.

[68] Augustine, *City of God*, 667 (my emphasis).

jealous of the little humanist science below with its cognitive invasion of the sky.'[69]

Harold Bloom combines historical-critical and literary interpretations in order to read the Babel narrative as a 'summit of J's art.'[70] Thus J is ironically reaching for the heavens or the summit like the builders of the Tower of Babel. Bloom's reading, like Shapiro's, continues to be influenced by rabbinic exegesis; therefore, he can understand why Yahweh destroys the Tower of Babel. 'Her [J's] tower is a broken tower to begin with, since that which rises against Yahweh must be broken by Yahweh. Incommensurateness is, as always, her rhetoric and her theme alike. We are godlike or theomorphic, or can be, but we cannot be Yahweh . . . Babylon or babbling is where Yahweh wishes us to live, except insofar as we become children of Abraham.'[71] Bloom understands well why Yahweh sees the building of the Tower of Babel as an affront: 'The purpose is fame rather than rebellion against Yahweh, though to seek fame is necessarily to rebel against Yahweh.'[72] But in judging Yahweh, Bloom imposes his literary theory concerning the 'anxiety of influence' upon the text, and consequently, the theological meaning of the story is lost:

> Yahweh *is* irony, and not just the spirit of irony. Perhaps he is the irony of mere maleness, when seen from J's marvelous perspective. We are children always, and so we build the Tower of Babel. J's Yahweh is a child also, a powerful and uncanny male child, and he throws down what we build up.[73]

Moving from the 'perhaps' of modern doubt to the suspicion of postmodern hermeneutics, Bloom asserts Yahweh's moral flaws as if he were merely a character in J's story: 'he [YHWH] reveals again that he is, in J, an antithetical imp or sublime mischief-maker, in no way morally or spiritually superior to the builders of Babel.'[74] Bloom's J is not a religious writer at all but rather a literary writer whose main character is a vain and capricious Yahweh.[75]

Regina Schwartz, in her analysis of 'the violent legacy of monotheism,' also finds Yahweh morally culpable. Relying upon the modern hermeneutics of suspicion that sees God as a projection of human desire, Schwartz develops a

---

[69] Shapiro, 'The Story,' 68.
[70] Bloom and Rosenberg, *The Book of J*, 191.
[71] Ibid., 192.
[72] Ibid.
[73] Ibid.
[74] Ibid.
[75] For a critique of the reduction of God to a character in a novel in postmodern hermeneutics, see Watson, *Text*, 224–25. 'If one wishes to avoid this conclusion while maintaining the irreducibility of the final form of the text, it is necessary to speak of the text as *mediating* the reality of Jesus rather than as *constructing* it' (Watson's emphasis).

postmodern reading which blames monotheism for generating ethnic and imperialistic violence:

> the Bible offers its own critique of the Wizard of Oz . . . In this remarkable myth, the division of people into peoples is not in their interests, but in the interest of maintaining the power of a tyrannical, threatened deity jealously guarding his domain. How did the victorious monotheistic party miss that one . . . ?[76]

Schwartz uses the results of historical-critical reading, especially source criticism, to uncover an original polytheism which has been imperialistically destroyed by a conquering monotheism, an analysis learned from post-colonial theory in literary studies.

Here we see the uncritical postmodern valorization of multiplicity over unity. Monotheism, particularly Judeo-Christian monotheism, is blamed for 'turning allegiance to one god into the obliteration of other gods.'[77] In her commitment to the suspicion of monotheism, however, Schwartz is blind to the possibility that Babel itself represents the attempt to unify humanity under one dominant authority, an imperialistic attempt to subjugate the whole earth to its own power. In contrast, Fritz Lang shows greater insight into the narrative when in *Metropolis* he emphasizes the subjugation of the workers in his modern retelling of the Babel narrative, which make Hitler's enthusiastic response to the film and his desire to hire Lang to film the Nazi revolution horribly ironic. Schwartz, focusing upon the effect of the text (the reader's response) and ignoring the purpose of the narrative (the intent of the writer), blames the text rather than misinterpretations of the text for the glorification of imperialistic violence, even though she questions whether it could 'really be a coincidence that biblical higher criticism and the ideology of radical modern nationalism were born in the same period in the same place?'[78] Even though she can see that 'in nationalism, the religious is secularized, and the national sanctified,'[79] her work remains a critique of monotheism rather than nationalism.

In a more subtle interpretation, Jacques Derrida interprets the narrative as condemning 'the colonial violence or the linguistic imperialism' that Schwartz argues the text teaches. Derrida asserts elsewhere that, 'Had their enterprise succeeded, the universal tongue would have been imposed by violence, by force, by violent hegemony over the rest of the world.'[80] Derrida therefore reads the text as a parable or allegory of deconstruction:

---

[76] Schwartz, *The Curse*, 38.
[77] Ibid., 17.
[78] Ibid., 10
[79] Ibid., 13
[80] As quoted in Bartholomew, 'Babel and Derrida,' 310.

The 'tower of Babel' does not merely figure the irreducible multiplicity of tongues; it exhibits an incompletion, the impossibility of finishing, of totalizing, of saturating, of completing something on the order of edification, architectural construction, system and architectonics . . . There is then (let us translate) something like an internal limit to formalization, an incompleteness of the constructure. It would be easy and up to a certain point justified to see there the translation of a system of deconstruction.[81]

Derrida interprets this impossibility as structural, as true not only of the human but also the divine: 'it also constrains the deconstructor of the tower.'[82]

But in his commitment to the inescapability of difference, Derrida misreads the narrative. He ignores or refuses to believe the narrative when the writer asserts at the beginning of the narrative that 'Now the whole earth used the same language and the same words' (Gen. 11:1). Bartholomew asserts:

it is clear that Derrida makes no attempt to read the Tower of Babel narrative closely within its context in Genesis or within the Hebrew Bible as a whole. He fails, firstly, to note that the narrative deals with the descendants of Shem, Ham and Japheth and treats the story as though it is dealing just with the Shemites.[83]

Consequently Derrida reads the narrative as the story of Semitic imperialism over other peoples: 'Before the deconstruction of Babel, the great Semitic family was establishing its empire, which it wanted universal, and its tongue, which it also attempts to impose on the universe.'[84]

Derrida insists that 'before language, languages,' that is, the plurality of languages precedes the unity of language, or better, the desire for a single language.

In his premodern interpretation of the Babel narrative as 'inspired Scripture,' Augustine also interprets the tower of Babel as an imperialist project. But in his more careful reading of the narrative, Augustine does not assert, against the writer's explicit statement, that the builders of Babel were trying to impose their own language upon all other peoples: 'Now those nations, according to the narrative, possessed "their own languages". But despite that statement the narrator goes back to the time when all men had the same language; and then he explains how the diversity of languages arose.'[85] Augustine is still able to criticize the construction of the tower of Babel as an imperialist project. Referring back to the tenth chapter of Genesis, he sees the tower as

---

[81] Derrida, '*Des Tours*,' 165–166.

[82] Ibid., 184.

[83] Bartholomew, 'Babel and Derrida,' 313.

[84] Derrida, '*Des Tours*,' 167.

[85] Augustine, *City of God*, 656.

the project of Nimrod, who, 'with his subject peoples, began to erect a tower against the Lord, which symbolizes his impious pride.'[86] However, Augustine mistranslates Nimrod's name as referring to a mighty hunter 'against' the LORD, rather than as a mighty hunter 'before' the LORD. Therefore, he interprets the tower as a direct assault against God.

Derrida notes that 'Babel,' before it came to mean confusion and incoherent speech by way of a pun in Hebrew, signified the gate or city of God. This helps us to see that the tower of Babel might not signify primarily humanity's attempt to storm heaven and overthrow God.[87] The tower of Babel represents humanity's attempt to ascend to God on its own power. M.C. Escher's woodcut of the tower of Babel depicts a man with arms outstretched toward the heavens, highlighting the religious motivation of the builders.[88] And as Barth and Bonhoeffer have so forcefully reminded us, religion is humanity's most powerful idol. Thus Updike's divinity school professor correctly understands the meaning of the biblical narrative when he criticizes the graduate student trying to prove the existence of God: 'You're trying to make God stand at the end of some human path . . . You're building a Tower of Babel.' Yahweh confuses their language not because he is afraid they will succeed in overthrowing him, but rather because they will succeed in creating an idol. As Augustine writes, 'what harm could be done to God by any spiritual self-exaltation or material elevation however high it soared?'[89] The success of the tower would harm humanity, not God. God is 'jealous' not out of selfishness but out of love for humanity. Yahweh wants us to know him, but if we try to reach God through our own strength, we reach only an idol. *The tower of Babel is a physical representation of ontotheology, not deconstruction.*

While Derrida is perhaps right to see the narrative as the story of 'God deconstructing,'[90] Yahweh is deconstructing ontotheology, not language. If we focus upon the multiplication of languages as a curse, it can cause us, as Umberto Eco has shown it has, to search for the perfect language of paradise.[91] Eco observes that it is not until after the eleventh century 'that the story of the confusion came to be perceived not merely as an example of how divine justice humbled man's pride but as an account of a historical (or metahistorical) event.

---

[86] Ibid., 658.

[87] This interpretation is stressed in J.L. Kugel's attempt to reconstruct the traditional reading of the Bible as it was practiced 'from, roughly, the third century B.C.E. through the first century C.E., although some of the interpretations of the Bible found in them doubtless go back still earlier,' in *The Bible As It Was*.

[88] See White, *Masterpieces*, 20–21.

[89] Augustine, *City of God*, 658.

[90] Derrida, *Des Tours*, 170.

[91] Eco, *Serendipities*, 23–51.

It was now the story of how a real wound had been inflicted on mankind, a wound that might, in some way, be healed.'[92]

According to the Bible, Yahweh does want to bless humanity, but only Yahweh knows the way. Derrida is right when he argues that God punishes the builders of Babel 'for having wanted thus to *make a name for themselves*',[93] but not because he is jealous of humanity as the postmodern Bible teaches. The postmodern prophet Derrida asks rhetorically: 'Can we not, then, speak of God's jealousy? Out of resentment against that unique name and lip of men, he imposes his name.'[94] Bartholomew summarizes Derrida's misunderstanding of Yahweh in the narrative: 'Out of God's jealousy and resentment against that single and unique lip of men, says Derrida, Yahweh violently imposes *his name*.'[95] But Yahweh does not violently impose his name; rather, he prevents the builders of the metropolis and the tower of Babel from violently imposing their name upon others.

As Genesis moves from primeval history to saving history in the following verse, Yahweh speaks to Abram, demonstrating that his desire is to bless humanity, not to violently impose his name: 'Go forth from your country, and from your relatives and from your father's house, to the land which I will show you. And I will make you a great nation, and I will bless you, and make your name great; and so you shall be a blessing . . . And in you all the families of the earth will be blessed' (Gen. 12:1–3). Contra Schwartz, Yahweh does not desire to bless some and curse others; rather, his desire is to bless all the families of the earth. But he desires that we be truly blessed, rather than worshipping an idol that cannot save.

On the day of Pentecost recorded in Acts, God reverses the confusion of Babel as his Holy Spirit descends upon the apostles. In order to help them proclaim the true way to heaven, Yahweh does not impose a single language but rather enables those gathered to understand one another, despite the confusion of tongues. 'Pentecost signifies the reverse of Babel, to be consummated in the new heavens and new earth in which linguistic pluralism celebrates the Messiah.'[96] In the book of Revelation, God's final pronouncement upon Babylon is announced: Like a great millstone thrown into the sea,

---

[92] Ibid., 29.

[93] Derrida, *Des Tours*, 169 (his emphasis).

[94] Ibid., 170.

[95] Bartholomew, 'Babel and Derrida,' 309. Bartholomew further points out that 'Derrida here follows Chouraqui's most unusual translation at this point in taking *Babel* to be God's name which God proclaims over the city! Generally Babel is taken to be the city's name, but according to Derrida, God punishes the people by proclaiming *his* name, Babel'. Later Bartholomew argues that this interpretation is 'virtually indefensible' (314).

[96] Ibid., 328.

'So will Babylon, the great city, be thrown down with violence, and will not be found any longer' (Rev. 18:21). But in the place of Babylon, the new Jerusalem, the city of God, *comes down* out of heaven and descends upon the earth: John is shown by the Spirit 'the holy city, Jerusalem, *coming down out of heaven from God*' (Rev. 21:10). And while the violent and unclean are excluded, the gates of the city are left open not only to Israel but also to 'the nations' (Rev. 21:25).

Bibliography

Alter, R., *The Art of Biblical Narrative* (New York: Basic Books, 1981)

Alter, R., and F. Kermode (eds.), *The Literary Guide to the Bible* (Cambridge, MA.: Harvard University Press, 1990)

Arnold, M., 'The Study of Poetry' in H. Adams (ed.), *Critical Theory Since Plato* (Fortworth: Harcourt Brace Jovanovich, rev. edn. 1992), 603–607

Augustine, *City of God*, tr. H. Bettenson (New York: Penguin Books, 1984)

Barth, K., *The Christian Life*, tr. G.W. Bromiley (Grand Rapids: Eerdmans, 1981)

Bartholomew, C.G., 'Babel and Derrida,' *TynBul* 49.2 (1998), 305–328

Bloom, H., and D. Rosenberg, *The Book of J* (New York: Grove Weidenfeld, 1990)

Caputo, J.D., and M.J. Scanlon (eds.), *God, The Gift, and Postmodernism* (Bloomington: Indiana University Press, 1999)

Carroll, R.P., 'Poststructuralist Approaches' in J. Barton (ed.), *The Cambridge Companion to Biblical Interpretation* (Cambridge: Cambridge University Press, 1998), 50–66

Derrida, J., *Of Grammatology*, tr. G.C. Spivak (Baltimore: The Johns Hopkins University Press, 1976)

—, '*Des Tours de Babel*,' tr. J.F. Graham, in J.F. Graham (ed.), *Difference in Translation* (Ithaca: Cornell University Press, 1985), 165–248

Descartes, R., *Meditations on First Philosophy*, tr. D.A. Cress (Indianapolis: Hackett, 1979)

Eco, U., *Serendipities*, tr. W. Weaver (San Diego: Harcourt Brace, 1998)

Eliot, T.S., 'Religion and Literature' in idem *Selected Essays* (San Diego: Harcourt Brace Jovanovich, 1960), 343–354

Feuerbach, L., *The Essence of Christianity*, tr. G. Eliot (New York: Harper & Row, 1957)

Fokkelman, J.P., 'Genesis' in R. Alter, and F. Kermode (eds.), *The Literary Guide to the Bible* (Cambridge, MA.: Harvard University Press, 1990), 36–55

Frei, H.W., *The Eclipse of Biblical Narrative* (New Haven: Yale University Press, 1974)

Gabel, J.B., et al., *The Bible as Literature: An Introduction* (New York: Oxford University Press, 1996[3])

Gadamer, H.-G., *Truth and Method* (New York: Crossroad, 1975)

Heidegger, M., *Identity and Difference*, tr. J. Stambaugh (New York: Harper & Row, 1969)

Ingraffia, B., *Postmodern Theory and Biblical Theology: Vanquishing God's Shadow* (Cambridge: Cambridge University Press, 1995)

Jeanrond, W.G., *Theological Hermeneutics: Development and Significance* (New York: Crossroad, 1991)

Kant, I., *Critique of Pure Reason*, tr. J.M.D. Meiklejohn (London: Dent, 1986)

Kermode, F., *The Genesis of Secrecy: On the Interpretation of Narrative* (Cambridge, MA.: Harvard University Press, 1979)

Kort, W., *'Take, Read': Scripture, Textuality, and Cultural Practice* (University Park: Penn State University Press, 1996)

Kugel, J.L. *The Bible As It Was* (Cambridge, MA.: Harvard University Press, 1999)

LaCocque, A., and P. Ricoeur, *Thinking Biblically*, tr. D. Pellauer (Chicago: University of Chicago Press, 1998)

Locke, J., *An Essay Concerning Human Understanding*, ed. P. H. Nidditch (Oxford: Oxford University Press, 1975)

Popkin, R.H., 'Spinoza and Bible Scholarship' in D. Garrett (ed.), *The Cambridge Companion to Spinoza* (Cambridge: Cambridge University Press, 1996), 383–407

Pynchon, T., *Gravity's Rainbow* (New York: Viking, 1973)

Rad, G. von, *Old Testament Theology*, vol. 1, tr. D.M.G. Stalker (San Francisco: HarperCollins, 1962)

Ricoeur, P., and A. LaCoque, *Thinking Biblically*, tr. D. Pellauer (Chicago: University of Chicago Press, 1998)

Sailhamer, J.H., 'Genesis' in G.E. Gaebelein (ed.), *The Expositor's Bible Commentary*, vol. 2 (Grand Rapids: Zondervan, 1990)

Shapiro, D., 'The Story of the Tower of Babel' in D. Rosenberg (ed.), *Genesis As It Is Written: Contemporary Writers on Our First Stories* (SanFrancisco: HarperCollins, 1996), 63–70

Schwartz, R.M., *The Curse of Cain: The Violent Legacy of Monotheism* (Chicago: University of Chicago Press, 1997)

—, 'Teaching a Sacred Text as Literature, Teaching Literature as a Sacred Text' in P. Franklin (ed.), *Profession 1998* (New York: MLA, 1998), 186–198

Shelley, P.B., 'A Defense of Poetry' in H. Adams (ed.), *Critical Theory Since Plato* (Fortworth: Harcourt Brace Jovanovich, rev. edn 1992), 516–529

Spinoza, B., 'Tractatus Theologico-Politicus' in *The Chief Works of Benedict de Spinoza*, tr. R.H.M. Elwes (New York: Dover, 1951)

The Bible and Culture Collective (G. Aichele, F.W. Burnett, et al.), *The Postmodern Bible* (New Haven: Yale University Press, 1995)

Thiselton, A., *New Horizons in Hermeneutics* (Grand Rapids: Zondervan, 1992)

Updike, J., *Roger's Version* (New York: Ballantine, 1986)

Vanhoozer, K.J., 'The Spirit of Understanding: Special Revelation and General Hermeneutics,' in R. Lundin (ed.), *Disciplining Hermeneutics: Interpretation in Christian Perspective* (Grand Rapids: Eerdmans, 1997), 131–165

Watson, F., *Text, Church, and World: Biblical Interpretation in Theological Perspective* (Grand Rapids: Eerdmans, 1994)

Westphal, M., *Suspicion and Faith: The Religious Uses of Modern Atheism* (Grand Rapids: Eerdmans, 1993)

—, 'Overcoming Onto-theology' in J.D. Caputo and M.J. Scanlon (eds.) *God, the Gift, and Postmodernism* (Bloomington: Indiana University Press, 1999), 146–169

White, K.J., *Masterpieces of the Bible* (Grand Rapids: Baker Book House, 1997)

Wolterstorff, N., *Divine Discourse: Philosophical Reflections on the Claim That God Speaks* (Cambridge: Cambridge University Press, 1995)

15

Imagination and Responsible Reading

Trevor Hart

To be human, we are often told nowadays, is to have our distinctive mode of being 'in communion'.[1] For the purposes of this chapter I am content simply to acknowledge that in some fundamental and vital sense this is so. To the extent that it is so, however, it follows that an activity basic (rather than accidental) to our humanity is that of relating to others. To be human, of course, is not simply to 'be related' in the passive sense, as the two telegraph poles outside my study window are 'related' in various ways to one another. To be human is *actively* to relate, as I must relate to my son Jonathan whose ninth birthday falls tomorrow, and who has spent much of the past few days sharing with me the burden of his hopes and desires in the expectation that some, at least, of the burden may transmit successfully across the gap which separates his world from mine, and evoke a suitable parental response (almost certainly involving *Star Wars* paraphernalia!). In the field of the human, relatedness has a moral as well as a 'natural' dimension, and at its heart lie the continuous attempts to understand and, reciprocally, to communicate with the other on which we all expend so much effort, consciously or otherwise. We are engaged in what might be described as an endless series of bids for self-transcendence,[2] seeking to move out beyond

---

[1] See, e.g., Macmurray, *Persons*, Moltmann, *Trinity*, Zizioulas, *Being as Communion*, McFadyen, *Call to Personhood*, Ricoeur, *Oneself as Another*, Torrance, *Persons in Communion*.

[2] For purposes of clarification I should state at the outset that I do not use this phrase in the technical sense invested in it, for example, by Karl Rahner. I mean, simply, that relationship to human persons entails the moral aspect of reaching out beyond the identifiable boundaries of selfhood deliberately to engage with otherness. It might be argued that, since my case supposes personhood to be constituted and sustained precisely in relation (rather than in isolation), this activity of reaching out is better

the apparent limits of our own particularity without abandoning or losing it, and to enter into or overlap more fully with the particularity of the other. I shall suggest duly that imagination is vital to this quintessentially human activity.

Understanding and Otherness: Problems and Possibilities

We are concerned chiefly at this consultation with questions pertaining to the status of texts as (whatever else they may be held to be for our purposes, at least) the media of such human exchanges. Texts (their composition and interpretation) represent, in literate societies, a fair proportion of our most significant bids to relate to others, appropriating to our purpose the tools of a publicly acknowledged linguistic currency. Hence 'hermeneutics' (a discipline or set of practices intended deliberately to minimize the risks or reduce the margins of failure in such exchanges) has tended to focus mostly on the interpretation of texts. But, as Schleiermacher saw, some analogous practice occurs (and must occur) much more widely, whenever one person relates to another (as an other) through symbolic media. (Schleiermacher focuses mainly on language, but admits that other types of 'personal influence' are equally desirous of careful interpretation if understanding is to follow.) Thus, the skilful interpretation of a text 'has no other goal than we have in listening to any piece of everyday speech'.[3] Both are ways in which we seek to understand, and thereby to facilitate appropriate patterns of relatedness to, the other.

Of course, face-to-face encounter with the living voice of the other often entails no *conscious* effort to translate whatsoever. Effort is only required where difficulty is apparent or misunderstanding most likely, and many of our daily oral exchanges do not fall into this category. Even when they do, the presence of the other to whom we are relating often makes further interrogation and immediate clarification possible. On the other hand, the very fact that we choose to cast certain things in textual form is an indication of our desire to say something quite carefully and precisely, and a recognition of the danger of

---

described as 'self-constitution' than 'self-transcendence' (the latter possibly being taken to indicate a ringfenced 'self' which first exists and must subsequently be 'transcended' or broken away from). In principle I have no difficulty with such an alternative phraseology, although it bears its own ambiguities, and would need to be worked out and defined more fully than is possible here. The paradox of a dynamic selfhood being ever more fully realized in the very act of its apparent 'breaching' lies at the heart of this chapter. If I prefer the language of 'self-transcendence' here, therefore, it is chiefly for its suggestion of a dynamic motion of exploration and return which, while there is an aspect of it which is as natural and inevitable as breathing, nonetheless has dimensions of a highly moral sort.

[3] Schleiermacher, *Hermeneutics and Criticism*, 21.

being misunderstood or 'saying the wrong thing'. We tend mostly, therefore, to be more conscious of both the need and the opportunity to interpret carefully when we approach a text than we are in face-to-face encounters with the living other. In fact, though, we produce lots of trivial and mundane texts requiring little of those who read them ('Gone for lunch – back at 2'), and can all think of conversations we have had where the presence of the living voice was of little practical benefit, and we left the exchange none the wiser than when we approached it. So we should not press the distinction too far, and are best advised to think more broadly of hermeneutics as furnishing us with a set of tools for making sense of all discourse, whether spoken or written.

It is not even helpful to limit the scope of our definition to 'all difficult discourse', since, as Schleiermacher maintains, in the strictest sense we should assume that 'misunderstanding results as a matter of course and . . . understanding must be desired and sought at every point'.[4] To hold this is not to suggest that all misunderstanding is significant, or that we should subject each apparently transparent utterance to a rigorous hermeneutic of suspicion. Such a project would make daily life both impractical and depressingly cynical! It is simply to recognize that every act of communication involves both parties in some responsible activity, even though it may often be so small as to go unnoticed on the part of either. As George Steiner argues, every act of understanding has the logical form of an act of translation, even though it may be intra- rather than inter-lingual, and no matter how unaware we may be of the fact of our performing the act.[5] Furthermore, if our ultimate purpose in understanding is to grasp *fully* what the other who expresses herself through utterance wishes to communicate,[6] then there is a sense in which in all but the most mundane and transparent of utterances (and perhaps even in these) we are bound to some degree of failure, since the 'fully' eludes even our most careful attempts to fathom it. If hermeneutics is indeed 'the art of putting oneself in possession of all the conditions of understanding' in this sense,[7] then it must be admitted at once (and Schleiermacher readily admits) that it is an art which can never achieve its goal, since 'every utterance is to be understood only via the whole life to which it belongs',[8] and in both its grammatical/objective aspects and its psychological/subjective aspects each such life is open-ended and in constant development, so that the task of

---

[4] Ibid., 22.

[5] Steiner, *After Babel*, 28f.

[6] '[T]he same thing in the [inner] thought which the utterer wanted to express' (Schleiermacher, *Hermeneutics and Criticisms*, 233).

[7] Ibid., 227. See also his bold insistence that the task of hermeneutics is 'to understand the utterance at first just as well and then better than its author', ibid., 23.

[8] Ibid., 9.

putting ourselves in the place of the author/other[9] is one which can at best be approximated to.[10]

The problems involved here (and the opportunities which enable us to respond to them) arise largely out of the complex relationships between general and particular aspects in the field of the human. For convenience we may disentangle three levels at which this distinction has significance: our own personhood, our experience of the world, and the ways in which language functions with respect to these.

In making sense of the world as we experience it, we are constantly involved in the tracing of patterns, identifying and making connections between discrete things. We trace both similarities (when we see two or more things as in some sense 'the same sort' of thing or even 'the same thing' when we posit a relationship of identity between two temporally discrete perceptions) and differences. In the strict sense no two objects of experience are ever *precisely* the same, so when we classify them as belonging to the same class (species, genus, type, etc.) we are effectively saying that the degree of similarity or overlap between the pattern each manifests is high, and of far greater significance than the genuine differences which nonetheless remain.[11] Since our use of language is inseparable from such judgements, the fashioning and deployment of common nouns, adjectives, adverbs and the like amounts in effect to a tacit conspiracy in which it is agreed to overlook degrees of difference up to a

---

[9] See ibid., 24.

[10] This inevitability of failure does not make this notional 'goal' in itself fruitless. On the contrary, held out before us as an ideal, it helps to keep our vision focused clearly on the mysterious depths of otherness, and prevents us from falling into the error of the complacent supposition that we have been entirely successful. Even the most successful of our bids for understanding must remain provisional and partial. Otherwise we may cease to adopt an attitude of attending or listening to the other, and impose our own perspectives onto him instead. It is true, of course, that interpretation may have many different 'goals' in different circumstances, and that a more obvious common goal might be described as 'grasping what someone is saying so as to be able to respond to their utterance (to relate to them) in an appropriate manner'. The point of Schleiermacher's apparent concern with fathoming the personal particularity of the other will be touched on again below.

[11] As I hope will be clear in what follows, I do not intend in this paragraph to endorse the postmodern preference for 'nominalist' over 'realist' accounts of ontology. What I have said is consistent with the claim that 'universals' of some sort exist. 'Overlooking difference up to a certain level' and 'discerning universality' may be taken to be two ways of saying the same thing. My point in what follows, though, will be that, if they do exist (i.e. if this is a helpful way of speaking about what is shared between particulars), 'universals' nonetheless never exist in the world in any pure or abstract form, but are mixed up with particularity in ways which are highly significant for our bids to understand otherness.

certain level in the interests of meaning. In the cases of analogical or metaphorical uses of terms we go further and transgress the conventional limits, permitting the application of common terms where the perceived levels of similarity are identifiably more slender. What we are doing in each case, though, is using words to chart or construct patterns of similarity and difference,[12] and thereby ordering our world into a meaningful whole for common indwelling.

The particularity which nonetheless marks this world in our experience of it is related, at least in part, to the particularity which marks our own personhood. The fact that we each occupy unique centres of perspective on the world, that our humanity is realized as a non-substitutable nexus within complex webs of relationships, that who and what we are is (as Ricoeur reminds us) constituted by and emerges in a narrative shaped by a radically particular cumulative stock of experiences, choices, actions, commitments, memories and hopes,[13] that we possess, as it were, a hypostatic fingerprint which goes way beyond the structure of our DNA, all this must be held in tension with the senses in which we may deem ourselves to share or indwell a common humanity or a common social tradition, and thus inhabit a shared world. Of course the matter must not be overstated (as it can be and often is), not least because, ironically, our very uniqueness as persons is constituted in significant part by our being related and relating to others. As David Ford writes: 'We live before the faces of others. Some are there physically, others in memory or anticipation. We have been formed face to face from our earliest days, deeper than conscious memory.'[14] This does not detract from but rather reinforces our own identity (*ipse*-identity in Ricoeur's phrase)[15] as the particular person we are and no other can ever be or become. It grants us an experience of the world and objects and events within it which no other can fully share, and we might therefore say that language, in deliberately overlooking the perspectival particularities which mark the world, thereby also overlooks the irreducibly particular dimensions of personhood, and attends instead to various levels at which some commonwealth of experience and outlook seem to be identifiable. Such deliberate oversight succeeds to the extent that our particularity has little practical bearing on our utterance, and fails to the extent that the significances run deeper perhaps than even the utterer, let alone the receiver and interpreter of utterance, is aware.

Language, we might say, is a necessary compromise which overlooks particularity in the interest of meaningful communication, and thereby facilitates a

---

[12] The question of the relative degrees of discovery and construction in our dealings with the world is one which cannot detain us here.

[13] Ricoeur, *Oneself as Another*, 115f.

[14] Ford, *Self and Salvation*, 17.

[15] See Ricoeur, *Oneself as Another*, 2.

properly human way of being in the world in relation. Yet appeals to the significance of belonging (or not belonging) to a particular community which shares
a 'common language' can easily be exaggerated. As persons who relate to
others, our identity is shaped at many levels, and many theoretical boundaries
of belonging and exclusion may be identified on a spectrum ranging from our
radically particular personhood to the most universal aspects of our humanity.
Although languages are an easily identifiable (and therefore convenient) symbolic marker of one level of our particular location as human persons (NB the
way languages function paradoxically both as a tool of reaching out to the other
and an efficient means of excluding those who do not belong to our group), the
significance of other levels should not be overlooked. Languages may be
common to (and even definitive of) particular human groups, but to some
extent the idea of a 'common language' is itself a fiction, since the ways in
which we deploy the language which we inherit and inhabit, and the sense of
the things which we say (or, if preferred, the 'noematic content of our speech
acts'[16]) are marked – more or less significantly, to be sure, but marked nonetheless – by other levels of our particular personhood.

This is true, for example, at the level of our belonging to groups *within* the
wider communities marked out by linguistic boundaries. An important part of
our personal identity consists in the 'set of *acquired identifications* by which the
other enters into the composition of the same'.[17] We each identify with many
such smaller communities: the nuclear family, the tribe, a football club, a political party, the church, some professional guild, or whatever. In some sense we
'recognize ourselves' in the ends, values, patterns of behaviour which characterize such groups. But part of such 'identifications with' is often the inheritance of a peculiar pattern of language use and associative context, each group
generating its own 'thesaurus', tacit familiarity with which is part and parcel of
what belonging to it means.[18] Non-members are not expected (perhaps not
intended) to share its secrets. Deliberately or otherwise, it effectively excludes
the uninitiated. At the level of our individuality (which includes but goes
beyond such membership) matters are equally ambiguous. As Steiner observes:

> No two human beings share an identical associative context. Because such a context
> is made up of the totality of an individual existence, because it comprehends not
> only the sum of personal memory and experience but also the reservoir of the par-
> ticular subconscious, it will differ from person to person. There are no facsimiles of
> sensibility, no twin psyches . . . Every counter of communication carries with it a
> potential or externalized aspect of personal content.[19]

---

[16] See Wolterstorff, *Divine Discourse*, 191.
[17] Ricoeur, *Oneself as Another*, 121.
[18] See Steiner, *After Babel*, 180.
[19] Ibid., 178–179.

In addition, therefore, as Schleiermacher observes, our utterance, as well as being shaped by the givenness of the language within which it is cast, has a reflexive shaping influence upon its linguistic environment (language being a dynamic organism and not a static system). Thus 'every person is . . . a location in which a given language forms itself in an individual manner'.[20] While, therefore, the notion of 'a private language' may be highly problematic, and while in practice every deployment of language for the purposes of relating to others is formally constrained by the public dimensions of language, it is nonetheless clear that the living reality of language must be viewed as made up of many layers ranging from the most general and shared to the most private 'concentric spheres of association'.[21]

Human acts of communication are like icebergs. Statements are cast out and retrieved 'at the surface' (of language and of our selves), but there is a vast hidden expanse which supports them invisibly, both in the case of the utterance and its responsible reception. Sometimes the significance of utterance is relatively shallow, and appropriation of it uncomplicated. But sometimes the hidden depths of association are vital to the bearing of its sense, either deliberately (when we assume the presence/absence of a particular associative set on the part of our readers/hearers) or tacitly (when words trigger for us associations or resonances the radical particularity of which we may ourselves remain unaware of). When depth matters in this way, the possibility arises within a 'common language' of exclusive rather than inclusive utterance. We run up against the paradox again: language is both a tool of the human need to relate to the other, but equally a marker of levels of particular belonging which (initially at least) distance us from the other. Hence the manifest need for *translation* at various levels, and the possibility of misunderstanding.

It is from a blunt recognition of this that Schleiermacher's account of the 'art of understanding' departs. He occupies an elusive position with respect to some of the debates which occupy contemporary hermeneutics. While he has a foot in the Romantic camp, he departs from the apparently odd and remarkably ambitious notion that interpretation has as its practical aim a mapping of the other's psychology or 'inner life'. Utterance is only rarely a matter of seeking to express some hidden fact of our own 'spirit', and far more commonly a matter of referring others to realities in a shared world. Hence the attention which, he insists, must be directed to the role of grammar and the objective/public dimensions of language (see below). Yet Schleiermacher certainly cannot be drafted into service by purely formalist accounts of meaning as a linguistic 'fact' to be discerned by observation of grammatical rules alone. Language is a personal, as well as a public, human phenomenon. And, as R.G.

---

[20] Schleiermacher, *Hermeneutics and Criticism*, 8.

[21] Steiner, *After Babel*, 180.

Collingwood (whose 'expressionist' theory of meaning is misunderstood if it be taken to rule out any significant objective or public dimension) insists, that which lies in the shared world is nonetheless experienced by particular persons in particular ways, and in this sense every reference to this world nonetheless has an irreducible personal and 'subjective' component, and is a bringing to expression of something mediated by our 'inner life'.[22] This means that responsible interpretation must hold both public and particular dimensions in a dynamic tension. If we would understand what people are *saying* (which, it might reasonably be suggested, is the proper immediate object of understanding rather than the 'persons' themselves), we can nonetheless hardly bracket out of consideration the particular persons who are saying it. So, Schleiermacher cannot dispense with the 'subjective/psychological' aspects (what we have preferred to call the personal particularity) of utterance in his hermeneutics, even though he admits from the outset the impossibility of complete success here. We can never understand an utterance 'fully', because in order to do so we should have to fathom the depths of the other's particularity completely, tracing every resonance to its end in the unique combination of factors which constitute personhood. It is not in any case clear that success of this sort would be desirable were we able to achieve it, since it would in some sense entail an abrogation of the other's particularity and an abandonment of ours. What we seek in our bids for understanding is sufficient depth of insight to enable us to relate properly to the other who speaks.

It would thus be perfectly possible to define the goals of understanding differently and in less rigorous terms than Scheiermacher does, thereby setting ourselves up neatly to be able to claim far higher levels of success. I suspect, though, that his pitching of notional standards high (arguably impossibly so[23]) and boldly facing the charge of constant failure in the technical sense is preferable; for in doing so he keeps us alert to the ever-present possibility of levels of misunderstanding which, while they may sometimes matter very little if at all for practical purposes, may often matter more than we recognize, and may be avoidable more often than we care to admit.

The fact that 'translation' or 'understanding' is 'not always possible and never perfect'[24] is not, though, a reason for exaggerating the problems which face us in the task, let alone for the sort of pessimism which posits insurmountable 'ugly ditches' of one sort or another and, in a counsel of despair, urges the abandonment of effort and a resort to 'playing with' utterances and texts

---

[22] See Collingwood, *Principles of Art*, esp. chs. 6, 11 and 14.

[23] '[T]o understand the utterance at first just as well and then better than its author' (Schleiermacher, *Hermeneutics and Criticism*, 23).

[24] Steiner, *After Babel*, 264.

instead. Recognition that every act of communication-understanding, every bid to relate to the human other, entails some level of translation, however slight, drives the logic of such proposals finally in the direction of a solipsism in which there is no one left to play with but ourselves, the task of transcending our personal particularity and engaging with otherness being one which we deem ourselves incapable of. Of course the momentum ought to be precisely the other way around. What Steiner refers to as the weight of 'abundant, vulgar fact', that 'We *do* speak of the world and to one another. We *do* translate intra- and inter-lingually and have done so since the beginning of human history'[25] undercuts any suggestion that the transcendence of our particularity (personal, sexual, social, ethnic, historical or whatever) is too difficult or impossible for us to achieve, and encourages us to make the effort even when it is clear that the difficulties are substantial and the potential for misunderstanding considerable. To give up on these grounds is in effect to turn our backs on what it means to be human, and the practical consequences of doing this in various spheres of life are easy enough to see, let alone imagine. Even if 'full understanding' of the other in Schleiermacher's notional sense is possible for God alone, the fact that we can approximate to it and can achieve some level of success even when the task is difficult, is vital to human well-being. When we are face to face with the living other, especially the other whose very otherness is more immediately apparent than any common 'nature' or shared experience between us, we have a duty to venture out into the 'far country' of their particularity in pursuit of the imaginative resources to love our neighbour as ourselves.

Migration between Nominatives: Imagination and Understanding

In his poem 'Swallows',[26] R.S. Thomas offers us a suggestive image for what Steiner calls the 'hermeneutic motion'.[27] Our encounters with otherness are endless migrations out from our particular 'perches of bone' only to return, eventually, with our own particularity enhanced, identifiably the same and yet somehow different. Steiner's preferred metaphor is that of a voyage of discovery and invasion of the world of the other, a voyage from which, like the imperial armies of old, we return bearing exotic trophies of our success, importing into our own world cargo which may infect it with alien and uncomfortable ideas and ways of seeing things, and telling colourful tales of the remarkable things we have seen and experienced so far from home. Such images draw

---

[25] Ibid.
[26] Thomas, *No Truce*, 49.
[27] Steiner, *After Babel*, 312f.

attention to the nature of every bid for understanding of the other as essentially a journey of imagination in which we are granted the capacity to transcend the boundaries of our own particularity and to engage with otherness in ways which plot something of its difference, before finally returning to ourselves with our horizons broadened and our 'self' in some sense more rounded and complete through the venture.

For this reason it might be argued that a training in the 'art of understanding' ought always to incorporate engagement with imaginative literature of one sort or another as a means to the cultivation of a disciplined imagination. For, what a great novel or poem does, in effect, is precisely to take the reader on journeys of imaginative self-transcendence, to lift us out of ourselves and relocate us temporarily somewhere else; to show us things we had not seen before, or familiar things now looking quite different because viewed from an unfamiliar perspective. The poet (using the term now inclusively for all creative writers) enlarges our vision, tracing patterns, threads and connexions which stretch out beyond the horizons of our known world, and leading us out (as we trace them with him) into the complex structure of things until, at last, we find ourselves in quite unfamiliar territory, our imagination stretched, sometimes to breaking point. Upon our return we discover that, while we are the same person we were, our personhood has nonetheless been transfigured in some way by the experience. We have seen and tasted more of reality than we had previously, and the texture and colour of our own world presents itself differently as a result.

Literature is, according to Ricoeur, 'a vast laboratory for thought experiments'[28] in which, under carefully controlled conditions, we are subjected to all manner of possible (and sometimes impossible) variations on human experience and outlook. As we read, we effectively leave our 'selves' behind in suspended animation and move out to become, in our imagination, someone other than ourselves. Sometimes we 'become' the central character about whom we are reading, identifying ourselves with their actions and experiences. The form of the novel facilitates this more fully than any other because (especially through the assumption of the voice of the grammatical first person) its narrative is able to put us inside the heads of its characters until we know them as well as they know themselves. The author can achieve this imaginative transition in her readers because she is the creator of her characters and responsible for fashioning their identity. She can fill out the picture from her position of authorial omniscience and omnipotence, granting us opportunities for indwelling alien particularity to a degree which could never arise in our real-life encounters with otherness.

---

[28] Ricoeur, *Oneself as Another*, 148.

C.S. Lewis, reflecting on the benefits of such imaginary migration between nominatives concludes that in and through it we seek and are granted

> an enlargement of our being. We want to be more than ourselves . . . We want to see with other eyes, to imagine with other imaginations, to feel with other hearts, as well as with our own . . . The man who is contented only to be himself, and there-fore less a self, is in prison. My own eyes are not enough for me, I will see through those of others . . . Literary experience heals the wound, without undermining the privilege, of individuality . . . in reading great literature I become a thousand men and yet remain myself. Here, as in worship, in love, in moral action, and in know-ing, I transcend myself; and am never more myself than when I do.[29]

Of course our being is enlarged more, and we are rendered more fully our-selves, by encounters with real rather than imaginary other or others; but the vital point is that both are encounters which occur through an *imaginative* engagement, and the *imaginary* or fictional, by virtue of its controlled and delib-erate nature and the possibilities of a more intimate becoming which the narra-tor's omniscience affords, can equip and train us better to handle our engagements with the actual others who face us in our lives.

According to Schleiermacher, hermeneutics must attend to two distinct levels of the other's particularity at once. It must adopt what he dubs 'grammat-ical' and 'technical' (otherwise 'psychological') approaches to the other. The grammatical pertains to the public context which forms the natural context for an utterance or text. Schleiermacher intends 'grammatical' first in the literal sense of locating utterance within an objective linguistic system with its shared rules and limits of use, but for the sake of convenience we might broaden this to include the wider cultural 'grammar' of a particular setting, of which actual lan-guage is an important part, but only a part. Since the diachronic dimension adds nothing unique to historical distance as such, we may treat *historical* otherness simply as a manifestation of this wider category of cultural otherness. Thus, in the case of our dealing with ancient texts, historical research is vital to our setting of the grammatical context. The 'technical' or psychological approach, on the other hand, is directed towards particularity rather than public context, and has to do precisely with attending to the ways in which a 'text' (literal or personal) differs from or transcends the level of the relevant vulgate, how the common stock of 'language' is modified by particular utterance and the partic-ular life from which it issues and of which it is a living expression. Neither approach can ever be exhausted due to the in-principle open-endedness of the respective realities concerned, but both must be pursued to the fullest extent possible, since each depends upon the other for its fruitfulness. Thus grammati-cal and technical are not so much two types or models of interpretation as two

---

[29] Lewis, *Experiment in Criticism*, 139–141.

aspects of every meaningful act of interpretation.

In this connection Schleiermacher refers to a closely related distinction between what he calls the method of 'divination' and that of 'comparison'. He writes:

> Each method refers back to the other. The divinatory is based on the assumption that each person is not only a unique individual in his own right, but that he has a receptivity to the uniqueness of every other person. This assumption in turn seems to presuppose that each person contains a minimum of everyone else, and so divination is aroused by comparison with oneself.[30]

The distinction here is subtly different to that between 'grammatical' and 'technical', but it too has to do with our approach to levels of generality and particularity in the other, and insists upon the need for both to be held in view at the same time in order for either to be meaningfully treated. It is with particularity, after all, that we must finally be concerned if we would respect the other rather than simply treating her as a type to be classified or committing some crass version of the fallacy of origins. In order for the particular to manifest itself as such, though, we must be able to compare it with or locate it within some more general pattern (whether this is something which we ourselves have in common with the other, or something proper to the other's original public context when this differs from our own). Correspondingly, our approach to the other's particularity is only possible at all because it is mixed up inextricably with elements of something shared and more or less familiar to us. It is this which, for all our irreducible 'uniqueness', renders us nonetheless receptive to the uniqueness of the other, that we 'contain a minimum' of everyone else already within ourselves.

Here we touch upon an aspect of Schleiermacher's hermeneutics which is perhaps the best known; namely, his appeal to the inevitable (although for him not ultimately vicious) circularity of every act of human understanding. In brief, we can grasp particulars as such only in relation to wider wholes or patterns within which they present themselves and of which they are already grasped as parts; yet grasp of the wider pattern is itself contingent on the knowledge of particulars. In order to recognize something we must in some sense already know it *in order* to be able to make sense of it. For our purposes here perhaps the sharpest question to arise out of this is whether there can ever be any genuine otherness or particularity at all or, if there is, whether we could ever know it. Surely, in order to fathom some genuinely particular aspect of the other, I must already be able to say that I 'know' it in some sense? To the extent that it is genuinely 'particular' (rather than simply something which I discover

---

[30] Schleiermacher, *Hermeneutics*, 150.

– possibly hidden – within the depths of my own prior experience or understanding) I shall be unable to recognize or make sense of it. We cannot understand something that we do not basically already know. Pessimistic appeals to 'big ugly ditches' which render understanding across cultures virtually impossible due to some fundamental incommensurability between them rest heavily on this idea. A universalistic denial of particularity is neither an attractive nor a necessary alternative. The answer lies in the recognition expressed in Schleiermacher's claim that 'we all contain a minimum' of the other within ourselves; namely, that generality and particularity are woven together in the manifold of the real, and that there is sufficient that we hold in common with the other – notwithstanding the uniqueness which characterizes both poles of the relation – for us to move out beyond our own particularity into unfamiliar territory. In order to pursue this further we need to return to the category of imagination, and its function in providing the vital conditions for belief and understanding.

One of imagination's characteristic roles is as that activity of the mind which, in various contexts, presents to the 'mind's eye' coherent and meaningful wholes for consideration. It is, we might say, the faculty which makes sense of things, locating particular bits and pieces within larger patterns, and in doing so goes beyond what is given, filling gaps, painting bigger pictures.[31] These patterns may be largely fictional (as in the plot of a novel), yet true in some sense to the way things are in the 'real world'. Or they may be patterns which pertain much more directly to our engagement with the world around us, enabling us to interpret individual perceptions, experiences, gestures, events and the like by relating them to wider patterns of phenomena. In one way or another, then, imagination has to do with identifying and/or constructing patterns of meaningfulness. But grasp of *meaningfulness* in this sense can, and I think should, properly be distinguished from the 'understanding' which arises when concepts and laws come into play. We can recognize a pattern without being able to understand it; but we cannot understand what we have not yet recognized as meaningful. And an important part of what imagination does in human life, I would suggest, is to present to us 'meaningful' or 'imaginable' states of affairs or worlds for our indwelling and consideration. This it does, we should note, without as yet any moral commitment to questions of truth or falsity; it is concerned simply with a certain sort of coherence. But, by showing us 'how things would be if' certain things were true, imagination breathes life into concepts in a way which not only makes them easier to grasp (they remain otherwise wraithlike and transparent), but actually has a degree of persuasive force which disarms our scepticism and makes 'belief in' possible. Only once the imagination is taken captive, we might say, can we really be much bothered

---

[31] See Warnock, *Imagination*.

to expend intellectual energy on understanding or moral effort in acting. It has been suggested that in matters much wider than theology, a certain sort of belief is the necessary condition for understanding. I suppose what I am suggesting here is that imagination is in fact the prior condition for belief, and thereby for understanding. We cannot understand, and shall be unlikely to entertain belief in, something which in broad outlines at least, we cannot imagine or grasp the meaning of.

Returning to our logical dilemma, then, we may now suggest that two conditions render our fathoming of the depths of particularity possible: The first is precisely this capacity of imagination to visualize or construct patterns, states of affairs, other than those given in our own experience. That we cannot understand something we do not already *know* seems to miss the mark: rather, we cannot understand something we cannot first *imagine*. But to this first condition must be added another, this time to do with the structure of reality itself. The imagination functions analogically, tracing meaningful connections, identifying the presence of the like in the very core of the unlike, offering metaphorical construals of the unfamiliar in terms of the familiar, and thereby cutting reality open at its joints for our appreciation. The artist, as Steiner reminds us, makes a wager on transcendence, investing faith in an overall meaningfulness which transcends the level of our own symbolic responses to the world. For the poetic image to succeed, though, the connections to which it points between distinct objects must be rooted in reality rather than imposed upon it. Thus, while particularity and genuine difference may (and must) be acknowledged and respected in the world, so too we must suppose there to be some analogical relation or set of relations which finally link all things together meaningfully, and render the imaginative journey out from one location to another possible. We can travel far through imagination's intuitive grasp of analogy, but where no analogy whatever exists, imagination runs aground, and with it the capacity to understand the other. In this sense every task of understanding the other is of similar sort to the artist's engagement with the world. It involves a wager on transcendence, and on our own concomitant capacity for acts of imaginative self-transcendence.

Going Beyond the Facts of the Matter

According to Schleiermacher, we are concerned in hermeneutics with 'determining the grammatically indeterminate via the grammatically determinate'[32] and putting ourselves 'in the place of the author on both the objective and the subjective side'.[33] Another way of putting this might be to say that in every bid

---

[32] Schleiermacher, *Hermeneutics and Criticism*, 233.

for understanding in the field of the human, we are concerned to go beyond the facts of the matter in pursuit of an encounter between persons. For, as we have already noted, the field of the human is irreducibly the field of the personal, and a purely 'grammatical' or 'objective' mode of approach to the other is necessarily impersonal.[34] Such impersonal relations to persons are important and necessary (we cannot relate to a person at all unless we are able to locate him meaningfully within wider patterns of things with which we are familiar); sometimes they are vital to our capacity to respond to the other in appropriate ways (a doctor must finally see her patient in terms of some type or class in order to make a proper prescription); but they will not suffice if we would gain some understanding of and relate to them as *a person*, and this must be our goal.

In his novel *Hard Times* Charles Dickens parodies a crude positivistic approach to the field of the human in his anti-hero Thomas Gradgrind. Gradgrind is enamoured of a form of political economy which sees nothing more in the human other than his senses present him with. He is 'A man of realities. A man of facts and calculations. A man . . . with a rule and a pair of scales, and the multiplication table always in his pocket sir, ready to weigh and measure any parcel of human nature, and tell you exactly what it comes to.'[35] As Gradgrind's disastrous dealings with his family and neighbours make clear, however, such a one-sided mode of relationship misses all that is most truly human, reducing the other to a categorial abstraction whose particular qualities, concerns, hopes, fears and pains – all the mysteries and complexities of human life – are deliberately overlooked in the interest of a precise and tidy accounting. In Martha Nussbaum's words, 'The cheerful fact-calculating mind plays round the surfaces of these lives, as if it had no need to look within, as if, indeed, it "could settle all their destinies on a slate".'[36] But human life will not be calculated in this way. It has to do not simply with 'facts', isolated packets of physical data to be perceived, measured and weighed precisely, and with the rules which govern or describe the relationships between these. The field of the human is a highly complex manifold in which physical events are mixed together with emotional, volitional, psychological and spiritual elements, all of which contribute to the mystery which is the life of a particular human person and which, within the field of the human, is vital to our bid for understanding.

There may be very few Gradgrinds among us in practice. Like all satirists, Dickens has taken something and exaggerated it into a grotesque form. Yet the point he makes is that whenever and to whatever extent we slip into *purely* impersonal and objectifying modes of approach to the human other we run the

---

[33] Ibid., 24.

[34] See Macmurray, *Persons*, 33.

[35] Dickens, *Hard Times*, 48.

[36] Nussbaum, '*Literary Imagination*', 885.

risk of dehumanizing the other (and thereby ourselves also in the process). Again, in relating to persons (participating in acts of human communication) we need both objective and personal modes to be held together as two aspects of the same interpretative activity:

> The impersonal attitude in a personal relation is the negative which is necessarily included in the positive personal attitude, and without which it could not exist. Even in the most personal of relationships the other person is in fact an object for us. We see his movements and his gestures; we hear the sounds he makes; if we did not we could not be aware of him at all. Yet we do not hear mere sounds or see mere movements or gestures. What we apprehend through these are the intentions, the feelings, the thoughts of another person who is in communication with ourselves.[37]

As Nussbaum observes, in this sense human life in its most distinctively human aspects involves a constant requirement and willingness to go beyond the evidence, beyond the facts;[38] and going beyond the facts is, as I have already suggested, a basic activity of human imagination.

It is Dilthey who perhaps offers the most developed account of understanding within the human field in terms of the activity of imagination.[39] The distinction he draws between knowledge of the physical world and knowledge of the human world corresponds to ours between 'objective' and 'personal' spheres of knowing, and he sees them as vitally interrelated in ways similar to those we have been suggesting. What Dilthey is particularly interested in is *how* we come to understand levels of the human which go beyond the phenomena of 'nature'. How is it that, when we see movements and gestures (or symbols such as those contained in texts), or hear sounds, we 'apprehend through these ... the intentions, the feelings, the thoughts of another person who is in communication with ourselves'? That we do this is vital to what it means to be human. But such things are not and can never be rendered or presented at the level of 'facts'. How, then, do we grasp them? What sort of process is involved in our apprehension of *Geist*?

Dilthey's answer is that we take certain physical phenomena as expressions or objectifications of the 'inner' or supra-physical life of the person who communicates with us by virtue of a capacity which such expressions possess to evoke corresponding patterns in our own minds.[40] In other words, put crudely, the inner life of one person transmits itself through such 'expressions' and is reproduced in some version (what Dilthey calls a *Nachbild*) in another mind. As

---

[37] Macmurray, *Persons*, 34.
[38] Nussbaum, '*Literary Imagination*', 898.
[39] For the following I am indebted in particular to the account in Hodges, *William Dilthey*.
[40] Ibid., 14.

Hodges notes, this 'power of expressions to evoke what they express' is, for Dilthey, 'the basis of all communication and all sharing of experience between human beings'.[41] Stated in this way alone it all sounds rather mechanistic; but Dilthey does not by any means see those who seek understanding as mere passive receivers. On the contrary, there is a vital corresponding *constructive* task of imagination to be engaged in in order for the relevant *Nachbild* to take root and grow in our consciousness so that we come to 'understand' what the other intends, desires, fears, or whatever the relevant manifestation of the personal may be. This constructive activity (effectively a reconstruction or 'living over again' [*Nacherlebe*] of some part of the other's inner world within our own) rests squarely on the fact that there is an identity of nature, a deep undercurrent of generality, spanning the distance between us. Put differently (and in terms of a reversal of direction), understanding is effectively a 'transposition of myself' into the other, perceiving the other as possessed of an inner life essentially like my own, and so, in Dilthey's classic phrase, attaining to a 'rediscovery of myself in the Thou' (*ein Wiederfinden des Ich im Du*).[42] Nussbaum offers a similar judgement: in going 'beyond the facts' in our dealings with the human other, she suggests, we are effectively involved in 'a projection of our own sentiments and inner activities onto the forms we perceive about us'.[43]

How are we to make sense of this? The terms in which it is all stated are not at first sight attractive ones to be sure. The idea that understanding has to do with the 'inner life' might seem to suggest that the 'grammatical' and public levels of human life and discourse are merely a conduit through which this inner life passes by virtue of an inconvenient necessity, and that all discourse is about attempts to bare our souls in public, which it clearly is not. But we do not have to endorse Romantic expressionism in its details in order to take the main point that Dilthey appears to be making here; namely, that while the grammatical/objective/public aspect of utterance and interpretation is vital to every act of human communication, nonetheless there is more than this to be taken into account if we would understand it as human (personal) communication. Wolterstorff puts it helpfully in terms of a quite different model, and is worth citing at length:

> Typically, there's something that the discourser wants to say, some speech action he wants to perform; his desire to do that may or may not be motivated by the desire to express some inner state. To perform that speech action, he . . . causally brings about some action which he believes will count-generate the speech action on which he has his eye. If all goes well on both sides, the interpreter, in discerning what counts as what, will perforce discern the content of that implemented action-plan; and

---

[41] Ibid., 14–15.

[42] Dilthey, *Gesammelte Schriften*, 191.

[43] Nussbaum, '*Literary Imagination*', 898.

typically the sequence of her discernment will reverse the sequence of its formation: the discourser started with a speech action he wanted to perform and then settled on an action he thought might count-generate it; the interpreter starts with that latter action and tries to discern what speech action might be count-generated thereby. But everything may not go well, even on the discourser's side. What he causally brings about may not count as what he thought it would count as – not count as the speech action that he intended to perform. Or it may count as quite a bit more than he had in mind; and with that more, he may be less than happy.[44]

It is with this problematic surplus which, I would suggest, goes beyond the level of grammatical determinacy even when things are going well, that we have typically to do in relating to and understanding the personal other. In Wolterstorff's terms, knowing the relevant locutionary action, we must go beyond it to discern what is not given in that action as such, the relevant illocutionary act (and its noematic content) which the speaker intended to perform. In discerning this, though, we are compelled to go beyond mere grammar (which may supply us with a set of possible meanings but cannot adjudicate between them) and consider the utterance in the context of its living and personal particularity. We should not overestimate the capacity of language alone to facilitate our relation to the other; as speakers we generally know and often intend more than we can say. As interpreters, on the other hand 'we always understand more than we know';[45] imagination enables us to grasp depths of personal being which go beyond the level of linguistic or conceptual determinacy.

It might also be supposed problematic to speak, as Dilthey does, of interpretation as involving an imaginative 'transposition of ourselves into' the other. Does this not sound rather like a *denial* of the other's particularity, a 'rediscovery' of ourselves in the other only possible because we have first hidden ourselves there, and in doing so obscured the other herself? Nussbaum's use of the language of 'projection' does little to allay fears of this sort. Yet this is not what either seems to intend. The point each is emphasizing is that *before* we can fathom the particularity of the other (logically if not temporally before) we must be able to identify the layers of shared human life which unite us to the other and which render possible the movement of imagination from the familiar into the unfamiliar by way of a series of analogical steps. We do not, to be sure, discover our own *particularity* in the other; but, knowing the other to be human, we move beyond her utterance by taking it as communicating some pattern (or part of a pattern) identifiable as or analogous to something in the structure of our own humanity. This form or pattern subsequently serves as the port from which our imaginative journeys of reconstruction embark to chart

---

[44] Wolterstorff, *Divine Discourse*, 183–184.
[45] Dilthey, cited in Hodges, *William Dilthey*, 14.

the unfamiliar territories of otherness, relying ever on the kindly trade winds of a shared human experience to bear us, paradoxically, ever closer to the shores of alien particularity. The more we intuit what is shared between us, the more clearly difference manifests itself as a departure from or modification of the known. What is shared in the field of the human thus enables the genuine particularity of the other to 'come to life' in our own imagination, at least to some extent. It is because we first discover something which we recognize as proper to our selves in the other (Schleiermacher's 'minimum of everyone else') that we can go on to plot the contours of the ways in which they nonetheless differ from us. Although the task is a distinct one, it is closely related to what we are doing when we indulge in a fictional imagining 'what it would be like if' to be someone else, and to the nurturing, education and disciplining of this insatiable curiosity in literature.

There is, of course, a sense in which even the 'grammatical' aspect of understanding entails an imaginative activity of just this sort. The classification of historical study (for example) together with other disciplines whose focus is the human condition as a 'science' should not be allowed to obscure this fact.[46] Of course there are precise and critical dimensions to a historian's training and activity: acquiring the relevant languages, learning to handle the sources, and so on. But, as Collingwood made plain, the task of historical understanding is one of imaginative construction all the same, and no less a respectable or reliable one for that. First, through his study of sources, the historian seeks to become a surrogate member of a human community to which he does not naturally belong, learning to speak, think and feel, as it were, as a viking, a renaissance Italian philosopher, a nineteenth century Russian peasant woman, or whatever. Immersion in the sources, and the careful construction of a patchwork account of the relevant 'world' from the available sources, facilitates some degree of success in this quest, and thereby enables the historian to judge, for example, the likely general patterns of association and response evoked by a text, an action, an event. Again, elements of shared humanity and particular modifications of its basic patterns combine to translate him imaginatively into this world and to become a connoisseur of its general qualities. 'The historian's picture of his subject, whether that subject be a sequence of events or a past state of things, thus appears as a web of imaginative construction stretched between certain fixed points provided by the statements of his authorities.'[47] Often the gaps will be relatively small, so that the effort of filling them comes naturally and is achieved almost without notice; but sometimes (even in the most respected historical accounts) gaps of considerable proportions must be stopped by a feat of imaginative intelligence, extrapolating from patterns of

---

[46] See on this Postman, *Technopoly*, 159f.
[47] Collingwood, *Idea of History*, 242.

behaviour or experience familiar to the historian and presenting a feasible account of how it might have been or probably was. This may sometimes be as far as he can proceed. But in order really to understand he will seek to go further, beyond the level of social and historical grammar, and into the particularity of the person who wrote, or acted, or suffered, or of some person in the story which a text tells. After all, as Schleiermacher reminds us, 'becoming one of the original readers' can have only so much value, since they themselves were compelled to do more, and to seek to put themselves imaginatively in the place of the other.[48] In order to do so, of course, the historian is able now to draw not only on what is familiar to him as the particular person he is. He is, by virtue of his prior successful labours, able to draw on his 'virtual' experience as a surrogate member of the relevant human group. His understanding of 'what most Jews in Paul's day' would likely have understood by a specific phrase furnishes a context within which the particularity of Paul's actual uses of it may be discerned.

Reading texts always involves some effort to go beyond the level of the words on the page, beyond even the wider 'factual' circumstances to which they relate (insofar as these can be discovered by the methods of careful objective study), and to penetrate into the field of the personal. Only thus can understanding occur as part of a genuine meeting of persons, and our own personhood be modified by it. But the demands upon us in this respect vary in their extent from text to text. Sometimes more is given in and with the text itself to furnish a given frame for our work of construction, sometimes less. In the case of certain sorts of documents it is important that we inquire about the author as a personal other, since what we know or do not know in this respect cannot but affect the way in which we read his text. We shall supply an inferred and hypothetical 'author' of our own to perform the relevant roles here even if we claim to eschew considerations of authorship altogether, and on the whole it is probably better to allow what we can discover of the *actual* author to serve. This I take to be true, for example, of Paul's epistles where only so much of Paul's context is given by way of clues within the text itself, yet understanding requires a fuller account to be supplied in order for his particular purpose in writing to become clear.

Other sorts of texts require less of us as readers in this respect. This is especially true of texts which fit identifiably into a particular genre (so that the author's basic purpose in writing is already declared) and which deliberately offer to us a self-contained world or narrative for consideration. Here, it is often urged, we not only *need* not but *should* not seek to press beyond the text in order to understand, but should limit ourselves to the text as it is given. This point, it seems to me, is well made but often misunderstood. That we need not

---

[48] Schleiermacher, *Hermeneutics and Criticism*, 24.

go beyond the text in pursuit of its author does not mean that we need not go 'beyond the text' at all. On the contrary, if we take the novel as an example of a relevant contemporary form then, as Nussbaum reminds us,

> we are reading a story [which] contains characters – men and women in some ways like ourselves. It represents these characters as very distinct one from another, endowing them with physical and moral attributes that make it possible for us to distinguish every one from every other. We are made to attend to their concrete ways of moving and talking, the shapes of their bodies, the expressions on their faces, the sentiments of their hearts. The inner life of each is displayed as having psychological depth and complexity. We see that as humans they share certain common problems and common hopes – and yet, as well, that each confronts these in his or her own way, in his or her concrete circumstances with the resources of his or her history . . . We see the novel's abstract deliberations . . . as issuing in each case from a concrete human life, and as expressing only a part of the content of that life's inner richness. And although we do not always have extended and explicit access to that complexity, we are always invited to wonder about it, to imagine it.[49]

So, while consideration of an 'author' in the literary sense is not always appropriate or possible, interrogation of the available depths of humanity from which an utterance issues always will be. In this respect, 'understanding' a fictional character in a story (and thereby grasping the sense of her utterance) is directly comparable to our attempts to understand someone who confronts us in living conversation.

E.M. Forster draws a distinction between what he calls 'flat' and 'rounded' characters in a novel.[50] Flat characters are those whom the novelist forms around a single basic idea or trait; two or three at most. In effect their reality extends no further than their identification with these simple ideas, and need not do so for the purposes of the plot. Round characters on the other hand are much more complex; we know much more about them, and their narrative identity is such that they could never be summed up in a single phrase. There is development, inner conflict, genuine struggle with the messiness of human life. We feel that they might surprise us at any moment as we learn more about them. They resist quick and easy classification. And, of course, they are what makes most novels worth reading, because the attempt to understand such characters takes us out on journeys of imaginative self-transcendence in which our own identity is transfigured through the enlargement of our world. But none of this can happen simply by remaining at the level of the text alone (whatever that might be supposed to mean). It is a supremely self-involving process in which our imagination is constantly stimulated to go beyond what

---

[49] Nussbaum, '*Literary Imagination*', 889.
[50] Forster, *Aspects of the Novel*, 75f.

the narrative itself offers us, bringing to it questions and concerns which arise naturally out of our own experience of what it is to be human, and thereby discovering the depths of humanity lurking latent within it. Here, too, that is to say, both 'grammatical' and 'technical' dimensions of understanding are vital if the text is to come to life for us.

Imaginative Exegesis?

What I have sought to do in this chapter thus far is to furnish a context for our reflection on how imagination (or lack of it) inevitably affects Christian readings of the Bible. In approaching the text as Scripture there is, of course, more to be taken into account than any general hermeneutic can allow for; but there is no less. And if we would press beyond the levels of discussion attended to here and ask what God has said and is saying to the church through the text, then (1) we shall be forced eventually to indulge in an extension by analogy of the sort of imaginative penetration of human otherness which I have outlined to God as an 'author' with depths of particular identity that cannot but have serious implications for our reading;[51] but (2) we must at least *begin* with the sorts of wider issues this paper has raised, attending to the text as a complex of acts of human communication; otherwise the 'grammar' of understanding will be wholly obscured, and the wax nose threaten to slide off the face of the text altogether, melted by the heat of a frenzied, random (and to my mind irresponsible) imagining. In this text of all texts, though, we might reasonably expect to find two things: (1) transforming depths of humanity plumbed (so that in engaging with it 'what we already know' of our humanity under God is supplemented, challenged, broken and restored through migration out into the particularity of otherness), and (2) the 'grammar' of the texts' various contexts stretched beyond its normal capacities as it seeks to accommodate God's particular and surprising activity in the world.

All this, I suggest, makes the imaginative aspects of interpretation vital, and leaves a 'scientific' refusal to do more than learn and apply the rules of the relevant linguistic set likely to miss all that is most relevant in the text, and thereby hardly 'scientific' in any proper sense at all. To interpret only at the level of generalities is to fish with a net too broad in its mesh to catch the text's true humanity. The dialectic between determinacy and indeterminacy in language is, Steiner suggests, part of its genius rather than a pathological failure. It is what grants language its remarkable capacity as a vehicle of human communication (a relatively stable system which places limits on meaning) and a tool

---

[51] There is not space in this chapter to trace the sort of thing which this would involve, but see Wolterstorff, *Divine Discourse*, 203f.

of sufficient flexibility to plot a world of experience which is never the same twice, open-ended and complex. We might liken it to a rope fixed securely to a point on a rock face, on the other end of which a climber hangs and skips across the rock, skilfully exploring its contours. Without the firm anchor the task of moving out beyond is an impossible one; but the point of mooring the rope in this way in the first place is precisely to allow such movement to occur. In this sense it is the very make-up and malleable nature of human language as such which permits the sort of imaginative self-transcendence to which this chapter has repeatedly referred.[52] The analogical imagination is bound up with the extension of language through metaphor. A thoroughly determinate (and inflexible) linguistic system would therefore trap us within our own particularity, and would, as Schleiermacher notes, render hermeneutics unnecessary: all we should need would be a good dictionary and a dose of common sense since 'there would only be grammar'.[53] But human life is not like this, fortunately.

Of course, the level and the sort of imagining demanded of us will vary quite significantly due to the multiplicity of genres within Scripture. A section of one of Paul's epistles is likely to demand much more, for example, than a portion of narrative, because a good deal of context will need to be supplied, and this may entail a considerable task of construction, rooted in the text (and perhaps other sources) but going beyond it. Jesus' parables, on the other hand, are deliberately self-contained and require little if any familiarity with the storyteller except at the most general of levels. That is, they are illuminated greatly by the sort of 'grammatical' detail supplied in Kenneth Bailey's writing (supplying the grammar of agrarian Palestinian society), but also appeal to basic human traits and types with which we can identify quite easily: greed, envy, laziness, pity, and so on. Their characters are, for the most part, 'flat' rather than 'rounded'. If we take the psalter as a further example, then we are dealing with an example which lies somewhere in between these other two in terms of its demands upon our imagination. As Christian readers, we share a considerable amount with the psalmist, not just in terms of a common humanity but also in our relatedness to the same God whose character shapes his hymnody. Again, 'grammar' is important; there are things we need to know about Jewish words and ideas. There are also particular contexts traditionally associated with particular psalms (e.g. David's sin with Bathsheba in the case of Psalm 51) which affect the ways in which we read their words. In order for them to become vehicles of our own praise, penitence, and invocation, though, we need to go beyond the level of 'knowing' such things and fuse the depths of humanity latent within the psalm with the patterns of our own relatedness to God. We

---

[52] See Steiner, *After Babel*, 236.

[53] Schleiermacher, *Hermeneutics and Criticism*, 233.

need to see things 'through David's eyes' to the extent we can, in order for the force of David's experience expressed in the psalm to modify the pattern of our own.

I want to end this chapter by (as a theologian rather than an exegete) risking the shift from a second-order to a first-order level of discourse, and offering an exegesis of some troublesome words from Paul in 1 Corinthians 14:33b–5.[54] These, I suggest, are words demanding a high level of imaginative activity from an exegete to arrive at an intepretation coherent with the overall shape of the epistle. According to Schleiermacher this is the basic exegetical task which renders the 'art' of hermeneutics necessary. We straddle 'grammar' and the particular situations in life which call forth utterance. We consider the shape of the whole text by relating its parts, and make sense of the parts in terms of the shape of the whole. In the dialectical toing and froing between these various aspects (which are present to varying degrees in all acts of understanding) we seek an interpretation which satisfies their respective demands. How, then, are we to make sense of Paul's notorious 'misogyny'? I offer the following:

> As in all congregations of the saints, women should remain silent in the churches. They are not allowed to speak, but must be in submission, as the Law says. If they want to inquire about something, they should ask their own husbands at home: for it is disgraceful for a woman to speak in the church.

Here Paul both invokes an assumed principle (i.e. within the wider social context) of female subordination to men, and demands on the basis of it that women should not speak, but be silent, in church. (There is no indication, for example, that these words are offered heavily laden with irony.) If these few verses were the sole scriptural basis for developing a theology of women's ministry, then the matter would be relatively straightforward, at least in terms of setting 'biblical teaching' alongside the demands of our own cultural context. But the fact that traditional views have sometimes been allowed to proceed *as if* these words were the only relevant consideration does not mean that it is so, and the first thing that we must notice about them is the stark contradiction which they present when set alongside the situation addressed in Chapter 11 where, not only were the women praying and prophesying in church, but Paul was prepared to enter into lengthy discussion concerning their deportment in so doing. There is, then, a problem of consistency attaching to these verses from the outset.

Scholars who have recognized this have sought to address the problem in various ways. Some have contended that the verb which Paul uses here (*lalein*)

---

[54] What follows is based substantially on a section of a booklet entitled 'Evangelicals and the Ordination of Women to the Priesthood' which I wrote for a series published by the Movement for Whole Ministry (No7; Edinburgh: Occasional Publications, 1994)

means 'to chatter' rather than 'to speak' in more general terms. In this case what Paul is addressing is a problem of 'disorderly' behaviour of the sort to be experienced in many churches in the moments before worship formally begins. If the pattern of seating in early Christian congregations can be supposed to match that of the synagogues (scholars remain uncertain whether or not this would have been the case) then all the women would be seated together and separately from the men. In such a circumstance it might be supposed that a reference to women 'chattering' in worship would not be unlikely. The reference to God as a God of 'order rather than disorder' in verse 33a seems if anything to support such a reading. But, while this provides an attractive (and a possible) solution to the question of Paul's meaning, its weakness lies in the fact that while *lalein* can mean 'to chatter', its more normal sense is simply 'to speak' and Paul uses it throughout the epistle to refer to the inspired or authoritative speech of those leading and participating actively in the congregation's worship.

Another proposed solution to the apparent inconsistency with Chapter 11 is to suppose that these two verses were not penned by Paul at all, but were added later by someone who took a quite different line on women's ministry. This is the view adhered to by Gordon Fee who furnishes strong literary grounds for such a supposition. But, even if this is the case, and even if it 'explains' the inconsistency of view contained within the epistle, it does little to resolve our problem as those who must presumably interpret this authoritative text in the form in which we have received it, and which, it must be supposed, is the form which God has seen fit to provide for us. The view that only the 'original' or 'authentic' form of a text or a portion of text can serve as authoritative would, if adhered to, leave our Bibles looking very different, and raises all manner of questions concerning the way in which we understand God as having inspired its contents. We do not have any manuscript versions of 1 Corinthians which lack these verses, and so, it would seem to me, they must stand for our purposes, less convenient though that may be for our argument.

Is there, then, a way of reading them which enables us at least to hold them together with the rest of 1 Corinthians rather than tearing the logic of its argument apart? I would suggest that there is. First, we must note a recurrent emphasis of Paul throughout the epistle which might be summed up thus: the gospel is undoubtedly a scandal and a stumbling block (see 1:23); let those who live by its authority then not do anything which might put up any additional barriers for those considering the gospel's claims, even when this means compromising the freedoms which we undoubtedly have in Christ (see 8:9; 10:32). Instead, Christians are to 'put up with anything rather than hinder the gospel of Christ' (9:12). The salvation of those for whom Christ has died is more important than the Christian's wish to exercise his or her new-found liberty. Thus we find Paul exhorting the Corinthians to abstain from eating meat sacrificed to idols if eating with someone likely to be shocked or offended by such behaviour. Similarly, as Chapter 11 indicates, women are to conform to those conventions of Jewish public worship which, if openly flouted, might well succeed in driving people away from the church and giving them false reasons for refusing to wrestle with the challenge of its gospel. So women should have their heads covered in church as they would in the synagogue. But now, in Chapter 14, I would suggest, Paul goes further even than this, pushing this same principle of willingness to sacrifice a genuine Christian liberty for the sake of the gospel to more extreme lengths.

Chapter 14 addresses the propriety of the exercise of spiritual gifts within the congregation, gifts which, Paul affirms, have been granted to everyone, and not to men alone (see vv. 23, 24, 26, 31). In verse 23 Paul expressly envisages a situation in which unbelievers come into the congregation, and asks how best the gifts of tongues and prophecy (which from 11:5 we know was something women were involved in) might be handled in this circumstance. His concern is that from what is seen and done in the congregation's midst, the unbeliever should only be encouraged and impressed, and perhaps even led to the point of belief and worship (vv. 24–5). What is vital is that such a person should not be offended by externals or things which are less than central to the gospel message. What is done must in all contexts 'be done for the strengthening of the church' (v. 26). It is in this immediate context that the words we are focusing on in particular arise. If we read them in the light of the flow of Paul's argument in the chapter, and of his paramount concern for the gospel's welfare, then, by supplying a conditional clause which (as so often in Paul's particular style) might be assumed in what he says, we get the following: As is the case in all the congregations of the saints, *if there is a risk of serious offence being taken*, women should remain silent in the churches. They are not (in this situation) allowed to speak, but must be in submission (as Jewish custom dictates). If they want to enquire about something, they should ask their husbands at home (rather than asking for themselves as they would ordinarily do); because (for some people) it is a cause of shame for a woman to speak in church.

To reconstruct the passage thus is to read it as a specific provision for the possible sensitivities of those unbelieving visitors to the congregation whom Paul mentions earlier in the chapter, and with whose scruples and problems of conscience he is concerned throughout the epistle. It is a pragmatic accommodation to conventional Jewish attitudes to women, for the sake of keeping the channels of communication uncluttered with unnecessary sources of offence. Let these supposed objectors first hear the gospel itself in all its clarity; and then, when they have received it, they can discover some of the practical ramifications of it as these ordinarily pertain within church life. Read thus, this is not a precept to be applied in every church and at all times. Indeed, we might suggest that the same concern in our own very different context would demand the precise opposite prescription. Unbelievers today are for more likely to be scandalized by a situation in which women are prohibited from speaking, or taking full part in the proceedings of worship.

Such an interpretation of the passage involves an imaginative construction of context which reads 'between the lines'. For some this will render it problematic. But, as I have indicated throughout this chapter, some reading between the lines or filling in of the gaps is involved in all interpretation, and therefore in our reading of Scripture generally. In the case of 1 Corinthians in particular more is needed of this sort than in some more straightforward passages of the Bible. Many commentators on this epistle observe the difficulty of interpreting those sections where Paul seems to be responding to some direct question or concern expressed by the Corinthian church, questions and concerns which he does not bother to reproduce in his answer. Might we not imagine them having asked him a straight question: 'What should we do if people who find the idea of women taking an active part in public worship scandalous come into the congregation on some occasion? In such a situation, do you allow the women to speak, and thereby to cause offence, or do you insist that they observe the traditional proprieties?' The interpretation offered here is one which fits together with the overall logic of the epistle, and more specifically enables us to avoid positing a blunt contradiction between this passage and sections of Chapter 11. The question we must ask ourselves quite bluntly is whether the traditional interpretation (which, we might note, does not avoid an interpretative filling of gaps but appeals to an alternative one) furnishes us with a more or less satisfactory account of the direction of Paul's thought in 1 Corinthians as a whole. I would contend that it creates more problems than answers, and should be set aside.

Bibliography

Collingwood, R.G., *The Idea of History* (Oxford: Oxford University Press, 1946)

—, *The Principles of Art* (Oxford: Oxford University Press, 1958)

Dickens, C., *Hard Times* (London: Penguin Classics, 1985)

Dilthey, W., *William Dilthey's Gesammelte Schriften*, vol. 7 (Berlin: B.G. Teubner, 1942)

Ford, D., *Self and Salvation* (Cambridge: Cambridge University Press, 1999)

Forster, E.M., *Aspects of the Novel* (London: Pelican, 1962)

Hodges, H.A., *William Dilthey: An Introduction* (London: Kegan Paul, Trench, Trubner, 1944)

Lewis, C.S., *An Experiment in Criticism* (Cambridge: Cambridge University Press, 1961)

Macmurray, J., *Persons in Relation* (London: Faber & Faber, 1961)

McFadyen, A.I., *The Call to Personhood* (Cambridge: Cambridge University Press, 1990)

Moltmann, J., *The Trinity and the Kingdom of God* (London: SCM Press, 1981)

Nussbaum, M.C., 'The Literary Imagination in Public Life', *New Literary History* 22 (1991), 877–910

Postman, N., *Technopoly* (New York: Vintage Books, 1993)

Ricoeur, P., *Oneself as Another* (Chicago: University of Chicago Press, 1992)

Schleiermacher, F.D.E., *Hermeneutics: The Handwritten Manuscripts*, ed. H. Kimmerle (Missoula: Scholars Press, 1977)

—, *Hermeneutics and Criticism*, ed. A. Bowie (Cambridge: Cambridge University Press, 1998)

Steiner, G., *After Babel: Aspects of Language and Translation* (Oxford: Oxford University Press, 1992^2)

Thomas, R.S., *No Truce with the Furies* (Newcastle: Bloodaxe Books, 1995)

Torrance, A.J., *Persons in Communion: An Essay on Trinitarian Description and Human Participation* (Edinburgh: T. & T. Clark, 1996)

Warnock, M., *Imagination* (London: Faber & Faber, 1975)

Wolterstorff, N., *Divine Discourse: Philosophical Reflections on the Claim That God Speaks* (Cambridge: Cambridge University Press, 1995)

Zizioulas, J.D., *Being as Communion: Studies in Personhood and the Church* (London: Darton, Longman & Todd, 1985)

16

A Response to Trevor Hart's

Nicholas Wolterstorff

In the following comments I will have to neglect almost entirely Professor Hart's various subsidiary theses and concentrate on his main thesis, with which I agree heartily: in the nature of the case, interpretation of both oral and written speech requires imagination, this feat of imagination in turn altering the interpreter. The thesis is nicely summarized in this sentence: 'every bid for understanding of the other [is] essentially a journey of imagination in which we are granted the capacity to transcend the boundaries of our own particularity and to engage with otherness in ways which plot something of its difference, before finally returning to ourselves with our horizons broadened and our 'self' in some sense more rounded and complete through the venture'. As I have put it in some of my own writing (see my *Works and Worlds of Art*), one of the goals of interpretation is first to discern, and then to indwell, the world which the work projects; and both of these activities – discerning and indwelling – require imagination.

Professor Hart does a fine job of developing this thesis. So, rather than summarizing it and then trying to find spots where I might cavil at his formulations or add an epicycle or two, let me amplify his thesis by briefly taking note of another point at which interpretation, in the nature of the case, requires imagination. This other point comes before we are ready to discern and to indwell the projected world; those require that we have already accomplished the feat of imagination to which I will be calling attention. This other point where imagination is required is hinted at by Hart, but not really developed.

If between locutionary and illocutionary acts there were a one to one relationship, such that for each locutionary act there was just one illocutionary act that the locutionary act could count as, and vice versa, then no imagination would be required on the part of listeners or readers in determining which illocutionary act the locutionary act they're confronted with counts as, nor would any imagination be required on the part of speakers or writers in determining which locutionary act to perform so as to perform the desired illocutionary act. Both speakers and listeners, writers and readers, would just operate the system. But in fact there is no such one to one correspondence.

As a consequence, the interpreter, when confronted with a locutionary act, or the written or spoken trace thereof, has no choice but to ask what the human being who performed that locutionary act is likely to have wanted to say thereby. And the answer to that question requires imagination of a greater or lesser degree. The reader or listener must to some extent imagine himself or herself in the position of the discourser, choosing an action plan from a whole array of options.

What is also required is *phronesis* – that is, good judgment. (As indeed *phronesis* is necessary for discerning the projected world.) Having imagined various alternatives as to what the discourser is likely to have wanted to say with these words, I need good judgment for settling on the best interpretation – on what in fact the discourser is likely to have wanted to say. A combination of imagination and good judgment, imagination and *phronesis*, is essential.

Once I have determined, by this combination of imagination and *phronesis*, what the discourser is likely to have wanted to say, and thereby, when things go normally, what the discourser said, then I am ready to discern the world projected by what he or she said, employing for this purpose various strategies of 'extrapolation,' to use one of Hart's words.

One of Professor Hart's subtheses is that biblical interpretation also requires imagination – to which I would add, *phronesis*. It requires imagination both at the point to which I am calling attention and at the point to which Hart calls attention. This is worth adding as a distinct subthesis because, when it comes to biblical interpretation, the need for imagination and *phronesis* would be denied by a good many Christians. There has always been a strand, in Protestantism at least, which insists that in biblical interpretation one should just drink in what the text says instead of engaging in imagination and judgment, or in any other way importing oneself into one's interpretation. Professor Hart argues that, in the nature of the case, this is impossible. I agree.

My own view, which so far as I can see Professor Hart shares, is that biblical interpretation, at least when engaged in by Christians and the church with the aim of grasping the 'what's said,' requires imagination and *phronesis* on two distinct levels. First, one has to use imagination and *phronesis* to discern what the human author or editor of some particular passage was saying. I am inclined to agree with Hart that the epistolary literature of the New Testament requires more expansive imagination and more subtle *phronesis*, at this point, than does the narrative literature. This is because many if not most letters occur in the context of some prior exchange between the parties, and take for granted a great deal of that exchange rather than detailing it. Accordingly, when confronted with letters written not to oneself but to someone else, one usually has no choice but to fill in some of that presupposed context. That requires imagination. To illustrate the point, Hart offers an interpretation of Paul's puzzling injunction, in 1 Corinthians 14, that women in the church should be silent, and highlights the points at which we have to imagine what context is being presupposed if we are to figure out what Paul was saying. Let me say that I find his interpretation of this passage highly plausible.

There is, as I see it, a second level at which imagination and *phronesis* are required in biblical interpretation, and that is when we go on to ask what God was saying by way of this particular piece of human discourse. It is often difficult in any case to discern what God was saying by way of some episode or other. What makes it especially challenging, when confronted with the Bible, to answer the question as to what God was saying by way of some particular passage, is that we must, to answer this question, interpret the passage in the light of the entire Bible. For the Bible is God's *one* book. It is not God's *opera omnia*, containing sixty-six or more books – the precise number depending on one's own preferred canon – but God's one book. Furthermore, since it's God's book, we cannot assume, as we can when dealing with human authors, that the author was absent-minded here or there, ignorant of certain things, self-contradictory at certain points, and so on.

My own basic complaint about the work of biblical scholars in the twentieth century is that they too seldom offer us interpretation at either of these levels. Often – so it seems to me – they avoid or neglect trying to figure out what Isaiah or Paul might have been saying by way of some passage and instead content themselves with offering philological comments and speculations as to the background and origins of the text. And even those who do offer an interpretation of what the human author or editor might have been saying avoid taking that last bold step – of helping us figure out what God might have been saying by way of this piece of human discourse.

I have expressed my agreement with Professor Hart's main thesis, that in the nature of the case, interpretation in general, and biblical interpretation in particular, requires imagination and *phronesis*. Another thesis of his with which I concur is not so much emphasized as assumed in what he says: both spoken speech and texts are means of human engagement.

In one context or another I have been writing on interpretation for some twenty years now; I would say the basic theme in everything I have written on the matter is that speech and texts are modes of human, more specifically, modes of *normative*, engagement. I am averse to the current fashion of assuming that interpretation consists just of me, or me and you, and *a text*. It is persons – Plato, Augustine, Anselm, whoever – that we are dealing with. When I read *The Confessions* I am interpreting what Augustine said; I am not just dealing with some impersonal object, the text of *The Confessions*. So too when I take up the Bible: I am not just taking up a text, an impersonal object, which somehow washed up on the shores of the Aegean; I am dealing with St. Paul, and by way of dealing with him, I am, awesomely, dealing with God.

This conviction, that interpretation is a mode of normative engagement with my fellow human beings, and with God, goes hand in hand with my insistence to my students, and my resolution to myself, that in interpreting texts we have responsibilities to their authors. In reading and interpreting *The Confessions* I have responsibilities to Augustine. I may not just engage in a play of interpretation, and I may not take cheap shots.

Having expressed my firm agreement with these two central theses of Professor Hart, let me now go on to take note of one point where I would be more emphatic than he is, and another where, perhaps, we disagree.

Hart observes that his discussion of 'tracing patterns' in reality does not commit him to nominalism; and he is correct. He wants to leave the nominalism/realism issue open, but I think it is important that we embrace realism.

There is a wave of fashion in favor of nominalism nowadays, with Nietzsche its patron saint. All there is in reality, insisted Nietzsche, is particulars bearing similarities to each other. However, the use of language requires our grouping things together. The groupings we make and employ have no grounding in reality: reality offers, for example, no reason for grouping red things together, or for grouping dogs together, and so forth. Our groupings are arbitrary impositions on the seamless fabric of experience performed in the service of our purposes, purposes which, for the most part, are attempts at gaining power over others. All language obscures from us the radical singularity of things. All of it is metaphor, mainly in the service of power, calling to our attention similarities among the radical particulars.

Each of us can continue this line of thought from here on; we have all heard it hundreds of times in recent years.

Now is obviously not the occasion to engage in systematic ontology; I shall have to content myself with announcing, in dogmatic fashion, that I think this is all just false. I hold that there are universals in the things – and entities with natures. There are, of course, particulars; but there are not just particulars. There really is the commonality of the color red, there really is the type, dog; and our scientists have really discovered the nature of water. As a corollary, our concepts – unless totally inept – are discernments of pattern and commonality, and of essences which are there to be noticed. When I perceive a dog *as a dog*, my perceiving it under the concept of a dog does not conceal from me its nature as a radical unessenced particular, but instead consists of my perceiving it as what it is, namely, a dog. It is a dog whether or not you or I or anyone else conceives or perceives it as a dog. Accordingly language, and the concepts which get expressed by language, are not – not for the most part, anyway –

simply ways of achieving our purposes in a radically particular world, ways which conceal that radical particularity from us; they are modes of discernment. I do not deny that some of our concepts have little more going for them than that they serve our purposes; and I do not deny that all of them, whatever else they do, serve our purposes or we wouldn't use them. But for the most part they serve our purposes by enabling discernment. Rather than concealing reality from us, they open it up to us. Given that I possess the concept of a dog, and that the object before me is a dog, I can now perceive it as it is, and correctly predicate of it what it is, namely, a dog. I couldn't do that if I didn't have the concept.

Secondly, though Hart and I both see texts as a medium of engagement among persons, it appears to me that we have somewhat different views about the goal of interpretation. Let me put that a bit more precisely. I don't believe there is any such thing as *the* goal of interpretation. A sizeable number of distinct activities are covered by our English word 'interpretation'; we must keep this in mind and not fall into the trap of asking 'What is interpretation?' – as if there were some one thing which constitutes interpretation. The question 'What is interpretation?' is void for vagueness, as the lawyers say. Before the question can be answered, you must tell me which mode of interpretation you are inquiring about. One of the most perplexing features of the hermeneutic tradition is that though it regularly professes to be adamantly opposed to all essentialism, it even more regularly assumes that there is an essence of interpretation; a strange lack of self-awareness!

With this point in mind, let me then say that most of the time a central goal of interpretation is and should be discerning what the discourser was saying – discerning, to use the jargon, which illocutionary act he or she performed. Not which one he or she *intended* to perform, but which one he or she *did* perform, if any. Once that goal has been achieved, one can then go on to pursue other interpretative goals, for example, to discern the world projected by the author's discourse.

Often, probably most of the time, when people speak of interpreting texts, I think what they are really doing is trying to discern what the author was saying by way of his or her text – trying to discern, for example, which illocutionary acts Plato was performing by inscribing and authorizing the text before us. Jacques Derrida is famous for recommending and practicing a 'play of interpretation' when having a text in hand. I find it striking that when people criticize his texts, he constantly insists that he did not say what they claim he said: they have got him wrong. Whatever Derrida may do with Plato, Dionysius, and so forth, he does not want readers engaging in plays of interpretation with his own texts. He wants them to discern *what he said*!

I am in short, a staunch defender of what I call 'authorial discourse interpretation' and of its centrality in our engagement with the speech and discourse of our fellows. Not, be it noted, interpretation for authorial intent, but interpretation for authorial discourse. Of course, since discourse is obviously intentional action, rather than autonomic action, considerations of intention will have to go into the discerning of that intentional action which is an act of discourse. Nonetheless, we must keep constantly before us the distinction between intentionally saying something, and *intending* to say something. I concede that there are activities rightly called 'interpretation' other than the activity of trying to discern authorial discourse, which it is appropriate on occasion to engage in; but I contend that authorial discourse interpretation is both theoretically defensible and unavoidably pervasive in human life.

If I understand Hart, he, under the influence apparently of a certain reading of Schleiermacher, is of a different view. At various points in his chapter he speaks of interpretation of texts as aimed at understanding 'the other.'

I do not believe that when interpreting Plato's *Republic* my aim is to understand Plato, or Plato's personhood. My goal is to understand what Plato said. I might *also* on some occasion try to understand Plato; but understanding Plato is a different activity from understanding what Plato said. My impression is that Hart often runs these distinct activities together. If I am to understand what Plato said, I cannot indeed be totally ignorant of Plato; but it is not Plato, that is, his personhood, that is the focus of my interest.

Hart speaks at one point of a 'bid for understanding of the other,' apparently regarding this as the goal of interpretation of texts. I am dubious. I concede that sometimes one's goal is to understand Plato, and appropriately so; but most of the time interpretation of texts and speech is not a bid for understanding the other, but a bid for understanding *what the other said*. In the case of understanding God's speech, this is what it has to be: I try to understand what God said while all the time acknowledging that understanding the person of God is beyond me in this life.

I judge that Schleiermacher would not disagree with what I have been saying – which implies that I think the received interpretation of Schleiermacher, with which Hart works, is mistaken. Schleiermacher explicitly says, near the beginning of what has been published as his *Hermeneutics and Criticism*, that the object of interpretation is a 'speech act' (*Akt des Redens*). A speech act, so argues Schleiermacher, is both an episode in the history of the language and an episode in the history of the life of a particular human being. It is both of these at once. Hence he says that both 'grammatical' interpretation and 'technical' (or 'psychological') interpretation are required. The issue pivots on what he has in mind by technical interpretation.

Let us distinguish between understanding what a person said (his speech act) and understanding why he said it. I submit that when Schleiermacher speaks about understanding the author, as he does, he is assuming that we have already understood what he said, and now wish to understand why he said it; that is to say, we want to render its occurrence intelligible. Schleiermacher assumes that to achieve that we must, to some extent, understand the person. And surely he was right about that; once we have grasped what speech act was performed, then, if we wish to render its occurrence intelligible, we have to understand something of the discourser's motivations and purposes; that requires that we understand something of the person. But when Schleiermacher talks in this context about understanding the person, he assumes that we have already understood what the person said; and I nowhere find him saying that *this* amounts to understanding the person.

In short, I read Schleiermacher as working with exactly the distinction I have been urging: between understanding what a person said, and understanding the person. The relevance of the latter to the former is that to understand *why* a person said what we have identified her as having said, we must to some extent understand *her*.

I interpret Hart as accepting the received interpretation of Schleiermacher and allowing that to lead him away from saying that the normal goal of interpretation is understanding what the person said – saying instead that the normal goal is to understand the person. I have made clear that in my judgment this is a mistake. But I trust I have also made clear that my disagreement on this point does not detract from my agreement with Hart's main point – that in the nature of the case, interpretation of the world projected by a text requires imagination. I have added that interpretation of what a person *said* also requires imagination, and that interpretation of what a person said, as well as interpretation of the world projected thereby, requires *phronesis* as well as imagination.

17

A First Retrospect on the Consultation

Walter Brueggemann

I thought it would be useful if I located myself a bit personally about the sense of 'crisis'. My church location came out of the Prussian union of which Schleiermacher was the architect. It was a union of Calvinists and Lutherans in Germany because the king got tired of them arguing about the Eucharist so he just said 'get together'. It's the same community out of which the Niebuhrs came and that means that this tradition of church faith has never been confessionally self-conscious. It is a kind of innocent pietism.

The second comment is that I studied under James Muilenburg at Union Seminary, New York. I think I probably started studying about the time that Prof. Childs went to Yale. One of my main memories of those days is that the field was dominated by the Albrightians and Muilenburg was an odd man out. At the SBL (Society of Biblical Literature) in those days the Albrightians used to laugh at anyone who did it differently. As a consequence, I am very alert to authoritarian scholarship since I have been on the other side of it.

The third locating comment that I want to make is that my teaching has been at two theological seminaries – in St. Louis and Atlanta – which gives one a different fix on things. I have to say that what I understand to be the crisis we've been talking about is not a felt crisis where I live; and the fracture between reason and faith really never happened very pronouncedly in my tradition. Therefore I'm not sure that I am completely in touch with our conversation and my response is in that context.

So I tried to think about what we mean here by 'crisis'. I anticipated, when I got invited to the consultation, that the crisis concerned historical criticism and the idea that *wissenschaftliche* study is a threat to faith. There has been some of that in the first paper by Walter Sundberg. Al Wolters argued that we stopped too soon, Christopher Seitz alluded to the same, and I suppose Craig

Bartholomew's paper was about that. But it struck me as we talked about it that the problem of historical criticism is not new and that it did not generate great passion among us as a problem. I suspect that is because we are all sort of agreed that while it is problematic we cannot do without it. I suppose what we would all agree on is that the key issue is to be critical of our criticism so that we know what we are doing.

Secondly, it seemed more likely to me that what goes under the slogan of 'post-modern' or, as Craig Bartholomew said, 'high-modern' interpretation that is marked by diversity and fragmentation is more likely the crisis that we are trying to talk about, because it is increasingly interpretation that does not take place in our orbit of faith. Sundberg, it seemed to me, was sort of suggesting that this diversity means that 'anything goes'. And Prof. Childs, while he didn't talk about post–modernity, talked about his experience of fragmentation[1] that I think is a part of this whole business. It is clear that fragmentation is a newer awareness among us and is more sharply felt. Many people do not read and many people have no mandate to read by what we might say is 'the rule of faith', whatever we take that phrase to mean. So I have wondered to what extent the crisis is a danger – that has seemed to be basically the way we have used the word – and to what extent the crisis is a possibility.

I think I understand the crisis as our having to unlearn old interpretative habits because our interpretation is now no longer privileged and can no longer count on heavy cultural, institutional support. I think I understand the crisis as the problem of having to learn new habits of interpretation that do not feel very easy or congenial. Now if the crisis is something like that (and I'm not sure about that), then I want to think about a response to that crisis and I want to misuse Hans Frei's phrase and talk about the response of 'generous orthodoxy'. I probably would put more emphasis on the generous than on the orthodox.

We are agreed, I think, in our conversations that there must be a critical reading of the text and then there must be a rereading. The rereading got highlighted, I think, particularly by MacDonald in his argument about typology, Wright on aesthetics, and Hart on imagination. These are readings that want to argue that there is a surplus in the text beyond what our critical readings can notice. We have in a variety of ways asked what are the warrants for rereading. How do you discipline and make sound judgements for rereading? We have several times in passing talked about the Trinity as a warrant for our rereading. I'm not sure we would know or agree on what that might mean, but I take it that all of us would agree that our rereading is under the aegis of the gospel and a sense of the whole in the single narrative of the gospel. I think it is an interesting question among us whether that rereading is generated by the text itself, or

---

[1] In a talk about his journey as a Christian scholar on the first evening at the consultation.

whether that rereading is an act of testimony and confession that the community does. Probably there would be some who would argue that it is intrinsic to the text, but I am mindful of Rex Mason's passion about saying that it is the community that has to undertake this. So that is an interesting question.

But what I really want to ask, if we agree that the warrant for rereading after critical reading is something to do with the gospel, is whether there are *other warrants for rereading* besides the gospel that I would name as being prior and provisional warrants that finally are on the way to the gospel. I want to develop that in a couple of directions.

I want to suggest that in the new postmodern situation – and how new it is we can talk about – that *wound* is a deep warrant for *rereading*. Were I to extrapolate that theologically, I would link the reality of the wound to the theology of the cross. And I must say that I have been surprised about how readily we have dismissed what I think might be called postmodern readings that do not stand by our warrants but are engaged with the text. Let me name three of those.

First of all, I think in feminist or liberationist hermeneutics what we are basically talking about is reading by people who have been wounded by the world or who have been wounded by an authoritarian church, and who cannot readily submit to any of those readings that appear to be hegemonic. I think Craig Bartholomew did not comment on it, but I am very interested in the question to what extent Derrida is simply a French intellectual and to what extent he is doing a very Jewish thing toward Christian hegemony. Regina Schwartz was mentioned, I think, in connection with *The Postmodern Bible*, but her more recent book, *The Curse of Cain*, purports to be an assault on the violence that is produced by monotheism. But I believe it is in fact a Jewish critique of Christian hegemony, and I believe that monotheism is one way in which she speaks about Christian hegemony.

Second, several people have observed about the energy of interpretation that is taking place in Africa. I am sure that is variegated and complex, but I want to suggest that what we may be seeing in the African church is a kind of interpretative energy that is post-colonial. It is a *rereading* of the text that is not submitted to our western colonial habits.

Third, Prof. Childs observed on Friday night – I think this is exceedingly important and he would know more about it than I would – that the generation of von Rad read differently out of their war and post-war wound from the next generation of German scholarship which doesn't have that particular experience of wound and displacement. As a consequence, much of the energy of theological interpretation has disappeared in recent scholarship.

Now that is a complicated list of feminists, liberationists, Jewish deconstructionists, African post-colonialists, and Germans who lived through the war. It suggests that those who read *through their hurt* often cannot go the way of our theological reading for reasons of lived reality. I submit that the fact that they often cannot go the way of our theological reading is not willful resistance but is because of deep woundedness. I suggest that very often these are not enemies of our reading who detract but they may indeed be allies and reading companions by whom we may be instructed.

Now if there is anything in that, that would suggest to me that we might want to rethink Christopher Seitz's confinement of what constitutes 'serious' reading. I had the impression that he was saying that the word 'serious' refers to academic reading and it may well be that there is very serious reading that could instruct the academy. The other side of this *reading out of wound* is that also in the academy we do read, for all of our claims of objectivity, through our wound. I have the impression, moreover, that perhaps postmodern readings or deconstruction might require serious academics to be more honest about how our woundedness is a warrant for our *rereading*. Mostly we keep our woundedness hidden in the posturing of the academy. But it is there and it is powerful:

First, the felt threat of *fragmentation* about which we have talked might indeed be one trigger for the response of reading by the 'rule of faith' as a way of guarding against fragmentation.

Second, perhaps best represented by the acerbic habits of James Barr or the 'minimalists', of which Britain seems to have a particular collection, the felt threat, I propose, that generates that sort of work – and obviously with reference to James Barr, those who know the interpersonal history in Edinburgh could fill that in better than I could – but the felt threat of *authoritarian reading* is a huge impetus to *rereading* where confessional readings are experienced as powerful silencers. Prof. Childs, and I understand what he meant, used the phrase 'the coercion of the text'. The problem I think very often is that what we may think is the coercion of the text is experienced by people as the coercion of our readings. Therefore while there has been some passion for confessional reading against fragmentation in our conversations, it seems to me we need to be vigilant that we don't undertake a kind of confessional reading that simply produces more of the other kind in response.

Third, I want to suggest that the felt threat of the text being *familiar* – whether it is the rational familiarity of Barr or the confessional familiarity of canon – is a way of killing the text. Therefore one of the warrants for *rereading* is the invitation to face the unfamiliarity of the text, 'the strange new world of the Bible' that does not conform to our controlled formulations, either rational or canonical. I am interested in a little bit of a taxonomy of a response to *fragmentation*, a response to *authoritarianism*, and a response to the *familiar*. And I take it that the openness to the unfamiliarity of the text is what is at issue in the papers we have heard on the aesthetic and on imagination, in which primary attention is given to the surplus that runs beyond all of our familiar methods and expectations, rational or canonical.

Now my last point. It was said somewhere in passing that one of the problems now is that *rereading* belongs to everybody, which I took to mean that it is so public and undisciplined that it has become amorphous and uncontained. It is possible to take the notion that the crisis is that *rereading* belongs to everybody, in generosity, that is, that we may have allies who see what we do not see and what we do not want to see. I suspect that many of those readings to which we object are engaged in what we might name here as ideological criticism. On the other hand, it is possible to regard those readings that are done by everybody as threats and distortions that must be disciplined. Quite clearly, our most faithful readings have often been misreadings. To extrapolate from MacDonald, perhaps the mistaken references in the text – that they were talking about something that they didn't know about – were not the last mistaken references: they reappear in our readings.

I have a colleague in homiletics who is reaching the conclusion that seminarians probably cannot learn to preach in the chapel but need to learn to preach by doing 'street preaching'. In our very bourgeois Presbyterian context, that's not going to happen soon, but it's an interesting taunt to the administration. I have reflected on that just in the last weeks and have concluded that the issue about street preaching, as distinct from church preaching, maybe concerns two things that would be of interest to us.

First, in street preaching, one may expect to be heckled, that is, the claims are directly *contested* as they are not in the usual decorum of the church. It occurs to me that our new crisis situation of hermeneutics is one in which our readings are contested to the roots by those who do not accept our premises. I suspect, moreover, that it is our past privilege of not being contested that is the crisis, or that the crisis is our surprise at being contested because we have grown content with not being contested. Second, in street preaching there is very little patience with intellectual, idealistic rhetoric. But one is regularly pressed to the question of *so what?* about material reality because those who listen on the street characteristically need bread. Whereas inside church preaching the luxury of second level rhetoric is affordable, it is not affordable on the street. Which is to say, as Dan Beeby suggested, that maybe the hermeneutical crisis comes down to the *praxis* that is yielded by our reading. That is, what are the payouts in the lived practice of the interpretative community?

My impression is that the only time we made direct reference to *praxis* was in Wolters' chapter on Zechariah, in which he simply lined out quickly what some of that agenda might be. I have no doubt that in future consultations it is important to work backwards to philosophical foundations, but I suspect it is equally urgent to work forward to ethical contradictions, and by and large our conversations did not approach that.

Finally, the question, I suspect, that the ordinary church reader wants to know about is what different kind of public life in the world will be imagined through and generated by this lining out of reality. I want to suggest the analogy that our hermeneutical crisis is parallel to preachers who have learnt to do very well in the church all of a sudden finding themselves on the street. Some of you must be like me about that, for I do not want to do 'street preaching'. It is my judgement that our crisis is the jarring resituation of our work as 'street preaching', which is deeply serious biblical theology – I am using 'serious' now as Seitz used it, I think – which is *highly contested* and which is regularly pressed to *concrete payout*. If you think about serious, highly contested, concrete payout, that is what the church does at its best, at its most faithful, and that is where God has now put us. We have had better places, but this is our place. Therefore I suggest that being generous and recognizing allies may protect us from excessive certitude about our chance of serious misreading that always haunts serious reading, academic or ecclesial.

Bibliography

Schwartz, R.M., *The Curse of Cain: The Violent Legacy of Monotheism* (Chicago: University of Chicago Press, 1997)

The Bible and Culture Collective (G. Aichele, F.W. Burnett, et al.), *The Postmodern Bible* (New Haven: Yale University Press, 1995)

Scripture and Hermeneutics Seminar

Cheltenham and Gloucester College of Higher Education is pleased to be working in partnership with the Bible Society in this hermeneutics project. It is based in the School of Theology and Religious Studies and is in keeping with the College's Christian foundation.

The origins of the College are in 1847 when The Rev Francis Close founded an evangelical College in Cheltenham for the training of teachers. The name Cheltenham and Gloucester College of Higher Education has been used since 1990. For some years immediately prior to this it was called The College of St Paul and St Mary, Cheltenham.

Theology and Religious Studies have always been key activities of the College. We teach at undergraduate and postgraduate levels and supervise research students. About three hundred students are involved in theology and religious studies each year. The College has now been given Degree and Research Degree Awarding Powers. The Masters programme includes MAs in Biblical Studies, Religion and Society, and Religious Fducation. lucre is a growing research culture. In the School of Theology and Religious Studies around thirty research students are working for MPhil/PhD awards, particularly in Biblical Studies.

We are delighted that the Scripture and Hermeneutics Seminar has been supported by a number of international experts. and we acknowledge their fine contribution to the consultations and to this first volume. We are also grateful for the encouragement and co-operation of Paternoster Publishing (UK) and Zondervan Publishing House (USA).

The College is launching an International Centre for Biblical Interpretation to initiate and promote new advanced work.

Dr Fred Hughes
Head, School of Theology and Religious Studies
Cheltenham & Gloucester College of Higher Education
PO Box 220, The Park, Cheltenharn GL50 2QF.
www.chelt.ac.uk/ah/sotrs

Scripture and Hermeneutics Seminar

In 2004 the **British and Foreign Bible Society (BFBS)** celebrates its bicentenary. The Society originated in the early years of the nineteenth century in a context of evangelical revival and social reform associated with people such as Wesley, Whitefield, Wilberforce and the Clapham Sect. Wilberforce organized a number of campaigns ostensibly aimed at the 'reform of manners'. The use of the phrase was itself a piece of opportunism, seizing on a passage in a speech by King George III to Parliament. The formation of the BFBS was one of the elements in Wilberforce's broad campaign to put the biblical narrative back in the center of British public life and so create a new societal imagination opposed to the cynicism and callousness of many of his contemporaries that allowed social evils such like the slave trade to flourish. Wilberforce was not a biblical scholar. He recognized, however, that genuine social and political reform did not take place in a vacuum but must be earthed in a moral and religious vision of what constitutes a just and humane society.

Over the last 200 years the BFBS, as the founding member of the now worldwide United Bible Societies fellowship, has been deeply concerned with Bible distribution making the scriptures available to increasing numbers of people in a language they can understand and at a price they can afford. If, and when, the Society intersected with the world of biblical scholarship at all it was over issues of translation and cultural relevance. It is a source of some considerable irony that during the period when the work of the Bible Societies in distribution and translation was flourishing, particularly overseas, historical–critical biblical scholarship was contributing to the increasing marginalization of the Bible and the churches in the public life of society in the west. That, of course, was not intentional and it is as well to remember the sanguine comment of Paul Tillich that it is to the credit of the Christian Churches that Christianity was the first world-wide religion to allow its primary text to go through the fires of historical critical research. We are not yet at the end of that process and in a postmodern context, where the traditional boundaries between what were previously discreet disciplines (such as philosophy, theology, cultural and literary theory, and socio-political analysis) are being surmounted all the time, questions to do with the credibility, authority and relevance of the Bible in the context of contemporary society are even more paramount.

It is for this reason that we at the BFBS are delighted to be partners in a new exciting interdisciplinary project we are calling 'the Scripture and Hermeneutics Seminar'. The hermeneutical recovery of the diverse and variegated traditions of the biblical story in the context of an equally diverse, pluralist and multi-cultural society remains high on our agenda. Consequently, we want to work in and with the world of critical scholarship and allow debate and reflection to flourish for the mutual benefit of all, so that, as the commissioned cover of the first volume suggests, the Book is once again open and able to address the complex realities of living in the third millennium.

Revd. Dr. Cohn J.D. Greene
Head of Theology and Public Policy (BFBS)

Name Index

Page numbers in roman text include references to works cited. Full bibliographic details can be found at the end of each chapter.

Subject Index

Addendum

Bibliography for Chapter 4

Aner, K., *Theologie der Lessingzeit* (Hildesheim: Georg Olms, 1964)

Baur, F.C., *Church History of the First Three Centuries* (London: Williams and Norgate, 1878)

Kausemann, E., 'Gottesgerechtigkeit bei Paulus', EVB, II, 181-93

Luther, M., Preface to the Latin Writings, *Luther's Works* (tr. J.J. Pelikan & H.T Lehmann,. vol. 34, Saint Louis: Concordia, 1960)

Luz, U., *Das Evangelium nach Matthus*, EKK, I/1 (Zürich: Benziger, 1985;2nd rev. edition, 1989)

Newman, J.H., *Essay in Aid of a Grammar of Assent* (London: Longmans, Green and Co., 1947)

Riches, J., 'Lessing's Change of Mind', *JTS* 29 (1978), 121-36

—, 'Lessing as Editor of Reimarus' *Apologie*' in *Studia Biblica* (JSNTSup. 2; Sheffield: Sheffield Academic Press, 1980) 247-54

—, *The Bible: A Very Short Introduction* (Oxford: Oxford University Press, 2000)

Stephen, L., *History of English Thought in the Eighteenth Century* (London: Rupert Hart- Davies, 1962)

Upkong, J.S., 'The Parable of the Shrewd Manager (Lk 16:1-13): An Essay in the Inculturation Biblical Hermeneutic', in G. West and M.W. Dube (eds.), *'Reading With': An Exploration of the Interface between Critical and Ordinary Readings of the Bible: African Overtures, Semeia* 73 (1996); 189-210

We want to hear from you. Please send your comments about this book to us in care of the address below. Thank you.

ZondervanPublishingHouse

Grand Rapids, Michigan 49530
http://www.zondervan.com